NEGOTIATING SEX WORK

Negotiating Sex Work

. . . .

Unintended Consequences of Policy and Activism

Carisa R. Showden
and Samantha Majic, Editors

University of Minnesota Press
Minneapolis
London

Published by the University of Minnesota Press
111 Third Avenue South, Suite 290
Minneapolis, MN 55401-2520
http://www.upress.umn.edu

Library of Congress Cataloging-in-Publication Data
Negotiating sex work : unintended consequences of policy and activism
Carisa R. Showden and Samantha Majic, editors.
Includes bibliographical references and index.
ISBN 978-0-8166-8958-3 (hc : alk. paper)
ISBN 978-0-8166-8959-0 (pb : alk. paper)
1. Prostitution—Government policy. 2. Prostitutes—Political activity. 3. Prostitutes—Labor unions. I. Showden, Carisa Renae. II. Majic, Samantha.
HQ118.N44 2014
306.74—dc23   2013028376

Printed in the United States of America on acid-free paper

The University of Minnesota is an equal-opportunity educator and employer.

21 20 19 18 17 16 15 14   10 9 8 7 6 5 4 3 2 1

Contents

Acknowledgments

THIS BOOK would not have been possible without the support and hard work of so many people. First and foremost, we must thank the authors in this volume. In addition to conducting thoughtful and path-breaking research, these women and men responded with patience and good humor to our seemingly never-ending comments and queries.

We were fortunate to work with Pieter Martin at the University of Minnesota Press, whose careful editorial guidance was essential for revising this manuscript and bringing it into production. We thank Kristian Tvedten, our editorial assistant at the Press, for keeping us organized and moving the book along in a timely manner. Indexing is a fine art, and Denise Carlson is a gifted artist. We thank her for her careful and creative work producing an index for us in a short time frame.

Over the course of developing and producing this volume, a number of institutions and individuals provided essential support. The annual meeting of the Western Political Science Association offered a forum to gather and discuss the initial material in this volume, and the Office of Undergraduate Research and the Office for the Advancement of Research at John Jay College/CUNY and a Professional Staff Congress-CUNY Research Grant (65157-00 43) provided funds for travel and editorial assistance. The two anonymous Press reviewers gave us thoughtful and engaged feedback that improved the individual chapters and the overall framework of the book. We are especially grateful to Kelley Burke for completing the volume's bibliography.

We cannot thank enough our partners, Erin Carlston and John Rasmussen, for their patience and support—and dinners cooked—along the way.

Finally, we express our greatest admiration, respect, and gratitude to all the sex workers who fight for justice every day.

Abbreviations

ABC	acceptable behavior contract
ACT-UP	AIDS Coalition to Unleash Power
AFDC	Aid to Families with Dependent Children
AIDS	acquired immunodeficiency syndrome
AIRC	Australian Industrial Relations Commission
ASBO	antisocial behavior order
BCCEW	British Columbia Coalition of Experiential Women
BEAVER	Better End All Vicious Erotic Repression
BNG	*Bound, Not Gagged*
CAB	community advisory board
CACTUS	Community Action Center for Injection Drug Users
CAL-PEP	California Prostitutes Education Project
CATW	Coalition against Trafficking in Women
CBO	community-based organization
CEDIM	State Council for Women's Rights
CES	Centre for AIDS Research
CGEL	Canadian Guild for Erotic Labour
CLC	Canadian Labour Congress
COYOTE	Call Off Your Old Tired Ethics
CPSS	criminalizing the purchase of sexual services
CRA	Canada Revenue Agency
CSQ	Comité SIDA Québec (Québec AIDS Committee)
CUPE	Canadian Union of Public Employees
ECP	English Collective of Prostitutes
EDA	Exotic Dancers' Alliance
EMPOWER	Education Means Protection of Women Engaged in Recreation
ESPU	Erotic Service Providers' Union
FFW	Foundation for Women
GAATW	Global Alliance against Trafficking of Women
GFATM	Global Fund to Fight AIDS, Tuberculosis, and Malaria

HIV/AIDS	human immunodeficiency virus/acquired immunodeficiency virus
ICCPR	International Covenant on Civil and Political Rights
IJM	International Justice Mission
ILO	International Labour Organization
KLPD	Korps Landelijke Politiediensten (National Force of Police Services)
LGBT	lesbian, gay, bisexual, transgender
LHMWU	Liquor, Hospitality and Miscellaneous Workers' Union
MAM	Museum of Modern Art (Rio de Janeiro)
MOU	memorandum of understanding
MP	Member of Parliament
MSDHS	Ministry of Social Development and Human Security (Thailand)
MSP	Minister of the Scottish Parliament
NBI	National Bureau of Investigation
NGO	nongovernmental organization
NIDA	National Institute of Drug Abuse
NIH	National Institute of Health
OIT	Organização Internacional de Trabalho (International Labor Organization)
PACE	Prostitution Alternatives, Counseling, and Education
PAR	participatory action research
PCV	Prostitutes' Collective of Victoria
PDAR	participant-driven action research
PEERS	Prostitutes Empowerment Education Resource Society
PEPFAR	President's Emergency Plan for AIDS Relief
PEPS	Promotoras Educadoras de Pares (Peer Health Promoters)
P.I.A.M.P.	Priject d'intervention aupres de mineu-e-s prostitute-ees (Outreach Project for Minors Involved in Prostitution)
PLWH	people living with HIV
PNETP	National Plan to Combat Human Trafficking
POWER	Prostitutes of Ottawa/Gatineau Work, Educate, Resist
PRA	Prostitution Reform Act (New Zealand)
RDS	respondent-driven sampling
ROKS	National Organization of Women's Shelters in Sweden
S&M	sadomasochism
SAA	Striptease Artists of Australia

SAGE	Standing against Global Exploitation
SAP	Swedish Social Democratic Party
SIU	Service Employees' International Union
SJI	St. James Infirmary
SOF	Semprevia Feminist Organization
SPOC	Sex Professionals of Canada
SPSS	Statistical Package for the Social Sciences
SSDI	Supplemental Security Disability Income
SSKF	National Federation of Social Democratic Women
STAR	Sex Trade Advocacy and Research
STI	sexually transmitted infection
SWEAT	Sex Worker Environmental Assessment Team
SWOLHCR	Sex Workers Organized for Labor, Human, and Civil Rights
SWOP	Sex Workers Outreach Project
SWU	Sex Workers' Union
SWUAV	Sex Workers United against Violence
TS	*trabajadora sexual* (sex worker)
TVPA	Trafficking Victims Protection Act
UCSF	University of California–San Francisco
UN	United Nations
UNESCAP	United Nations Economic and Social Commission for Asia and the Pacific
UNODC	United Nations Office on Drugs and Crime
USAID	United States Agency for International Development
WHISPER	Women Hurt In Systems of Prostitution Engaged in Revolt
WISE	Workers in Sex Employment

.

The Politics of Sex Work

Carisa R. Showden and Samantha Majic

I N THE UNITED STATES and across the globe, sex workers—individuals who exchange sexual services for cash or other goods—often conduct their work clandestinely. The recent *politics* of sex work, however, are a much more visible matter. In 2008 in San Francisco, for example, prostitutes' rights activists spearheaded Proposition K, a ballot measure that would have barred local police officers from arresting or investigating or prosecuting anyone for selling sex. Advocates claimed this would free up $11 million per year in police resources and allow prostitutes to form collectives and defend their rights as workers (YesOnPropK.org 2009). However, they were eventually defeated by a strong campaign by the mayor and district attorney, who claimed Proposition K would limit law enforcement's ability to curb human trafficking and provide services for victims. As then District Attorney Kamala Harris stated, "We can not give a green light or a pass to predators of young women" (*NBC Bay Area* 2008). Similar concerns were also expressed that same year in Norway, when it became the second country in the world (after Sweden) to criminalize the purchase of sexual services from prostitutes. When the law passed, Justice Minister Knut Storberget stated, "We want to send a clear message to men that buying sex is unacceptable. Men who do it are taking part in an international crime involving human beings who are trafficked for sex" (Fouché 2007).

These debates about the dangers of sexual commerce continued in 2009 at a panel discussion at Harvard Law School that considered the civil rights implications of legalizing or decriminalizing prostitution. Here a sharp division occurred between two professors who supported removing prostitution from the purview of criminal laws and a psychologist and former prostitute who vehemently opposed this practice (Young 2009). Continuing the now decades-long sex wars debate, when the professors stated that prostitution occurs in many contexts and is experienced differently based on one's social location and the broader cultural, political, and economic context, the emphatic response from many audience members (comprising social workers, law students, and scholars) was "but prostitution *is* violence against women!" Such sentiments were apparent again at a 2011 Women's World Conference in Ottawa, Ontario, that brought together almost 2,000 women from 92 countries, many of whom were concerned about prostitution and human trafficking. However, it also highlighted deep divisions in the feminist movement when sex workers and others supporting the decriminalization of prostitution claimed they were silenced and outnumbered by anti–sex work groups that hurled negative epithets at them in the common spaces and during the conference's various exhibits and panels (Purvis 2011).

This cursory review of recent events indicates that the politics of sex work are not only visible but also (almost) exclusively about *prostitution* and contests for power between those who view it as legitimate work and those who view selling sex as a form of coercive sexual exploitation (or sex trafficking). Further, with increased globalization, "trafficking in women" has become the metonymic frame for sex work (and prostitution in particular) in both political discourse and policy practice. As a result, the current politics reflect and reproduce the long-standing, persistent "agent/victim" debate about prostitution (and sex work in general). In the standard form of this debate, agents choose (freely) and victims have no choice.

Through both theoretical and empirical arguments, this volume provides a timely and necessary intervention in this debate on two interrelated levels. First, it emphasizes sex workers' *political* agency, thereby rejecting the choice/no choice dichotomy that persists in so many discussions of sex work and generates instead a definition of agency as both capacity and action. "Agent" is not an identity (nor is "victim"). It is both a capacity relative to different structural positions people occupy and a way of negotiating structures; thus agents are mobile and their capacities are activated in different ways depending on specific, variable contexts. The chapters in this volume thus indicate how sex workers are political agents who negotiate various social, political, legal, and economic structural circumstances across the globe to challenge the political processes that have largely relegated their voices to the margins. In so doing, they challenge how policymakers, interested groups, and the broader public regard sex workers' agency and their perceived lack of legitimate place in the polity.

In addition, by focusing on political agency, the volume's second intervention is a necessary critique of the broader sex-trafficking debates that dominate the current politics of sex work. With the erasure of political agency produced by having trafficking synecdochically cover all forms of sex work—and "trafficking victims" represent all sex workers—these essays serve as a timely intercession, providing theoretical and empirical evidence for sex workers' political agency while critiquing the dominance of the trafficking/victim narrative. Without erasing the knowledge that some persons are trafficked—and victimized—the chapters here contest the totality of that framework. This contest is necessary given the near stranglehold that the trafficking and victimization frameworks have on public policymaking.

Sex Work Politics and the "Agent/Victim" Debate

Currently, it is not difficult to equate sex work with victimization. For just some examples of how the media has focused on reporting prostitution experiences that involve violence, coercion, and exploitation (often by third parties), one only needs to look at *New York Times* columnist Nicholas Kristof's numerous columns on sex trafficking to learn the story of "a teenage girl, Long Pross," who was brutally beaten by a brothel owner in Cambodia (Kristof 2009); or the *New York Times Magazine*'s story of Lucilla, a Brooklyn teenager who worked for a pimp who took all her money after every "trick" (Lustig 2007); or Lauren Hersh's recent column on sex trafficking in the *Huffington Post* for Human Trafficking Awareness Day exhorting readers that "a paradigm shift is necessary to recognize the definitive link between prostitution and trafficking and that those who buy sex fuel trafficking . . . There is nothing victimless about this crime" (Hersh 2013). Even the U.S. Department of State's 2010 *Trafficking in Persons Report* has an entire section titled "Victims' Stories" that narrates individual experiences with coercive labor, often in prostitution (U.S. Dept. of State 2010). While few would deny that violence and other forms of exploitation occur in the sex industry, the popular media and political leaders' emphasis on this has constructed not only sex work as a universally violent and exploitative activity that primarily harms women (and, increasingly, young girls) but also sex workers as victims who are coerced into this activity by male pimps and/or traffickers.

This emphasis on the relationship between sex work and victimization is not new, particularly in the United States. Activists, scholars, and
political leaders have expressed repeated (albeit sporadic) concern about
women being coerced in to the sex trade (or "sex trafficking") in response
to changing socioeconomic and political conditions. Most notably, at the
beginning of the twentieth century, the growing immigration of men to
the United States from Europe fueled social reformers' fears that (white)
women were now more vulnerable to the criminal trafficking rings these
immigrants allegedly ran (Meil-Hobson 1987). Mirroring the trafficking
discourse that would emerge over one hundred years later, charges
that an international syndicate was trafficking women mobilized the U.S.
Immigration Service to send hundreds of agents to cities as underground
investigators (Meil-Hobson 1987, 142), culminating in the passage of the
Mann-Elkins Act by Congress in 1911, which forbade the transportation of
women across state lines for immoral purposes (Brandt 1987).

In the late 1970s and early 1980s, the AIDS epidemic and the social
impacts of reconstruction and development in the Southeast Asia region
in the aftermath of the Vietnam War drew public and political attention to
victimization in the sex industries internationally. Sex tourism; mail-order
brides; militarized prostitution; and coercion, violence, and trafficking in
the movement and employment of women from their home countries to
more affluent regions for work in the leisure and sex industries became
the focus of those opposed to prostitution (Kempadoo 2005). These "real-
world" events also coincided with the so-called feminist "sex wars"—the
heated debates in predominantly Western academic circles over feminist depictions of women's sexuality in pornography that consumed the
attention of many theorists and activists through the early 1990s (Abrams
1995). From these debates, a network of feminists, scholars, and activists
coalesced around the notion that sex work epitomized women's subordination and constituted the foundation of women's victimization and
male dominance (Barry 1984; Schotten 2005). Thus their policy objective
became abolitionism, or "ending demand" for commercial sex by criminalizing clients and pimps but not sex workers.

Since the 1990s, abolitionist advocates and their allies have focused
public and political attention toward the "traffic in women," which they
understand as a dangerous manifestation of global gender inequalities
(Bernstein 2010, 45). In the past thirty years, labor—particularly women's
labor—has become more mobile, visible, and service intensive as broader

economic deregulation and technological changes facilitate more rapid and accessible travel and communication across borders (Kongar 2008; Godfrey 1995). On the one hand, these socioeconomic developments have facilitated the growth of high-paying service jobs and a growing, traveling professional class. On the other hand, they have also contributed to growing wage disparities and poverty, particularly for women from the global south who are increasingly migrating, often in search of low-paying factory or domestic work (Beneria 1999; 2003; Beneria and Bisnath 2003; Beneria and Sen 2001; Buvinich 2001; Ehrenreich and Hochschild 2003; Harris-White 2003; Koopman 1991).

The sex industry was not immune to these trends, and it grew more technologically sophisticated and global (Bernstein 2007). Sex work is among the many types of work that women migrate for, and through today's rapidly expanding and integrated communication and policing networks, it is more visible now to the public and political officials alike. It is therefore unsurprising that sex work was equated with sex trafficking in the public eye when media attention to the plight of Latin American and Asian women illegally trafficked to work in brothels in Western Europe, among other regions, illustrated the dangers of prostitution and made it seem inconceivable that anyone would choose this as legitimate work (Gozdziak and Collett 2005; Soderlund 2005).

Still as political officials and the public continue to equate sex work with trafficking and victimization, the actual number of victims is unknown. As Laura Maria Agustín (2007, 36–41) notes, the few statistics that exist on trafficking in general and sex trafficking in particular are obtained from a limited number of (often unnamed) sources who rarely reveal their research methods and are then recited and recirculated through the media, academic, and political outlets that are working to proclaim and denounce the sex-trafficking crisis. As a result, government statements and press releases (such as those already cited) seem to conflate sex-trafficking estimates with all other forms of trafficking into other industries, making the problem appear both extremely overwhelming and extremely vague (O'Neill-Richards 2000). For example, a Bureau of Public Affairs "fact sheet" states, "Of the estimated 600,000 to 800,000 people trafficked across international borders annually, 80 percent of victims are female, and up to 50 percent are minors. *Hundreds of thousands* [italics ours] of these women and children are used in prostitution each year" (Bureau of Public Affairs 2004, 1).

Yet despite the numeric discrepancies in estimating the extent of the trafficking problem, the trope of the trafficking victim remains a pervasive cultural myth (Doezema 1998) and, as a result, a number of abolitionist groups are leading efforts to raise awareness about and end the practice, such as the Coalition against Trafficking in Women (CATW), "a non-governmental organization that . . . works internationally to combat sexual exploitation in all its forms, especially prostitution and trafficking in women and children, in particular girls" (CATW 2011). Other groups advocating this position include Standing against Global Exploitation (the SAGE Project), Women Hurt In Systems of Prostitution Engaged in Revolt (WHISPER), and Fight Slavery Now! Their combined focus is on the sex worker who is most often a prostitute (and occasionally a dancer in a club) from the global south or an emerging Eastern Bloc nation who has migrated—or been trafficked—for this work. For these groups, the continued criminalization of prostitution is essential for apprehending, punishing, and ending pimps', traffickers', and clients' demand for prostitution (Hotaling 2007; Hotaling et al. 1997; Hotaling et al. 2003). For women in prostitution, they propose decriminalizing their participation so they may be diverted from the criminal justice system to social services that help them exit the trade.[1] As a result of their efforts, (women's) victimization in the sex industry is an integral issue to the international women's movement—it now is part of the United Nation's Fora on Women and a key interest of women's organizations and networks worldwide (Kempadoo 2005).

Consequently, many policymakers and members of the public do not understand women in the sex industry as agents with legitimate, and variable, claims on and opinions about the policy process. Thus policy design has favored efforts to "rescue" women. This is most apparent in the United States, which is leading global efforts against human trafficking. As Elizabeth Bernstein writes, a "coalition of strange bedfellows" (2010, 65)—an alliance of abolitionist feminists and religious groups—has formed to lead these efforts. Here, as Ronald Weitzer (2010) writes, abolitionist groups such as CATW formed coalitions with conservative Christians like Senators Sam Brownback and Rick Santorum and antiprostitution organizations like International Justice Mission and the Family Research Council. Although these feminists and conservatives would have opposing views about a number of issues related to sex and sexuality (such as reproductive rights), this alliance is arguably possible because all parties have a similar gendered understanding of their subject—the sex worker. Specifically, they view her universally as a "total victim"—that is, poor, foreign, and naïve—and therefore not capable of speaking up for her own interests. This, combined with their opposition to prostitution and support for victims of crime, allowed them to rally their constituencies, influence trafficking policy in the United States and internationally, and dominate the debate over any policy and funding related to prostitution (Berman 2006).

Together, these "strange bedfellows" have "secured a growing proportion of federal monies for both international and domestic anti-trafficking work, as well as funds for the prevention of HIV/AIDS" (Bernstein 2010, 51). For example, in May 2003, Congress passed the Global AIDS Act and barred the use of federal funds to "promote, support, or advocate the legalization of the practice of prostitution" (Public Law 108-25 2003). The accompanying National Security Presidential Directive (NSPD-22, 1) asserted, "Our Policy is based on an abolitionist approach to trafficking in persons. The United States Government opposes prostitution and any related activities, including pimping, pandering, or maintaining brothels as contributing to the phenomenon of trafficking in persons" (The White House 2003; Lachynsky 2005). The Global AIDS Act required nongovernmental organizations (NGOs) it funded to have a policy explicitly opposing prostitution and sex trafficking (Bernard 2006). Public health officials and sex workers' rights advocates argued this requirement would compromise sex workers' health by limiting the range of service providers (see for example ACT-UP 2003; Cohen 2005). Lacking powerful allies in Congress, this rights-based perspective was minimized until a United States Court of Appeals decision found the policy, known as the "gag rule," violated the First Amendment rights of U.S. organizations (U.S. Agency for International Development v. Alliance for Open Society International Inc. 2006).

The Trafficking Victims Protection Reauthorization Act (TVPA) also refused the notion that prostitution may be legitimate work by expanding the state's police powers. Specifically, the 2003 TVPA required all applicants for funding to state that they do not promote or support prostitution and expanded financial support for local law enforcement engaged in antitrafficking activities (Trafficking Victims Protection Reauthorization Act 2003). Sex workers' rights activists were vocal in the TVPA's creation process, arguing it effectively conflated all forms of prostitution with sex trafficking. These scholars and activists also criticized the TVPA for putting women at risk for experiencing criminal penalties if they do not cooperate with law enforcement out of fear of encountering their trafficker (Kempadoo 2005; Chapkis 2005). In essence, if a woman does "not fit the stereotype of an innocent girl forced into prostitution" (Sex Workers Project at the Urban Justice Center 2005, 25), she becomes a criminal. However, again lacking allies in Congress (or elsewhere), their perspective was often, and continues to be, minimized.

At the state and local level, numerous U.S. jurisdictions have also implemented policies that reflect abolitionist influence and the broader understanding of sex work as a universally victimizing activity. In recent years, this is most apparent in lawmakers' and advocates' efforts to "end demand" for prostitution (and, by extension, human trafficking) with initiatives targeting men who buy sexual services. Today, at least forty-seven states have "demand reduction" programs related to prostitution (Shively et al. 2008, 96). While many of these are punitively oriented (such as "reverse stings," where police departments used female officers as decoys to arrest male solicitors), various jurisdictions have developed programs with an "educational" orientation, such as john schools, where men arrested for prostitution solicitation pay a fine and take a class to learn about the consequences of their actions after they are arrested.

The framework of sex work as universally victimizing to women is central to U.S. domestic and foreign policy, but it is not limited to the United States. While in all countries in Western Europe, as well as Australia and New Zealand, selling sex is no longer a crime, the need to end demand and "save women" is articulated in many nations' sex work policies. European-style abolitionism is expressed perhaps most notably in Swedish law, which was codified as the *Kvinnofrid* law, or the Violence against Women Act, and includes the criminal offense of "gross violation of a woman's integrity." Indeed feminist abolitionism is today colloquially known as the "Swedish model": criminalize traffickers, pimps, and the purchase of sex because of the understanding that patriarchal dominance allows men to buy sexual services from women.

But competing with the victim frame enshrined in Swedish law are policy regimes that recognize sex workers' agency by focusing on sex work as labor and, thus, trying to improve women's standing as legitimate workers. In the Netherlands, most notably, a combination of harm reduction and economic rights promotion has emerged over the past two decades as municipal governments have used legalization and regulatory mechanisms to reshape sex workers' economic and political standing. Specifically, zoning, mandatory health checks for sex workers, the registration and licensing of workers, and brothel occupational health and safety inspections have been implemented.

For example, in the 1990s municipal governments used their zoning powers to create areas where street-based prostitution would be tolerated (*tippelzones*, or safe parks) while elsewhere prostitution was criminalized (Hubbard, Matthews, and Scoular 2008; Kuo 2002). These parks were viewed as especially important when brothels were outlawed. But once the brothel ban was lifted in 2000, cities could "impose standards on the off-street trade," which local governments believed "dispense[d] with the need for *tippelzones*," thus most have been dismantled in the years following brothel legalization (Hubbard, Matthews, and Scoular 2008, 142). With both the *tippelzones* and the legalized brothels, access to health and police resources was increased (at least for some prostitutes). Meanwhile, brothel regulation specifically focuses on minimum dimensions for working areas, running hot and cold water, fire escapes, condom provision, and the protection of prostitutes' "physical and mental integrity, [allowing] no under-age workers and none without a valid residence permit" (Kilvington, Day, and Ward 2001, 82). Additionally, in the four years after the brothel ban was struck down, "the number of prostitutes registered for tax purposes doubled" (Hubbard, Matthews, and Scoular 2008, 142).

While the Netherlands has tried to acknowledge sex workers' agency through a regulatory policy regime, New Zealand has done so through the unique step of decriminalization—removing sex work–specific laws from the criminal code in an effort to meet both harm minimization and economic and civil rights objectives.[2] New Zealand's 2003 Prostitution Reform Act (PRA) was developed in part based on scholarly participatory research studies conducted with both female and male sex workers, giving them a voice in policy construction (much like the research described in chapters 2 and 3 of this volume). The New Zealand Prostitutes' Collective worked to construct an image of sex workers as professionals practicing safe sex rather than as disease vectors, and the public health community argued that criminalization, rather than sex worker attributes, put public health at risk: "Their data showed sex workers' had high levels of STI awareness but that pressures from clients and managers, combined with police harassment, discouraged condom use" and that "criminalization enabled violations of sex worker's rights, mistreatment and exploitation by massage parlour managers, strip club owners and clients" (Harrington 2012, 341).

The PRA allows only New Zealand citizens and permanent residents to engage in sex work (legally), a provision crafted to meet some policymakers' concerns that decriminalization would result in an increase in human trafficking for prostitution (Harrington 2012, 343). However, studies conducted postreform have in fact found evidence that the harm minimization goals are being met, at least to some degree. A Christchurch School of Medicine study—also using participatory research methods—reports that the most serious health risks sex workers faced were from stigma, and "after the PRA, sex workers felt more able to complain to police about violence and to stand up to exploitative managers," reducing the damage to their emotional health by empowering them in their efforts to be health conscious and stand up for their rights (Harrington 2012, 341, 348).

In contrast with both the Netherlands and New Zealand, some Australian states attempt to acknowledge sex workers' agency through a system of mixed regulatory schemes. In two states, prostitution is not illegal but most related activities are (e.g., living on the earnings of another's prostitution, soliciting, and keeping a brothel); in five states, brothels and/or escort agencies are legal and regulated but public soliciting (i.e., street-based work) is prohibited; and in New South Wales, legalization of brothels coincides with the decriminalization of some street-based sex work (Sullivan 2010). In the states where brothels are more heavily regulated but private prostitution is allowed, sex workers now have the right to housing (landlords are not allowed to refuse to rent to them) and banks are not allowed to refuse them credit due to their work. The courts have upheld these legal protections when sex workers have had to seek redress from landlords and banks that have declined to comply (Sullivan 2010, 92). Where licensing requirements are loosened or absent and some street work is decriminalized, sex workers can exercise more power vis-à-vis sex-business operators. For example, more kinds of brothels, including private, sex worker–owned brothels, are allowed in some municipalities and brothels are required to provide safe-sex equipment, such as condoms (Sullivan 2010, 101–4). Still, workers are heavily regulated and considered disease vectors who must be tested regularly for sexually transmitted infections (STIs).

The approaches taken by the Netherlands, New Zealand, and Australia thus indicate how states may acknowledge sex workers' agency through policy, even amid a broader political context that focuses on their victimization; however, they also have many unintended consequences for shaping the ways in which sex workers are then able to exercise their capacities for agency and articulate their demands. In all three countries, distinctions between legal and illegal sex work and sex workers are starker than ever, so that improvements in the conditions for some workers (e.g., citizens in legal brothels) comes at the expense of others (e.g., those who wish to work on the street and/or in small brothels and those without citizenship who now face even harsher criminal penalties).[3] Regulated brothels have to respect workers' health and safety rights, but one aspect of regulation in the Netherlands and Australia, for example, has been the consolidation and corporatization of brothels in some states as zoning and building permits can be limited; thus, fewer entities are able to set up shop legally. The flip side of corporatization in the limiting of brothel permits is when the size of brothels is also limited, as in Queensland, Australia, where no more than eight sex workers can work at any one time, limiting legal employment opportunities even further (Sullivan 2010). Thus as many chapters in this volume make clear, legalizing the selling of sex still exists in an overall policy framework that makes sex work, for all intents and purposes, impossible for many to do legally. Further, legalization is difficult to do in ways that both respond to and facilitate sex workers' self-articulated needs and interests.

Given the very visible political power plays evident across regulatory regimes, we think it is fair to say that the sex worker as "victim" ideal is codified in different ways, either explicitly in the law or implicitly through its implementation. One of the major contributions of the chapters in this volume is that they engage with the intersections of policy, culture, identity, and history to complicate this "victim" ideal and, in doing so, show us how and why the politics of sex work *work* as they do. Our contributors also focus on the concern that, trafficked or not, sex workers' rights and self-defined needs are too often deemed to be the product of false consciousness or endogenous preferences. Even where sex workers are afforded some measure of protection and self-determination, victimization rhetoric and stigma occlude the agency of strategic choices and consciousnesses already raised, in part, because states are better at regulating individuals than they are at promoting freedom.

Thus to see the agency sex workers have, the authors in this volume look at what sex workers *do*, not at who they are, by examining how sex workers make sense of their lives, their work, their dissatisfactions, their legal positions, and their family options. Our authors analyze the difficulties sex worker outsiders (and insiders) have reconciling the preconceived *notions* of "sex worker" and "victim" identities and needs with the complicated *lived experiences* of persons who exchange sex for money or other goods. Following Susan Dewey and Patty Kelly, the authors in our volume thus demonstrate how sex work can be a source of "precarious autonomy" (2011, 10) that is fraught with problems yet can still be an option chosen by a knowing, reasonable agent. Therefore, as the following chapters make clear, the "agency" of sex work isn't a "free choice" or liberation through selling sexual services, it is a complex, knowing negotiation.

Complicating the Politics of Sex Work

The chapters that follow examine many of the ways in which sex workers are struggling for agency and recognition and the role that state and non-state actors have in facilitating—or hampering—these efforts. Political agency and civic standing are the central animating themes of this volume, and they are explored through examinations of sex workers' interactions with political processes that illustrate how sex workers, who are key political actors with diverse demands and capacities, achieve their civic, legal, and policy goals. The chapters are thus unified by their attention to the relations between the multiple sites of and actors in sex work politics. Through their multiple disciplinary lenses, the chapters highlight the different levels of power plays.

In developing this volume, we deliberately sought out scholarship from a range of fields—and scholars who work across fields—precisely because of the multiplicity of actors, institutions, and interests in sex work politics. This interdisciplinary approach is part of what enables us to make a unique, substantive contribution to the literature on this topic. The initial impetus for this book was a successful conference panel at the Western Political Science Association Meeting in March 2010, where we gathered four scholars who considered the politics of sex work from sexuality studies, political science, policy studies, and legal perspectives. Following this, we circulated a call for abstracts among academic departments and relevant listservs in the United States and abroad. We received over sixty abstracts, and from these—based on thematic coherence—we selected and cultivated the chapters that now appear in this volume. The authors included represent a range of academic (and activist) disciplines and, thus, their works employ a variety of interdisciplinary methods. Without this multimethod approach, we could not persuasively and consistently support our argument about the multiple levels of sex work politics and the complex nature of political agency.

We begin presenting our argument about sex workers' political agency in part 1, "Sex Work and the Politics of Knowledge Production," by considering how knowledge about sex work and sex workers is generated. Arguably, the persistence of the victim/agent debate is, in part, an epistemological problem; victimization and agency remain dichotomously and ideologically cast terms in part because of the ways in which knowledge about sex work and sex workers is generated and then used to produce public policy. Therefore, to see sex workers as agents requires rethinking not just *what* we know about sex work and sex workers but *how we know* it.

Of course, debates over methodology in studying sex workers have been raging for decades, going back at least to the "feminist sex wars" era. At issue are appropriate sampling methods, ideological biases in the framing of questions and study populations, generalizability, and procedures for conducting, replicating, and disseminating research. For example, street-based sex workers and incarcerated populations are overrepresented in research on prostitution, and study samples are frequently not compared to control groups, or they are chosen only from researchers' or subjects' contacts who agree with the assumptions about prostitution as violence against women. Many researchers also do not share their survey tools or interview questions, which makes replication impossible (Norton-Hawk 2003; Shaver 2005; Weitzer 2005a).

Addressing these issues matters because they get to the heart of what it means to do "good" social science *and* because research shapes what we know about sex work and sex workers. How do sex workers make sense of violence, victimization, and opportunities for agency? How do the ways in which sex workers evince agency demonstrate how to negotiate the broader structural conditions in which people find themselves embedded? How do sex workers simultaneously challenge and reaffirm these conditions? How do some policy interventions improve, or deteriorate, the material and psychological well-being of sex workers? The way research is conducted determines how and whether we can answer these and other policy questions.

Therefore, one unique contribution of our volume is its insistence on a new model of knowledge production. Rather than just rehashing the victimization/agency debates, the chapters in part I recognize and attempt to intervene in them by offering new models of how to carry out sex work research; in doing so, they defend and develop models of "subject–subject" research rather than models that perpetuate "researcher–object" relationships.[4] To do this, all three chapters in this section offer self-critical reflections on the process and product of community-engaged sex work research while further complicating the meaning of the "community" under study. These chapters' reflective stances illustrate one of their key methodological arguments—it is essential for researchers to be aware of their unique subject positions in relation to sex workers and how these positions influence the knowledge that is produced by the research. Such explicit self-awareness leads to more nuanced—and more "objective"—results. This methodological argument in part I reframes our understandings of how sex workers negotiate competing policy interests—as well as how sex workers articulate their own understandings of their work and themselves—at the apex of the trafficking narrative's hold on policy discussions and popular consciousness. Thus, our volume challenges the popular wisdom in part by challenging how that wisdom has been generated.

Michele Tracy Berger and Kathleen Guidroz (chapter 1) kick off this challenge. Using their own experiences researching street-based and indoor prostitution and telephone sex work, they discuss the current limits of available research approaches for preparing social scientists to confront the stigma of sexuality in their research and the role that their own sexuality plays in conducting research with sex workers. Berger and Guidroz argue for a politics-of-location approach that foregrounds sexuality as an important dimension of experience that shapes research on the sex industry *and* other types of qualitative inquiry. By highlighting the role of sexuality in many kinds of research projects, they challenge social science researchers to address more adequately the role of personal and professional stigma in their research processes. A politics-of-location approach is the critical inquiry stance that can resituate sexuality—and sex work research more centrally—in social science research practices.

Both Alexandra Lutnick (chapter 2) and Raven Bowen and Tamara O'Doherty (chapter 3) "operationalize" a version of the politics-of-location approach as they describe and analyze the participatory research studies they have conducted. Both chapters demonstrate the epistemological gains from peer-produced, methodologically complex research design and implementation. Lutnick's Sex Worker Environmental Assessment

Team (SWEAT) study was a participatory research study with sex workers in San Francisco, California, that sought to discover their preferred legal framework for the sex industry. Using both qualitative and quantitative methods, Lutnick's study—a combined effort of researchers at the University of California–San Francisco and the St. James Infirmary, a peer-run sex worker health clinic—is an example of how transparent, rigorous, and participant-inclusive research can be conducted successfully. Not only did the researchers learn more about the population under study, but the peer investigators gained intellectual and career development skills.

Similarly, Bowen and O'Doherty's chapter analyzes the ethical guidelines developed by Bowen in her participatory research with the grassroots, sex worker–driven organization called Prostitution Alternatives, Counseling, and Education (PACE) Society. The authors describe how Bowen's ethical guidelines for collaborative research were operationalized in O'Doherty's study of victimization of off-street sex workers in Vancouver, British Columbia, in each stage of the research project, from design through dissemination. The authors then explain the challenges and successes they experienced and offer suggestions for implementing this model in future research projects.

Taken together, these three chapters highlight how to generate knowledge about sex workers, from sex workers, in a way that provides them with the resources they need to tackle the problems they see in the industry (as opposed to the "problems" other people want to solve or focus on). These studies clarify the ways that academics and sex workers (who are sometimes the same people) can work together more productively. The chapters then suggest how to make both the politics of sex work and the politics of *sex work research* more visible and less polarized. The chapters in parts II and III build on the politics of participation and the political knowledge produced by the differently situated researchers and subjects that have been set out in part I.

Part II, "Producing the Sex Worker: Law, Politics, and Unintended Consequences," moves from considering how research produces knowledge about sex workers to how public policy creates rather narrow (and often contradictory) categories for understanding sex workers socially and legally. Political science research indicates that policy shapes political subjects in a variety of ways, particularly by "socially constructing" the *subjects* of policy. As Anne Schneider and Helen Ingram have written extensively, social constructions—the cultural characterizations or popular images of the persons or groups whose well-being and behavior is affected by public policy—have a powerful influence on public officials and shape the design of policy. These constructions send messages about what government is supposed to do *and* about which groups citizens belong to, which ones are deserving, and what participatory patterns in the policy process are appropriate for them in society (Schneider and Ingram 1993; 1995; 1997).

The chapters in this section add to and complicate these findings by exploring further how societal, legal, and policy regimes at the local, state, and international levels interact to produce and construct sex workers as citizen-subjects. As we already discussed, sex work–related policy is often motivated by and developed with particular notions of agency and victimization in mind. Consequently, the chapters in this section indicate further how local and national policies that often claim to "protect" or "save" women (and men) from the abuses of sex work often socially construct sex workers as nonagentic victims and further marginalize them in the political process. This is particularly apparent in Annie Hill's (chapter 4) discursive analysis of *Paying the Price*, a British Home Office report that describes prostitution as violence against women while arguing for proactive policing of prostitution to combat this violence. As Hill argues, the creation and publication of this document illustrates an ironic shift in British prostitution policy where, on the one hand, it develops a "sympathetic" view of prostitution among members of the public. But on the other hand, it limits spaces where sex workers—especially those who do not or will not fit themselves into the "victim" framework—could be active as citizens who exercise their demands for social, legal, and political rights.

In a different context, that of Canadian body-rub parlors, Cheryl Auger (chapter 5) also uses discourse analysis to examine critically the municipal codes licensing these sex work venues in Canada's twenty largest cities. She reveals how licensing bylaws actually construct sex workers as ugly, deviant, and abnormal, which ultimately undermines their health, safety, and standing as full citizens. Drawing on the insights and methods presented in part I, Auger argues that these policies would improve if sex workers were involved in their development and implementation. This would also go some way toward treating sex workers as full members— that is, citizens—of the democratic polity and toward improving their health and safety.

Following from Hill and Auger's examination of the unintended con-sequences of domestic policies, the next two chapters consider how the interplay of domestic and international trafficking policies has similar out-comes for the agency interests of sex workers. First, Thaddeus Gregory Blanchette and Ana Paula da Silva's (chapter 6) political ethnography analyzes the discourses employed by the main agents in Brazil's National Plan to Combat Human Trafficking. Although Brazil's policy program claimed to protect victims and circumscribe trafficking, Blanchette and da Silva explain how it actually criminalizes victims and subverts labor protections for sex workers in a country where prostitution is legal. Ulti-mately, Brazil's antitrafficking policy constructs women in prostitution not as workers but as dangerous subjects in need of state surveillance that lim-its their mobility both internationally and within Brazil.

Next Edith Kinney (chapter 7) draws on her field research in Thai-land from 2004 to 2005 and 2007 to examine the tensions between "crime control" and "rights-based" approaches to human trafficking and exploi-tation in the Thai sex industry. Specifically, she considers how, over the past three decades, Thailand's sex industry has been the target of advocacy campaigns by state institutions and a host of antiprostitution, sex workers' rights, public health, and faith-based NGOs attempting to ameliorate the negative impacts of sex tourism, HIV/AIDS, human trafficking, and com-mercial sexual exploitation. Her analysis indicates that despite increased collaboration between NGOs and state agencies to develop a gender-sensitive, rights-based response to human trafficking in Thailand, in prac-tice, many interventions compound rights violations against exploited migrants. Failure to listen to, and take seriously, the claims and needs artic-ulated by the "victims" themselves contributes to many of these counter-productive policies. The failures Kinney points to remind us of where we started in this volume: with the need to construct knowledge and public policy with—rather than for—sex workers.

In part, the first four chapters in part II demonstrate how various domestic and international laws and policies socially construct sex work-ers (often as victims and/or criminals); in turn, sex workers must navigate these constructions in their political efforts to express and develop their agency. But such limiting social constructions are not solely produced by policies that increase criminal penalties against sex work and/or human trafficking. For example, Joyce Outshoorn's chapter (chapter 8) explores the Netherlands, whose policy practices are often heralded, as we already noted, as examples of the successful *legalization* of sex work. To consider whether the Dutch model deserves the praise, Outshoorn explores whether legalization has improved sex workers' civil rights, finding this is largely a function of a sex workers' nation of origin. She explains how Dutch policy ultimately constructs two categories of sex workers, and, hence, citizens: the modern, assertive native Dutch sex worker and the helpless immigrant who is either a trafficking victim or an enterprising migrant profiteer.

In addition to criminalization and legalization, decriminalization policies also socially construct sex workers' agency in limiting ways. But the point of our final chapter in this section is not only to show that all state actions—as exercises of power—produce citizen-subjects. Gregg Bucken-Knapp, Johan Karlsson Schaffer, and Pia Levin (chapter 9) also illuminate how feminists as and with policymakers shape these conditions of subjectivity in important ways. To illustrate this point, they examine the discursive interplay between sex workers and government officials at the national level, particularly as this pertains to decriminalization and efforts to "end demand" in Sweden and Finland in the 1990s and 2000s. Drawing on comparative political theory, they argue that the difference between these countries is largely rooted in feminists' different deployments of particular discourses. In Sweden, feminists successfully used discourses of gender equality in conjunction with causal stories characterizing female prostitutes as having abusive life histories, leading to a consensus among political elites that banning the purchase of sexual services would serve the purposes of gender equality and female protection. In Finland, however, no similar hegemonic discourse existed. While feminist policymakers pushed for similar bans, the responding interest groups, policymakers, and sex workers successfully mobilized ideas regarding the rights of individuals to make decisions regarding one's own body without state interference.

While part II considers the myriad ways that state actors and public policy construct who the "sex worker" is and what her needs are, part III, "Negotiating Status: The Promises and Limits of Sex Worker Organizing," examines sex workers' *own* organizational efforts to combat laws that interfere with their self-defined needs and contribute to ideas of them as deviant, sinful, or total victims. These chapters both build on and challenge political science research documenting that policies have "feedback" effects that influence and reflect participatory patterns. An example of this feedback effect in the American context is Suzanne Mettler's work demonstrating that large, nationalized and smoothly administered programs and policies such as the GI Bill and various New Deal Policies helped constitute politically efficacious citizens who are more active in political and civic life than those connected to government through particularistic, variable, state-level policies (Mettler 1998, 2005). And as Joe Soss compares Aid to Families with Dependent Children (AFDC) recipients with those receiving Supplemental Security Disability Income (SSDI), he finds that AFDC recipients felt more negative toward government and, hence, less civically efficacious than those in the universal SSDI program (Schram and Soss 1998; Soss 1999; 2000). Similar relationships are apparent in the realm of criminal justice policy and programming (which many persons engaged in prostitution encounter), where research indicates citizens who interact with prisons and other elements of the "carceral state" are less likely to participate in politics and carry out other responsibilities of citizenship (Lerman and Weaver 2010).

While not rejecting the policy feedback effects that both Mettler and Soss found in their studies, our contributors find that, across a range of locations, these feedback effects are muted and redirected as they are filtered through sex workers' resistance to the discursive constructions they face. The policy feedback model would assume that criminalization and marginalization would silence sex workers, but these stigmas in some ways create conditions of community, as sex workers find they have to articulate their interests collectively in order to fight the carceral state. The ways in which this collective action happens, though, are of course mediated through the individual and collective interests of citizens living on the margins of respectability. So while public policy shapes their responses, it rarely silences them. Sex workers indeed exercise a wide field of agency.

Since the 1970s, sex workers across the globe have been working inside and outside the state to change public and legal understandings of and responses to their labor by creating their own formal and informal support systems and organizations. Chapters in this section examine some of sex workers' more current self-organizational efforts (and the results thereof), and they consider the specific dilemmas raised both by the illegal, quasi-legal, and stigmatized nature of sex work and by the highly innovative political and social actions they produce. Here, then, is another view on the politics-of-location approach discussed in part I. Because of their marginal position, sex workers' efforts at self-definition are sometimes engaged through channels easily overlooked by "traditional" research and thinking about politics, such as worker-based collectives, blogs, and discursive productions. But these efforts are often better suited to some of the unique obstacles sex workers face in contesting the politics of social construction where sex and labor mix.

For example, as Gregor Gall (chapter 10) explains, unionization has often been advocated as a means of promoting labor rights for sex workers. But despite valiant efforts by sex workers, initially in the global north and later in the global south, unionization (as traditionally defined) has proved difficult to implement and inappropriate to the specific labor needs and interests of sex workers. Therefore Gall both describes and argues for forms collective action and interest representation by sex workers that do not follow a traditional unionization model. Drawing on earlier sex worker self-organization efforts by groups such as Call Off Your Old Tired Ethics (COYOTE) in the United States and the Red Thread in the Netherlands, Gall contends that emphasizing civil, political, and human rights might actually be the better strategy for achieving the economic and labor rights that sex workers are also seeking. This is partly because political rights activism is better suited to the nature and needs of sex worker activists who face, in Gall's terms, "extra-workplace political and legal regimes" that require collective action independent of operators, employers, and other third parties. Sex workers' demands for economic justice are thus necessarily situated in an interlocking political-economic perspective. Further, those early advocacy groups were organized by the workers themselves rather than by outsiders and thus fulfill important aspects of democratic self-development that modern polities ideally seek to encourage.

Following Gall's more general analysis, Valerie Feldman's chapter (chapter 11) looks at a specific example of sex workers' (nonunion) self-organizing, the sex-worker blog *Bound, Not Gagged*. This blog, and the off-line activism that accompanies it, overcomes some of the organizational limits of unionization efforts; for example, workers can still be solitary laborers but also group members and social activists. The blog and ancillary efforts also serve as a bridge between those spaces that allow insiders to engage in private resource mobilization and debates and discussions with outsiders—namely, non–sex workers—who may or may not be sympathetic to the sex worker–agency and self-development model and arguments. The blog then crafts a new public face for sex workers—combating the "abject, abnormal" model Auger discusses—while the sex workers debate and refine their insider identities as well.

Like many other groups, sex workers' resistance and self-definition efforts are often mediated by the structures they employ and engage with, such as NGOs. And so the final two chapters in this section illustrate and build on many of the findings in scholarship on "NGO-ization," which considers NGOs' roles in evaluating and administering self-help, social service, and training programs with participatory consequences for marginalized communities. This research acknowledges that while NGOs often become more hierarchal and less likely to act as "critical outsiders" when they work with governments to deliver services (Alvarez 1999), they also provide space for marginalized groups to gather, heal, and develop civic skills and political capital (Magno 2008). Moreover, as Sonia Alvarez writes, these NGO collaborations with government provide a seat at the table for many groups previously excluded from policy development and implementation processes (Alvarez 1999), which may further empower and enable then to promote social change (Courville and Piper 2004; Magno 2008).

Both Yasmin Lalani (chapter 12) and Sarah Beer and Francine Tremblay (chapter 13) examine the political balance many sex workers, state and governmental agencies, feminists, and NGOs negotiate; while many claim to be allies working in the best interests of sex workers, critics claim these efforts further marginalize sex workers (and advocacy for their concern) in political and social life. First, Lalani considers two community-based sex worker NGO efforts to combat HIV/AIDS and sexually transmitted infections among the larger community in Iquitos, Peru. Both organizations engage in political advocacy for sexual minorities in addition to health promotion. Using a gender relations framework, Lalani demonstrates how sex workers' community building and organizing in the wake of the HIV/AIDS epidemic positioned them as actors with social agency, not only to protect themselves against HIV and sexually transmitted infections through successful condom negotiation, but also to transmit their knowledge of HIV/AIDS prevention to male clients. As grassroots groups, the community organizations had fraught negotiations with state authorities as they tried to reduce the stigma associated with sex work and become respected health educators. Their actions provoke new questions about the limits of what sex workers can achieve or aim for when addressing HIV in the Amazon. To the degree that the women's successful social activism was predicated on their role as sex workers (who are outsiders to formal regimes of power), Lalani's work also raises provocative questions about the difficulties for success when state or NGO "insiders" are the primary agenda setters trying serve the needs of marginalized "outsiders."

Finally, Tremblay and Beer trace the emergence and activities of Stella, a health and social services nonprofit NGO created by sex workers' rights activists in Montréal, Canada. Drawing on social movement theory and multimethod qualitative research, the authors consider how Stella's engagement with the policy process both benefited and compromised their broader struggle for the political recognition and destigmatization of persons engaged in prostitution. They illustrate that while Stella's receipt of government funding and engagement in city and provincial political processes (concerning street prostitution and, later, HIV/AIDS prevention) increased their public profile, this also led them to formalize and professionalize their organization, thereby challenging their inclusion of and connection to their grassroots. While attending to the potential problem of delegitimizing radical critiques proffered by the community when activist groups work with the state, Tremblay and Beer also defend a more sanguine view about the dangers of working with the state than other contributors to this volume (and other scholars who have studied the compromises that grassroots groups must make when they become partial agents of state interests or rely too heavily on state relief [Daniels and Brooks 1997; Densham 1997]). If Lalani's work suggests that an outsider location is necessary for achieving some of the very insider goals put forth by the state, then Tremblay and Beer seem to counter that the benefits of working with and inside the state to advance group interests largely outweigh the deficits.

Notes

1. For some recent examples of this perspective, see Farley (2005; 2007), Farley et al. (2003), Farley and Kelly (2000), Hotaling et al. (2003), Hughes (2003), Hughes and Raymond (2001).

2. As Phoenix (2007, 8–9) notes, only New Zealand and the state of New South Wales, Australia, have decriminalized prostitution, and even these cases are limited; New South Wales decriminalized only brothels, and New Zealand has a few regulations and criminal sanctions still in place regarding age and citizenship status requirements.

3. Harrington (2012); Hubbard, Matthews, and Scoular (2008); Kilvington, Day, and Ward (2001); Scoular (2010); Sullivan (2010); and Wijers (2008) all detail

and compare the positive and negative aspects of the different regimes as they have been implemented in different countries and the various municipalities within them.

4. Disagreements over methods in sex work research are debated at length elsewhere. See, for example, Weitzer (2005a; 2005b), Raymond (2003), Farley (2005), Agustín (2007), Raphael and Shapiro (2004), and Kuo (2002, especially chapter 1).

References

Abrams, Kathryn. 1995. "Sex Wars Redux: Agency and Coercion in Feminist Legal Theory." *Columbia Law Review* 95, no. 2: 304–76.

ACT-UP. 2003. "Global Gag Rule." http://www.actupny.org/reports/globalgagrule .html.

Agustín, Laura Maria. 2007. *Sex at the Margins: Migration, Labour Markets, and the Rescue Industry*. London: Zed Books.

Alvarez, Sonia. 1999. "Advocating Feminism: The Latin American Feminist NGO 'Boom.'" *International Feminist Journal of Politics* 1, no. 2: 181–209.

Barry, Kathleen. 1984. *Female Sexual Slavery*. New York: New York University Press.

Beneria, Lourdes. 1999. "Globalization, Gender and the Davos Man." *Feminist Economics* 5, no. 3: 61–83.

———. 2003. *Gender, Development and Globalization: Economics As If All People Mattered*. New York: Routledge.

Beneria, Lourdes, and Savitri Bisnath. 2003. *Global Tensions: Opportunities and Challenges in the World Economy*. New York: Routledge.

Beneria, Lourdes, and Gita Sen. 2001. "Class and Gender Inequalities and Women's Role in Economic Development—Theoretical and Practical Implications." In *Gender and Development: Theoretical, Empirical and Practical Approaches*, ed. Lourdes Beneria and Savitri Bisnath, 14–32. Northampton, Mass.: Edward Elgar.

Berman, Jacqueline. 2006. "The Left, the Right and the Prostitute: The Making of a US Antitrafficking in Persons Policy." *Tulane Journal of International and Comparative Law* 14: 269–94.

Bernard, Edwin. 2006. "US Anti-Prostitution Gag for HIV Work Unconstitutional, Rules US Judge." *AIDSmap News*, May 12. http://www.aidsmap.com/en/news/D03B0C8F-CCA5-4FF0-B976-8D920F4E6B80.asp.

Bernstein, Elizabeth. 2007. *Temporarily Yours: Intimacy, Authenticity, and the Commerce of Sex*. Chicago: University of Chicago Press.

———. 2010. "Militarized Humanitarianism Meets Carceral Feminism: The Politics of Sex, Rights, and Freedom in Contemporary Antitrafficking Campaigns." *Signs: Journal of Women in Culture and Society* 36, no. 1: 45–71.

Brandt, Allan. 1987. *No Magic Bullet: A Social History of Venereal Disease in the United States since 1880.* New York: Oxford University Press.

Bureau of Public Affairs. 2004. *The Link Between Prostitution and Sex Trafficking.* Washington, D.C.: U.S. Department of State, Bureau of Public Affairs.

Buvinich, Mayra. 2001. "Projects for Women in the Third World: Explaining Their Misbehavior." In *Gender and Development: Theoretical, Empirical and Practical Approaches*, ed. Lourdes Beneria and Savitri Bisnath, 499–511. Northampton, Mass.: Edward Elgar.

Coalition against Trafficking in Women (CATW). 2011. "An Introduction to CATW." http://womenintheworld.org/solutions/entry/coalition-against-trafficking-in -women.

Chapkis, Wendy. 2005. "Soft Glove, Punishing Fist: The Trafficking Victims Protection Act of 2000." In *Regulating Sex: The Politics of Intimacy and Identity*, ed. Elizabeth Bernstein and Laurie Shaffner, 51–66. New York: Routledge.

Cohen, Susan A. 2005. "Ominous Convergence: Sex Trafficking, Prostitution and International Family Planning." *The Guttmacher Report on Public Policy* 8, no. 1: 12–14. http://www.guttmacher.org/pubs/tgr/08/1/gr080112.html.

Courville, Sasha, and N. Piper. 2004. "Harnessing Hope through NGO Activism." *Annals of the American Academy of Political Science* 592, no. 1: 39–61.

Daniels, Cynthia R., and Rachelle Brooks, eds. 1997. *Feminists Negotiate the State: The Politics of Domestic Violence.* Lanham, Md.: University Press of America.

Densham, Andrea. 1997. "The Marginalized Uses of Power and Identity: Lesbians' Participation in Breast Cancer and AIDS Activism." In *Women Transforming Politics*, ed. Cathy Cohen, Kathleen Jones, and Joan Tronto, 284–301. New York: New York University Press.

Dewey, Susan, and Patty Kelly. 2011. *Policing Pleasure: Sex work, Policy, and the State in Global Perspective.* New York: New York University Press.

Doezema, Jo. 1998. "Forced to Choose: Beyond the Voluntary v. Forced Prostitution Dichotomy." In *Global Sex Workers: Rights, Resistance and Redefinition*, ed. Kamala Kempadoo and Jo Doezema, 34–50. New York: Routledge.

Ehrenreich, Barbara, and A. Hochschild. 2003. *Global Women: Nannies, Maids and Sex Workers in the New Economy.* New York: Henry Holt.

Farley, Melissa. 2005. "Prostitution Harms Women Even If Indoors: Reply to Weitzer." *Violence against Women* 11, no. 7: 950–54.

———. 2007. *Prostitution and Trafficking in Nevada: Making the Connections.* San Francisco, Calif.: Prostitution Research and Education.

Farley, Melissa, Ann Cotton, Jacqueline Lynne, Sybille Zumbeck, Frida Spiwak, Maria Reyes, Dinorah Alvarez, and Ufuk Sezgin. 2003. "Prostitution and Trafficking in Nine Countries: An Update on Violence and Post-Traumatic Stress Disorder." In *Prostitution, Trafficking and Traumatic Stress*, ed. Melissa Farley, 33–74. Binghamton, N.Y.: Haworth Press.

Farley, Melissa, and Vanessa Kelly. 2000. "Prostitution: A Critical Review of the Medical and Social Science Literature." *Women and Criminal Justice* 11, no. 4: 26–64.

Fouché, Gwladys. 2007. "Prostitutes Fume as Norway Bids to Criminalise Sex Purchases." *Sunday Times Online*, July 22.

Godfrey, Brian. 1995. "Restructuring and Decentralization in a World City." *Geographical Review* 85, no. 4: 436–57.

Gozdziak, Elzbieta, and Elizabeth Collett. 2005. "Research on Human Trafficking in North America: A Review of the Literature." *International Migration* 43, no. 1–2: 99–128.

Harrington, Carol. 2012. "Prostitution Policy Models and Feminist Knowledge Politics in New Zealand and Sweden." *Sex Research and Social Policy* 9, no. 4: 337–49.

Harris-White, Barbara. 2003. "Development and Productive Deprivation: Male Patriarchal Relations in Business Families and their Implications for Women in South India." In *Global Tensions: Opportunities and Challenges in the World Economy*, ed. Lourdes Beneria and Savitri Bisnath, 209–22. New York: Routledge.

Hersh, Lauren. 2013. "Global Sex Trafficking and the Guy Next Door." *Huffington Post*, January 11. http://www.huffingtonpost.com/lauren-hersh/global-sex-trafficking-th_b_2451378.html.

Hotaling, Norma. 2007. "San Francisco's Successful Strategies: Prevention Services for Girls and the First Offender Prostitution Program." http://www.familyimpactseminars.org/s_mifiso6co8.pdf.

Hotaling, Norma, Autumn Burris, Julie Johnson, Yoshi Bird, and Kirsten Melbye. 2003. "Been There, Done That: SAGE, a Peer Leadership Model among Prostitution Survivors." In *Prostitution, Trafficking and Traumatic Stress*, ed. Melissa Farley, 255–66. Binghamton, N.Y.: Haworth Maltreatment and Trauma Press.

Hotaling, Norma, N. Dutto, P. Gibson, J. Coleman, T. Jackson, D. Nothmann, A. Cassidy, S. Sawyer, and P. Grant. 1997. *Social Justice, Health Education, Program Planning for Prostitutes and Solicitors* (unpublished outline). Cited in Hughes, Donna. 2004. *Best Practices to Address the Demand Side of Trafficking*, 33, note 113. Washington, D.C.: U.S. Department of State. http://www.uri.edu/artsci/wms/hughes/demand_sex_trafficking.pdf.

Hubbard, Phil, Roger Mathews, and Jane Scoular. 2008. "Regulating Sex Work in the EU: Prostitute Women and the New Spaces of Exclusion." *Gender, Place and Culture* 15, no. 2: 137–52.

Hughes, Donna. 2003. "Accommodation or Abolition?: Solutions to the Problem of Sexual Trafficking and Slavery." *National Review Online*, May 1. http://www.nationalreview.com/articles/206761/accommodation-or-abolition/donna-m-hughes.

Hughes, Donna, and Janice Raymond. 2001. *Sex Trafficking of Women into the United States*. Amherst, Mass.: Coalition against Trafficking in Women.

Kempadoo, Kamala. 2005. "From Moral Panic to Global Justice: Changing Perspectives on Trafficking." In *Trafficking and Prostitution Reconsidered: New Perspectives on Migration, Sex Work and Human Rights*, ed. Kamala Kempadoo, Jyoti Sanghera, and Barbara Pattanaik, vii–xxxiv. Boulder, Colo.: Paradigm Books.

Kilvington, Judith, Sophie Day, and Helen Ward. 2001. "Prostitution Policy in Europe: A Time of Change?" *Feminist Review*, no. 67: 78–93.

Kongar, Ebru. 2008. "Is Deindustrialization Good for Women? Evidence from the United States." *Feminist Economics* 14, no. 1: 73–92.

Koopman, Jeanne. 1991. "Neo-Classical Household Models and the Modes of Household Production: Problems in the Analysis of African Agricultural Households." *Review of Radical Political Economics* 23, no. 3–4: 148–73.

Kristof, Nicholas. 2009. "Sex Trafficking: Time to Launch a 21st-Century Abolitionist Movement." *Seattle Times*, January 8.

Kuo, Lenore. 2002. *Prostitution Policy: Revolutionizing Practice through a Gendered Perspective*. New York: New York University Press.

Lachynsky, Paul. 2005. "Over 100 Groups Urge Bush to Enforce Anti-Prostitution Policy to Aid Sexually Exploited Women and Children." *Medical News Today*, August 8. http://www.medicalnewstoday.com/releases/28834.php.

Lerman, Amy, and Vesla Weaver. 2010. "Political Consequences of the Carceral State." *American Political Science Review* 104, no. 4: 817–33.

Lustig, Jessica. 2007. "The 13-Year-Old Prostitute." *New York Times Magazine*, April 1.

Magno, Cathryn. 2008. "Refuge from Crisis: Refugee Women Build Political Capital." *Globalisation, Societies and Education* 6, no. 2: 119–30.

Meil-Hobson, Barbara. 1987. *Uneasy Virtue: The Politics of Prostitution and the American Reform Tradition*. New York: Basic Books.

Mettler, Suzanne. 1998. *Gender and Federalism in New Deal Public Policy*. Ithaca, N.Y.: Cornell University Press.

———. 2005. *Soldiers to Citizens*. Oxford: Oxford University Press.

NBC Bay Area. 2008. "Voters Choose Not to Legalize Prostitution in San Francisco." November 4. http://www.nbcbayarea.com/news/elections/local/Voters_Choose_Not_to_Legalize_Prostitution_in_San_Francisco.html.

Norton-Hawk, Maureen. 2003. "Social Class, Drugs, Gender and the Limitations of the Law: Contrasting the Elite Prostitute with the Street Prostitute." *Studies in Law, Politics and Society* 29, no. 1: 123–39.

Office of the Press Secretary. 2003. *Trafficking in Persons National Security Presidential Directive*. Washington, D.C. http://www.fas.org/irp/offdocs/nspd/trafpers.html.

O'Neill-Richards, Amy. 2000. *International Trafficking of Women to the United States*. Washington, D.C.: Central Intelligence Agency.

Phoenix, Jo. 2007. "Regulating Prostitution: Different Problems, Different Solutions, Same Old Story." *Community Safety Journal* 6, no. 1: 7–10.

Public Law 108-25. 2003. *Global AIDS Act.* http://www.gpo.gov/fdsys/pkg/PLAW-108publ25/pdf/PLAW-108publ25.pdf.

Purvis, Lara. 2011. "Hostile Clashes Dominate Women's Conference." *Xtra! Canada's Gay and Lesbian News,* July 18. http://www.xtra.ca/public/Ottawa/Hostile_clashes_dominate_womens_conference-10497.aspx.

Raphael, Jody, and Deborah L. Shapiro. 2004. "Violence in Indoor and Outdoor Prostitution Venues." *Violence against Women* 10, no. 2: 126–39.

Raymond, Janice. 2003. "Ten Reasons for *Not* Legalizing Prostitution and a Legal Response to the Demand for Prostitution." In *Prostitution, Trafficking and Traumatic Stress,* 315–32. Binghamton, N.Y.: Haworth Press.

Schneider, Ann, and Helen Ingram. 1993. "Social Construction of Target Populations: Implications for Politics and Policy." *American Political Science Review* 87, no. 2: 334–47.

———. 1995. "Social Construction (Continued): Response." *American Political Science Review* 89, no. 2: 441–46.

———. 1997. *Policy Design for Democracy, Studies in Government and Public Policy.* Lawrence: University Press of Kansas.

Schotten, C. Heike. 2005. "Men, Masculinity, and Male Domination: Reframing Feminist Analyses of Sex Work." *Politics and Gender* 1, no. 2: 211–40.

Schram, Sanford, and Joe Soss. 1998. "Making Something Out of Nothing: Welfare Reform and a New Race to the Bottom." *Publius* 28, no. 3: 67–88.

Scoular, Jane. 2010. "What's Law Got to Do With It? How and Why Law Matters in the Regulation of Sex Work." *Journal of Law and Society* 37, no. 1 (March): 12–39.

Sex Workers Project at the Urban Justice Center. 2005. *Behind Closed Doors: An Analysis of Indoor Sex Work in New York City.* New York: Sex Workers Project at the Urban Justice Center. http://www.sexworkersproject.org/publications/reports/behind-closed-doors.

Shaver, Francis. 2005. "Sex Work Research: Methodological and Ethical Challenges." *Journal of Interpersonal Violence* 20, no. 3: 296–319.

Shively, Michael, Sarah Jalbert, Ryan Kling, William Rhodes, Chris Flygare, Laura Tierney, Dana Hunt, David Squires, Christina Dyous, and Kristin Wheeler. 2008. "Final Report on the Evaluation of the First Offender Prostitution Program." Cambridge, Mass.: Abt Associates. https://www.ncjrs.gov/pdffiles1/nij/grants/222451.pdf.

Soderlund, Gretchen. 2005. "Running from the Rescuers: New US Crusades against Sex Trafficking and the Rhetoric of Abolition." *NWSA Journal* 17, no. 3: 64–87.

Soss, Joe. 1999. "Lessons of Welfare: Policy Design, Political Learning and Political Action." *American Political Science Review* 93, no. 2: 363–80.

———. 2000. *Unwanted Claims: The Politics of Participation in the US Welfare System*. Ann Arbor: University of Michigan Press.

Sullivan, Barbara. 2010. "When (Some) Prostitution Is Legal: The Impact of Law Reform on Sex Work in Australia." *Journal of Law and Society* 37, no. 1 (March): 85–104.

Trafficking Victims Protection Reauthorization Act. 2003. H.R. 2620.

U.S. Agency for International Development v. Alliance for Open Society International Inc. 2006. U.S. District Court for the Southern District of New York.

U.S. Department of State. 2010. *Trafficking in Persons Report 2010*. Washington, D.C. http://www.state.gov/g/tip/rls/tiprpt/2010/.

Weitzer, Ronald. 2005a. "Flawed Theory and Method in Studies of Prostitution." *Violence against Women* 11, no. 7: 1– 16.

———. 2005b. "The Growing Moral Panic over Prostitution and Sex Trafficking." *Criminologist* 30, no. 5: 2–5.

———. 2010. "The Mythology of Prostitution: Advocacy Research and Public Policy." *Sex Research and Social Policy* 7: 15–29.

The White House. 2003. Trafficking in Persons National Security Presidential Directive. Washington, D.C.: Office of the Press Secretary. http://www.fas.org/irp/offdocs/nspd/trafpers.html.

Wijers, Marjan. 2008. *Prostitution Policies in the Netherlands*. Amsterdam, the Netherlands: International Committee on the Rights of Sex Workers in Europe. http://lastradainternational.org/?main=documentation&document=1994.

YesOnPropK.org. 2009. "Worker Safety Is Public Safety." http://www.yesonpropk.org.

Young, Stephanie. 2009. "Freedom to Sell Sex? Prostitution Debate Continues." *Harvard Law Record*, December 4. http://hlrecord.org/?p=11594.

· I ·

Sex Work and the Politics of Knowledge Production

CHAPTER 1

Researching Sexuality

The Politics-of-Location Approach for Studying Sex Work

Michele Tracy Berger and Kathleen Guidroz

QUALITATIVE RESEARCHERS customarily consider how the visible aspects of their identity (i.e., race and gender) affect how their interviewees might respond to them. Other aspects of the researcher's identity, such as sexuality, are concealable and likely to remain invisible throughout the research encounter. However, qualitative social science research on sex work often brings the issue of sexuality (for both the researcher and the researched) to the front and center in unanticipated ways. Yet researchers' silence around sexuality seems to be the norm, and with a few exceptions (Bellamy, Gott, and Hinchliff 2011; Brak-Lamy 2012; Manalansan 2006) scholars' published works do not address the methodological questions concerning the range of potential sexual encounters and expressions in field research. This chapter reflects a collaboration of our thinking about the politics of sexuality in conducting sex work research from a critical feminist perspective.[1]

In the past thirty years, anthropologists and sociologists have expressed reservations about including qualitative field reflections that focused on certain identity categories such as race, social class, and gender. Today, however, it is unthinkable for social science researchers not only to ignore how all aspects of their identities shape field experiences but also not to grapple with the complicated role of identity (e.g., gender, race, nationality) in the field. Conceptualizing sexual identities, behaviors, and desires is important in the research encounter, and we propose a politics-of-location approach (Anthias 2002; Lorenz- Meyer 2004; Mohanty 1995; Rich 1986) as part of the methodological preparation in feminist sex work research. Adrienne Rich (1986) and later Chandra Mohanty (1995) were the first to acknowledge how one's locations or positions serve as a source of knowledge—as "the historical, geographical, cultural, psychic, and imaginative boundaries which provide the ground for political definition and self-definition" (Mohanty 1995, 68).

Anthropologists were the first scholars to rethink the importance of the researcher's stance vis-à-vis sexuality in fieldwork (see Kulick and Willson 1995; Markowitz and Ashkenazi 1999). They called for a reconsideration of sexuality in relation to field research, and they challenged earlier positivist theories that make sexuality suspect or abstract or relegate it to unanalyzed field notes. A politics-of-location approach extends anthropologists' ethnographic inroads into thinking about how a researcher's own views on sexuality shape research outcomes and could further help prepare researchers—before they formally begin their research on sex work—to anticipate and comprehend challenges that may arise during the research process. As Dagmar Lorenz-Meyer (2004) concedes, "practical methodological questions usually take precedence over a thorough inquiry into the researchers' own epistemic locations, agency and convictions" (1). We believe when researchers acknowledge that their sexuality is embedded in the multiple stages of qualitative research, this acknowledgment benefits social science research on sex work. Feminist researchers, in particular, will realize their goal of reflexivity (see Callaway 1992; Harding 1993) toward sexuality and understanding sex workers in their various environments.[2]

The politics-of-location approach to sex work research that we develop here builds on the more general framework developed by feminist self-reflexive researchers (Bloom 1997; Flowers 1998; Gluck and Patai 1991; Haraway 1988; Harding 1993; Harstock 1988; Kirsch 1999; Letherby 2003; Naples 2003; Seymour 1998; Visweswaran 1994; 1997; Wolf 1996). From this work our approach specifically acknowledges the importance of recognizing one's "positionality" (Anthias 2002)—the ongoing shifting locations of the self—throughout the research process to the "finished" product (Thapar-Björkert and Henry 2004; see also Geller and Stockett 2006). What our approach adds to the positionality framework is an explanation of how sexuality is coconstitutively produced in the research encounter with the potential to shape both data collection and analysis. Where the positionality literature emphasizes "multivocality" and the interview encounter as a "partnership" (Hesse-Biber and Leavy 2004, 141), a "coconstruction of . . . understanding" (Miller and Crabtree 2004, 188), or an opportunity for "erasing boundaries" (Visweswaran 1997), the politics-of-location approach in sex work research posits both researcher and respondent sexualities as shifting positions vis-à-vis each other and the knowledge they are (co)producing. And yet despite advances by feminist anthropological research on subjectivities and selfhood (see Boellstorff 2007) and by positivist-oriented social science research on the sex industry, neither approach has looked specifically at sexual subjectivities when researching sex work.

Thus what we pursue here is a *feminist* rethinking, reimagining, and retelling of how sexuality is not only performed but also produced throughout the research encounter for both researchers and respondents. Employing a politics-of-location approach enables researchers to understand how sexuality manifests itself in their fieldwork experiences and in their interactions with other scholars. This approach also contributes to scholars' capacity to make epistemologically useful assessments about participants' experiences of sex work and the sex industry. Finally, it encourages researchers to reflect on the ongoing challenges of researching sex work in the academy.

In this chapter we discuss the possibilities of a politics-of-location approach from our positions as sex work researchers engaged in fieldwork but also as European American and African American, and as queer-identified women. Examples from our research encounters illustrate the methodological and epistemological challenges of studying sex work without an attendant discussion about sexuality. Since the topic of sex work involves explicitly examining sexuality (albeit sexuality that is commercialized and often illegal), we argue that this research tends to have a unique impact on the researcher's professional and personal life. It often requires the researcher to confront the "whore stigma" (among other contested terrains about human sexuality) in both field research and academic communities (Chancer 1993; Pheterson 1989; 1993; 1996); however, current training in qualitative methods, particularly in the social sciences, lacks appropriate guidance for explicating researcher location and stance, sexual stigma, and the heterosexism embedded within the organization of commercial sex.

We believe that the politics-of-location approach we present in this chapter offers valuable epistemological insights to researchers who confront these challenges as they study sex work. After briefly discussing our own positions as sex work researchers, we consider three main analytical points that are often present while researching the commercial sex industry: sexuality in fieldwork, researcher positionality, and professional stigma. In the sections that follow we suggest how—in hindsight—a politics-of-location approach toward sexuality could have contributed to our initial qualitative research with sex workers and given us a framework to understand, respond to, and counter the stigma we faced within the academy.

Positioning Ourselves

Our "home" disciplines are political science (Berger) and sociology (Guidroz), and we came to sex work research through our feminist interests in gender, race, social class, power, and sexuality. Our qualitative research on sex work has taken place within the United States with a variety of sex worker populations, including women who engage in both sex for drugs and sex for monetary exchanges (Berger 2004), telephone sex operators (Guidroz and Rich 2010), call girls and escorts (Guidroz 2001), and dominatrixes (Guidroz 2008). Although the women (and some men) we studied occupy different dimensions of the sex industry, ranging from street-level prostitution to indoor commercial sex work, in our studies we faced similar challenges to how our sexuality was coconstructed with actors inside and outside the academy (e.g., our research participants, graduate student peers, academic professors and mentors, and other professional colleagues). Across venues and respondents our sexual identities, behaviors, and desires were constructed beyond the interview context (O'Connell Davidson and Layder 1994). As we discuss in the rest of this chapter, sexuality became a layered process throughout our research as we were confronted with and made aware of how our respondents viewed us, how we saw ourselves, and how we were perceived in the academy.

Berger came to the study of sex work after making connections about African American women's sexual representations within video culture and black popular culture. Moreover, during the late 1990s, she was aware of the shift in feminist attention in the United States to global sexual slavery issues. She felt that this focus on global issues provided easier victim/oppressor sex work narratives than the more complicated ones emerging on urban streets in America around race, crack cocaine, and sex work in the mid-1990s. Berger wanted to apply interdisciplinary multiracial feminist theories in an empirical sex work research project. She recognized the limitations of criminology's approach to sex work, as explained in her field notes (Berger 1998): "Studying female lawbreakers had solely been in the domain of criminology. I felt that these accounts lacked an analysis of the structure of sex work as a practice. If there were drugs involved, researchers (criminologists) suggested that all sex work practices and meanings were related to and subsumed under drug use—I found this to be an inadequate explanation both methodologically and substantively for explaining urban women's participation in sex work."

Berger entered her field research in Detroit, a large midwestern city, to understand the meanings women—particularly women of color—assigned to their street-level sex work and crack cocaine use. She interviewed sixty women and then followed and collected life histories from a "deep sample" of women who were HIV positive and became politically active in their communities (Berger 2004).

Guidroz decided to focus on sex work research because she was interested in women's labor experiences, such as sexual harassment. She recognized the dearth of scholarship on the labor of "bad girls"[3] for whom sexuality is "part of the job description." This interest was partially rooted in her experience growing up in New Orleans, where she regularly visited the French Quarter and observed gendered representations of commercialized sexuality (e.g., the infamous Bourbon Street). As a researcher, Guidroz's qualitative research (i.e., interviews) has centered primarily on two groups of sex workers: self-identified escorts (including call girls and dominatrixes) and telephone sex operators in different regions of the country. Her more recent research has two threads: (1) participants in commercial sadomasochism (S&M) and (2) grassroots and formal organizing for sex industry workers.

At the time, we were aware of how our race, age, and class (i.e., education) locations might affect our respondents' responses to us and vice versa. Here we briefly discuss two locations: race and class. By studying mostly lower-income women of color in a primarily African American city and functioning as a graduate student within a predominately white and male political science department, Berger was keenly aware that her minority status and research interests made her susceptible to additional unwanted scrutiny (and unstated judgment) by some professors and peers, as this 1998 field note indicates:

To explore the sexual dimensions of stigmatized women's lives meant a discussion of taboo subjects, and sometimes to doubly or triply "other" myself as an African American female researcher. I know that if I was doing a traditional [political science] research project on lobbying, I would not have at times felt shame and isolation as I tried to explain this project to colleagues. The nature of the research was in effect, to almost strip myself of the credibility of being someone pursuing a Ph.D., both inside and outside the field. Studying street level sex work was often to have my being sexualized in ways that I could not control.

In contrast to Berger, in Guidroz's research, respondents were primarily white and there was more class homogeneity due to her use of snowball and targeted sampling (see Shaver 2005). While there were some differences in educational attainment among respondents (ranging from high school diplomas to doctoral degrees), these differences did not greatly affect their middle-class status. Because the educational background of the respondents approximated Guidroz's background, many related to her from their own experience of the role of "student" despite their distinction through sex work participation.

Sexuality in Sex Work Field Research

As graduate students we were steeped in the available literatures on feminist and qualitative methodology and sex work. None of these literatures were sufficient, however, to prepare us for the complex features of sexuality both in and out of our field research. Likewise, there were also gaps on the topic of qualitative sex work research, mainly due to the lack of methodological scholarship—feminist and otherwise—on techniques of gaining access to and recruiting sex workers and other participants in the sex industry, complications that could arise in the field, and how to employ commodified sexuality as a category of analysis.

Such experiences meant that both of us were highly sensitized to sex workers' often marginalized and stigmatized position in society and maintained an awareness of racial status and social class barriers between our respondents and us. However we were still not prepared to handle how *sexuality* emerged in the research process with our respondents as well as our professors, mentors, and academic colleagues. We had to continually adjust our research expectations when some respondents were hesitant to describe their experiences using explicit sexual terms or when others showed no hesitation describing their interactions and encounters with their customers in explicit detail. Sometimes respondents divulged how their work lives compared with or interfered with their private lives, which meant disclosing multiple narratives. And because their work lives involved dealing with sexual harassment, stigma, and/or gender violence, hearing these experiences made us question whether we should offer help, give advice, or stay silent. A few respondents asked us to participate in their sex work encounters; and still others indicated wanting us to become their sexual partners beyond the research context. These experiences, combined with our sexualization by our academic peers, meant (re)negotiating our own sense of our sexual selves along with our variously positioned research participants.

Social scientists' interest in sex work research continues to grow (Kempadoo 1999; Parsons 2005; Weitzer 2010). However, discussions of the researcher's and the respondent's sexuality as an interactive, constructed, and relevant experience during the research encounter (i.e., gaining access, establishing rapport, interviewing, etc.) and for later analysis are rare. The current lack of dialogue and methodological preparation among researchers to understand issues of sexuality, which we assume to include sexual identities, behaviors, and sexual desire (Schwartz and Rutter 1998), is a critical epistemological issue. Although it is often unacknowledged, ignored, or suppressed, a researcher's sexuality is often braided through many components of a qualitative project on sex work, including how researchers develop rapport with respondents, what they discuss with peers and mentors, and ultimately what they reveal in their scholarship. While quantitative researchers engaged in knowledge production might consider how individuals respond to issues of sexuality in surveys, in this chapter we focus on qualitative research that requires repeated face-to-face contact, including interviews, ethnography, and participant observations.

Altogether, we had no academic models that shed any light on these issues. In consulting various texts (e.g., a broad qualitative literature; see Sanders 2006), there was a general silence about how to negotiate sexuality—ours and sex workers'—while conducting field research. We felt that we were competent collecting data in the field; however, we also recognized the necessity of talking competently about sex work to others. Sexuality, metaphorically and ironically, had become the elephant in the room.

As the two of us compared notes on our field experiences, what was shockingly obvious is that we failed to anticipate our own complicated responses to sexuality during our qualitative research. For example, as part of Guidroz's "research bargain" (Warren and Karner 2010, 95), she attended "sex clubs" in Washington, D.C., in order to meet sex industry participants in a field setting, gain their trust prior to interviewing, and make observations to supplement her analysis. She watched open sexual and sadomasochistic encounters, mostly involving women who were nude or seminude, as part of a predominantly male audience (and at times standing shoulder-to-shoulder). Guidroz's observations of women in these sexual/sadomasochistic "scenes" alongside men mirrored what Sheila Rowbotham experienced while watching the Beatles' *Magical Mystery Tour* movie in 1967, in which members of the band enter a "strip tease" with a group of men. Viewing this part of the movie, Rowbotham later wrote, was like "watch[ing] another woman as if I were a man. . . . I was being asked to desire myself" (qtd. in Smith 1987, 52). While observation is a technique many qualitative researchers employ, in this instance Guidroz missed opportunities to better understand the participants she was observing and the context within which they engaged with the sex industry. In other words, Guidroz's preoccupation with the *gender* dynamics of these sexualized encounters interfered with her understanding of the *sexual* dynamics to these gendered encounters.

Of course, our ultimate goal as researchers is to have a more complete and accurate understanding of the sex industry. Nonetheless, ours is primarily a cautionary tale that can push researchers to use the politics-of-location approach to highlight the role of sexuality as a site of legitimate meaning making during the research process and to contribute to destigmatizing the study of sex work in the academy. Later we provide more detailed examples of how the politics-of-location approach could be utilized in the field and in the academy.

For researchers and their participants, sexuality can manifest itself in multiple ways, including trepidation about discussing sexual topics, unexpected arousal from such discussions or observations, and misperceptions by respondents and their associates (e.g., employers, friends, partners, or clients) about the purpose of conducting such research. Negotiating sexuality in the field begins when a researcher gains access to respondents and continues through building rapport and maintaining respondents' trust. In our research we negotiated not only the broad palette of sexuality but also overt heterosexism. An example of the former took place when a male-to-female transgender respondent (whose clientele were men) asked Guidroz to accompany her during the respondent's first visit to a lesbian bar with which Guidroz was already familiar. It was not clear whether the respondent wanted Guidroz to help her meet women socially or to recruit female clients. When women approached them in the bar, Guidroz wondered not only whether the respondent would "pass" as a woman but also about their ability to "pass" as something other than a researcher–respondent dyad, such as two female friends visiting a lesbian bar. Guidroz questioned her own professional and sexual "authenticity" (see Brak-Lamy 2012 on "seduction" behaviors in fieldwork). If Guidroz disclosed the true nature of their relationship to others at the bar, then the trust established between the respondent and her would have been violated. Like other field experiences Guidroz had, this encounter within the context of the bar entailed multiple layers of identity, yet she left it out of her dissertation. A politics-of-location approach would have enabled Guidroz to extend her focus from "sex workers' labor experiences" exclusively to one that explored the "seamlessness" between a sex worker's work life, her or his personal life, and a researcher's involvement in either or both of them (Statham, Miller, and Mauksh 1988, 12). In other settings there was also explicit flirting, seduction, and propositions from respondents and other participants in the field. These occurrences led to changes in the way we began to understand research on sexual experiences and practices.

Based on our research experiences with sex workers, we began to raise questions that contribute to a politics-of-location approach: Should we disclose our own sexual identity or interests if that seems important to our respondents (Letherby 2003 refers to a researcher's "sense of the self")? Or do we try to protect ourselves through nondisclosure or "bracketing" elements of the encounter (see Denzin 1989)? How do we as social scientists analyze the myriad sexual practices and opportunities presented to us? At times, issues of sexual identity and/or orientation were definitely taboo—as we stated earlier, the sex industry remains a mostly heterosexist environment—though Berger was surprised to find some respondents describing bisexual, lesbian, and heterosexual women "pimping" other women, as well as lesbian and bisexual women who were engaged with other women of similar orientation in organized sexual events and drug use.

Given that our sexual identity is simultaneously being constructed with that of our respondents' (Lerum 2001; Markowitz 1999), we must be aware that this construction is sometimes problematic for researchers (e.g., Goode 1999). There is often talk among researchers about the ways that research impacts our lives; indeed, much of the qualitative research process is about building relationships. Thus how could sexuality not be part of this experience? Despite this, researchers like us have not been forthcoming about the explicit sexual conversations they had, how the conversations affected them, and their ways of understanding respondents' lives. Our own ambivalence and indecision in the field suggest there is not one "correct" way to respond to a particular fieldwork situation.

Researcher Positionality: Negotiating the Role of "Sex Work Researcher"

For research on commercial sex work, a politics-of-location approach does not require researchers to fall within or adopt the same identity categories as their respondents to "truly understand" or to identify with them (Wahab and Sloan 2004; see also England 1994). Instead it suggests that, within this role, they demonstrate a willingness to explore commonalities and differences between researchers and their study populations and to theorize and write about issues of sexuality as (or if) they present themselves in all phases of the research process.

In our role as sex worker researchers, neither of us personally adopted the "whore" label nor attempted to transcend those boundaries as some feminist scholars studying sex worker communities have done in order to better understand their participants and to participate in the destigmatizing of sex work (Bell 1995; Chapkis 1997). We did not find that option appealing for a variety of complicated reasons including the nature of the work, the safety of it, and its legality. Granted, there were contradictions in our research: we both felt pressured to differentiate ourselves from sex workers and avoid being labeled as such by respondents, others associated with our field research, or those in the academy (more on this in the next section). On reflection, we have wondered how navigating professional stigma and our reluctance to write more honestly about sexuality affected our analyses of our respondents' accounts (see Bradley-Engen 2009). While we realize that intrepid researchers often embark on a diversity of qualitative projects that leave them feeling vulnerable and uncomfortable in the field, few research experiences exist where the researcher is likely to feel as unsupported and even scorned as they are when researching the sex industry. Several researchers who have also participated in the sex industry as sex workers have identified this phenomenon (see Bradley-Engen 2009; Flowers 1998; Frank 2002), and it's highly, though differently, acute for non–sex worker researchers of sex work as well.

A hallmark of qualitative research is a complex relational process of seeking potential respondents and/or potential research sites, building and sustaining rapport with research participants, exiting from the research site, and changing (if not ending) the relationship that was established with respondents (Feldman, Bell, and Berger 2003). We therefore believe the researcher's ongoing presentation of self to sex worker participants is a critical part of access and rapport building, which in turn requires thoughtful choices *before* and *while* conducting the research. How we presented ourselves as non–sex worker researchers was as important in facilitating the data-gathering process as it was for reducing or eliminating barriers between sex workers and ourselves.

For example, Guidroz's key informant initially believed that Guidroz was interested in meeting sex workers to gather enough information about sex work and to begin working in the industry. When he learned Guidroz was not entering the industry as a worker, he asked her whether she was looking for a girlfriend or lover among the sex workers he knew. After he fully understood she was a graduate student and why she was engaging in research on the sex industry, he then encouraged her to begin "swinging" in order to get to know other individuals with "alternative lifestyles" (though not the focus of her research) and invited her to "*meet up*" where "play couples" (see Frank 2007) attended such events. Her field notes (e.g., "*Was it an invitation from him for sex?*") on this part of her research never entered her analysis or her published work in sociology and, as a result, the opportunity to apply a politics-of-location approach to this encounter was lost. Had she taken this analytic opportunity, she could have explored the power dynamics in this interaction in which the informant did not accept her assertion of her own location. How did this refusal contribute to the coconstitution of both the researchers' and informants' sexual positionalities?

In her role as a researcher, Berger found it difficult to negotiate the broader context of sexuality that saturated the field experience, not primarily because of respondents' reactions to her presence but because of other actors (often male) whom she had to initially rely on for access. She recruited participants in multiple locations, but when she was on the street or in court, it was clear that primarily African American men (on the street as substance users, clients, or boyfriends/pimps, and in court as bailiffs and police officers) controlled and shaped most social interactions. In several instances, male bailiffs asked to be interviewed, which she agreed to in order to learn more about the local context of substance use and street-level sex work. Most often during these interviews, the bailiffs proceeded to sexually harass Berger and refused to offer useful information unless she agreed to an explicit date with them. In the following field notes (1998), Berger describes her experience:

> I was very aware in the field that I was not like the women there. Too closely identifying with them on the street I felt carried risks. Even people who were supposed to be serving these women often regarded the women as worthless and judged people who had interest in them as either sexual deviants or naive. People in the field (particularly men), including judges, bailiffs and police officers, however, who were not a part of the research felt freer to tell me their likes and dislikes about women on the street. They also felt freer to engage me in personal discussions of sexuality. Because they were able to help me sustain access in order to interview some respondents, I had to decide how much of a sexual awareness/persona I was going to share with them.

The reality for Berger was that she had to fend off propositions while in the field. Her location as both observer and participant—and as a graduate student conducting research while simultaneously being sexualized—in relation to those with whom she came in contact necessitated exerting a great amount of emotional energy in developing strategies of avoidance and deflection. These strategies included figuring out what schedules certain bailiffs worked (in order to avoid them), making sure she left before a lunch break (where she might be asked to join a bailiff for lunch), and setting up on-the-spot interviews with potential respondents (so she did not have to linger in a particular courtroom).

The ways in which Berger was propositioned also speak to sexuality's coconstitutive relationship with race. As an individual, Berger dealt with advances that were based on perceived ideas of racial solidarity (i.e., a seemingly available heterosexual African American woman "should" be receptive to sexual advances by an African American man). She was also studying a group of women (many were African American) who were "understood" to be sexually deviant, which tended to overwhelm other aspects of their identities (e.g., as mothers, sisters). As a result sexuality, as embedded with racial histories, defined the field experience. These encounters that Berger faced both in the field and later in the academy stem from the long history of perceiving African American women as hypersexual and sexually deviant (Collins 1991). For Berger—like Guidroz—multivocality was missing; she was slotted into roles or positions she had little voice in creating or choosing and she had to keep negotiating them throughout the researching and writing processes.

In contrast to our experiences, Wendy Chapkis (1997) suggests that in her research on the sex industry she drew on the multiple dimensions of being a marginalized researcher in sociology (see Chapkis 1986) and made explicit her self-reflective work on gender and sexuality issues. She took up massage and practiced massage (in California and Amsterdam), purchased sexual services (in California), and engaged in sex work (only in Amsterdam) while studying women who offered massages and sexual services. Her dynamic role as participant and observer gave Chapkis another lens for understanding the physical and emotional demands and scheduling of this type of labor. By engaging in nontraditional and potentially stigmatizing activities and then revealing these activities to her respondents, Chapkis attempted to create opportunities for trust and rapport building. By revealing these activities to fellow scholars, Chapkis provides one model (and we would argue a courageous one) of how to employ a politics-of-location approach in empirical sex work research. At the same time, her work raises many questions about how other researchers (especially male) might be received if they adopted similar strategies. A researcher conducting sex work research involving participant observation must navigate a complicated terrain of being both insider and outsider (see also Kanuha 2000). This particular research method requires perhaps the most meticulous deployment of the politics-of-location approach, as the boundaries between researched and researcher can blur within a short span of time.

Rapport with respondents in long-term qualitative research is built over many conversations and with what some researchers call "commitment acts," whereby researchers demonstrate interest in respondents' lives outside of the formal interview or research context (e.g., attending holidays and birthday parties, babysitting, attending rallies or meetings; see Feldman, Bell, and Berger 2003). Besides accompanying a respondent to a lesbian bar, another one of Guidroz's commitment acts was meeting a respondent at a sex toy shop, standing near the dressing room, and providing feedback on the lingerie the respondent came out wearing. The respondent wanted Guidroz's opinion on wearing particular lingerie outfits with clients. What should sex work researchers do when respondents want the researcher to give them "professional tips" about how to interact with a potential client or where to obtain birth control? Beyond the interviews, our respondents asked us about a multitude of topics, ranging from our advice on their profession (such as where and how to advertise their services and how to deal with a difficult customer, coworker, or boss) to steps toward "leaving the life" through advanced education (seen as our domain) or securing other types of employment. This type of information sharing—while important for maintaining rapport—can create discomfort for a researcher and therefore make analysis more difficult. While much has been written on dealing with respondents' discomfort or resistance during interviews (Miller and Crabtree 2004), a politics-of-location approach can help a researcher be attentive to these moments when they arise by making respondents aware of the researcher's positionality and subjectivity and therefore reducing internal concerns and conflicts in the field (see Liong 2012).

Both of us found that "heterosexuality" is assumed by most people to be part of a "researcher's positionality." We often faced choices about how we would handle our sexuality in the field. This was especially tangible for Guidroz when she attended open S&M events and was purposefully ambiguous in her self-presentation (to appear as neither dominant nor submissive). Lacking visual "cues" such as leather and studs or a collar, during informal conversations with other attendees, she was asked whether she would play the "top" or "bottom" role with men or women during hypothetical S&M encounters (Guidroz 2008). As much as possible, she tried not to answer the question. When a researcher is asked a direct question about her or his sexuality, providing an answer that others might interpret as "deviant" (Liong 2012) could place a barrier between the researcher and research participants. It is not a given that such questions will arise; nonetheless, conducting research on the sex industry might necessitate learning about sex work in various settings. If a sex work researcher avoids the more "difficult" contexts in order to ward off questions about his or her sexual preferences, then the researcher's data collection, analysis, and contributions to her or his discipline could be inhibited.

Additionally, if the researcher is single she or he may also be perceived to be sexually or romantically available. For example, at the time of her research Guidroz was single and several respondents in both escort and telephone sex work propositioned her to observe or take part in their commercial and private sexual activities. Guidroz immediately reflected, "Is this a 'come-on'? Did I do something to encourage it?" In all instances, and regardless of whether Guidroz wanted them to take place, Guidroz felt compelled to decline all offers and respond with excuses similar to Markowitz's (1999, 167) reliance on a professional-ethical distance both in the moment and when writing up her findings. Guidroz disclosed nothing about her private life that could have been interpreted as sexual openness by her respondents.

To not reflect on how these everyday sexual interruptions, innuendos, or interludes are implicated in our research leaves less room for deepening rapport. In the hypermasculinized environment of the Detroit drug culture of the 1990s, Berger often felt unsafe and sought to desexualize herself, choosing to wear baggy clothes and downplay any signifiers of femininity. If Berger were in a similar situation today, using a politics-of-location approach, she might choose to share her concerns with her respondents about the behavior of several men both on the street and in court and listen to their thoughts. Opening up about her own vulnerability in the field based on gender, sexuality, and race might have deepened rapport between the women and her and elicited new insights about the everyday sexism that many have to confront in order to survive.

Although both of us established and maintained strict boundaries in our roles as researchers, we now understand how our research could have been strengthened, not weakened, by a more fluid approach of acknowledging and discussing sexuality while doing fieldwork. Fluidity in research does not mean that researchers will abandon established research standards and aspire to have sex with their respondents (see Goode 1999); however, fluidity in talking openly about sexuality, fully observing participants in the field, and analyzing the sum of our data will yield a greater understanding of the sex industry.

We do not advocate these changes for the simple notion of adding "racy" vignettes for titillation, voyeurism, or even personal fascination with the subject. We believe, as others have argued (England 1994; Lerum 2001), that there are important epistemological connections to be made when we are more aware of how sexuality emerges in our research encounters and shapes our position as researchers. Such awareness could help produce more robust and richer knowledge. Specifically, Guidroz has felt unable to bring more of how her respondents revealed their sexual interest about her during those "moments of eroticization" into her published works. Incorporating their sexual interest into her analysis would have also allowed her to discuss how she understood the context of their work in additional publishing venues.

However, the publisher of Berger's book, *Workable Sisterhood*, allowed her to reflect on the disquieting ways that women in the study were hypersexualized and how, in turn, she as a researcher was also subject to being hypersexualized as part of her fieldwork experience. It is often the case in publishing that lengthy fieldwork reflections are left out of the main body of the text and relegated to the end of the book as a "research note" or as an appendix. After a discussion with her editor about why her reflection on how sexuality permeated the fieldwork experience was important to her central arguments, Berger's editor agreed to allow those sections to remain in the methods chapter. By including in a central chapter her struggles when issues of sexuality unexpectedly arose in the field, Berger made reflexivity a core part of the research method, giving readers additional insight into the particular dimensions of how sexuality intersects with stigma in ways that affect both researcher and participants.

Professional Stigma and the Academic Sex Work Researcher

Another kind of stigma, professional stigma, can be part and parcel of the sex work research experience. Because a politics-of-location approach addresses sexuality as a legitimate area to theorize, study, and document throughout different phases of the research process, it could help reduce professional stigma for the sex work researcher. Some professors and mentors chose, on occasion, to sexualize us or encouraged others to sexualize us. We received blatant propositions from both professors and peers. But lacking a way to confront, manage, and most importantly disclose to our professors the complicated ways issues of sexuality arose during our research had specific consequences for not only how we approached our topics but also how we handled—or how we thought we should handle— our research endeavors. Thus we were both insiders and outsiders in the academy and in the research field, and this made "inside" and "outside" difficult to name or separate because both places were sites that demanded critical interrogation.

Given the renaissance in the publishing of sex work research and the global sex workers' rights movement, few social science departments can legitimately ignore or outright block a student or colleague who wishes to pursue this line of research. Still, a receptive climate for sex work research is not guaranteed, and the liabilities of conducting sex work research are not imaginary. Graduate students and untenured professors interested in sex work research must navigate a plethora of academic gatekeepers (e.g., peers, mentors, dissertation and personnel committee members, university administrators, institutional review boards, journal and book editors, and funding agencies) when they start, fund, and publish their research. These gatekeepers may or may not see the value of social science research on sex work, and if they do, they may raise criticisms to researchers who openly write about utilizing the politics-of-location approach to sexuality in the field. In other words, sexuality might be privately acknowledged by the researcher but publicly doing so can have real, material consequences.

Another area of ongoing concern for researchers conducting sex work research is obtaining internal and external funding for both short- and long-term research studies. Public funding for research on sex-related topics has decreased significantly in the last decade, causing concern for sex researchers about a new dependency on for-profit pharmaceutical companies as providers of funding (Clark 2005). Grants and fellowships from public and nonprofit agencies often have either unreasonable or "unscientific" (e.g., moralistic) restrictions attached to grant applications (see Kempner 2008 and Lutnick in chapter 2 of this volume) or have been eliminated entirely (e.g., the Social Science Research Council's Sexuality Research Fellowship Program). Given current funding challenges, sex work researchers may choose to conduct research on phenomena that are not illegal or illicit or do research that is not qualitatively focused, thus bypassing extra and possibly hostile responses to their work. Besides funding challenges, we also believe the widespread stigma that still pervades research on sex work and the silence about sexuality in the qualitative research process continue to be insidious hindrances to current and future academics seeking tenure and who have much to contribute to existing empirical knowledge about the sex industry.

Being feminist researchers within the academy *and* feminist researchers of sex work involves elements of professional and personal stigma. Just providing frank sexual descriptions with academic colleagues has its challenges for researchers. While Guidroz's graduate school department was generally receptive to her research topic (i.e., there was already a sociology professor who did research on prostitution),[4] Berger had difficulty doing her project in political science, a discipline that until recently has not taken up the study of sex work across multiple subfields. Sociology, in comparison to political science, has had a longer and more varied history of scholarship exploring the sex industry and feminists' self-reflexivity within field research. In either academic field, however, there can be repercussions from studying sex work.

During our research, we became increasingly aware of not only the persistent social labeling of sex workers but also the stigmatizing effect of researching the sex industry. When other academics showed an interest in our work, we tried to deflect and prevent the voyeuristic tendencies that had been arising as our research progressed. We did not want to be seen as a "sex object" or perceived as "kinky," sexually available, or promiscuous. As a result, our own emotional management led to conflicted feelings over disclosure versus openness with mentors, students, and colleagues and also served to reinforce the "us versus them" dichotomy between academics and sex workers. At that point in our professional careers, given the power differences with our mentors and other academic colleagues (e.g., committee members), we were unable to openly acknowledge or challenge stigma directed at us. A politics-of-location approach provides researchers with the insight to recognize and challenge patterns of professional stigma as experienced through complex social locations.

Male researchers run the risk of being labeled "perverts" by colleagues and respondents alike (or implicitly heralded as "oversexed"); however, female researchers' academic peers may use potentially damaging and misleading labels like the women we study receive. Lynn Chancer's (1993) path-breaking essay "Prostitution, Feminist Theory, and Ambivalence: Notes from the Sociological Underground" confirms, among other things, the taboo nature of studying sexuality. Several colleagues asked Chancer if she had at one time been a prostitute. Chancer's observation written almost two decades ago on the challenges of studying sex work is still salient: "There must be something about openly participating in studies of *sex*—especially (though not exclusively) if the study is conducted by a woman, especially (though not exclusively) if the study is about sex-for-sale, i.e., plain, blatantly commercial sex—which situates *prostitution* along a wider continuum of activities that produce awkward and loaded reactions, in academia and beyond, in other women as well as men" (Chancer 1993, emphasis added).

Having experiences similar to Chancer's, we both felt pressured to differentiate ourselves from sex workers in the field, in the academy, or both. In the field, for example, Guidroz had an exchange with one of her respondents that touched on the issues of the "good girl / bad girl" split and shame. She wrote the following in her field notes after the interview:

One major point of distance on my part: She asked me if I had ever considered sex work. Without thinking, I immediately responded, "No!" The look on her face told me I just put a space (or a gulf?) between us. It [her facial expression] said back to me "You're not one of those women like me who would do this." Was this feminist ambivalence [see Chancer 1993] on my part? I wanted to reconnect with her. I then said, "Well, that's not totally the truth. It would be a lie to say I've never considered it. I think most women consider it when they try to support themselves." Then I added, "Actually, I've considered it in two ways. One, economically. And two, for research." We then talked about uncomfortableness [sic] (mine) when someone says, "You could strip, or be an escort, etc." She said, "You could do this; men love red hair." She added, ". . . look how long I've been in it—five years."

We had failed to understand the complex ways that our research topics would contribute to our sexualization by others inside academe. In spite of our efforts to self-protect, our peers and colleagues expressed clear misconceptions of us as sexually willing, potential sex workers. For example, Guidroz was invited via e-mail by a male editor of a peer-reviewed journal to "*offer a submission*" (his emphasis) to the journal. His e-mail contained a host of other explicit sexual innuendos—including whether she had a "*vicarious interest*" in sex work—a topic he had raised in person to her previously at an academic conference. Guidroz felt his sexual advances demonstrated that he did not take her seriously as a researcher in sociology. She found the message so offensive that she never answered it or attempted to publish in that journal. Although Guidroz found other publishing outlets, this experience sent a clear cue about the kinds of responses she might expect, even from other scholars working in the area of sexuality.

Male students and professors who were not in the field often asked Berger surreptitiously if what they heard about women who used crack cocaine was true: "Would they do anything for a rock?" Berger's field and academic experiences helped her to question how she was going to represent marginalized women, who were active in illicit activities, in her academic work, given the prevailing worldview of them as unknowable and unworthy of public concern. Ultimately she sought to disrupt traditional assumptions about her respondents as inarticulate and predatory. Instead she focused on analysis that included their complex and contradictory perceptions about how sex work shaped aspects of their lives.

Other researchers have chosen to withhold their knowledge about the link between sexuality and fieldwork from other scholars. Consequently, their research experiences are less accessible to scholars engaged in data collection, analysis, and theory building (see Altork 1996). Increasingly, scholarship about qualitative fieldwork encourages (and expects) researchers to think critically about race, class, and gender, so why does sexuality receive a pass? Again, if other areas of social experience including race and gender can be "active" in the research process, it strikes us as odd that any researcher should be penalized for theorizing about sexuality to explain the context of field research.

In anticipation of additional academic misunderstanding and rejection, a sex work scholar may withhold or censor his or her work from others in their discipline. Stigma from the academic world can also affect our data analyses. In Guidroz's previous writing on sadomasochism, for example, she asked herself, "Did I 'stick to the facts' and make sex seem sterile or boring enough to be considered credible?" Moreover, there are epistemological implications of leaving "off the record" the ways peers and colleagues have commented on our work. What happens when a scholar uses a politics-of-location approach about sexuality in work that is to be peer reviewed? Rose Jones (1999) highlights such an experience with a reviewer. Jones's research was on HIV/AIDS transmission in Saint Lucia, and she writes about being sexually propositioned by both men and women. In the context of her article, she draws on these encounters to understand and elucidate the fluidity of relationships among respondents and of those between herself and respondents. Later, in answering a solicitation for manuscripts on ethnographic work and sex research for a highly ranked academic journal, her work was denied because her discussion of sex and sexuality (her own and her respondents') played an "active role in the ethnographic process" (37). Giving reasons why the article would not be published, a reviewer wrote: "Although I appreciate the author's candidness about her [ethnographic] experiences [including] . . . her discovery that female lovers would approach her . . . [this] do[es] not need to be recounted in the *active voice*. Some researchers may be concerned about the ethics of that [and] since the author may have a long and interesting career, she may wish to preserve some anonymity" (37, emphasis in original).

To Jones, the reviewer's response participated in a discourse of distance—anthropology's conventional sexual discourse—that separates "our" sex and sexuality from our respondents (Jones 1999). A politics-of-location approach rejects the prevailing discourse of distance about sexuality that is prevalent in social science writings on sex work research. Sexuality is one concealable aspect of a researcher's identity that inevitably will collide with the respondents' (or other field participants) in ways that are impossible to anticipate prior to entering the field. We now believe that discussions about sexuality as part of the fieldwork process, and as one's research develops or matures, are appropriate.

For example, we have been asked repeatedly and in a myriad of ways, "Did you go native?" and we were left without an effective and appropriate response because we found the question offensive. The frequency with which we heard this question is a reminder to understand and call attention to how particular bodies and subjects are always located within discourses predicated on racial, gender, sexual, and class hierarchies. How could the politics-of-location approach have helped us respond to the sometimes uninformed and misguided questioning from our colleagues? Rather than hoisting one's academic armor when confronted with this line of questioning, sex work researchers should adopt equally in their conversations and writing the lens that sexuality is "an interactive, constructed, and relevant experience" (see Lerum 2001) in sex work research. Rather than shrinking from the question, distancing ourselves from our respondents, or attempting to defend our choice to not "go native," today we would answer more openly with "Yes" or "No" and why we did or did not utilize the research strategy of experiencing buying and selling sex. We would have also used the "Did you go native?" question as a way to talk about and problematize our complicated identities in and out of the field that needed constant attention and negotiation. We can respond effectively to our academic gatekeepers by continuing to position ourselves in our research endeavors.

New Directions for Sexual Reflexivity in Research

Research and the qualitative process reflect a two-way street, and feminist researchers have pointed to the multiple ways we are implicated in respondents' lives (Bloom 1997; DeVault 1999); in particular, according to England, "the intersubjective nature of social life means that the researcher and the people being researched have shared meanings and we should seek methods that develop this advantage" (England 1994, 82). We find the idea of the "sexed anthropologist" useful here; it is the "recognition that ethnographers are viewed as sexual beings and placed into gender categories—male, female, homosexual, heterosexual, bisexual, neuter, androgynous, and more—by the people studied" (Markowitz 1999, 162). This is an encouraging beginning on which we can draw our analysis and invite other researchers to make a discussion of sexual matters integral to the research experience. We ask other researchers to consider what kinds of things we might learn from our respondents and whether this changes or influences how we conduct research and what we potentially do in our personal lives.

We agree with Keri Lerum (2001) that to maintain an "academic armor" in the face of sexuality in the research process does a disservice to knowledge production and constitutes a willful self-blinding. Rather, we promote a feminist self-reflexivity—defined by feminist geographer Kim England (1994, 82) as the "self-critical sympathetic introspection and the self-conscious analytical scrutiny of the self as researcher"—that in turn treats research as "an ongoing inter-subjective activity" (England 1994, 82).

We are not suggesting that making explicit the researcher's experiences of sexuality through the interaction with respondents will be an easy or simple process without possible professional consequences. Undertaking research on the sex industry may have professional repercussions from colleagues, professional associations, journal editors, department chairs and other administrators, and even other feminists. But we believe that this collective effort toward making sexuality visible will yield better and more accurate data. We believe that qualitative researchers who have conducted sex work research have important epistemological insights about sexuality that are suppressed in field notes as well as in official papers, conferences, and articles. We believe that the scholarly community as a whole loses when these insights are left out of the conversation and not subject to debate and discussion.

We recommend that researchers contemplate how they would handle comparable situations in other research contexts. Moreover, a politics-of-location approach can encourage the researcher to record and reflect on such moments and decide whether such moments will be discarded or productively used later on for theory building. Social scientists' increasing interest in the sex work industry means it is crucial for researchers to deal with issues of sexuality in all stages of their research. We have argued that a politics-of-location approach can have a decisive impact on the research process, encounter, and product. In this chapter, we made the case for exposing the missing dimension of sexuality within the research process. We assert that any researcher interested in studying the sex work industry must understand that this field of study comes with some unique challenges that include navigating one's academic status and prestige, sexism, and the difficulty in securing external funding.

A politics-of-location approach offers a useful perspective on how researchers can engage and explore why and how sexuality operates within the research encounter. As this approach is premised on meaningful struggle and identification with people who have been marginalized, it undercuts concerns about sharing the exact same history or experience with respondents. We have used the arena of sex work to throw these issues into relief, and we also assert that they are relevant to many aspects of the research encounter. Karla Poewe (1999) argues that a meaningful encounter of "any significance for an ethnographic work involves both full-bodied experiences as well as edited thought" (202). Sexuality is part of those full-bodied experiences and can greatly enhance our understanding of our respondents and ourselves. A revision of our inherited research "canon" could further empower researchers to approach controversial topics, such as commercial sadomasochism (see Kleinplatz and Moser 2006), with knowledge and confidence about both overt and covert elements of sexuality instead of ignorance and trepidation.

Despite funding challenges, there are a few indications of increasing openness and receptivity to sex work scholarship (e.g., college courses on the sex industry).[5] This does not mean that professional stigma has ceased or abated. To what extent are graduate students' professors and mentors advocating and supporting the multiple meanings of sexuality within the research encounter? If we are not careful—if we do not include the broader context of methods *and* sexuality—we might miss the potential for a transgressive methodological movement to bridge gaps between "us" as researchers and "them," our respondents. Ongoing attention to the methodology we use for sex work research will provide a continuing space for research in the academy, and it will help us be more reflective researchers.

Notes

Our gratitude goes to Kamala Kempadoo and Jodi O'Brien for comments on earlier versions of this manuscript.

1. We use the term "sex work" to represent the diverse array of consumer activities where sexual services or products are sold or purchased. Carol Leigh (1997), a feminist and a proprostitution activist, has written that she first used the term sex work at a feminist conference in 1979 or 1980 and this later influenced other scholars and activists. Others simply refer to the "sex industry" or the "sex work industry" to represent sex-for-sale services, products, and all participants.

2. Our thinking on this point was influenced by Kamala Kempadoo's insights.

3. This reference to "bad girls" comes from the long-standing dichotomous separation of women into two classes based on perceived sexual activity, promiscuity, virginity, and so on.

4. Albeit for Guidroz there was some initial misunderstanding on the part of some professors of the nature of sex work encounters, in particular submissive male customers' "scenes" with female dominatrixes.

5. On this point, we are much encouraged by the scholarship of the editors and contributors of this volume, in particular, Samantha Majic's (2011) recent publication in *Perspectives on Politics,* a top-tier political science journal.

References

Altork, Kate. 1996. "Walking the Fire Line: The Erotic Dimension of the Fieldwork Experience." In *Out in the Field: Reflections of Lesbian and Gay Anthropologists,* ed. Ellen Lewin and William Leap, 107–39. Champaign: University of Illinois Press.

Anthias, Floya. 2002. "Beyond Feminism and Multiculturalism: Locating Difference and the Politics of Location." *Women's Studies International Forum* 25, no. 3: 275–86.

Bell, Shannon. 1995. *Whore Carnival.* New York: Automedia.

Bellamy, Gary, Merryn Gott, and Sharron Hinchliff. 2011. "Controversies and Contentions: A Gay Man Conducting Research with Women about Their Understandings of Sexuality, Sex and Sexual Problems." *Culture, Health and Sexuality* 13, no. 6: 699–712.

Berger, Michele Tracy. 1998. "Workable Sisterhood: A Study of the Political Participation of Stigmatized Women with HIV/AIDS." Unpublished PhD diss., University of Michigan, Ann Arbor.

————. 2004. *Workable Sisterhood: The Political Journey of Stigmatized Women with HIV/AIDS.* Princeton, N.J.: Princeton University Press.

Bloom, Leslie Rebecca. 1997. "Locked in Uneasy Sisterhood: Reflections on Feminist Methodology and Research Relations." *Anthropology and Education Quarterly* 28, no. 1: 111–22.

Boellstorff, Tom. 2007. "Queer Studies in the House of Anthropology." *Annual Review of Anthropology* 36, no. 1: 17–35.

Bradley-Engen, Mindy S. 2009. *Naked Lives: Inside the World of Exotic Dance.* Albany, N.Y.: State University of New York Press.

Brak-Lamy, Guadalupe. 2012. "Emotions during Fieldwork in the Anthropology of Sexuality: From Experience to Epistemological Reflexions." *Electronic Journal of Human Sexuality* 15. http://www.ejhs.org/volume15/Emotions .html.

Callaway, Helen. 1992. "Ethnography and Experience: Gender Implication in Fieldwork and Texts." In *Anthropology and Autobiography,* ed. Judith Okely and Helen Callaway, 29–48. New York: Routledge.

Chancer, Lynn Sharon. 1993. "Prostitution, Feminist Theory, and Ambivalence: Notes from the Sociological Underground." *Social Text* 11, no. 4: 143–71.

Chapkis, Wendy. 1986. *Beauty Secrets: Women and the Politics of Appearance.* Cambridge, Mass.: South End Press.

————. 1997. *Live Sex Acts: Women Performing Erotic Labor.* New York: Routledge.

Clark, Justin. 2005. "Sex: The Big Turnoff." *Psychology Today,* January 1. http:// www.psychologytoday.com/articles/200502/sex-the-big-turnoff.

Collins, Patricia Hill. 1991. *Black Feminist Thought: Knowledge, Consciousness and the Politics of Empowerment.* Boston: Unwin Hyman.

Denzin, Norman. 1989. *Interpretive Interactionism.* Newbury Park, Calif.: Sage.

DeVault, Marjorie. 1999. *Liberating Method: Feminism and Social Research.* Philadelphia: Temple University Press.

England, Kim V. L. 1994. "Getting Personal: Reflexivity, Positionality, and Feminist Research." *Professional Geographer* 46, no. 1: 80–89.

Feldman, Martha S., Jeannine Bell, and Michele Tracy Berger. 2003. *Gaining Access: A Practical and Theoretical Guide for Qualitative Researchers.* Walnut Creek, Calif.: AltaMira Press.

Flowers, Amy. 1998. *The Fantasy Factory: An Insider's View of the Phone Sex Industry.* Philadelphia: University of Pennsylvania Press.

Frank, Katherine. 2002. *G-Strings and Sympathy: Strip Club Regulars and Male Desire.* Durham, N.C.: Duke University Press.

————. 2007. "Playcouples in Paradise: Touristic Sexuality and Lifestyle Travel." In *Love and Globalization: Transformations of Intimacy in the Contemporary World,* ed. Mark Padilla, Jennifer S. Hirsch, Miguel Munoz-Laboy, Robert E.

Sember, and Richard G. Parker, 163–85. Nashville, Tenn.: Vanderbilt University Press.

Geller, Pamela L., and Miranda K. Stockett, eds. 2006. *Feminist Anthropology: Past, Present, and Future*. Philadelphia: University of Pennsylvania Press.

Gluck, Sherna Berger, and Daphne Patai, eds. 1991. *Women's Words: The Feminist Practice of Oral History*. New York: Routledge.

Goode, Erich. 1999. "Sex with Informants as Deviant Behavior: An Account and Commentary." *Deviant Behavior: An Interdisciplinary Journal* 20, no. 4: 301–24.

Guidroz, Kathleen. 2001. "Gender, Labor, and Sexuality in Escort and Telephone Sex Work." Unpublished PhD diss., George Washington University, Washington, D.C.

———. 2008. "'Are You Top or Bottom?': Social Science Answers for Everyday Questions about Sadomasochism." *Sociology Compass* 2, no. 6: 1766–82.

Guidroz, Kathleen, and Grant Rich. 2010. "Commercial Telephone Sex: Fantasy and Reality." In *Sex For Sale: Prostitution, Pornography, and the Sex Industry*, ed. Ronald Weitzer, 139–62. New York: Routledge.

Haraway, Donna. 1988. "Situated Knowledges: The Science Question in Feminism and the Privilege of Partial Perspective." *Feminist Studies* 14, no. 13: 575–99.

Harding, Sandra. 1993. "Rethinking Standpoint Epistemology: What Is 'Strong Objectivity'?" In *Feminist Epistemologies*, ed. Linda Alcoff and Elizabeth Potter, 49–82. New York: Routledge.

Harstock, Nancy C. M. 1988. "The Feminist Standpoint: Developing the Ground for a Specifically Feminist Historical Materialism." In *Feminism and Methodology*, ed. Sandra Harding, 157–80. Bloomington: Indiana University Press.

Hesse-Biber, Sharlene Nagy, and Patricia Leavy, eds. 2004. *Approaches to Qualitative Research: A Reader on Theory and Practice*. Oxford: Oxford University Press.

Jones, Rose. 1999. "Husbands and Lovers: Gender Construction and the Ethnography of Sex Research." In *Sex, Sexuality and the Anthropologist*, ed. Fran Markowitz and Michael Ashkenazi, 25–42. Champaign: University of Illinois Press.

Kanuha, Valli Kalei. 2000. "'Being' Native versus 'Going' Native: Conducting Social Work Research as an Insider." *Social Work* 45, no. 5: 439–47.

Kempadoo, Kamala, ed. 1999. *Sun, Sex, and Gold: Tourism and Sex Work in the Caribbean*. Lanham, Md.: Rowman and Littlefield.

Kempner, Joanna. 2008. "The Chilling Effect: How Do Researchers React to Controversy?" *PLOS Medicine* 5, no. 11: 1571–78.

Kirsch, Gesa E. 1999. *Ethical Dilemmas in Feminist Research: The Politics of Location, Interpretation, and Publication*. Albany: State University of New York Press.

Kleinplatz, Peggy J., and Charles Moser, eds. 2006. *Sadomasochism: Powerful Pleasures*. Binghamton, N.Y.: Harrington Park Press.

Kulick, Don, and Margaret Willson, eds. 1995. *Taboo: Sex, Identity, and Erotic Subjectivity in Anthropological Fieldwork.* London: Routledge.

Leigh, Carol. 1997. "Inventing Sex Work." In *Whores and Other Feminists,* ed. Jill Nagle, 225–31. New York: Routledge.

Lerum, Kari. 2001. "Subjects of Desire: Academic Armor, Intimate Ethnography, and the Production of Critical Knowledge." *Qualitative Inquiry* 7, no. 4: 466–83.

Letherby, Gayle. 2003. *Feminist Research in Theory and Practice.* Philadelphia: Open University Press.

Liong, Chan Ching Mario. 2012. "Under the Shadow of Deviance: Positionality, Subjectivity, and Masculinity of the Male Feminist Ethnographer in a Patriarchal Field Setting." Paper presented at the Seventh International Conference on Interdisciplinary Social Sciences, Barcelona, Spain. http://umu.diva-portal.org/smash/record.jsf?pid=diva2:564490.

Lorenz-Meyer, Dagmar. 2004. "Addressing the Politics of Location. Strategies in Feminist Epistemology and Their Relevance to Research Undertaken from a Feminist Perspective." *Women Scholars and Institutions,* 13b: 783–805. http://www.cec-wys.org/docs/Lorenz-Meyer_ENG_final_web.pdf.

Majic, Samantha. 2011. "Serving Sex Workers and Promoting Democratic Engagement: Rethinking Nonprofits' Role in American Civic and Political Life." *Perspectives on Politics* 9, no. 4: 821–39.

Manalansan, Martin F., IV. 2006. "Queer Intersections: Sexuality and Gender in Migration Studies." *International Migration Review* 40, no. 1: 224–49.

Markowitz, Fran. 1999. "Sexing the Anthropologist: Implications for Ethnography." In *Sex, Sexuality and the Anthropologist,* ed. Fran Markowitz and Michael Ashkenazi, 161–74. Champaign: University of Illinois Press.

Markowitz, Fran, and Michael Ashkenazi, eds. 1999. *Sex, Sexuality and the Anthropologist.* Champaign: University of Illinois Press.

Miller, William L., and Benjamin F. Crabtree. 2004. "Depth Interviewing." In *Approaches to Qualitative Research: A Reader on Theory and Practice,* ed. Sharlene Nagy Hesse-Biber and Patricia Leavy, 185–202. Oxford: Oxford University Press.

Mohanty, Chandra. 1995. "Feminist Encounters: Locating the Politics of Experience." In *Social Postmodernism: Beyond Identity Politics,* ed. Linda Nicholson and Steven Seidman, 68–86. Cambridge, U.K.: Cambridge University Press.

Naples, Nancy. 2003. *Feminism and Method: Ethnography, Discourse Analysis and Activist Research.* New York: Routledge.

O'Connell Davidson, Julia, and Derek Layder. 1994. *Methods, Sex and Madness.* New York: Routledge.

Parsons, Jeffrey. 2005. "Contemporary Research on Sex Work." *Journal of Psychology and Human Sexuality* 17, no. 1/2: Special issue.

Pheterson, Gail. 1989. *A Vindication of the Rights of Whores*. Seattle, Wash.: Seal Press.

———. 1993. "The Whore Stigma: Female Dishonor and Male Unworthiness." *Social Text* 11, no. 4: 39–64.

———. 1996. *The Prostitution Prism*. Amsterdam, the Netherlands: Amsterdam University Press.

Poewe, Karla. 1999. "Afterword: No Hiding Place: Reflections on the Confessions of Manda Cesara." In *Sex, Sexuality and the Anthropologist*, ed. Fran Markowitz and Michael Ashkenazi, 197–206. Champaign: University of Illinois Press.

Rich, Adrienne. 1986. *Blood, Bread and Poetry: Selected Prose 1979–1985*. New York: W. W. Norton.

Sanders, Teela. 2006. "Sexing Up the Subject: Methodological Nuances in Researching the Female Sex Industry." *Sexualities* 9, no. 4: 449–68.

Schwartz, Pepper, and Virginia Rutter. 1998. *The Gender of Sexuality*. Thousand Oaks, Calif.: Pine Forge.

Seymour, Craig. 1998. "Studying Myself/Studying Others: One (Professional) Boy's Adventures Studying Sex Work." In *Prostitution: On Whores, Hustlers, and Johns*, ed. James E. Elias, Vern L. Bullough, Veronica Elias, and Gwen Brewer, 361–67. New York: Prometheus Books.

Shaver, Frances M. 2005. "Sex Work Research: Methodological and Ethical Challenges." *Journal of Interpersonal Violence* 20, no. 3: 296–319.

Smith, Dorothy E. 1987. *The Everyday World as Problematic: A Feminist Sociology*. Boston: Northeastern University Press.

Statham, Anne, Eleanor M. Miller, and Hans O. Mauksh, eds. 1988. *The Worth of Women's Work: A Qualitative Synthesis*. New York: State University of New York Press.

Thapar-Björkert, Suruchi, and Martha Henry. 2004. "Reassessing the Research Relationship: Location, Position and Power in Fieldwork Accounts." *International Journal of Social Research Methodology* 7, no. 5: 363–81.

Visweswaran, Kamala. 1994. *Fictions of Feminist Ethnography*. Minneapolis: University of Minnesota Press.

———. 1997. "Histories of Feminist Ethnography." *Annual Review of Anthropology* 26, no. 1: 591–621.

Wahab, Stephanie, and Lacey Sloan. 2004. "Ethical Dilemmas in Sex Work Research." *Research for Sex Work* 7 (June): 3–5.

Warren, Carol A. B., and Tracy Xavia Karner. 2010. *Discovering Qualitative Methods: Field Research, Interviews, and Analysis*. 2nd ed. New York: Oxford University Press.

Weitzer, Ronald, ed. 2010. *Sex for Sale: Prostitution, Pornography, and the Sex Industry*. 2nd ed. New York: Routledge.

Wolf, Diana L., ed. 1996. *Feminist Dilemmas in Fieldwork*. Boulder, Colo.: Westview.

CHAPTER 2

Beyond Prescientific Reasoning

The Sex Worker Environmental Assessment Team Study

Alexandra Lutnick

S EX WORK, the exchange of sexual services for some type of payment, is primarily a criminal offense in the United States. Moralistic interpretations of sex work, coupled with its illegal status, result in the "whore stigma" being projected onto sex workers (Benoit et al. 2005) by researchers, academics, policymakers, law enforcement officials, and the general public. It is this legal and social labeling that results in sex workers being categorized as a hidden population in research studies. Hidden populations are best categorized by three characteristics. First, the size of group membership is unknown, making it particularly difficult to obtain a random sample. Second, to acknowledge membership in the group may result in being the target of societal scorn or hate, as well as legal prosecution. Because of the stigma and illegal nature of their behaviors, members of hidden populations are often distrustful of nonmembers (Benoit et al. 2005; Heckathorn 1997). Finally, the more threatening or sensitive the topic, the greater the likelihood is that members will hide their involvement (Lee and Renzetti 1990).

Conducting research with hidden populations such as sex workers poses unique methodological challenges. Probability-based sampling frames are not feasible because a full listing of all adults engaged in sex work does not exist. Consequently, much of the research conducted with hidden populations relies on convenience samples that are better suited for research that is still in the exploratory stage (Sudman and Kalton 1986; Sudman, Sirken, and Cowan 1988). Likewise, convenience samples of institutional and clinical populations, such as prisoners or individuals in drug treatment programs, offer limited generalizability (Watters and Biernacki 1989) since their characteristics may differ from their counterparts outside of those settings. Therefore, working with hidden populations requires careful consideration in determining the strongest methodology that best fits the study question.

The methodologically troubling nature of some sex work research has been well documented (Shaver 2005; Wahab and Sloan 2004; Weitzer 2010). For example, targeted sampling often results in those workers who are the most visible (i.e., street-based workers) being oversampled (Shaver 2005). Some studies will sample only one group of sex workers, or rely on small convenience samples, yet present their findings as if they represent the diversity of people trading sex (Wahab and Sloan 2004; Weitzer 2010). Furthermore, as the criterion for scientific knowledge is falsifiability (Phillips 2000), findings that include the exact wording of questions asked allow other researchers to replicate the study and determine whether the findings are replicable. In sex work literature, though, it is rare for authors to share the exact wording of the questions used (Weitzer 2010). Relying on research that is not transparent about its methodological choices and its limitations inhibits accurate theorizing and misguides service providers and policymakers about the needs of this population. To facilitate a more nuanced understanding of sex work and sex workers, research that reflects the heterogeneity of sex workers is needed (Benoit and Shaver 2006).

To illustrate the ways that methodologically rigorous, transparent, and participatory research with female sex workers can be conducted, this chapter will explore the methods of a study conducted by the University of California–San Francisco (UCSF), and the St. James Infirmary (SJI), a peer-run occupational health and safety clinic for sex workers (Lutnick 2006). Because the results of this study have been published elsewhere (Lutnick and Cohan 2009), the intent of this chapter is to show how researchers can rethink how they work with hidden populations—particularly sex workers—by describing the ways this study challenged the hierarchical approach to research that is common in much of the work involving hidden populations. Instead of relying on a hierarchical approach, where outside researchers enter a community to gather data and do not integrate community members into the research process, we employed a participatory approach that integrated sex workers throughout the entire research process, respected sex workers' positionality, and provided opportunities for skill development and community empowerment. This study can serve as a model for those who want to conduct research with hidden populations and not perpetuate the exclusionary impact of nonparticipatory approaches.

Participatory Research as a Challenge to Exclusionary Approaches

Research that forges community and academic partnerships is well suited for research with hidden populations, such as sex workers, who have historically been excluded from decision-making positions within research and who may be distrustful of outsiders (Clements-Nolle and Bachrach 2003; Israel et al. 1998). Unlike research that is conducted within the community, participatory research is community *based* and conducted *with* the community (Israel et al. 1998; Minkler 2004). As summarized by Barbara Israel and her colleagues (1998), participatory research recognizes the community as a unit of identity, builds upon and enhances the community's strengths and resources, facilitates a collaborative partnership for all phases of the research, integrates knowledge and action, promotes a co-learning and empowering process, is iterative, and disseminates the findings to all members of the partnership. Thus a key underpinning of this approach is to blur the line between the "researcher" and the "researched" by bringing communities into the process of knowledge production (Minkler and Wallerstein 2003). These collaborative research partnerships also offer steps toward reducing inequitable power differentials within social science research (Sanders 2006) by offering control of certain, or all, aspects of the process to community members.

The principal investigator of this study, Dr. Deborah Cohan, an associate professor in the Department of Obstetrics, Gynecology and Reproductive Sciences at UCSF and, at that time, the medical director of SJI, was committed from the beginning to conducting such community-based research with sex workers. Prior to entering medical school, Dr. Cohan did some community-based HIV activist work and, through that experience, recognized that she could often learn more from those "in the field" than those in the ivory tower. Once in medical school, volunteering as a medical provider at a women's needle exchange program in San Francisco provided Dr. Cohan with the opportunity to get to know several sex workers who subsequently expanded her perspective on the sexual and reproductive choices women make. It was Dr. Cohan's clear commitment to learning from others, and her extensive time investment with sex workers through her volunteer work and as the medical director of SJI, that established her as someone the sex worker community could trust (Cohan, pers. comm., September 10, 2011).

Reflecting participatory research's commitment to being based in and working with the community, Dr. Cohan had a series of conversations with the peer staff at SJI, along with consultants and collaborators from UCSF and the San Francisco Department of Public Health, about key issues relevant to sex workers in San Francisco that they wanted to see studied. In 2004, Dr. Cohan received funding from the National Institute of Health (NIH)/National Institute of Drug Abuse (NIDA) to conduct the study that emerged from her conversations with sex workers and other key stakeholders. These issues formed the basis of the emergent Sex Worker Environmental Assessment Team (SWEAT) study, where the threefold goal was to examine the individual-level psychological risk factors associated with the prevalence of HIV, sexually transmitted infections (STIs), and viral hepatitis among female sex workers in San Francisco; to characterize social capital among subpopulations of female sex workers in San Francisco; and to investigate whether diminished social capital is associated with an increased prevalence of HIV, STIs, and viral hepatitis.

When the study began in 2004, Measure Q (the Angel Initiative) was on the ballot in Berkeley, California. The initiative was authored by Robyn Few, a former sex worker, and named for Angel Lopez, a San Francisco prostitute who was murdered in 1993. If passed, Measure Q would have made enforcement of prostitution laws the lowest priority, required the Berkeley Police Department to provide semiannual reporting about their prostitution-related enforcement activities, and required the Berkeley City Council to lobby the state legislature to decriminalize prostitution. Although the initiative had the support of key Bay Area politicians such as the then state senator John Burton and former San Francisco district attorney Terence Halinnan (Marshall 2004), Measure Q was defeated receiving only 36.5 percent of the votes (League of Women Voters 2004).

Despite a long history of prostitution policy reform efforts in the San Francisco Bay Area, such as the work of COYOTE ("Call Off Your Old Tired Ethics"),[1] the San Francisco Task Force on Prostitution in 1993 (SFTF 1996),[2] and Measure Q, no studies had been conducted in California that examined sex workers' attitudes about the various legal approaches to sex work. While a diverse group of constituents has supported attempts to decriminalize prostitution, others have criticized them for excluding the input of more marginalized sex workers (No on K 2008). Therefore, the peer research staff indicated that it would be beneficial if the SWEAT study was also able to assess the participants' perspectives on the regulatory frameworks (i.e., criminalization, decriminalization, and legalization) that can be applied to sex work to ensure that a diverse group of female sex workers' opinions were represented and that sex workers had the opportunity to speak for themselves. This peer feedback, coupled with the research team's knowledge that no other researchers had measured perspectives on the law among a diverse sample of sex workers, resulted in adding an additional aim to the study to assess the preferred type of regulatory framework among this sample of women.

Sex Worker Integration

While participatory research ensures that the community is involved in all phases of the research, this does not mean that all parties are involved in the same way for all activities. In fact, there is never a perfect equilibrium of power (Wallerstein and Duran 2003). The classification of peer involvement is informed by the degree of control community members have over the research process and the level of collaborative decision making between the community members and researchers (Balcazar et al. 2004). Susan Torres-Harding et al. (2004) explore the various levels of peer involvement in the research process. At the most basic level, community leaders and representatives are consulted as the research is planned and implemented. More formal types of involvement include convening community advisory boards as part of the planning and execution of study protocols. A way to get peers even more involved is to employ them as outreach workers. The most integrated approach is one where community members are hired as project employees in roles such as interviewers, outreach workers, and coinvestigators (see Benoit et al. 2005; Boynton 2002; Dorfman, Derish, and Cohen 1992; Parsons 2005; Shaver 2005).

Within the United States, studies exist that have been conducted by sex workers-turned-academics-and-researchers, but this work seems to be solely among individuals who worked in legal sectors of the sex industry, such as exotic dancing or phone sex (Flowers 1998, Frank 2002; Pendleton 1997). This is not to say that there are no individuals conducting research who have been or are currently involved in the illicit sector of the sex industry, rather it is to point out that those individuals have chosen to keep that aspect of their identity hidden. In fact, my personal experience with sex worker activist groups leads me to believe that a number of professional researchers at the principal investigator or project director level have current or past experience in the illicit sex industry. Although some of the staff of the SWEAT study were comfortable with their involvement in the sex industry being public knowledge, one aspect that designates this study as being unique from other participatory research with sex workers was and is that, in my role as project director, I was willing to have my previous involvement in the illicit sex industry known.

The SWEAT study was unique in that it used the most integrated approach of community involvement where sex workers were represented at all levels of the research process, except for the principal investigator (Dr. Cohan). I was hired as the project director since Dr. Cohan wanted someone with a master's degree and experience in both the sex industry and conducting research. We then circulated a job posting through UCSF, the SJI, and to individuals in our personal networks who we knew had the requisite skill set and hired eleven additional research team members, comprising an ethnically diverse group of women and transgender individuals with current or former involvement in the sex industry. Peer research team members helped create the qualitative and quantitative instruments, played key roles in developing the study protocol, developed educational pamphlets for study participants, conducted all interviews, and assisted with data analysis.

The likelihood that research will be relevant to and valued by community members is enhanced when peers are involved in all aspects of the project. In the SWEAT study, by employing sex workers we increased the ability of our research to be sensitive and relevant to the participants and the larger sex worker communities. Including sex workers also provided recognition of the valuable knowledge we hold. As peers, we brought with us an understanding of the working conditions and dynamics that enhanced the development of appropriate surveys. We pilot tested the qualitative and quantitative instruments among the research team and then with other members of the sex worker community. We did not assume that research participants would identify with certain terms (i.e., sex work) or characterize their experiences with trading sex in a particular fashion and therefore used neutral language in our instruments to allow the participants to define for themselves what their experiences have been. For those community members who may be wary of outsiders, the peer involvement may have granted the research process legitimacy and enhanced access to the community. We also played a key role in data analysis and assisted Dr. Cohan in interpreting the findings.

To help ensure that the quantitative survey and protocols were sensitive to potential sources of risk and discomfort to research participants, we also established a community advisory board (CAB) composed of sex workers, staff from SJI and other community-based organizations that serve sex workers, in addition to individuals who interact with sex workers in their professions, such as taxi cab drivers. The CAB members offered guidance in the development of study tools, generated ideas regarding recruitment and follow-up, helped recruit the initial study participants, and assisted in furthering community support by talking about the study with individuals from their own personal and professional networks.

Even with the aforementioned advantages, peer involvement in research studies also presents some challenges. Peer researchers may mistakenly assume common cultural understandings. This can result in not following up on vague statements since the researcher assumes a common meaning. Researchers may also project their own feelings onto the participant's narrative and not recognize the ways in which their own experience is biasing the data collection and analysis. Research participants may engage in identity management and not reveal certain information that they fear will result in the researcher viewing them differently. Inevitably, there are costs and benefits to being an "insider" or "outsider" and thought must be given to the traits needed to create the shared meanings necessary for instrument creation, interviewing, and data analysis.

Negotiating "insider" status within participatory research requires the researcher to establish clear boundaries between researchers and participants so that neither group compromises expectations of confidentiality or friendship (Kirsch 2005). Some have suggested that it may be helpful to offer participants the option of whether they want to be interviewed by a peer in case someone does not feel comfortable sharing personal information with an interviewer who is from their peer network (Benoit et al. 2005; Shaver 2005). As sex workers are not a homogenous population, the SWEAT research staff and participants often differed in identities such as race/ethnicity, age, educational level, class, gender identity, and types of sex work performed. It may be that these other differences influence whether someone is viewed as an insider (Agustín 2004; Hockey 1993; LaSala 2003; Mullings 1999) and that the type of sex work the staff have engaged is more important than simply having engaged in sex work (Agustín 2004). Additionally, because interviewing requires the establishment of trust and rapport, it may be that for some people, having a peer interviewer may not be as important as having an interviewer who is intuitive, sensitive, and receptive (Corbin and Morse 2003). In our mock run-through of the interviews with fellow research team members, and our pilot interviews with other sex workers, we received feedback about our interview styles to ensure that we created a respectful interview experience for the participant. During the study, at the end of each interview we created space for the participants to provide us with feedback about how they experienced the interview.

Skill Development and Capacity Building

A goal of participatory research is to create an infrastructure that supports the intellectual and career development of community members (Keys et al. 2004). Some of the peer research staff had prior experiences working on research studies, yet many did not. Recognizing the diversity of research experience and skills among the research team, Dr. Cohan and I conducted extensive trainings to ensure uniformity in data collection. All research staff received an orientation to research in general and this project in particular and trainings on qualitative and quantitative data collection. Sessions were conducted with the quantitative interviewers, where they conducted mock interviews with each other and provided feedback about questions or phrasing that did not seem appropriate or were not clear in their intent.

Because all research team members brought with them specific skills, we explored how we could contribute to individual and community capacity building. Dr. Cohan and I provided opportunities through one-on-one and group work for members of the research team to develop research skills in sampling strategies, questionnaire development, data analysis, manuscript preparation, and presentations. Additionally, two of the team members became certified as phlebotomy technicians. To address the power differentials sometimes found in academic and community partnerships, Dr. Cohan and I also made long-term academic and career mentorship available. All research team members were hired through UCSF members have listed this project on their resumés, have used Dr. Cohan and me as references for employment, and have gone on to be hired for other research positions. Some of the team members were working on their master's degrees during the study and have since acquired those degrees, and two of us are currently pursuing doctoral degrees. This process of utilizing and enhancing the skills of the peer research team is an integral component of the trust and respect required for a successful research partnership. By facilitating opportunities for peer staff to learn skills that would benefit them beyond the study, sex workers became more than just hidden subjects.

Awareness of the Political Climate and the Politicization of Science

When conducting research with hidden populations in general, and participatory research in particular, it is imperative to be aware of and attentive to the political climate because it can pose challenges in receiving funding. The SWEAT proposal was submitted to NIH/NIDA for review during George W. Bush's first term as president. His administration's policies are described as having "subverted scientific integrity through the government" (Kamerow 2008, a2903). During this time, NIH researchers were questioned by Congress about the merits of their funded studies that focused on sex work (Kaiser 2003; Kempner 2008), program staff at NIH cautioned grant applicants to remove terms like "prostitutes" from their grant applications to reduce the projects' visibility (Kaiser 2003), and the U.S. Agency for International Development released their "Prostitution Pledge," which restricted federal funds to those organizations who signed a statement that they were opposed to prostitution and sex trafficking (Busza 2006; Kempner 2008).

An awareness of the political climate allowed us, in the SWEAT study, to challenge the current climate, or at least have a sense of the politics that the study would challenge. In a conversation with a project officer at NIDA, Dr. Cohan received feedback that if she left the term "sex work" in the title, her chances of the proposal being funded would be severely compromised. Thus the proposal, which was originally titled, "Social Capital, Self-Efficacy and Sex Worker Health," became "Ethnography of an HIV-Risk Population." It was fortunate that Dr. Cohan received this advice so that this study could be funded and that we could collect data that offered new insight into female sex workers' perspectives about preferred legal frameworks. Yet it also serves as an example of the ways in which sex workers are rendered invisible before the research even begins. In response to that erasure, as well as an acknowledgment of the participatory approach, we locally renamed the project the SWEAT Study. Although we were disappointed that through the title we had to cater to the idea that sex workers are an HIV-risk population, as opposed to highlighting our resourcefulness and resilience, we were appreciative that we received the funding to carry out this important study.

Reflexivity

Within sex work research there are three dominant discourses. Some authors absolutely condemn sex work, others romanticize it, and still some normalize it (Weitzer 2000). To report findings based solely within one of these frameworks is to ignore the diversity of people and experiences involved in sex work and instead rely on dichotomous explanations such as exploitation versus work or empowered agent versus victim. This "mental set" employed by researchers who rely on one discourse results in their forming a hypothesis early on about the group being studied and threatens the validity of the conclusions (Phillips 2000). Recognizing that all researchers bring their own systems of meaning and values with them to the research process, we were all aware that our position as peers may introduce bias to the study. To address this we employed a reflexive approach where we acknowledged the beliefs we brought with us to the study and exposed them to critical examination. At the beginning of both the qualitative and quantitative phases of the study, research team members wrote reflection pieces that we shared with each other about what we thought were the ideal legal policies. Talking about our assumptions and preferences with each other fostered an environment in which we could assess whether our interview instruments and data analysis were biased by our individual views. Although I personally believe that criminalization limits sex workers' control over working conditions and the ability to receive legal support if and when we are victims of crimes, I did not let my personal views compromise my ability or willingness to hear alternative perspectives. Instead, with the assistance of other research team members, we developed nonleading qualitative and quantitative questions to assess the participants' perspectives. Furthermore, as a team, we were committed to sharing the findings that emerged from the data whether or not they were in accordance with our personal views. This process of explicitly ana-lyzing our subjective biases offers a more objective approach to the study of sex work. By acknowledging potential sources of bias, and collectively processing those sources, we were able to minimize the potential for bias in our lines of questioning and analysis.

Another method we used to minimize the potential of compromising the validity of our conclusions was to rely on grounded theory to inter-pret the qualitative data (Corbin and Strauss 1990; Strauss and Corbin 1998). In grounded theory, codes of the interview text are derived directly from the interview data and consist of subject areas that, by virtue of the time the participant spent discussing them and/or their recurrent nature, seem important.[3] Dr. Cohan and I had all interviews transcribed verbatim and we analyzed them using NVivo 2 (by QSR International). We read through several interviews and then chose three for open coding where we made notations in the margins about content or analytic thought. Dur-ing open coding we would read through a section of the interview and ask ourselves "What is this about?" without restricting ourselves to existing theoretical explanations. We then synthesized the codes generated from open coding into one list complete with memos that described the mean-ing of the codes. The final coding list was used with all remaining inter-views. By having a sex worker (myself) and a non–sex worker (Dr. Cohan) analyze the interviews, and by using grounded theory, we minimized the potential for bias to enter into our analysis.

Our qualitative analytical approach not only facilitated a reflexive process, but it was also pivotal for developing the questions for the quan-titative instrument. The women were asked a series of nonleading, open-ended questions about what they thought their sex work experiences and lives would be like if trading sex was not illegal. We also inquired about whether they thought trading sex should be illegal and if not, what they felt would be a preferred regulatory framework. Through our analysis of the women's responses, we discovered that half of the women never used the terms criminalization, decriminalization, or legalization in their responses. This indicated that the quantitative questions should not rely on those terms because individuals may assign different meanings to them than we intended or they may be unfamiliar with some of the terms. Therefore, in the quantitative instrument we provided statements for the participants to respond to that gave specific examples of situations that would occur in one of the three frameworks.

Respecting Sex Workers' Positionality

We undertook a variety of measures to communicate our respect for the sex workers who were research participants. To ensure their privacy and safety, in addition to the requisite approval from the Committee on Human Research at UCSF, as an added measure of security for the research participants we obtained a Federal Certificate of Confidentiality. This ensured that all test results and data remained confidential and protected from subpoena. During the consent process we ensured the participants were aware that we had this certificate and explained the ways in which it protected them. Recognizing that some sex workers may not want to provide legal identification or may not have any legal identification, we did not ask participants for identification and did not require that they provide us with their legal names.

Informed by our ethnographic and qualitative work, it was clear that to achieve a diverse sample of women engaged in sex work we could not rely solely on street outreach or institutional-based samples. After reviewing the sampling methodologies available, we decided that respondent-driven sampling (RDS) had the greatest potential of increasing the diversity of sex workers in the sample and respecting their positionality. Based on the work of Heckathorn (1997; 2002), RDS is similar to snowball sampling in that researchers identify the initial participants (called "seeds") and enroll them into the study. Using the data collected from our ethnographic and qualitative work, we identified a list of characteristics (i.e., race/ethnicity, drug use, age, and type of sex work) that were desired in the "seeds." These initial participants were chosen in a nonrandom fashion, as members of hidden populations are rarely represented in public data sets. Then those women who enrolled in the study were given three coupons with which they could recruit their peers. Participants received an initial incentive for participating in the study ($40), along with a secondary incentive of receiving payment for successfully recruiting their peers into the study ($10 for each recruit who enrolled in the study). The anticipated result is that because of the peer referrals and depth of the waves, the final sample will include those population members who might otherwise be missed by methods such as street outreach, snowball sampling, and venue-based approaches (Semaan et al. 2009).

The dual-incentive approach of RDS is respectful of sex workers' positionality. Sex workers who may not participate if a non–peer researcher approached them, for example, might be more willing to participate because of the peer influence involved in the recruitment process. The premise behind this is that sex workers are better than outreach workers and researchers in their ability to recruit other sex workers into a study. Similarly, the issue of masking—sex workers hiding their activities from researchers—is diminished in RDS as peer recruiters have the ability to offer a coupon to a group member without having to disclose the person's identity to the research team. With peer recruitment, RDS overcomes the human subjects' violation inherent in snowball sampling, where research participants provide researchers with the name and contact information of other community members. Consequently, peer recruitment offers a higher level of privacy and confidentiality for potential participants, as they choose whether to show up at the study sites (Semaan et al. 2009). Using RDS for the SWEAT study resulted in a heterogeneous sample of women involved in sex work. Slightly less than half (48 percent) identified as African American, 31 percent as Caucasian, and 8 percent Latina; 52 percent reported current injection drug use; and while women reported more than one type of sex work conducted in the past 30 days, 68 percent reported street-based work, 56 percent independent outcall, and 48 percent independent in-call. Another example of the ways in which RDS facilitated a diverse sample is that only 5 percent of the women had ever received services from the St. James Infirmary.

In addition to sampling methodology, we attempted to address other factors that can influence sex workers' enrollment in the study. To increase opportunities for women to participate and minimize bias related to the type of sex work performed, we held both morning and evening shifts. Offering financial compensation for participation and peer recruitment showed respect for the women's time and effort. Not everyone who trades sex for some type of payment identifies with the term "sex worker." Instead of assuming that it was acceptable to refer to the women as sex workers, we asked all research participants whether they identified with this term. As it ends up, only 54 percent stated that they did. For those who did not identify with the term, the interviewers inquired whether it would be OK if during the interview we used the term to refer to exchanges of sex acts or nonsex sexual services (i.e., exotic dancing or phone sex). Of those who did not identify with the term sex worker, none objected to using the term for the interview. To ensure a shared meaning, interviewers explained our definition of sex work to all participants.

We strived to acknowledge and respect the positionality of sex workers, and the samples from both the qualitative and quantitative phases represent a diversity of women involved in sex work. However, there are some key limitations of our study. The research findings do not represent the views of all sex workers. Interviews were only conducted in English, which effectively excluded non-English-speaking sex workers. Similarly, we only interviewed women and restricted inclusion to individuals who were eighteen years of age or older. Male and transgender sex workers, non-English speakers, and individuals younger than eighteen may all have different perspectives on this issue. It is possible that neither the qualitative nor quantitative phase represented the views of socially isolated sex workers. To have known about the study would require some level of connectivity to other sex workers or community agencies that serve sex workers.

The physical location, hours of operation, and incentives offered may also have been a barrier for some sex workers. It is possible that some women were not able to participate because we had limited hours during which we conducted interviews and only one study site. Future work may want to explore alternative means of participation such as Internet-based surveys, venue-based sampling, mobile vans, and conducting interviews in participants' homes or vehicles. With over half of the sample reporting being homeless, and $650 being the median amount of money earned in the past month from sex work, it would be helpful if other research projects examine whether offering $40 for a ninety-minute interview and specimen collection is an appropriate amount for sex workers who have more financial resources. As some sex workers make far more than $40 for ninety minutes of work, it may be that the financial loss involved by participating in the study prevented some sex workers from enrolling.

Dissemination

When conducting research with hidden populations such as sex workers, the intent is often to produce knowledge that will inform service delivery and/or influence policy changes that will hopefully improve the lived experiences of the population. Following a participatory model of research, we were committed to disseminating the findings of this study beyond the traditional academic conferences and journals. It was our hope that this more expansive dissemination strategy would reach sex workers, service providers, policymakers, and researchers so that the findings from this study were accessible and could not only influence the ways in which we think about what type of regulatory system this group of women preferred but also highlight the ways in which research can be conducted in a truly participatory approach with sex workers. We created a blog (since removed) to keep people up-to-date on the research as it was being conducted. We also presented findings at academic conferences (e.g., International AIDS Conference, Sex Work Matters: Beyond Divides Conference, and the Western Political Science Association) and sex worker–produced conferences (such as the Desiree Alliance's Re-visioning Prostitution Conference), published in peer-reviewed journals and the sex worker–created zine *$pread*, shared the findings with staff and clients at SJI and with staff at other community-based organizations, and participated in interviews conducted by mainstream and sex worker reporters. In our publications we shared the exact wording of the questions asked in our qualitative and quantitative instruments (Lutnick 2007; Lutnick and Cohan 2009).

Expanding the range of dissemination may enhance the collective understanding about the diversity of sex workers and their experiences. However, research with hidden and oftentimes stigmatized populations can pose personal and professional challenges for researchers. Throughout our dissemination process we were mindful of our status as peers and carefully negotiated how we chose to discuss the peer element of the study. Concerns existed among the research team about the potential negative consequences of being identified as sex workers in a public forum such as a journal article or interview with the media. These concerns are not unfounded. In an interview with a local weekly paper in San Francisco (Smith 2008), I chose to acknowledge my previous involvement in the illicit sex industry to highlight the participatory nature of our study. The reporter either misunderstood or intentionally misrepresented my involvement in the sex industry and our sampling methodology and felt that the peer element compromised the objectivity of the study. According to Smith: "In any other field, 'research' conducted by outlaws, aimed at informing political debate about whether their chosen activity should be illegal, would be labeled conflict-of-interest-riddled propaganda. But the work of researchers in sociology, anthropology, political science, and related genres consists in large part of wedging technical-sounding terms into mischaracterized opinion essays, making it difficult to glean unbiased specks of truth."

Although disseminating research findings both within and outside of the typical academic channels is recommended (Fernandez-Pena et al. 2008), when the research is conducted in a participatory fashion and sex workers are part of the research team, caution is advised when deciding how best to disseminate the findings. To prevent nonconsensual identification as a sex worker, authors and presenters need to consult with the team members to explore whether they feel comfortable having their names attached to documents that identify the study as peer based. For those studies where not all the research team is composed of sex worker peers, language such as "peers and interested others" can help highlight the participatory nature and occlude connections of any one researcher to sex work. When researchers choose to acknowledge their membership in a hidden population, they should be aware of the personal and professional risks involved. Researchers who have participated or are still involved in sex work may face a loss of trust within the research community as their sex worker status can raise questions about their objectivity (Flowers 1998). Some will question the quality of the research, particularly its validity, reliability, and objectivity, since community members were involved in the development of the research instruments, data collection, and analysis (Israel et al. 1998; Minkler and Wallerstein 2003).

Conclusion

The likelihood that research will be relevant to and valued by community members is enhanced when peers are involved in all aspects of the project. Our inclusion of peers at the formative stages of the research where the aims and questions were decided, all the way through to analysis and presentation of the data, is cutting edge and ensured that the research was relevant to and respectful of the needs of sex workers. Including sex workers provided recognition of the valuable knowledge we hold. As peers, we brought an understanding of the working conditions and dynamics that enhanced the development of appropriate surveys. Furthermore, since we were connected to other community members, we played a pivotal role in facilitating recruitment methods that would bring a diversity of sex workers into the study.

The participatory approach used in our study can serve as a model for researchers who want to work with sex workers or other hidden populations. Research that forges community and academic partnerships offers many benefits. By engaging local knowledge, the quality and validity of the research is improved. Involving community members in data analysis can improve external validity and can facilitate a more nuanced understanding of an issue compared to instances when analysis is conducted solely by an outside researcher in isolation. Participatory approaches provide not only monetary but also professional validation of community members' work and unique knowledge. Lastly, inherent to a participatory approach is the belief that research is never value-free. Consequently, participatory approaches encourage a self-reflexive role to examine the biases individuals bring with them to the research process. This self-reflexivity can provide the opportunity for research partners to monitor that their biases are not impacting the research process.

It may be that other researchers are limited by finances or time available to achieve the same level of integration that was utilized in the SWEAT study. Even if others do not have the financial capability to conduct fully integrated participatory work, ways exist to bridge the academic and community divide. Individuals from the community can be hired to assist with data collection through which researchers can create opportunities for them to enhance their skill sets. Community advisory boards can be formed to provide critical community feedback and support to the project. Likewise, researchers can meet with community members and key stakeholders to hear what they consider to be the most pressing research needs of their community and explore ways in which researchers can facilitate that work. It is my hope that by sharing what we did with this study, others may think about ways in which they can begin to incorporate more of a participatory approach into their work.

Notes

1. COYOTE was founded in 1973 by Margo St. James to call attention to the double standard in the law, where women were being arrested for prostitution and the male clients never faced any charges. Since its inception, COYOTE has advocated for the decriminalization of prostitution, as communicated through their slogans such as "Outlaw poverty, not prostitution," "A blowjob is better than no job," and "No bad women, just bad laws" (Lutnick 2006; Lutnick and Cohan 2009).

2. The San Francisco Task Force on Prostitution was established by the San Francisco Board of Supervisors. In 1996 it issued its final report, which

recommended that the City of San Francisco decriminalize prostitution (Lutnick and Cohan 2009).

3. One of the essential operations of grounded theory is the process of asking questions while analyzing the data. First, there are sensitizing questions: "What is going on here?" "Who are the actors involved?" "How do they define the situation?" "What is the meaning to them?" "What are the various actors doing?" These questions help us understand what the data might indicate. Second, there are theoretical questions: "What is the relationship of one concept to another?" "How do events or actions change over time?" "What are the larger structural issues here and how do these issues play into or effect what I am seeing?" These questions help us to see process and variation and to make connections between and among concepts. As interview transcripts and summary statements are read and questions are posed and events are observed, coding categories will be developed (Strauss and Corbin 1998).

References

Agustín, Laura. 2004. "Alternate Ethics, or: Telling Lies to Researchers." *Research for Sex Work* 7 (June): 6–7.

Balcazar, Fabricio. E., Renée R. Taylor, Gary W. Kielhofner, Karen Tamley, Tom Benzinger, Nancy Carlin, and Sabrina Johnson. 2004. "Participatory Action Research: General Principles and a Study with a Chronic Health Condition." In *Participatory Community Research: Theories and Methods in Action*, ed. Leonard A. Jason, Christopher B. Keys, Yolanda Suarez-Balcazar, Renée R. Taylor, and Margaret I. Davis, 17–36. Washington, D.C.: American Psychological Association.

Benoit, Cecilia, Mikael Jansson, Alison Millar, and Rachel Phillips. 2005. "Community-Academic Research on Hard-to-Reach Populations: Benefits and Challenges." *Qualitative Health Research* 15, no. 2: 263–82.

Benoit, Celia, and Frances M. Shaver. 2006. "Critical Issues and New Directions in Sex Work Research*." *Canadian Review of Sociology/Revue canadienne de sociologie* 43, no. 3: 243–52.

Boynton, Petra M. 2002. "Life on the Streets: The Experiences of Community Researchers in a Study of Prostitution." *Journal of Community and Applied Social Psychology* 12, no. 1: 1–12.

Busza, Joanna. 2006. "Having the Rug Pulled from Under Your Feet: One Project's Experience of the US Policy Reversal on Sex Work." *Health Policy Plan* 21, no. 4: 329–32.

Clements-Nolle, Kristen, and Ari Max Bachrach. 2003. "Community Based Participatory Research with a Hidden Population: The Transgender Community

Health Project." In *Community-Based Participatory Research for Health*, ed. Meredith Minkler and Nina Wallerstein, 332–44. San Francisco, Calif.: Jossey-Bass.

Corbin, Juliet, and Janice M. Morse. 2003. "The Unstructured Interview: Issues of Reciprocity and Risks When Dealing with Sensitive Topics." *Qualitative Inquiry* 9, no. 3: 335–54.

Corbin, Juliet, and Anselm Strauss. 1990. "Grounded Theory Research: Procedures, Canons, and Evaluative Criteria." *Qualitative Sociology* 13, no. 1: 3–21.

Dorfman, Lori E., Pamela A. Derish, and Judith B. Cohen. 1992. "Hey Girlfriend: An Evaluation of AIDS Prevention among Women in the Sex Industry." *Health Education Quarterly* 19, no. 1: 25–40.

Fernández-Peña, José Ramón, Lisa Moore, Ellen Goldstein, Pamela Decarlo, Olga Grinstead, Carolyn Hunt, Daniel Bao, and Hank Wilson. 2008. "Making Sure Research Is Used: Community-Generated Recommendations for Disseminating Research." *Progress in Community Health Partnerships* 2, no. 2: 171–76.

Flowers, Amy. 1998. "Research from Within: Participant Observation in the Phone-Sex Workplace." In *Prostitution: On Whores, Hustlers, and Johns*, ed. James E. Elias, Vern L. Bullough, Veronica Elias, and Gwen Brewer, 390–95. Amherst, Mass.: Prometheus Books.

Frank, Katherine. 2002. *G-Strings and Sympathy: Strip Club Regulars and Male Desire*. Durham, N.C.: Duke University Press.

Heckathorn, Douglas D. 1997. "Respondent-Driven Sampling: A New Approach to the Study of Hidden Populations." *Social Problems* 44, no. 2: 174–99.

———. 2002. "Respondent-Driven Sampling II: Deriving Valid Population Estimates from the Chain-Referral Samples of Hidden Populations." *Social Problems* 49, no. 1: 11–34.

Hockey, John. 1993. "Research Methods: Researching Peers and Familiar Settings." *Research Papers in Education* 8, no. 2: 199–225.

Israel, Barbara A., Amy J. Schulz, Edith A. Parker, and Adam B. Becker. 1998. "Review of Community-Based Research: Assessing Partnership Approaches to Improve Public Health." *Annual Review of Public Health* 19: 173–202.

Kaiser, Jocelyn. 2003. "Politics and Biomedicine. Studies of Gay Men, Prostitutes Come Under Scrutiny." *Science* 300, no. 5618: 403.

Kamerow, Douglas. 2008. "Politics and Science: A Cautionary Tale for the Presidential Candidates." *BMJ* 337: a2903.

Kempner, Joanna. 2008. "The Chilling Effect: How Do Researchers React to Controversy?" *PLOS Medicine* 5, no. 11: e222.

Keys, Christopher B., Susan McMahon, Bernadette Sánchez, Lorna London, and Jaleel Abdul-Adil. 2004. "Culturally Anchored Research: Quandries, Guidelines, and Exemplars for Community Psychology." In *Participatory Community Research: Theories and Methods in Action*, ed. Leonard A. Jason, Christopher B.

Keys, Yolanda Suarez-Balcazar, Renée R. Taylor, and Margaret I. Davis, 177–98. Washington, D.C.: American Psychological Association.

Kirsch, Gesa E. 2005. "Friendship, Friendliness, and Feminist Fieldwork." *Signs: Journal of Women in Culture and Society* 30, no. 4: 2163–72.

LaSala, Michael C. 2003. "When Interviewing 'Family': Maximizing the Insider Advantage in the Qualitative Study of Lesbians and Gay Men." *Journal of Gay and Lesbian Social Services* 15, no. 1: 15–30.

League of Women Voters of California Education Fund. 2004. "Measure Q Prostitution Enforcement." http://www.smartvoter.org/2004/11/02/ca/alm/meas/Q.

Lee, Raymond M., and Claire M. Renzetti. 1990. "The Problems of Researching Sensitive Topics." *American Behavioral Scientist* 33, no. 5: 510–28.

Lutnick, Alexandra. 2006. "The St. James Infirmary: A History." *Sexuality and Culture* 10, no. 2: 56–75.

———. 2007. "Survey Says: Job Satisfaction." *$pread Magazine*, Spring, 44–48.

Lutnick, Alexandra, and Deborah Cohan. 2009. "Criminalization, Legalization or Decriminalization of Sex Work: What Female Sex Workers Say in San Francisco, USA." *Reproductive Health Matters* 17, no. 34: 38–46.

Marshall, Carolyn. 2004. "Bid to Decriminalize Prostitution in Berkeley." *New York Times*, September 14. http://www.nytimes.com/2004/09/14/national/14porn.html?_r=0.

Minkler, Meredith. 2004. "Ethical Challenges for the 'Outside' Researcher in Community-Based Participatory Research." *Health Education and Behavior* 31, no. 6: 684–97.

Minkler, Meredith, and Nina Wallerstein. 2003. "Introduction to Community Based Participatory Research." In *Community-Based Participatory Research for Health*, ed. Meredith Minkler and Nina Wallerstein, 3–26. San Francisco, Calif.: Jossey-Bass.

Mullings, Beverly. 1999. "Insider or Outsider, Both or Neither: Some Dilemmas of Interviewing in a Cross-Cultural Setting." *Geoforum* 30, no. 4: 337–50.

No on K. 2008. "No on K: Say No to All Human Trafficking." http://noonk.net.

Parsons, Jeffrey T. 2005. "Researching the World's Oldest Profession." *Journal of Psychology and Human Sexuality* 17, no. 1/2: 1–3. Special issue.

Pendleton, Eva. 1997. "Love for Sale: Queering Heterosexuality." In *Whores and Other Feminists*, ed. Jill Nagle, 73–82. New York: Routledge.

Phillips, D. C. 2000. *The Expanded Social Scientist's Bestiary*. Lanham, Md.: Rowman and Littlefield.

Sanders, Teela. 2006. "Sexing Up the Subject: Methodological Nuances in Researching the Female Sex Industry." *Sexualities* 9, no. 4: 449–68.

San Francisco Task Force on Prostitution. 1996. *The San Francisco Task Force on Prostitution: Final Report*. San Francisco, Calif.: Submitted to the Board of

Supervisors of the City and County of San Francisco. http://archive.org/details/sanfranciscotask19sanf.

Semaan, Salaam, Scott Santibanez, Richard S. Garfein, Douglas D. Heckathorn, and Don C. Des Jarlais. 2009. "Ethical and Regulatory Considerations in HIV Prevention Studies Employing Respondent-Driven Sampling." *International Journal of Drug Policy* 20, no. 1: 14–27.

Shaver, Frances M. 2005. "Sex Work Research: Methodological and Ethical Challenges." *Journal of Interpersonal Violence* 20, no. 3: 296–319.

Smith, Matt. 2008. "Dubious UCSF Study Claims Cops Extort Sex." *SF Weekly*, September 10. http://www.sfweekly.com/2008-09-10/news/dubious-ucsf-study-claims-cops-extort-sex/.

Strauss, Anselm, and Juliet Corbin. 1998. *Basics of Qualitative Research: Techniques and Procedures for Developing Grounded Theory*. 2nd ed. Thousand Oaks, Calif.: Sage.

Sudman, Seymour, and Graham Kalton. 1986. "New Developments in the Sampling of Special Populations." *Annual Review of Sociology* 12: 401–29.

Sudman, Seymour, Monroe G. Sirken, and Charles D. Cowan. 1988. "Sampling Rare and Elusive Populations." *Science* 240, no. 4855: 991–96.

Torres-Harding, Susan R., Richard Herrell, and Carole Howard. 2004. "Epidemiological Research: Science and Community Participation." In *Participatory Community Research: Theories and Methods in Action*, ed. Leonard A. Jason, Christopher B. Keys, Yolanda Suarez-Balcazar, Renée R. Taylor, and Margaret I. Davis, 53–70. Washington, D.C.: American Psychological Association.

Wahab, Stephanie, and Lacy Sloan. 2004. "Ethical Dilemmas in Sex Work Research." *Research for Sex Work* 7 (June): 3–5.

Wallerstein, Nina, and Bonnie Duran. 2003. "The Conceptual, Historical, and Practice Roots of Community Based Participatory Research and Related Participatory Traditions." In *Community-Based Participatory Research for Health*, ed. Meredith Minkler and Nina Wallerstein, 27–52. San Francisco, Calif.: Jossey-Bass.

Watters, John K., and Patrick Biernacki. 1989. "Targeted Sampling: Options for the Study of Hidden Populations." *Social Problems* 36, no. 4: 416–30.

Weitzer, Ronald. 2000. "Why We Need More Research on Sex Work." In *Sex for Sale: Prostitution, Pornography, and the Sex Industry*, ed. Ronald. Weitzer, 1–16. New York: Routledge.

———. 2010. "The Mythology of Prostitution: Advocacy Research and Social Policy." *Sexuality Research and Social Policy* 7: 15–29.

CHAPTER 3

Participant-Driven Action Research (PDAR) with Sex Workers in Vancouver

Raven Bowen and Tamara O'Doherty

HISTORICALLY, academics, practitioners, and policymakers have treated sex workers, like many other marginalized groups, as the *subjects* of research by limiting—or denying—their opportunities to participate in designing and guiding research. Typically, researchers will approach sex workers with projects that have already been conceptualized, designed, funded, and approved by ethics boards and academic institutions. As a result, sex workers are excluded from key phases of knowledge production about their lives and work—the research instruments have been finalized, research assistants have been hired, and the data analysis strategies have been decided. Generally, the only remaining role for sex workers to fill is as participants in the data collection phase of the research. Although some researchers involve members of a community of interest as consultants, or hire individuals to perform tasks such as project coordination or data entry, crucial phases of research remain out of reach for community members. In this chapter, we hope to expand the dialogue around inclusion to demonstrate that participant-driven research (where participants are research collaborators and the source of research topics) may offer the most potential for empowering the communities that are subjects of research. Here, we discuss the challenges, successes, and benefits of participant-driven action research (PDAR) as a mechanism to address issues of power in knowledge production within marginalized communities.

PDAR is an expansion of participatory action research, a methodology by which investigators and communities can collaborate in research technologies and processes. Such research can take many forms. Alexandra Lutnick's discussion of the SWEAT study (chapter 2 of this volume) is an excellent example of a complementary collaborative research approach wherein community members have expanded roles as participants, as research assistants who collect data, and as members of the research advisory committee. These research partnerships provide much-needed opportunities for inclusion but, most importantly, they offer evidence that it is possible to make more fundamental changes wherein research topics *emerge* out of the community through interactions and relationships with its members.

Under the PDAR framework, community members are not only participants but also the architects of research frameworks and processes. In this way, PDAR acknowledges the leadership roles that sex workers can take in research rather than confining them to narrow roles as data sources. Through this process, research is created, guided, interpreted, (re)presented, and utilized by the community of interest. As a result, the research enterprise becomes more accessible and relevant to community members and the production of knowledge through research becomes a tool *of and for* the community. Thus PDAR expands the roles available to participants, from data collection and advisory capacities to the research conceptualization, design, analysis, and praxis phases.

The Development of Our Research Orientation

Our research orientation was shaped by our experiences working in a grassroots, sex worker–driven organization called PACE (Prostitution Alternatives, Counseling, and Education) Society. PACE Society was founded in 1994 by Paige Latin who, along with other former sex workers, garnered the support of friends and allies to raise money for an outreach and support service for street-based sex workers. PACE is a Federal Charitable Society and is one of two Vancouver-based organizations providing outreach, one-on-one support, and advocacy to active and former street-based sex workers. Originally PACE was structured like a typical nonprofit organization (i.e., with an executive director and board of directors), but with the leadership and inclusion of sex workers, it began to operate in a nonhierarchical manner. Decisions were made based on consensus so that all staff, managers, and members had equal say.

We both became involved with the PACE Society (and PDAR) as an extension of our own work as community activists, providing frontline services for other local nonprofit groups on youth justice and women's rights in the Vancouver area. Raven was the chair of the board of PACE Society in 1995. She soon resigned to accept employment with the organization. From 1996 to 2000, Raven provided outreach and direct support services to sex workers and youth at risk of sexual exploitation and then served as executive director until 2006. As executive director, she worked to ensure that sex workers filled decision-making roles within the organization. As a result, all of PACE Society's programs and services were designed, implemented, and evaluated by sex workers. For example, PACE Society materials, such as operating policies, were developed by sex workers who were employed at the organization and who received its services. The PACE Society board of directors, of which Tamara served as chairperson from 2001 to 2004, comprised people with diverse experiences and backgrounds—sex workers, academics, activists, and other community members were all dedicated to promoting sex worker leadership within the organization and in the community at large. Within this collaborative environment, sex workers were encouraged, individually and collectively, to explore opportunities for increased social involvement—a crucial step in addressing some of the marginalization experienced by street-based workers, who are typically relegated to the fringes of society.

In addition to the outreach and support components of PACE Society, staff and board members also created and took part in many research projects. For example, in 2001, Len Cler-Cunningham, former executive director of PACE (1994–2000), copublished the findings from a study on sex workers' experiences of victimization in Vancouver (2001). Sex workers at PACE Society also took part in both the implementation and the evaluation of a support and education project funded by the National Crime Investment Fund. This project produced educational materials targeted at youth and an asset-based peer support tool that inventoried sex worker's strengths and mobilized these toward personal and career goals. Since some PACE Society staff and board members were former sex workers, they also had experience as research subjects and thus as the objects of the research "gaze." They had experienced stigma and exclusion through their past participation in positivistic and hierarchical research projects. They expressed their frustration about how these kinds of research designs corralled them into specific roles, controlled how their stories were "made sense of," and how their experiences and lives were (re)presented publically.

One of the key areas of concern identified by PACE members was how knowledge about sex work was produced and used by the health, welfare, and legal systems. Sex workers identified the link between academic research and social policy and social spending; they saw that their organizations were constantly struggling for funding, which limited their ability to advocate for sex workers' rights and safety initiatives. When organizations do not have funding to send representatives to conferences, experts' meetings, or other policy forums, they are unable to voice the concerns and needs of their members. Sex workers at PACE therefore expressed the desire to see more accurate information about their working conditions produced so that policies affecting the sex industry are grounded in their lived experiences.

In 2005, as a demonstration of resistance to the misrepresentation and exclusion of sex workers from knowledge production, Raven organized policy development workshops with sex workers at PACE Society who wanted to change the way research was performed in Vancouver. These individuals learned about policy development and research ethics by working with experts such as researchers Ted Palys and John Lowman from Simon Fraser University and government policy analyst Esther Shannon. These experts were invested in sex workers gaining a greater understanding of the roles of policy and research in order to increase sex workers' abilities to realize roles as collaborators in research. In 2006, Raven published *Research Ethics: A Guide for Community Organizations* (hereinafter, *Community Guidelines*) to establish some minimal "rules of engagement" for research with sex worker communities (Bowen 2006). The *Community Guidelines* were created to (1) ensure that sex workers who participate in any form of research are knowledgeable about their rights to privacy, confidentiality, informed consent, and the right to withdraw from research, in accordance with Canadian research standards (and that this protection is the acknowledged responsibility of sex workers, community organizations, and researchers);[1] (2) increase the accuracy and quality of research about hidden and criminalized populations *because* research informs social/welfare and enforcement policies; and (3) ensure that community groups become full partners in the production of knowledge about and with their service populations. By increasing knowledge among service providers about research ethics, goals, and potentialities, we strove to encourage egalitarian partnerships with academic researchers and community organizations.

The *Community Guidelines* explained what potential research participants should know prior to agreeing to research; it assisted potential participants and organizations in identifying key questions to ask when approached to participate in research. As a result, many sex workers in Vancouver have access to these community guidelines and now question the research designs, approaches, and uses of data, as well as the motives and intentions of researchers, prior to taking part in studies. The community's use of the guidelines is a clear demonstration of their desire to be a part of knowledge production. The guidelines also serve as an invitation by sex workers to the research community to do more research and to collaborate in mutually beneficial ways.

These experiences with PACE showed us how valuable it is to involve sex workers in all stages of the research process; and so when we entered academia, participatory research methodologies appealed to us as a meaningful way to involve sex workers in the creation of knowledge about themselves. We also believed that sex worker leadership in research was in itself a political act. Our shared philosophies of increasing sex worker participation in knowledge production and of respecting sex workers' rights in research activities thus led to the collaboration that eventually became Tamara's (2007) research on victimization with off-street sex workers. The research, which employed PDAR, was completed in partial fulfillment of a master of arts degree in criminology.[2] The project comprised a self-administered survey and in-depth interviews with sex workers that explored women's experiences of victimization in off-street venues such as massage parlors, escort agencies, and private work environments. Raven was one of Tamara's key community mentors and helped to facilitate the study. For Raven, the project provided an opportunity to operationalize the community-based guidelines developed by sex workers. In the following sections, we illustrate our PDAR approach through our reflections on Tamara's research project. This contribution presents our experiences of undertaking scholarly yet community-based research.

Sex Work Researchers and PDAR

For decades sex workers have been voicing their concerns about research performed on their communities and they have objected to the stereotypical and sensationalist representations that often appear in media and academia (Brock 1998; Kempadoo and Doezema 1998; Pheterson 1989). In our experience, sex workers are willing to engage in research *because* they have been subjected to the often harmful policies that have been created based on inaccurate and overgeneralized research findings and that have been erroneously transformed into "common sense" wisdom and social stereotypes. Both sex workers and academics express concern over researchers benefitting "off the backs of sex workers": researchers earn academic degrees, further their progress toward tenure in universities, and gain reputations in the academic community as a result of the information provided to them by sex workers (Hubbard 1999; Jeffrey and MacDonald 2007; O'Neill 2010). However, some academics have taken great pains to learn from the criticisms raised by sex workers and a growing number are working in research partnerships with sex workers in Canada.[3] These partnerships have created research best practices and hence more nuanced representations of sex workers' lives.

Yet despite these potential benefits, collaborative research methods are not typical in academia and researchers may struggle to gain equal recognition for their work. Researchers may even face stigma by association for their work with marginalized groups such as sex workers (see, for example, chapter 1 in this volume). But even with these challenges, researchers who choose collaborative research designs can benefit from enhanced reputations in their communities of interest: they can develop a kind of "street cred" or social capital that may facilitate future projects in hard-to-reach communities. This has certainly been the case for Tamara. The relationships she built as a result of using PDAR for her master's thesis research enabled her to conduct a second, more expansive, study for her current PhD research. Such research collaborations may also inspire community activists to undertake research degrees as it did for Raven, who defended her master's thesis in March 2013. This kind of community–academy collaboration may also benefit the community and therefore reduce the perception some hold that the benefits of research are only unidirectional. For example, participatory research may carry an "emancipatory potential" for traditionally silenced and criminalized groups (Hubbard 1999) by encouraging greater political activism from community members as they may see changes to their conditions and may benefit from challenges to stereotyping about their community. It also may reveal new research directions that might have been overlooked due to a lack of in-depth knowledge regarding the issues affecting community members. All of this can ultimately build social and cultural capital among sex workers and researchers;[4] support joint goals toward social justice; and challenge existing policies that serve to criminalize and ostracize sex workers, directly affecting their health and leaving them susceptible to violence.

The PDAR Approach: Research With Rather Than Research On

While many styles of collaborative research feature key principles of inclusion—participation, individual and collective action, social change, and empowerment—the degree of participant involvement at various stages reflects a researcher's valuation of participants.[5] Maggie O'Neill, one of the principle advocates for community-based collaborations, argues that by reorienting the subject–object paradigm, researchers and participants can all be repositioned as subjects, thus enabling "mutual recognition" and allowing the "critical recovery" of history for oppressed groups (2010).

Other researchers, such as Sandra Kirby, Lorraine Greaves, and Colleen Reid (2006), and Stephanie Wahab (2003), also ensure that collaboration occurs at all stages of the research process: design, method, analysis and "knowledge uptake" (Kirby, Greaves, and Reid 2006, 46). Debbie Pushor (2008) explains that the specific division of labor within projects will differ and work will not always be equally shared, but all collaborative projects should feature the goal of more equitable power sharing over decision making. This sense of mutuality is a hallmark of participatory research.

PDAR, as we have experienced it, extends the participatory approach and encompasses five broad steps: *conceptualization, research design, implementation, analysis and (re)presentation, and action.* The remainder of this chapter explains how we employed these steps in our own participant-driven action research by detailing each step as it related to Tamara's master's research. Tamara's study consisted of two elements: (1) an interview segment exploring ten women's working conditions, safety, stereotypes of prostitution, and law reform; and (2) an anonymous, self-administered survey dealing specifically with interpersonal violence and other forms of victimization in the workplace, such as theft and client refusals to wear condoms. The methodology was designed to facilitate the greatest amount of meaningful involvement by women with experience in the sex industry to ensure that they had opportunities to guide the research. Our overarching objectives included contributing to academic and legal knowledge about prostitution and effecting legal change to increase safety for sex workers.

Conceptualization

In PDAR, research topics are created as a result of interactions with community members (Wahab 2003). Particularly among oppressed groups, members tend to share anecdotal information about experiences they have had or barriers they face in their daily lives. Researchers can work with marginalized communities such as sex workers to identify what they already know and don't know about an issue. This information, or lack of it, can be transformed into a topic for exploration that reflects sex workers' lived experiences. Conversations that emerge from these interactions can lead to project ideas that have goals toward social change or community education.

Researchers note that those who participate in the early stages of research will intimately affect the research direction, approach, and methods (Kirby, Greaves, and Reid 2006). Tamara conceptualized her research based on, and therefore reflective of, the personal and professional experiences, political viewpoints, and biases of each of the people who would eventually become her "collaboration team." This was important because the sociopolitical positions of academic and community members ultimately affect what they prioritize and what they miss or ignore when conducting research. By employing a diverse collaborative team, it is possible to reduce any biases or blind spots that might exist.

Linda Tuhiwai Smith (1999) asks researchers to consider two specific questions prior to engaging in research with indigenous populations: *whose interests does it serve* and *who will benefit from it*? While these questions are central to conceptualizing research, they can also serve as anchors for PDAR at every stage of the research project. In this research project, the collaborative team was committed to centering the work on these questions; in effect, the questions became a part of our philosophical common ground from which the collaborative team could suspend individual politics and work in a consensus-driven framework. Since three of the members of the collaborative team were already colleagues, working under a consensus-based peer-driven framework, this structure was familiar and posed no problems. The fourth member of the team took part anonymously; she heard of the project and joined the team after we had decided on the research topic. We were all committed to informing policies with empirically sound evidence developed with sex workers as active and equal members of the collaboration.

In PDAR, the shape of a project emerges through the conceptualization of the research. The sex workers who had encouraged Tamara to pursue research in the first place agreed to take part as "collaborators" in the research project. Once the collaborative team was established, a research topic (victimization) and a general target group (off-street workers) quickly emerged over a casual meeting in a local pub—a space that the sex workers had identified as safe. In the collaborators' experiences, off-street sex work was safer than street-based sex work but they wanted to know if their experiences held true across a wider population of off-street sex workers. To explore this further, the collaborative team opted to focus exclusively on off-street venues.

The idea to research violence in off-street commercial sex venues therefore came from the community rather than from Tamara; this was an important distinction that resulted in a unique research experience for all parties involved in the project. While crucial to the success of Tamara's project, participating in but not controlling the community process through which the research topic emerged does not appear to be a particularly common strategy in academia. If researchers decide on topics themselves, then the projects are still originating via a more hierarchical structure—especially if the researchers are outsiders to the communities they wish to study. These projects can still be participatory if members of the community find value in the research topic and shape the project's design and its implementation.

Even if a researcher is an insider to the community and that individual decides on a research topic on his or her own, that person is not engaging in collaborative research unless multiple individuals from the community are involved. Joey Sprague (2005, 192) cautions against "privileging" insider researchers; she argues that we are all limited by our standpoints, or our "locatedness," in relation to any given social issue. For Sprague, the solution to this epistemological issue is to include a diverse group, including social researchers, or outsiders. While the individuals on the collaborative team in Tamara's research were all women with experience in the off-street industry, they each had different experiences in relation to the sex industry and with prior research—for example, some had significant involvement as both principal investigators and participants.

After making the decision to focus on off-street sex work, Tamara and her team decided to explore victimization specifically; this was important to the team because one of the most enduring ideas about sex work is that it is rife with violence. With this starting point, Tamara searched the academic literature for information on off-street sex work and found a significant void. This paucity of research about the topic was known intuitively among sex workers and was reinforced by the lack of literature. Taken together, this highlights the differing roles parties can play in the collaboration and demonstrates that community members may "know" about the gaps in academic research done on their groups because they have been the subjects. Sex workers "live" in the research gaps and in the misrepresentations and they are consciously aware of when their experiences are not represented; Tamara became empirically aware of this. Although the way of "knowing" (i.e., that the topic of off-street victimization was a research gap) came about differently for Tamara and the collaborative team members, they felt united and prepared to begin the process of designing a research project that was meaningful to all involved.

Research Design

We have separated the conceptualization and research design phases here to highlight the fact that research design begins with the identification of a topic, which in PDAR is often a result of informal dialogue over multiple occasions. But when participants begin to create the lines of inquiry and chose the methods to employ, a more structured process develops, even if this process is conducted in informal environments (Wahab 2003), as demonstrated in the previous section. Collaborative research may potentially transform researchers, participants, and the community at large; however, it also raises many challenges that are not present when a researcher operates on an individual basis (Dupont 2008). Debbie Pushor (2008) describes a variety of administrative items that are beneficial to successful academic research collaborations, such as clarity in coordination and leadership of the team, discussion about the division of labor, rights to the data and the research tools, and copyright issues. In our experiences, attention to these practical details was necessary, but it is not an area that most texts on research methods devote much time to.

Fortunately, the collaborators were prepared for dialogue on the administrative items that Pushor speaks of because some had participated in the *Community Guidelines* project. We discussed expectations, time requirements, confidentiality, and rights to authorship at the onset of the project. In paying attention to rights and responsibilities, we brought transparency to the process. For example, confidentiality, or the promise not to disclose particular information, is a key concern for nearly all researchers (Palys and Atchison 2007; Shaver 2005). John Lowman and Ted Palys (2007) recommend that researchers employ strict confidentiality to effectively protect research participants. This requires researchers to maintain confidentiality even in the event that a third party, such as a criminal court, subpoenas a researcher to testify in court.[6] Confidentiality was also a concern for sex workers and members of the collaborative team, since some members knew each other and others took part anonymously. Tamara had to engage in multiple group and individual meetings with participants in order to support their safe participation in the research design phase.

In participant-driven form, the collaborative team chose the methods. To do this, researchers can inform participants about the different research methods, the strengths and weaknesses of each in relation to the particular subject area, and then support the participants in choosing the method they would like to employ. Here, the collaborative team felt strongly that quantitative methods could be used to gather evidence that would be accepted in formal legal settings. But the team also wanted to employ qualitative methods to allow sex workers to contextualize the data arising from the research. Over a four-month time period, we used our connections to sex workers, along with outreach to other sex workers who advertised their services in public online forums, to purposively sample the off-street community. We invited anyone who identified as a woman engaged in off-street commercial sex work to participate in the research project. In the end, the team decided to use a mixed-method approach, which included both a questionnaire (N = 39) and interviews (N = 10).

The success of the research project was most certainly connected to the effort that went into creating an appropriately worded and thorough questionnaire. Choices in language proved to be instrumental to success; by using insider language we showed a strong level of knowledge about the sex industry. We also used terminology that would not offend; for example, the term *prostitute* often carries a negative connotation and while most of the participants would agree they engage in forms of prostitution, they resisted being labeled *a prostitute*. While some preferred *escort*, *masseuse*, or *companion*, we agreed upon the terms *sex worker* or *sex industry worker* to refer to most forms of erotic labor.

The process of developing the questionnaire was tedious. The team went through about twenty five versions of the survey before we had to stop revising and simply start the research. We began with a survey developed by Dr. John Lowman and Laura Fraser (in 1996), as Dr. Lowman was a well-known and trusted researcher whose work was also conducted in Vancouver. The team revised this survey, developing numerous original lines of query about topics such as coworkers as potential perpetrators of victimization, requests for unsafe sex acts as a form of victimization, and sex workers' grounds for refusing to provide services to clients. When we reviewed the results later, we found that all these new questions produced valuable information in the study: coworkers ended up being the most likely source of victimization for masseuses, refusal to wear a condom was the most likely form of victimization for escorts, and nearly all participants detailed grounds upon which they would refuse to provide sexual services. Working with a small group of sex workers to customize a research tool was time consuming but invaluable to the collaborative process. Coproduction of research tools is where participants' ideas, experiences, and priorities are most evident.

Occasionally issues arose on which the collaborators disagreed. For example, there were minor disagreements about the terminology used in the survey, but with discussion we came to agreement based on informal acknowledgment of a basic consensus decision-making structure: team members could (1) agree, (2) disagree but live with the decision, or (3) disagree and require a change. Consensus was attainable in this project because the sex workers involved initiated it and there was a collaborative spirit, a sense of ownership, and a commitment to seeing the project succeed.

While we are advocates for remunerating any individual who takes part in sharing his or her experiences, Tamara's project was not funded. In situations where funding is not available, there are creative ways to compensate individuals for their time and wisdom. For example, researchers could offer collaborators reference letters for those who wish to work in traditional labor markets, special limited-edition copies of the final research project (made unique by collaborators through artwork, special bindings, signatures, etc.), or special certificates or plaques for contributing to the project. It is important to discuss with participants how they would like to be recognized for their work and how they would like to celebrate or mark their contributions. This could also be done as a "roast" celebration or through art, such as the creation of collages.

In this case, at the end of Tamara's master's research, we celebrated the project and Tamara provided hard copies of the final product to the collaborators. One of the collaborators spent an incredible amount of time revising the survey. To recognize her intellectual rights, we signed a contract recognizing her coauthorship of the instrument and providing her the rights to use it for future research purposes. Tamara also provided scholarly and work-related references for the collaborators to acknowledge the research skills acquired by the collaborators and maintained the collaboration through the dissemination phase.

Implementation

Once we established who was doing what and through what method, community members guided researchers through their networks, vouching for them as individuals and introducing the research project and team to key individuals through sex worker–established mechanisms of communication. Due in large part to the considerable time spent preparing the research tools, implementing the study went quite smoothly. Tamara initially believed that this stage featured the least amount of involvement from the collaboration team; they functioned to assist in recruiting participants, and Tamara checked in with each member periodically to give them updates on the number of surveys that had been received or the number of interviews that had been completed. However, the collaborators' roles in recruitment were actually quite significant, and Tamara's ignorance to their level of involvement in this stage speaks volumes to the sustained divide between researchers and community members that exists even in collaborative styles of research.

While Tamara had worked in the community for years and had many strong individual relationships with sex workers, the combination of her outsider status and her legal background carried with it all of the potential negative outcomes of the previous decades of research done *on* the sex worker community by other academics. At the time, she was not fully aware of the degree to which her allies and collaborators were involved in negotiating sex workers' involvement in the project. And in addition to the collaborators, PACE staff members (many of whom were former sex workers) who were more visible among sex workers in the community shared the opportunity to work *with* Tamara and the collaborators to collectively produce knowledge about off-street victimization. Potential participants would check in with the members of the collaborative team to ask who Tamara was and whether she could be trusted. This "vouching" was significant because collaborators risked their reputations to support the project. Their willingness to do this demonstrates their degree of investment in the project and perhaps their sense of ownership over the research process itself. Their activities in essence moved Tamara from an "outsider" position to that of an ally or "trusted outsider."

Analysis and (Re)presentation

The analysis phase involved structuring and organizing data to present and represent a community, a context, or a phenomenon. As Howard Becker (1996) argues, it is not a question of *whether* we interpret the phenomena or findings based on our own frames or reference, the question is *how accurately* we interpret them (57). Drawing out themes or conducting data analyses is a subjective endeavor where interpretation can alter data to conform to the interpreters' expectations and experiences. Due to the inherent subjectivity of the analysis and representation phase (Strauss and Corbin 1998), it is crucial to involve collaborators as a way of increasing the breadth of the analysis (Becker 1996), thereby increasing the likelihood of accuracy in representations.

Kirby, Greaves, and Reid (2006) write that the analysis and interpretation phase is the most contentious part of collaborative research as it is the most likely point where conflict will occur. They argue that it is a "process fraught with the issues of difference" (51). This phase is also the part of the research process where some academics seem to be reluctant to share decision-making power. We do not dispute the fact that some forms of data analysis, such as using Statistical Package for the Social Sciences (SPSS) software and interpreting statistics, require skills and training that community members may not have. The academic in a collaborative team is often useful here. We were concerned about the "top-down" decision-making power over data analysis and interpretation, so we supported the full participation of sex workers at the data analysis and interpretation stages, as we did in every other stage of the research process. We learned that the analysis stage is the hardest stage to manage collaboratively. As Ted Palys and Chris Atchison (2007) note, it "comes down to whether it's better to ask people what *they* think is important, and incorporate their answers into our efforts to make sense of their behavior, or to ask only what *we* [researchers] think is important and then try to infer what they must have been thinking in order to give such answers" (9). Likewise, Ida Dupont (2008) concedes that while involving community members in the data analysis and writing process is challenging, providing the opportunity to dialogue in such a manner is a key step in empowering communities (205).

As Tamara was undertaking this research in partial fulfillment of her degree, she knew that ultimately she had to be the author of the thesis. But many research projects are not done for such specific purposes and therefore can feature collaborative writing. Sex workers are rarely offered opportunities to write or contribute directly to knowledge derived from their work and lives. Most often, their stories are interpreted and told through the lens of the researcher or are confined to quotations. Each research project is unique and it is possible to devise creative ways for sex workers to directly contribute their feelings and interpretations of projects through poems, vignettes, anecdotes, introductory statements, reflections, project dedications, nonidentifying photography, artwork for report covers, and so on. In this case, all the research-related activities were done collaboratively, but Tamara undertook the labor-intensive work of writing, entering data, and conducting and transcribing the interviews, while the collaborators guided the direction of the research, helped to decide on appropriate methods and research tools, assisted in recruiting participants, and contributed to the analysis of the data.

Kirby, Greaves, and Reid (2006) mention that challenges can occur if members of a collaboration team have conflicting opinions about the final conclusions of research. This was certainly true in our experience, but it was not an issue that detracted from the collaboration. Differences in interpretation should occur, particularly when you have a very diverse collaboration team. Similarly, Katherine Borland (1991) explains that the process of collecting information and unintentionally misrepresenting the experiences of her participant (who then rejected the text), forced a reconceptualization of the data to incorporate both the researchers' interpretation of the participant's experiences and the participant's representation of her own experiences. This kind of interchange is possible in sex work research when sex workers provide feedback on preliminary findings and drafts, thus providing opportunities for representations to be challenged (Wahab 2003).

To illustrate this, in an effort to make data analysis more collaborative, Tamara used SPSS and NVivo software to organize her data and then forwarded anonymized computer files to the collaborative team members along with descriptive statistics derived from the surveys and themes that emerged from the interviews (such as the positives and negatives about working the in the industry, myths participants wished to dispel, and sex worker experiences reporting victimization to authorities). The collaborators posed questions about these preliminary data outputs, suggested explanations for certain trends, interpreted the data based on their lived experiences, and at times challenged what was being presented.

For example, many of the women who participated in this project had negative views of escort agencies and in one of the early drafts of the thesis, Tamara initially presented these views as a generalization that escort agencies were exploitative and unconcerned about their employees. Members of the collaborative team caught and corrected this generalization in their review of themes. They explained that their experiences with agencies were much more complex than how Tamara had (re)presented them to be.

Action

The actions that follow participant-driven research make the process meaningful and relevant to community members and researchers. The action focus here is on praxis. The activities that have been part of, or will follow, the final printing of the research study function to empower community members in their social change and equality-seeking efforts. The utilization of research findings as part of the creation of subsequent community-based projects or advocacy work is a tangible outcome that makes the coproduction of knowledge worthwhile.

For action-based research, producing useful research is merely the starting point. As Dupont (2008, 197) argues, "The empowerment of research participants is as important as the contribution to knowledge and policy development." Therefore, to move participatory research into participatory *action* research, researchers must consider the "social value" of research and "[their] obligations to research participants beyond simply doing no harm" (Dupont 2008, 197). Rather than a final step in the research process, the finished report signifies the beginning of one of the most important phases: publication, distribution, and for us, dissemination and action.

The development of transferable skills among sex workers as a by-product of collaboration with researchers is a powerful contribution to sex worker movements. For example, as a result of all the collaborative work that has taken place in Vancouver over the past twenty-five years and sex workers' own desires to make change happen, sex workers formed a nonprofit organization called Downtown East-side Sex Workers United against Violence (SWUAV). This group brought about a legal challenge to Canada's criminal prohibitions related to prostitution (*SWUAV and Kiselbach v. Canada*, 2008).

Through the collaborative process, the team encouraged Tamara to initially take the lead on speaking engagements and the distribution of the report through academic publications and conferences; this process would support the ongoing anonymity of participants and collaborators. Since Tamara was uncomfortable speaking for a group of individuals she knew were entirely capable of speaking for themselves, a compromise was reached; Tamara has spoken, and continues to speak, about the study alongside sex workers who choose to be public about their experiences. Tamara very rarely accepts engagements where there is not at least one sex worker involved in the presentation of the work.

As a demonstration of the action phase in PDAR, the master's research project was used in a Canadian legal challenge (Bedford v. Canada 2010) to the criminalization of consensual adult sex work. The findings provided evidence of the diversity of sex work experiences; this evidence calls into question generalizations about prostitution and requires academics, legal practitioners, public policymakers, and others to make room for differences in experiences that extant generalized statements ignore. Tamara also submitted an expert's report as evidence to support the SWUAV and Sheryl Kiselbach court case.

In another example of the action phase in PDAR, when conducting community-based research projects among sex workers, Raven was able to engage sex workers in what she calls "participatory action advocacy," where sex workers shared the findings of research projects with funders, community groups, the public, and other stakeholders to garner support for harm reduction programming and improved reporting of violence experienced by sex workers.[7] Ultimately, research projects are unique and each can offer differing opportunities for action in ways that are comfortable for participants. In our technological age, sex workers can more safely participate in dissemination online and by using various forms of digital media. We encourage researchers and sex workers to work together to find creative ways to share project results and to act for social change.

Conclusion

The benefits of participant-driven action research span beyond bridging an "artificially" created divide between researcher and participant (Reinharz 1992, 181). Tamara gained innumerable skills and knowledge from the process. The data derived from the study have begun to fill a void in the academic literature and it has been used to support sex worker's advocacy efforts. The collaborative team also benefitted: they built upon their knowledge of research ethics by doing research, and they gained new skills in understanding specific details of creating questionnaires, managing workloads, understanding statistics, and learning about the requirements of academic publishing.

Our insider and "trusted outsider" privilege clearly influenced our methodological frameworks: we used PAR principles as social activists in environments where community members set the agenda. In this context it followed that participatory action research, for us, would emerge as participant-driven action research. We believe that as oppressed communities increase their capacities and forge new access routes toward social change for their communities, participant-driven collaborations with researchers will soon become the norm. As young academics, we are excited by this; however, it may be challenging for some researchers to adjust to this method, where the direction of research expertise flows not *from* but *to* the researcher.

By sharing our experiences with PDAR, we are encouraging partnerships and the transfer of knowledge, skills, and experiences between sex workers and academics. We also hope to inspire further debates on community-driven research approaches. We recommend that researchers demonstrate an investment in their populations of interest by giving their time to relevant community groups prior to conceptualizing research. This can be done by engaging with local organizations as part of a preliminary work plan—a "pre- pre"-research activity. The challenges and issues that community members face will become apparent through the resulting relationship building—and so will the community's ideas for responses and solutions. By valuing the community members' knowledge and abilities, PDAR offers increased potential for the empowerment of oppressed and marginalized groups.

If we approach research *with* participants who codetermine topics and methods and codevelop tools, in addition to shaping interpretations and (re)presentations, then knowledge has its best chance of being collectively produced. Both academics and sex workers can enter into research activities through a process of respect and recognition and leave mutually enriched with insights, new epistemological approaches to understanding our world, new jargon and frames of reference, stories, negotiable social capital (i.e., credibility and "street cred"), and new perspectives that are the derivatives of each other's lived experiences, and most importantly, of the research collaboration.

Notes

1. The Community Guidelines are based on Canada's Tri-Council Policy Statement, which sets the standards for academic research institutions to follow in granting ethical approval for research with humans. For the most current Tri-Council Policy Statement, see http://www.pre.ethics.gc.ca/default.aspx.

2. The full thesis is available at: http://24.85.225.7/lowman_prostitution/HTML/odoherty/ODoherty-thesis-final.pdf.

3. For example, see Benoit and Millar (2001), Jeffrey and MacDonald (2007), Lewis et al. (2005), Pivot Legal Society (2006), and Shannon et al. (2009).

4. See Benoit et al. (2005), Hubbard (1999), and Sanders (2006).

5. For a detailed discussion of the distinction between research *with* and research *on*, see O'Neill (1996).

6. Unlimited confidentiality is also recommended by Bowen (2006b) and the West Coast Cooperative of Sex Industry Professionals (n.d.).

7. See, for example, R. Bowen (2006a), R. Bowen (2007a), and R. Bowen (2007b).

References

Becker, Howard. 1996. "The Epistemology of Qualitative Research." In *Ethnography and Human Development: Context and Meaning in Social Development*, ed. R. Jessor, A. Colby and R. Shweder, 53–71. Chicago: University of Chicago Press.

Bedford v. Canada. 2010. ONSC 4264.

Benoit, Cecilia, Mikael Jansson, Alison Millar, and Rachel Phillips. 2005. "Community-Academic Research on Hard-to-Reach Populations: Benefits and Challenges." *Qualitative Health Research* 15, no. 2: 263–82.

Benoit, Cecilia, and Alison Millar. 2001. *Dispelling Myths and Understanding Realities: Working Conditions, Health Status and Exiting Experiences of Sex Workers.*

http://www.hawaii.edu/hivandaids/Working%20Conditions,%20Health%20
Status%20and%20Exiting%20Experience%20of%20Sex%20Workers.pdf.

Borland, Katherine. 1991. "'That's Not What I Said': Interpretive Conflict in Oral
Narrative Research." In *Women's Words: The Feminist Practice of Oral History*,
ed. Sherna B. Gluck and Daphne Patai, 63–75. New York: Routledge.

Bowen, Raven. 2006a. "From the Curb: Sex Workers' Perspectives on Violence
and Domestic Trafficking." Working Paper 03-06, Providing Alternatives Counselling and Education (PACE) Society, Vancouver, British Columbia. http://
bccec.files.wordpress.com/2010/01/final-report-violence_and_domestic
_trafficking_bccew.pdf.

———. 2006b. *Research Ethics: A Guide for Community Organizations*. Produced for
PACE Society. http://bccec.files.wordpress.com/2007/12/community_research
_-guidelines_feb2006_draft_.pdf.

———. 2007a. "Bad Date Reporting and Response: Experiences and Insights from
Sex Workers and Community Stakeholders, Discussion Document." Working
Paper 03-07, Providing Alternatives Counselling and Education (PACE) Society, Vancouver, British Columbia. http://bccec.files.wordpress.com/2010/01/
confronting_bad_dates_prelim_discussion_doc_1.pdf.

———. 2007b. "Protection for All: Bad Date Reporting and Response Strategies." Working Paper 08-07, Providing Alternatives Counselling and Education
(PACE) Society, Vancouver, British Columbia. http://www.pace-society.org/
library/protection-for-all-bad-date-reporting-and-response-strategies.pdf.

Brock, Deborah. 1998. *Making Work, Making Trouble: Prostitution as a Social Problem*. Toronto, Ontario: University of Toronto Press.

Cler-Cunningham, Len, and Christine Christensen. 2001. *Violence against
Women in Vancouver's Street Level Sex Trade and the Police Response*. Produced
for PACE Society. http://www.pace-society.org/library/sex-trade-and-police
-response.pdf.

Downtown Eastside Sex Workers United against Violence Society v. Canada
(Attorney General). 2008. BCSC 1726, 90 B.C.L.R. (4th) 177.

Dupont, Ida. 2008. "Beyond Doing No Harm: A Call for Participatory Action
Research with Marginalized Populations in Criminological Research." *Critical
Criminology* 16, no 3: 197–207.

Hubbard, Phil. 1999. "Researching Female Sex Work: Reflections on Geographical Exclusion, Critical Methodologies and 'Useful' knowledge." *Area* 31, no. 3:
229–37.

Jeffrey, Leslie, and Gayle MacDonald. 2007. *Sex Workers in the Maritimes Talk
Back*. Vancouver, British Columbia: University of British Columbia Press.

Kempadoo, Kamala, and Jo Doezema. 1998. Introduction to *Global Sex Workers:
Rights, Resistance and Redefinitions*. New York: Routledge.

Kirby, Sandra, Lorraine Greaves, and Colleen Reid. 2006. *Experience, Research, Social Change: Methods beyond the Mainstream*. 2nd ed. Peterborough, Ontario: Broadview Press.

Lewis, Jaqueline, Eleanor Maticka-Tyndale, Frances Shaver, and Heather Schramm. 2005. "Managing Risk and Safety on the Job: The Experiences of Canadian Sex Workers." *Journal of Psychology and Human Sexuality* 17, no. 1/2: 147–67. Special issue.

Lowman, John, and Laura Fraser. 1996. *Violence against Persons Who Prostitute: The British Columbia Experience*. Technical Report No. TR1996-14e. Ottawa, Ontario: Department of Justice Canada. http://184.70.147.70/lowman_prostitution/HTML/violence/Violence_Against_Persons_Who_Prostitute.pdf.

Lowman, John, and Ted Palys. 2007. "Strict Confidentiality: An Alternative to PRE's Limited Confidentiality Doctrine." *Journal of Academic Ethics* 5, no. 2–4: 163–77.

O'Doherty, Tamara. 2007. *Off-Street Commercial Sex: An Exploratory Study*. Unpublished Master's thesis, Simon Fraser University, Vancouver.

O'Neil, Maggie. 1996. "Researching Prostitution and Violence: Toward a Feminist Praxis." In *Women, Violence and Male Power*, ed. Marianne Hester, Liz Kelly, and Jill Radford, 130–156. Buckingham and Philadelphia: Open University Press.

———. 2010. "Cultural Criminology and Sex Work: Resisting Regulation through Radical Democracy and Participatory Action Research (PAR)." *Journal of Law and Society* 37, no. 1: 210–32.

Palys, Ted, and Chris Atchison. 2007. *Research Decisions: Quantitative and Qualitative Perspectives*. 4th ed. Toronto, Ontario: Thomson Nelson Canada.

Pheterson, Gail. 1989. *A Vindication of the Rights of Whores*. Seattle, Wash.: Seal Press.

Pivot Legal Society. 2006. *Beyond Decriminalization: Sex Work, Human Rights and a New Framework for Law Reform*. https://d3n8a8pro7vhmx.cloudfront.net/pivotlegal/pages/84/attachments/original/1345748276/BeyondDecrimLongReport.pdf?1345748276.

Pushor, Debbie. 2008. "Collaborative Research." In *The Sage Encyclopedia of Qualitative Research*, ed. Lisa M. Given, 91–94. Thousand Oaks, Calif.: Sage.

Reinharz, Shulamit. 1992. *Feminist Methods in Social Research*. New York: Oxford University Press.

Sanders, Teela. 2006. "Sexing Up the Subject: Methodological Nuances in Researching the Female Sex Industry." *Sexualities* 9, no. 4: 449–68.

Shannon, Kate, Thomas Kerr, Steffanie Strathdee, Jean Shoveller, Julio Montaner, and Mark Tyndall. 2009. "Prevalence and Structural Correlates of Gender

Based Violence among a Prospective Cohort of Female Sex Workers." *British Medical Journal* 339: b2939.

Shaver, Frances. 2005. "Sex Work Research: Methodological and Ethical Challenges." *Journal of Interpersonal Violence* 20, no. 3: 296–319.

Smith, Linda Tuhiwai. 1999. *Decolonizing Methodologies: Research and Indigenous Peoples*. London: Zed Books.

Sprague, Joey. 2005. *Feminist Methodologies for Critical Researchers: Bridging Differences*. New York: Altamira.

Strauss, Anselm, and Juliet Corbin. 1998. *Basics of Qualitative Research: Techniques and Procedures for Developing Grounded Theory*. Thousand Oaks, Calif.: Sage.

Wahab, Stephanie. 2003. "Creating Knowledge Collaboratively with Female Sex Workers: Insights from a Qualitative, Feminist and Participatory Study." *Qualitative Inquiry* 9, no. 4: 625–42.

West Coast Cooperative of Sex Industry Professionals. n.d. "Collaborate with Us!" http://www.wccsip.ca/collaborate.html.

· II ·

Producing the Sex Worker

Law, Politics, and Unintended Consequences

CHAPTER 4

Demanding Victims

The Sympathetic Shift in British Prostitution Policy

Annie Hill

A T THE DAWN OF THE TWENTY-FIRST CENTURY, the British government moved to modernize sex crime legislation. This initiative was part of a generalized political project to renew Britain. Prime Minister Tony Blair declared in *Modernising Government* that "the Government has a mission to modernise—renewing our country for the new millennium. We are modernising our schools, our hospitals, our economy and our criminal justice system" (Cabinet Office 1999, 4). Regarding sex crime, members of Parliament across the political spectrum agreed that offenses for homosexual acts should be removed from the criminal code, while new legislation should criminalize diverse activities such as the sexual grooming of children through the Internet and the covert filming of people in public and private places. By 2000, sex crime had garnered sufficient attention that New Labour moved to overhaul the Sexual Offences Act of 1956 (1956 c. 69. 4 and 5. Eliz. 2).

The last overhaul of the Sexual Offences Act had occurred a half century earlier, despite significant shifts in societal attitudes about what constituted sex crime. Since the 1950s, child pornography and marital rape had become criminal offenses, while homosexual encounters started to lose their status as sexually criminal and culturally deviant acts. To stitch the widening gap between law and social norms, New Labour endeavored to refashion sex crime legislation into a coherent strategy fit for the new millennium. To that end, Parliament passed the Sexual Offences Act of 2003 (2003 c. 42). The new Sexual Offences Act introduced offenses against necrophilia, bestiality, voyeurism, and sex trafficking; strengthened existing offenses against child sex abuse, rape, incest, indecent exposure, and "cottaging"; and removed past offenses that targeted (male) homosexual acts such as buggery and gross indecency.[1] However, one long-standing category of sexual offense—prostitution—was largely excluded from this revision of sex crime law. The Sexual Offences Act of 2003 replaced almost every single sex crime statute in England and Wales, but it left five provisions standing. These provisions all related to prostitution, specifically the "suppression of brothels," defined as any premises where more than one person offers sexual services.

As the British government modernized sex crime law, it remained remarkably mute about the crime of sex work. At first New Labour subordinated concerns about sex work to privilege "new crimes" such as bestiality and to decriminalize "old crimes" such as buggery. By the time the Home Office initiated a review of prostitution policy, the Sexual Offences Act had already received royal assent and passed into law.[2] This timing was crucial; it meant that the prostitution policy debate occurred after and outside of the general review of sexual offenses. Instead, the prostitution policy debate took place during a full-blown moral panic over the sex trafficking of Eastern European women to Britain. Narratives of sexual slavery and images of foreign trafficking victims incited a human rights discourse that also lent itself to depictions of domestic sex workers as victims and placed a moral imperative upon the state to save them too.

In what follows, I analyze New Labour's articulation of the problem of prostitution in this context and its coordinated strategy to protect and govern sex workers. In framing sex work as a policy issue, New Labour locates the problem of prostitution within prostitutes themselves, and its strategy employs rehabilitative interventions that require sex workers to change their conduct. I argue that rehabilitative interventions to divert women from sex work are part of a state-level sympathetic shift toward prostitutes. By "sympathetic shift" I mean to name New Labour's depiction of prostitutes as victims of gender-based violence as opposed to "sex offenders" deserving of traditional sanctions. While the sympathetic shift evinces good intentions, New Labour's prostitution strategy does not adequately address the structural conditions that make sex work a viable way of earning a living. Instead, the government supports mandatory rehabilitative measures as the first of several steps aimed at modifying the behavior of sex workers. Under the prostitute-as-victim paradigm, the penalties for prostitution extend beyond traditional sanctions to a whole range of medicobehaviorist exercises that turn the problem of prostitution into a personal one. Further, New Labour retains the state's ability to punish prostitutes when rehabilitative measures fail.

Situating the Sympathetic Shift

In practice, New Labour's sympathetic shift enables the criminal capture of women whose behavior is characterized as deviant, destructive, and undesirable. Although viewing sex workers as victims adduces a sympathetic stance, victim status effectively mobilizes disciplinary interventions to convert prostitutes into desirable citizen-subjects in line with neoliberal norms: an individualized prescription demanding that sex workers change even if their circumstances do not. Describing neoliberal governmentality, Aihwa Ong argues that "neoliberal policies of 'shrinking' the state are accompanied by a proliferation of techniques to remake the social and citizen-subjects . . . The neoliberal subject is therefore not a citizen with claims on the state but a self-enterprising citizen-subject who is obligated to become 'an entrepreneur of himself or herself'" (2006, 14). Sex workers are not entitled to make demands on the state for redistributive justice, occupational opportunities, or expunged criminal records, but the state can demand that sex workers be victims amenable to reform. This neoliberal strategy operationalizes disciplinary mechanisms that individually address the defects of sex workers and forestall a larger analysis of the social, economic, and political contexts in which they live and work. It also effectively silences demands for social and structural change that would recognize sex workers outside of the typical victim and villain narrative.

In Britain, these state interventions stretch the law's remit beyond sanctions for specific criminal acts to rehabilitative miscellany such as mandatory meetings with what the Home Office terms "moral welfare organisations." In this way, New Labour expresses sympathy for sex workers while elaborating a rehabilitative regime premised on individual responsibility and self-governance. The state is thus positioned as helping prostitutes and giving them the services and skills needed to become proper citizen-subjects.

To grasp how British governmentality and human rights discourse produced a neoliberal strategy for rehabilitating prostitutes, I will conduct a rhetorical analysis of the Home Office paper that launched the prostitution policy review and created an authoritative picture of prostitution. I then examine one policy outcome from the sympathetic shift as it moved

from discursive frame to a policing action targeting street-based sex workers. But first, in the next section, I lay the foundation for this analysis by
recounting the recent legal history of prostitution and New Labour's
reaction to fears about sex trafficking. The sex trafficking panic informed
the prostitution policy debate, enabling a conflation of sex work and sex
trafficking, with these discrete phenomena described under the same
umbrella term of "violence against women." All women involved in prostitution could thus be construed as victims of gender-based violence, while
sex work was cast as a "driver" for sex trafficking, a "safe haven" for sex trafficking, or sexual slavery itself.

The State of "Not Illegal"

To create a coordinated prostitution strategy, New Labour had to harmo-
nize prostitution provisions codified piecemeal over almost two centuries.
In Britain, prostitution is "not illegal." This double negation correctly
reflects the precarious status of prostitution and the legal jeopardy experienced by many prostitutes. Prostitution is not illegal because the law does
not prohibit the exchange of sex for money or material goods by two consenting adults in a private location. Prostitution is not practicably legal,
either, due to the criminalization of associated activities such as soliciting
in public, advertising "tart cards" in phone booths, and working alongside
other sex workers indoors (i.e., in a brothel). It is also illegal to run or manage a brothel, still referred to by the Crown Prosecution Service as "a place
where people of opposite sexes . . . are allowed to resort for illicit intercourse, whether the women are common prostitutes or not."[3] Additionally,
under Britain's brothel ban, ancillaries such as maids, managers, partners,
and receptionists can be charged with "living on earnings of prostitution,"
a criminal offense introduced in the Sexual Offences Act of 1956.

These restrictions prohibit both the safest and the most dangerous
forms of sex work: women working together in private and women engaging in public solicitation, respectively. What Britain tolerates is the least visible form of sex work: women working alone indoors. This arrangement
creates an extremely narrow space in which women may engage in prostitution without flouting the law. The reason indoor prostitution is permissible,
and other forms of sex work are not, finds its fullest theoretical expression
in the *Report of the Departmental Committee on Homosexual Offences and
Prostitution*, known as the Wolfenden report, published in 1957.

The Wolfenden report famously argued that sexual acts conducted privately between consenting adults were not the law's business (Home Office and Scottish Home Department 1957, 10). By distinguishing between public and private sex, Wolfenden et al. circumscribed the power of public morality based on a right to privacy. While the supposed immorality of certain sexual practices might outrage the British public, the report held that the law should not intervene in people's private lives if their acts do not harm others or society at large. This emphasis on community harm bolstered an argument for decriminalizing homosexual acts as crimes without victims and simultaneously provided grounds for robustly criminalizing public prostitution. The report explained the distinction, and evident bias, thus:

> If it were the law's intention to punish prostitution *per se*, on the ground that it is immoral conduct, then it would be right that it should provide for the punishment of the man as well as the woman. But that is not the function of law. It should confine itself to those activities which offend against public order and decency or expose the ordinary citizen to what is offensive or injurious; and the simple fact is that prostitutes do parade themselves more habitually and openly than their prospective customers, and do by their continual presence affront the sense of decency of the ordinary citizen. (1957, 87)

Wolfenden et al.'s general attempt to free law from its entanglement with morality—that is, to punish because an act does harm, not because it is deemed immoral—is followed by a defense of criminalizing prostitutes because they "affront the sense of decency of the ordinary citizen" (1957, 87). The line between morality and decency, between what injures and what offends, is crossed with confidence when considering women engaged in commercial sex due to their habitual publicity and the harm it is said to cause. The report cites the public nature of prostitution as contributing to broken homes and fragmented communities. The point (or "simple fact") being that prostitutes, as public women, harm ordinary citizens. Therefore, prostitutes ought to be punished in contradistinction to homosexuals and, curiously, prostitutes' clients, who are cast as either acting *in* private or acting out *a* private, not-for-profit sexuality.

Fifty years later, New Labour echoed the Wolfenden report by claiming that sex workers harm communities and that all public manifestations of prostitution should be repressed. New Labour scrapped proposals for minibrothels and tolerance zones, plans previously floated by the Labour Party, because they would draw attention to the presence of sex workers and a robust sex trade. New Labour feared that allowing such sites could suggest it approved of sex work or, worse, sex trafficking. Organized off-street sex work might pose the same problem as its on-street counterpart: it places prostitution in public view and, with the conflation of sex work and sex trafficking, it risks the accusation that New Labour negates women's human rights. According to Phil Hubbard et al., "The conflation of exploitation and prostitution in policy discourse has ensured that prostitution and trafficking law have now become inseparable" (2008, 140). Indeed, the specter of sex trafficking motivated New Labour's move from tolerance zones to coercive rehabilitation and from responding to sex workers as workers in a variegated, diffuse, licit, and illicit sex industry to understanding them uniformly as victims of gender-based violence.

In the early days of Tony Blair's premiership, the Labour government leaned toward legalizing brothels and creating tolerance zones in which street sex work could be conducted. Blair's Home Secretary David Blunkett, former head of the Home Office, initially indicated his support for licensing commercial sex districts and, as late as 2006, there was talk of permitting minibrothels in order to end the requirement that indoor sex workers work alone (Laite 2006). By the end of the Blair government, however, New Labour had turned from tolerance to take a hard line on prostitution by foregrounding personal responsibility and community safety and claiming that sex workers caused litter, noise, obscenity, anti-sociality, criminality, and damage to communities (Home Office 2004, 2006). Concurrently, the government began to employ a victim discourse that chimed with sex trafficking narratives and portrayed prostitutes as powerless and exploited.

The abolitionist advocacy of key Labour politicians, such as Home Secretary Jacqui Smith and Deputy Leader Harriet Harman, ensured that the government would no longer consider tolerating sex work. In 2007, Prime Minister Gordon Brown appointed Jacqui Smith as the first female Home Secretary. Smith became the primary spokesperson for post-Blair abolitionism, opposing one-sided prostitution policies that criminalized women while letting clients get off virtually scot-free. Smith tried to tackle demand by lobbying for provisions that targeted clients and treated sex workers as victims. Sex workers would still be processed through the

criminal justice system, but these interventions were rebranded as rehabilitative measures. Smith wished, ultimately, to follow the Swedish prostitution model by *outlawing the purchase of sexual services in all circumstances*,
but she had to settle for a strict liability offense of "paying for sexual services of a prostitute subjected to force," tougher "kerb-crawling" offenses
against clients, and the reclassification of strip clubs as "sex encounter venues" in order to restrict licensing.[4] The abolitionist position, elaborated
in two Home Office documents, *Paying the Price: A Consultation Paper
on Prostitution* (2004) and *A Coordinated Prostitution Strategy and a Summary of Responses to "Paying the Price"* (2006), aimed to eliminate sex work
and to "challenge the view that street prostitution is inevitable and here to
stay" (2006, 1).

The Home Office declared that its coordinated "strategy will focus on
disrupting sex markets by preventing individuals, particularly children
and young people, from being drawn into prostitution; by providing
appropriate protection and routes out for those already involved; by protecting communities from the nuisance associated with prostitution; and
by ensuring that those who control, coerce or abuse those in prostitution
are brought to justice" (2006, 1). Whether prostitutes are viewed as sympathetic victims of vice or active agents of community decline certainly
influences how they are treated, but it does not affect the underlying inter-
ventionist logic that their behavior must be changed. When addressing
prostitution policy, the British government debated disciplinary tactics;
it did not consider dismantling the state project of criminalizing women
because they receive material goods in exchange for sex. Prostitution,
although more frequently framed as a form of gender violence, continued
to be treated as a municipal problem best addressed by criminal justice
mechanisms.

The next section performs a rhetorical analysis of *Paying the Price: A
Consultation Paper on Prostitution*, the Home Office paper that initiated the
prostitution policy review. Specifically, I examine New Labour's construction of sex work as destructive to the self and the community, as it places the
plight of prostitutes in the personal realm, outside of economic conditions
and the political climate. In this inaugural paper, the Home Office makes
clear that the prostitute is to be confronted as a problem: a sympathetic
victim to be rehabilitated or a social nuisance to be removed from public
view. In the new millennium, it would remain the law's business to punish
prostitutes for their own good and the greater good of the community.

Constructing a Consensus:
The Partial View of *Paying the Price*

The Cover

In Britain, a green paper is a genre of governmental discourse that offers multiple perspectives on an issue and seeks public comment before the introduction of new policy. The Home Office opened the review of prostitution policy in 2004 by publishing a green paper titled *Paying the Price: A Consultation Paper on Prostitution.*[5] Its cover image is composed of mottled shades of violet and presents a girl standing in a doorway; the door's window and the girl's coat are fractured to look like stained glass. Frowning, the girl gazes directly at the audience positioned on the street in front of her. Titled *Girl Inside*, the illustration was created by a reformed prostitute, referred to only as Ruth. Ruth joined The Magdalene Group, a "charity with a Christian ethos" that, according to *Paying the Price*, helped her "to leave this way of life." Describing the image, Ruth explains, "The coat she is wearing is like the fragments of the glass, which to me represented my brokenness. I felt shattered."[6]

The "sympathetic visibility" accomplished through this illustration presents Ruth both as an instrument of pathos and as proof of prostitution's harm (Hesford 2011, 130). While *Girl Inside* is a personal interpretation of prostitution, its placement on the cover of *Paying the Price* privileges

Figure 4.1. Girl Inside.

British Home Office. 2004. Paying the Price:
A Consultation Paper on Prostitution.
London: Home Office Communication
Directorate. The cover illustration was created
by a freelance artist who was involved in
prostitution for several years.

it as a general representation of sex work. As synecdoche, Ruth can stand in for every prostitute. Her figure by the door, on the street, encased in lines, expresses the difficulty of escape from "this way of life." *Girl Inside* is a confrontational cry for help, constituting the audience as potential rescuers as opposed to prospective clients. She dares readers to do nothing and the pages that follow provide tactics for helping prostitutes become healthy, whole, law-abiding, and self-governing citizen-subjects.

This provocative image solicits the sentiment of a British public already primed on sex trafficking narratives and images of sex slaves. The prostitute-as-victim paradigm is persuasive in a climate of heightened anxiety about the sexual enslavement of women and girls and the damage wrought by their exploitation. Writing on women's human rights discourse, Wendy S. Hesford describes a strategy evident here: "The rhetorical appeal to women as a unified group—rhetorical identification—has been a fundamental strategy of women's human rights campaigns, which anchor their call to action in the experiences of individual victims" (2011, 138).

Yet *Girl Inside* can tap into other connections, and also functions through rhetorical disidentification, by inviting the public to appreciate the alterity of a street sex worker. The girl and the window, the prostitute and her surroundings, are drawn in pieces. The mimetic relation between the girl and the glass reveals the cross-contaminating potential of prostitute and place and ties the presence of prostitutes to broken windows, which communicate a community's lack of social control and inability to contain criminal elements (Kelling and Coles, 1996). The "broken windows" criminological theory advocates zero tolerance of urban disorder and the use of discretionary policing to fix signs of community decay. Further, it suggests that prostitutes and other social deviants *are* "broken windows": embodied signs of a community's moral and economic decline. As such, they also need to be removed and fixed in order to protect the community and prevent worsening conditions.

Girl Inside captures New Labour's approach by depicting sex work through a visual economy of destruction. This image of sex work is authorized by the Home Office's imprimatur, which sanctions the abolitionist agenda, at the same time that the paper is authenticated by the illustration of one former prostitute. In this way, the notion that sex work is an activity that shatters the self and society is disseminated as a transparent representation of reality rather than as a contestable point of view. For New Labour, this partial view of sex work is the whole picture.

The Content

Premised on the prostitute-as-victim paradigm, *Paying the Price* proposes a three-part antiprostitution strategy consisting of *prevention, protection and support*, and *justice*. It defines justice as "bringing pimps, traffickers and exploiters to justice, and delivering justice to those affected, including the families of young people coerced into prostitution and the communities blighted by prostitution" (Home Office 2004, 7). The paper is also organized around this strategy and traverses three modes of regulation: victimological (prevention), rehabilitative (protection and support), and criminological (justice). Chapter 3 of the paper concerns "Routes into Prostitution," primarily for individuals under eighteen years of age, and ways to prevent children and teens from entering prostitution. Chapters 4 and 5, "Protection and Support for Children Abused through Prostitution" and "Supporting Adults in Prostitution" respectively, outline services to divert women and children involved in prostitution. The bulk of the paper, however, is devoted to criminological mechanisms to stop prostitution. Chapters 6–9 are titled "Exploitation—the Role of Criminal Law," "Protecting Communities," "Links to Serious Crime," and "Considering the Options," which provides a brief overview of alternative regulatory approaches, using models from countries such as Australia and Sweden.

In the section on prevention, the paper identifies seven risk factors for entering prostitution, each tied to individual problems or interpersonal abuse: violence or abuse in the home, truancy, living in foster care, homelessness, drug abuse, alcohol abuse, and debt (Home Office 2004, 24). Several factors suggest economic motivations, but the proposal for addressing poverty (referred to narrowly as "debt") amounts to the claim that "appropriate advice and support can help people to avoid, manage and escape from debt" (31). Skirting structural issues such as entrenched poverty and unemployment, the paper zeroes in on the personal to protect sex workers by "ensuring that coercers and abusers are deterred, stopped and brought to justice" and pledging that "we must also prevent abuse by taking steps to avoid children and young people getting into a situation where they may be vulnerable to commercial sexual exploitation" (17). The paper persistently depicts sex workers as "vulnerable" and "coerced" "young people," "children," and "victims" in need of "protection," "help and advice," and "a pathway out." Such a charitable view is engendered by reliance on the trope of underage seduction and procurement, which figures sex workers as exploited children, and the concomitant vilification of men as "coercers," "users," "abusers," "pimps," and "traffickers." Male sex workers are not visible in this account because they disrupt the gender-based violence schema of men sexually exploiting women.

Despite putting the image of a prostitute on the cover, *Paying the Price* does not present the diverse perspectives and experiences of sex workers, although a range of different views on sex work is represented in its bibliography. *Paying the Price* gives short shrift to sex work sites other than the street (e.g., flats, brothels, hotels, and homes) and sidelines male sex workers. According to Mary Whowell and Justin Gaffney, "Although the [British prostitution] strategy claims gender neutrality, there is no substantive analysis of the issues male sex workers may face, or how these issues may be different from (or similar to) those of female sex workers; they are in essence rendered invisible" (2009, 101). Additionally, sex workers and sex work organizations responded to the paper, but their input was not reflected in subsequent policy changes. While the executive summary of *Paying the Price* notes that prostitution is a "complex area," it nevertheless depicts prostitutes as a homogenous group (of women) engaging in the same kind of activity (street prostitution) and experiencing a shared shattering of the self. Hesford argues that stereotypic portrayals of prostitutes are appealing because of their ability to divert attention from the issue's complexity and an audience's potential complicity: "Stereotypes of prostitutes as social deviants or as helpless victims maintain their rhetorical appeal because they keep the audience's focus on the [O]ther and thereby deflect attention from the national and international policies, economic and sociopolitical forces, and cultural traditions that contribute to the material conditions that drive many women to work in the sex industry" (2011, 132).

New Labour claims to let sex workers speak and be rendered visible. Yet "they" are the socially excluded group who "we" must address through rehabilitative interventions; such a hierarchical relation is predicated on notions of victimhood and a salvationist state (Phoenix 2009). *Paying the Price* declares, "It is crucial that the [policy] debate is based on an accurate picture of the issues and an understanding of the dreadful realities of the impact of prostitution" (Home Office 2004, 7). But the paper fails to acknowledge that sex work can be something other than a public problem or devastating private experience. Hence the paper inaugurating the prostitution policy debate erases those who experience sex work as something other than life shattering. It silences sex workers who argue that prostitution be viewed as a form of labor. It overlooks people who engage in sex work to support themselves and their families. And it fails to provide viable options to anyone who cannot exit prostitution due to economic need or a criminal record kept by the state. A dissenting view not found in *Paying the Price* is that of Caroline Stellar, a sex worker quoted in "Statements from Women Working in the Sex Industry"; she explains, "None of us need to attend meetings to look at why we do this job. We know why we do it: to support our families. It pays better than many other jobs and, for women like me with a criminal record, it is often the only job we can get. If they want to help me, then get rid of my criminal record, tell me where I can find a job that pays a decent wage that will cover my rent and let me raise my child without worrying how we will eat" (Safety First Coalition n.d.).[7]

In its 114 pages, *Paying the Price* eschews the economics of prostitution for sex workers and the competing perspective that prostitution deserves legal recognition as work. Prostitution is always a devastating experience in *Paying the Price*, whose very title declares that sex work takes a substantial personal and social toll. The paper was not titled, for example, *Earning a Living*. It follows that the executive summary encapsulates the problem this way: "The paper demonstrates that prostitution can seriously damage the individuals involved, and the communities in which it takes place. If we are to comprehensively address social exclusion, promote civil renewal and achieve a real reduction in anti-social behaviour and criminality—including a real reduction in violence against women—we need an in-depth debate on tackling prostitution. It is a complex area. Organized criminality, including trafficking and substantial drug misuse, and sexually and drug transmitted infection, are all part of the problem. Systematic abuse, violence and exploitation are endemic" (Home Office 2004, 7).

The Home Office links prostitution to organized crime, trafficking, drugs, disease, abuse, violence, and exploitation, but it overlooks how the state structures fundamental issues of poverty, crime, education, and employment. The agentic violence envisioned by *Paying the Price* is committed by pimps, traffickers, clients, drug dealers, partners, family members, and the prostitutes themselves. The state is not implicated in the conditions of possibility that make prostitution a viable means of self-support and a potentially dangerous activity. The state becomes visible only when it steps in to rescue women and help them solve their personal problems (Phoenix and Oerton 2005; Scoular and O'Neill 2007).

Moreover, New Labour's goal to effect a "real reduction in violence against women" by suppressing antisocial behavior and criminality begets the question, whose antisocial behavior and criminality would be targeted? The final section of this chapter analyzes the British policy for governing the purported antisociality and criminality of street-based sex workers. The category of the "persistent" prostitute reveals how the coordinated strategy extends the state's criminal capture of women who sell sex. Despite the avowed aim of turning prostitutes into responsible citizens, New Labour removes autonomy from sex workers and hands discretionary power to state actors. The sympathetic shift thus exercises the state's power to punish and to rescind victim status when sex workers do not change their behavior. In this context, a victim discourse justifies state action in the classical mode of retaliatory punishment by foregrounding its current correlate: coercive rehabilitation.

Reforming Persistent Prostitutes

Two years after publishing *Paying the Price*, the Home Office released a white paper, titled *A Coordinated Prostitution Strategy and Summary of Responses to "Paying the Price,"* that unveiled its prostitution policy proposals. A white paper outlines future policy, often considered by Parliament in the form of a bill, and creates another opportunity for public comment before the proposals become official policy. This paper announced that prostitution policy reform would "provide an opportunity to remove the outdated (and widely considered to be offensive) concept of 'common prostitute'" from the criminal code (Home Office 2006, 39). The term "common prostitute" was coined in the Vagrancy Act of 1824—An Act for the Punishment of Idle and Disorderly Persons, and Rogues, and Vagabonds, in England. The offense targeted "any common prostitute wandering in the public streets or public highways, or in any place of public resort, and behaving in a riotous or indecent manner" (1824 c. 83. 5 Geo. 4). It did not outlaw loitering or soliciting *per se* but a particular type of woman who committed these acts. The offense created a status crime and a new kind of criminal.

For nearly two centuries, a woman's commonness (i.e., her sexual availability to more than one man) and public presence (her visibility on the street) have been the law's business in Britain. The Sexual Offences Act of 2003 did not completely expunge "common prostitute" from the criminal code; the Policing and Crime Act of 2009 removed the last remnant of the term by replacing a portion of the Street Offences Act of 1959 that read, "It shall be an offense for a common prostitute to loiter or solicit in a street or public place for the purpose of prostitution" (1959 c. 57. 7 & 8 Eliz. 2) New Labour thus delivered on its pledge to remove the "common prostitute." However, the Policing and Crime Act of 2009 replaced the "common prostitute" with another criminal: the "persistent" prostitute (2009 c. 26).

The offense of persistent prostitution emerged in the Policing and Crime Act of 2009, the primary legislation codifying the recommendations from *A Coordinated Prostitution Strategy*. While this legislative innovation might appear to contradict the sympathetic shift toward prostitutes, it chimes with a rehabilitative mode of correction that aims to bring prostitutes back to "correct" conduct and into contact with the softer side of criminal justice. It protects on-street prostitutes by stipulating that they cannot be arrested for loitering or soliciting on a first offense; instead, police officers must issue an official caution at least twice before making an arrest for persistent prostitution. Conduct is deemed persistent if it takes place two or more times in a ninety-day period. By contrast, the Policing and Crime Act removed the proviso that "kerb crawlers" be persistent and permits the arrest of clients for a first offense. Tackling demand, or targeting male "users" and "abusers" of sex workers, is occurring in tandem with the sympathetic shift toward prostitutes.

An example of the sympathetic shift in practice is the staged approach for rehabilitating street-based sex workers. The rehabilitative strategy for street-based sex workers is divided into four stages. The first stage, *voluntary referral*, entails contact with an outreach worker for referral to a range of services premised on finding routes out of prostitution. In *A Coordinated Prostitution Strategy*, the Home Office asserts that drug intervention referrals allow counselors to seek, in its words, the "voluntary engagement of drug-using offenders" (2006, 38). The second stage, *precharge diversion*, involves contact with police who are empowered to issue drug intervention referrals, conditional cautions, and "prostitutes' cautions" that further encourage women to engage with rehabilitative services. Conditional cautions stipulate the conditions for avoiding criminal charges and are distinct from "prostitutes' cautions," which are a technique used to designate women as prostitutes. Revealing the roots of this approach, in *Tackling Anti-Social Behaviour and Its Causes*, the Home Office explains the system of cautioning women suspected of prostitution:

This system of "prostitutes' cautions" is regulated by Home Office Circular 108 of 1959, which initially applied to the Metropolitan Police service. It refers to a system of cautioning whereby a woman, who has not previously been convicted of loitering or soliciting for the purpose of prostitution, will not be charged with that offence unless she has been cautioned by the police on at least two occasions and the cautions have been formally recorded. The system was seen as a practical step to divert from prostitution women and girls who were taking to that way of life. Two officers would need to witness the activity and administer the caution. They would then ask the woman if she were [sic] willing to be put in touch with a "moral welfare organisation" or a probation officer. Providing appropriate sources of support is crucial to helping a prostitute to make changes to their lifestyle and exit prostitution. (Home Office n.d.)

If the woman is not diverted from sex work at either stage one or stage two, charges are brought against her for soliciting or loitering for the purposes of prostitution. She thus enters the third stage, *postcharge diversion*, which often includes mandatory drug testing. The Home Office reports that a "high proportion of those currently tested under Inspector's discretion are women involved in prostitution. Measures introduced in the Drugs Act 2005 are being implemented incrementally . . . to give police powers to test for drugs after arrest (alongside the continuing power to test after charge)" (2006, 39). The extension of drug testing prior to the filing of criminal charges is based on a woman's status as a "persistent" prostitute, an identity established by police through "prostitutes' cautions," and the interrogation of her body is enforced at the Inspector's discretion. According to Jane Scoular et al., "While there may be an element of voluntarism in this approach to policing, it is clear that if women are not ready to 'reform,' the next stage of compulsory rehabilitation will follow soon after" (2009, 43).

The fourth stage, *prosecution*, marks an end to the purportedly voluntary measures. If convicted of the charges against her, a woman's "penalty will vary according to persistence, to address the underlying issues which may be preventing an individual from succeeding on a voluntary basis to find a route out of prostitution" (Home Office 2006, 39). Completing the rebranding of criminalization as rehabilitation, the Home Office also refers to the prosecution stage as the "new rehabilitative approach to loitering and soliciting" (39). It appears any measure used to divert a woman from sex work can count as rehabilitation. The Home Office contends that diversion schemes are a type of support because they give women the necessary push to change and the "choice" to avoid criminal penalties. For women engaging in prostitution beyond stage two, the unvarnished punitive side of the rehabilitative approach comes to the fore. The Home Office confirms that the state retains the power to punish women who persist in street prostitution. Although personal circumstance seemed to count when counseling was offered at earlier stages, at this point a woman's reasons for engaging in prostitution no longer matter. The end-stage priority of the coordinated strategy is reducing recidivism and protecting communities: "Under this staged approach those women (and men) who respond to informal referrals and seek help from support services to leave prostitution, and those who engage with the [Criminal Justice Integrated Team] to receive treatment and other support, may avoid further criminalisation. However, for those individuals who, *for whatever reason*, continue to be involved in street prostitution, the criminal justice system will respond with rehabilitative interventions to reduce re-offending and to protect local communities" (2006, 39, emphasis mine).

The Home Office reverts to the familiar standby of retaliatory law enforcement, situating sex workers as victimizers of the community in a portrayal reminiscent of the "common prostitute" as threat to the moral order of society. The seeds of this policy were sown by *Paying the Price*, which, in an illustrative passage, moves smoothly from the paradigm of prostitute-as-victim to prostitute-as-criminal victimizing the community: "The victims of the so-called 'trade' are the young boys and girls, and the men and women trapped in it. But communities are also victims as street-based prostitution increases the general level of disorder and creates a climate of criminality. Those who choose to be involved should understand what it is like to live in an area in which kerb crawlers habitually harass young women, and where used condoms and dirty needles are regularly dumped in front gardens" (2004, 12).

The sweeping reference to "young boys and girls" and "men and women trapped in" the trade is juxtaposed with "those who choose" to engage in prostitution. The many victims of prostitution (e.g., boys, girls, men, women, homeowners, and communities) are contrasted with prostitutes who, *pace* the "broken windows" theory, bring crime and disorder in their wake. The Home Office indicts persistent sex workers as women who harm the community and instigate a climate of criminality. In this reckoning, the poor living conditions in a community are not shared by sex workers but caused by them; young women, in particular, are singled out as being harmed because men mistake them for prostitutes. This reference to young women is a return to the well-worn accusation that sex workers harm other women by encouraging sexual harassment on the street. Johanna Kantola and Judith Squires argue that such prostitution policy insists that "innocent women are to be protected from the manifestations of conspicuous sexuality . . . it is the resident women and their children who are constructed as victims, not the prostitutes" (2004, 80). For sex workers victimizing communities just by being there, disciplinary mechanisms include "prostitutes' cautions," conditional cautions, "acceptable behaviour contracts" (ABCs) for minors, and "antisocial behaviour orders" (ASBOs) for adults. Targeting street sex work, the British government aims to protect communities by reforming sex workers or removing them from sight.

The staged approach mandates the steps women must take to leave street prostitution. What women do not have is the choice to remain in sex work. Under Britain's rehabilitative regime, it is unclear where women are to go after they exit prostitution at the government's behest. The coordinated prostitution strategy is short on economic and occupational options for women supporting themselves through sex work. The Home Office provides "routes out" of prostitution, but routes into alternative employment are not an evident part of its plan.

The Home Office presents its carrot-and-stick strategy as balancing the needs of two opposing groups—prostitutes and communities—and asserts that "any strategy will need to ensure the involvement of communities, and balance the competing need to alleviate the harm done to communities with the protection of those trapped in prostitution" (2004, 73). Such a strategy excludes the involvement of those who choose sex work. Their needs are not placed in the balance of an abolitionist approach to prostitution. While New Labour's rehabilitative rhetoric extends the status of victim to more women by claiming that they are forced, tricked, or trapped in the sex trade, it maintains a clear juridical cordon around women who do not get with the rehabilitative program.

Conclusion

Despite the possibilities opened up by the prostitution policy review, the sympathetic shift toward prostitutes in Britain creates a criminological spectrum that shuffles women between the poles of prostitute-victim and prostitute-criminal, with either designation requiring contact with criminal justice personnel. The Home Office depicts disciplinary mechanisms as rehabilitative interventions, but these measures operate on a principle of punishment because women cannot refuse them. Although the strategy of *sympathy before sanction* appears to treat prostitutes as "victims first," it signals the ambiguous nature of sympathy when tied to legal processes that withhold penalties if women obey but deliver punishments when they fail to follow orders.

Distinctions between rehabilitation and criminalization collapse when women are refused a real choice in the matter. New Labour stressed the coercion and force used to make women enter prostitution without seeing the coercion it sanctioned via exit strategies. By so doing, the Home Office ignored the harm of forcing women to leave prostitution under threat of "further criminalisation" when economic alternatives are not viable or when sex work is what they prefer to do. This strategy extended sympathy—and the power of the criminal justice system—by requiring that women submit to various interventions, including drug tests, before being charged with a crime. On what grounds could such extralegal action be justified? The answer appears to be that rehabilitative measures are enacted out of concern for, and in the best interests of, sex workers. Rehabilitative measures enable the criminal justice system to enter the lives of women whose conduct is at odds with neoliberal notions of responsible citizenship and self-governance, even though their conduct is not (yet) deemed criminal. All the while, this augmentation of criminal justice camouflages the traditional penalties still levied against sex workers who persist after being caught and cautioned.

The irony is that the new coordinated prostitution strategy is, rather, a rehash of the old. New Labour's effort to modernize prostitution policy reiterates a moral division between the good and the guilty, refining the binary that once separated innocent women from prostitutes and using it to divide women *within* prostitution. In this way, the Home Office revives the Fallen Woman and refashions her as a modern victim who is either amenable to reform or recalcitrant.

In the late nineteenth century, Josephine Butler and antivice advocates fought against the state regulation and registration of prostitutes (Walkowitz 1980). The Social Purity Movement then capitalized on the positive shift in sentiment toward prostitutes to co-opt Butler's rebellion and turn it into a crusade for the moral improvement of prostitutes. The Social Purity Movement bifurcated into the rehabilitation of Fallen Women and the repression of unrepentant whores. Well over a century later, New Labour successfully breathed new life into the concept of prostitute *qua* victim in order to remake prostitution policy in an abolitionist vein. The result? Britain's sympathetic shift effectively curtailed tolerance and ushered in a more forbidding future for sex workers.

Notes

1. "Cottaging" is a British term that refers to anonymous sexual encounters among men in a public restroom. Despite the lack of legal specification for the term "buggery," in this context it refers to anal penetration of a man by another man. Historically, the term has also referred to anal penetration of a woman by a man; vaginal penetration of an animal by a man or woman; and vaginal or anal penetration of a woman or a man by an animal. Sexual intercourse with an animal ("bestiality") was outlawed in the Sexual Offences Act 2003.

2. The Home Office is the lead governmental department for immigration, passports, counterterrorism, policing, drugs, and crime.

3. Under the Sexual Offences Act of 1956, a brothel was defined as premises in which more than one woman offers sexual services at the same or at different times, whether or not they are "common prostitutes." Payment need not be involved for premises to be deemed a brothel (Crown Prosecution Service, http://www.cps .gov.uk/legal/p_to_r/prostitution_and_exploitation_of_prostitution/#a14). Replacing the Act of 1956, and moving legal language toward gender neutrality, the Sexual Offences Act of 2003 states, "It is an offence for a person to keep, or to manage, or act or assist in the management of, a brothel to which people resort for practices involving prostitution (whether or not also for other practices)" (2003, c. 42, 32).

4. These provisions came into force through the Policing and Crime Act of 2009. The Swedish model is again gaining currency in the British (and Irish) context as Scotland, Northern Ireland, and the Republic of Ireland are considering the "Nordic model" of criminalizing the purchase, but not the sale, of sex. Labour MSP Rhoda Grant was quoted in the *Guardian* stating, "Scotland has recognised prostitution as violence against women for some time, but unfortunately there has been a lot of talk and little action. It was time to do something about it. If you

recognise prostitution is violence against a woman then this makes a lot of sense" (Topping 2012).

5. Before changing policy, the Home Office publishes consultation papers inviting commentary on the issue from members of the public. The Home Office posts consultation papers online and, in the case of *Paying the Price*, six thousand hard copies also circulated and almost one thousand responses were received.

6. This biographical information is written inside the cover page of *Paying the Price*. The description of The Magdalene Group was obtained from its website, http://www.magdalenegroup.org/.

7. The Safety First Coalition released "Statements from Women Working in the Sex Industry" after collecting responses to prostitution policy reform. The Coalition formed in Ipswich following the murder of five street-based sex workers by Steve Wright in 2006. I obtained the document from the headquarters of the English Collective of Prostitutes in London.

References

Cabinet Office. 1999. *Modernising Government*. London: Stationery Office Ltd.

Crown Prosecution Service. n.d. "Keeping a Brothel." Prostitution and Exploitation of Prostitution. http://www.cps.gov.uk/legal/p_to_r/prostitution_and_exploitation_of_prostitution/#a14.

Hesford, Wendy S. 2011. *Spectacular Rhetorics: Human Rights Visions, Recognitions, Feminisms*. Durham: Duke University Press.

Home Office and Scottish Home Department. 1957. *Report of the Committee on Homosexual Offences and Prostitution*. London: Her Majesty's Stationary Office.

Home Office. 2004. *Paying the Price: A Consultation Paper on Prostitution*. London: Home Office Communication Directorate.

———. 2006. *A Coordinated Prostitution Strategy and a Summary of Responses to "Paying the Price."* London: Her Majesty's Stationery Office.

———. n.d. *Tackling Anti-Social Behaviour and Its Causes*. http://www.nationalarchives.gov.uk/ERORecords/HO/421/2/P2/CPD/SOU/REHABCON.HTM.

Hubbard, Phil, Roger Matthews, and Jane Scoular. 2008. "Regulating Sex Work in the EU: Prostitute Women and the New Spaces of Exclusion." *Gender, Place and Culture* 15, no. 2: 137–52.

Kantola, Johanna, and Judith Squires. 2004. "Discourses Surrounding Prostitution Policies in the UK." *European Journal of Women's Studies* 11, no. 1: 77–101.

Kelling, George L., and Catherine M. Coles. 1996. *Fixing Broken Windows: Restoring Order and Reducing Crime in Our Communities*. New York: Free Press.

Laite, Julie. October 2006. "Paying the Price Again: Prostitution Policy in Historical Perspective." *History and Policy*. http://www.historyandpolicy.org/papers/policy-paper-46.html.

National Archives. 1824. Vagrancy Act 1824. Office of Public Sector Information.

———. 1956. Sexual Offences Act 1956. Office of Public Sector Information.

———. 1959. Street Offences Act 1959. Office of Public Sector Information.

———. 2003. Sexual Offences Act 2003. Office of Public Sector Information.

———. 2009. Policing and Crime Act 2009. Office of Public Sector Information.

Ong, Aihwa. 2006. *Neoliberalism as Exception: Mutations in Citizenship and Sovereignty*. Durham: Duke University Press.

Phoenix, Jo. 2009. "Frameworks of Understanding." In *Regulating Sex for Sale: Prostitution Policy Reform in the UK*, ed. Jo Phoenix, 1–28. Bristol, U.K.: Policy Press.

Phoenix, Joanna, and Sarah Oerton. 2005. *Illicit and Illegal: Sex, Regulation and Social Control*. Portland: Willan Publishing.

Safety First Coalition. n.d. "Statements from Women Working in the Sex Industry."

Scoular, Jane, and Maggie O'Neill. 2007. "Regulating Prostitution: Social Inclusion, Responsibilisation and the Politics of Prostitution Reform." *British Journal of Criminology* 47: 764–78.

Scoular, Jane, Jane Pitcher, Rosie Campbell, Phil Hubbard, and Maggie O'Neill. 2009. "What's Anti-Social about Sex Work? Governance through the Changing Representation of Prostitution's Incivility." In *Regulating Sex for Sale: Prostitution Policy Reform in the UK*, ed. Jo Phoenix, 29–46. Bristol, U.K.: Policy Press.

Topping, Alexandra. 2012. "Government Under Pressure to Review Prostitution Laws in England and Wales." *Guardian*, December 26. http://www.theguardian.com/society/2012/dec/26/government-pressure-review-prostitution-laws.

Walkowitz, Judith. 1980. *Prostitution and Victorian Society: Women, Class, and the State*. Cambridge, U.K.: Cambridge University Press.

Whowell, Mary, and Justin Gaffney. 2009. "Male Sex Work in the UK: Forms, Practice and Policy Implications." In *Regulating Sex for Sale: Prostitution Policy Reform in the UK*, ed. Jo Phoenix, 99–120. Bristol, U.K.: Policy Press.

CHAPTER 5

Criminalized and Licensed

Local Politics, the Regulation of Sex Work, and the Construction of "Ugly Bodies"

Cheryl Auger

JUST MONTHS after the Ontario Superior Court ruled that a number of provisions in Canada's Criminal Code violate sex workers' constitutionally protected rights to security of person and freedom of association (Bedford v. Canada 2010), a Toronto city councilor suggested creating a red-light district on Toronto Island, located just off the city shore and accessible by ferry.[1] Giorgio Mammoliti said, "I've always suggested that the best way to deal with this is to create one area that is away from the rest of the city and residential community for the most part," adding that a state-run red-light district would take sex work out of the hands of organized crime and would generate "a couple hundred million" dollars over time for the city (quoted in Alcoba 2011). Mammoliti's suggestion was written off by Toronto Island's councilor as "ludicrous" and it seems unlikely to gain political traction. Yet it reveals how some politicians understand sex work as deviant and undesirable, which in turn justifies laws, policies, and regulations intended to control where and how sexual commerce takes place. His desire to segregate sex workers in a special red-light zone highlights a contradiction in law and order approaches, which seek to simultaneously exclude and include criminalized groups in order to implement various sociomoral priorities.

While the Ontario Superior court case raised the tricky issue of how to govern and regulate sex work and launched a debate about how municipal governments and cities should govern sex businesses, many cities already regulate sex industries through zoning provisions and licensing schemes written into business licensing bylaws.[2] In this chapter I pose two questions: first, how and to what extent do Canadian municipalities regulate sex work through business licensing bylaws? And second, how do these licensing bylaws socially construct sex workers? I show that Canadian municipalities employ a wide variety of licensing practices to regulate and control some of the commercial sexual relations in strip clubs, erotic massage parlors, and escort services. Many of these policies are intended to minimize nuisances associated with sex work and offer consumers some form of protection; however, several of the bylaws place onerous burdens on sex workers while failing to offer them more than the most basic workplace health and safety provisions.

I therefore argue that many of these licensing bylaws found across Canada construct sex workers as deviant outsiders. Drawing on Iris Marion Young's (1990) exploration of the construction of "ugly bodies," I demonstrate how Canada's municipal bylaws governing different sectors of the sex trade establish the sex worker's body as an important site of surveillance and regulation intended to maintain moral and social order. By working with the federal Criminal Code, these bylaws construct sex workers as unnatural, abnormal, and abject, and this is evident in how these bylaws reinforce stereotypes about "the prostitute" as a threatening sexual deviant, while upholding dichotomous notions of good and bad femininity, moral and immoral sex and sexualities, and public and private spheres. As a result, the concurrent processes of criminalization and regulation have both exclusionary and inclusionary tendencies: on the one hand, they seek to eliminate or eradicate commercial sex, but on the other hand, they also must recognize sex work—even if it is considered undesirable—in order to control and police it. All of this reinforces the idea that sex workers are not full citizens or members of the community and justifies the denial of their human rights, including the right to security of person.

Sex Trade Policies in Canada

Laws, policies, and regulations governing the sex industries are influenced by Canada's division of powers. Canada's Constitution Act specifies the legislative powers of the federal and provincial governments. The federal government has a range of responsibilities, including trade and commerce, raising money and taxation, currency, banking, defense, and the criminal law. The act also grants the federal government power over the provinces and limits the provinces' ability to raise money through taxation. However, provinces are responsible for the municipal level of government. They decide the structures, responsibilities, and financial system of local governments. Local governments are not part of the federal system because they are subordinate to provincial and territorial governments, but they have a range of responsibilities, including police and fire protection and providing services related to health and welfare, like housing and education. The constitutional division of powers both limits cities' options to respond to sex work and provides latitude for the creation of a range of local bylaws.

In Canada, prostitution has never actually been illegal. Instead, the federal Criminal Code criminalizes most of the *practices associated with* prostitution and other sexual services for sale. So while it is not illegal to engage in sex work or exchange sex for money or other goods, Section 213 of the Criminal Code makes it illegal to communicate for the purposes of prostitution in a public place, including in a car or even a large window open to public view (Jeffrey 2004). Section 210 of the Criminal Code also contains provisions against bawdy houses, making it illegal to be "an inmate of a common bawdy house," be found in a common bawdy house without a lawful excuse, or keep a common bawdy house. Section 212 prohibits procuring and living on the avails of prostitution, also known as pimping. The sex trade laws are mostly enforced on the streets. Only about 20 percent of Canada's sex trade is based in the streets, yet 90 percent of Section 213 charges occur on the street (Standing Committee on Justice and Human Rights 2006). While most indoor workers are unlikely to face federal charges, many types of indoor sex work, like erotic massage and even escort services, are subject to municipal regulations, including zoning and business licensing bylaws. In Canada, then, some sex workers are simultaneously criminalized and licensed.

While cities have little power relative to the federal and provincial governments, their respective provinces grant them the right to regulate businesses through licensing and zoning. The municipalities, as we see in the following pages, attempt to avoid overstepping their jurisdictional authority related to the criminal law by using euphemistic language and outlawing practices associated with prostitution and the sex trade. The Canadian federal system's division of powers means that sex workers are subject to contradictory yet mutually reinforcing forms of regulation and control. The interplay of the different forms of regulation constructs the sex worker as abject and contributes to the sex worker's status as a noncitizen and a nonmember in the polity and community. The criminal laws and bylaws both recognize sex work, even if only to police it, as they write sex workers out of political and social membership.

Method

As Canada waits for the courts to decide the fate of its federal prostitution laws, cities have started to discuss and debate what role they might play in regulating different sectors of the sex industry, and cities are increasingly important in debates on how to regulate commercial sex.[3] Yet there is not much research on municipal politics and sex work in Canada (Benoit and Shaver 2006). The research on Canada that does exist in this area mainly consists of case studies that show how specific cities license sex work, especially strip clubs and massage parlors, and the impact these regulations have on the lives and work conditions of sex workers. This work suggests that municipal licensing regulations are problematic policies, in part because the federal Criminal Code makes it difficult to perform sex work in a safe manner (Lewis and Maticka-Tyndale 2000; Maticka-Tyndale, Lewis, and Street 2005; STAR 2006). In addition, authors argue that municipal and federal regulations violate sex workers' basic labor rights and expose sex workers to unnecessary risks (van der Meulen and Durisin 2008). Pivot Legal Society (2006) reports that many sex workers suggest the quasi-legal nature of their work combined with restrictive licensing tends to give control to the state and the employer, invades their privacy, and makes it harder for them to protect their rights and security. A few scholars have started to explore how local regulations contribute to the construction of sex workers as a social problem (Bruckert and Dufresne 2002; Ross 2009).

International research also suggests the importance of looking at local and municipal forms of sex work regulation. In other jurisdictions where sex work is decriminalized or legalized, municipal forms of regulation are sometimes used to control where sex work takes place, if at all. In New Zealand, for example, where prostitution was decriminalized, territorial authorities have a number of regulatory options, including deciding on the location of brothels. Some cities used this authority to narrowly restrict brothel locations, making it extremely difficult for small owner-operated brothels to gain local approval (Knight 2010).

I was inspired to explore licensing regimes across Canada after hearing complaints from workers at strip clubs and erotic massage parlors in

Toronto about the cost of their license and what they saw as arbitrary rules making their jobs more difficult. In order to determine the extent to which Canada's municipalities are involved in regulating sex industries, I looked at municipal codes in Canada's twenty largest cities by population at the time that I began my study. I used Statistics Canada's population and dwelling counts by metropolitan area (2006 data) to help determine which cities to examine.[4] Based on the largest census metropolitan areas, I looked at licensing in twenty cities from across the country because prostitution and the sex trades are generally associated with cities and urban spaces, both in academic scholarship and in the media. Historically, the so-called respectable classes associated cities with dirt, disease, overcrowding, and disorder, and the sex worker was the paradigmatic symbol of urban life and all of its risks (Hunt 2002). In addition, I wanted to begin filling a gap in existing sex work research by further exploring how and why local governments regulate sex industries and by examining how the federal criminal laws influence the policy options other levels of government have.

I searched municipal codes and licensing bylaws available online and in some cases I called or e-mailed city employees for clarification. I discovered that fourteen of the twenty cities have licensing schemes governing "adult entertainment parlors" or strip clubs, "body-rub parlors" or erotic massage parlors, and escort or dating services (see Figure 5.1 in the section on municipal licensing). I found that there is a significant amount of variation in how cities target and regulate adult industries. This variation is not surprising considering bylaws governing commercial sex were created over long periods of time. For example, in Toronto, the bylaws licensing strip clubs and body-rub parlors were created in the 1970s as part of an effort to clean up vice on Yonge Street. At the time, federal politicians amended the Municipal Act to allow cities to license and limit the number of body-rub parlors in the city (Brock 1998). Yet the bylaws licensing holistic practitioners were not enacted until the late 1990s. The holistic bylaws are different from the body-rub bylaws. While the body-rub bylaws remain in place, the newer holistic category was introduced to ensure body-rub attendants were not pretending to offer holistic services by requiring holistic practitioners to have government-recognized training. It was intended to separate erotic massage parlors from spas offering holistic services, like reiki or massage; however, in practice many of Toronto's erotic massage parlors are licensed under the holistic category. It is somewhat surprising, however, how similar some of the bylaws are, considering they were passed over different periods and in different provinces.

After using the bylaws to determine what kinds of licenses sex workers, operators, and owners may need in Canada's different cities and what rules govern these businesses, I analyzed the bylaws using discourse analysis. Discourse analysis is a qualitative, interpretive, and constructionist methodology that attempts to "uncover the way that reality is produced" by policies (Hardy, Harley, and Phillips 2004, 19). It involves exploring how policies actively construct categories and it can help illustrate dominant relations of power (Crawford 2004; van Dijk 1993). Although policies are usually intended to respond to problems, they also send messages about deserving and undeserving citizens to the public and to policymakers (Schneider and Ingram 1993).

In the following analysis, I therefore critically examine how the discourse of the bylaws contributes to the reproduction of dominance and naturalizes the social order that continues to oppress sex workers.

Unnatural, Abnormal, and Ugly: The Political Construction of Sex Workers as Deviants

In *Justice and the Politics of Difference* (1990), Iris Marion Young looks at the construction of "ugly bodies and the implications of unconscious fears and aversions for the oppression of despised groups" (124). She outlines three important and interrelated elements in the creation of ugly bodies and unconscious fears: reason, respectability, and abjection. According to Young, modern discourses on reason helped to create categories of deviancy and deficiency, or ugly bodies, rooted in nature and the idea of what is natural. In addition, an effort to understand social phenomena that privilege reason/rationality over "embodied knowledge" relies on hierarchal standards used to assess the objects or bodies under appraisal. Young writes, "Bodies are both naturalized, that is, conceived as subject to deterministic scientific laws, and normalized, that is, subject to evaluation in relation to a teleological hierarchy of the good" (127). This hierarchal standard of assessment locates the young, white, healthy, and strong male body as hierarchically superior to those that fall outside of this supposedly natural and normal category. Modern scientific reason involves systems of logic and surveillance, which assist in the classification of subjects and objects, natural and unnatural, normal and abnormal. The sex worker is frequently considered "bad" because she challenges norms of femininity by the public nature of her work and her nonmonogamous and thus immoral sex. By challenging norms of femininity, the sex worker is also challenging supposed scientific laws about female behavior.

Similarly, the sex worker challenges ideals of female respectability. The ideal of respectability "consists in conforming to norms that repress sexuality, bodily functions, and emotional expression" and is linked to an idea of order where everything is under control and in its proper place (Young 1990, 136). Respectability also plays a role in understanding how "ugly bodies" are constructed. Norms of respectable behavior are closely connected to behavior that is considered orderly, like chastity, cleanliness, and frugality. Norms of respectable behavior are gendered, however, meaning that things that may be acceptable for men are not acceptable for women. Respectability treats masculinity and femininity as mutually exclusive and yet complementary. The ideal of respectability sees women under men's paternalistic control and care (Young 1990, 137). Sex workers are not respectable, according to this logic, because they usually are not under men's control or care as wives in the private sphere of the home. They also disrupt the ideal of femininity through their financial independence and work in the public sphere. Respectable women are expected to only engage in sexual relations with one man within the confines of a romantic relationship. Sex workers, by the nature of their work, are not usually sexually monogamous.

Those who fall outside of the ideal of respectable behavior might be considered unnatural, abnormal, and abject, where "the abject is other than the subject, but is only just the other side of the border . . . the abject provokes fear and loathing because it exposes the border between self and other as constituted and fragile, and threatens to dissolve the subject by dissolving the border" (Young 1990, 143). The abject is a social and political construction that changes over time but is linked to the persistence of oppression "partly through interactive habits, unconscious assumptions and stereotypes, and group related feelings of nervousness or aversion" (Young 1990, 148). Those who are at the bottom of the sexual and gender hierarchies, established by a belief in modern scientific reason, or otherwise fall short of the ideal of respectability are thus subject to abjection. They are turned into "others" and are considered objects of law. As a result, they become social and political outsiders. But these processes of othering are contradictory in the sense that they must recognize the sex worker while they simultaneously "disacknowledge" her labor (Sanchez 2004). The sex worker is recognized in law, not to ensure her rights but to ensure that she is controlled (by the state and society) in order to maintain sexual and racial boundaries. As a result, she is both written into law and written out of political membership. The tension between the sex worker's erasure and recognition highlights her role as a limit concept marking the boundaries between the social and antisocial, between order and disorder (Sanchez 2004).

In light of this, Young's theory seems to draw on and contribute to sociological theories of deviance (Goffman 1963) by exploring the construction of deviant identities; however, unlike scholars of deviance, Young is less concerned with how people *manage* their deviant identities. Instead, Young explores the processes that produce relations of dominance and oppression and asks how attending to group differences can undermine oppression and contribute to justice. Young's theory is helpful because it relates the construction of the "other" to group difference and, as such, raises important concerns about how oppressed groups can participate in political decision making and help end human rights abuses (Young 2000). She suggests that oppressed groups should be afforded opportunities for participation in public life and that group differences should be acknowledged in public policy in order to reduce oppression (1990, 11). By linking the construction of the deviant abject to oppression, Young's theory helps to highlight a relationship between deviance and human rights, where "the deviant" label (or any other) helps to justify denying some groups, like sex workers, the full range of human rights that is guaranteed to more respectable members of the community. Her theory also helps to highlight the contradictory processes of othering, where the "other" is included in laws and policies to maintain order but is otherwise excluded from full social and political membership.

Local Variation: Municipal Licensing

With this background of social construction of a normative order in mind, we can now examine Canada's various municipal regulatory schemes to get a better understanding of how these processes of social construction take place. There is a great deal of local variation in the licensing schemes across Canada, and the types of sex businesses requiring licenses differ significantly. Some municipalities like Toronto, Ottawa, and Oshawa only license adult entertainment parlors (strip clubs) and body-rub parlors (erotic massage parlors). Other cities, like Vancouver, license those and dating and escort services. Yet others, like Winnipeg, still only license escort agencies. In Victoria, the Escort and Dating Service bylaw includes body painting studios, body-rub parlors, encounter studios, escort and dating services, and model studios. In some instances, only owners and operators require licenses. In Ottawa, for example, owners and operators of adult entertainment parlors and body-rub parlors are licensed but erotic dancers and body-rub attendants are not individually licensed. In other cities, erotic dancers and body-rub attendants are also required to obtain licenses.

The licensing fees for sex industries across Canada are quite high compared to other licensing categories. In Saint Catharines, Ontario, body-rub parlor owners pay the highest licensing fee under the bylaw, $3,100 per year. In Vancouver, body-rub parlors, body painting studios, and model studios pay a license fee of $9,250 annually. High licensing fees mean that many people who might like to work independently and run their own massage parlor or escort service cannot afford the fees. License fees for workers are not as onerous, but initial licensing fees range from $95 for body-rub attendants in Kitchener to almost $400 for erotic dancers in Toronto, and workers in all areas are subject to annual renewal fees.

Many of the municipalities that license body-rub parlors and escort services attempt to get around the jurisdictional limitations imposed by the constitutional division of powers by implementing policies that are intended to curtail prostitution.[5] For example, escorts in Barrie, Ontario, are explicitly prohibited from touching their clients (Bylaw 2005-276, 7.4.1.0.0). In most city bylaws, erotic dancers are prohibited from sexual contact with customers and neither adult entertainers nor body-rub attendants are permitted to handle cash or offer services that have not been filed with the city. Many cities require dancers and body-rub attendants to provide clients with a bill listing services and prices, followed by a serialized receipt of payment.

Existing sex work bylaws include a range of measures to control sex workers yet they fail to offer sex workers many of the protections associated with citizenship, including the rights to privacy and security of person. The bylaws also contribute to sex workers' tenuous citizenship status by constructing them as deviant outsiders who threaten social order in Canada's cities.

CITY	LICENSING SCHEME	LICENSEE
Toronto, ON	Adult entertainment parlor	Owner, operator, attendant
	Body-rub parlor	Owner operator, attendant
	Holistic massage	Owner, attendant
Vancouver, BC	Adult entertainment store	Owner
	Body-rub parlor, body painting studio, and modeling studio	Owner
	Dating service	Owner
	Social escort service	Owner, escort
	Health enhancement center	Owner
Calgary, AB	Dating and escort service	Owner, escorts
	Exotic entertainers	Owner, entertainer
Edmonton, AB	Escort license	Escort, agency, independent
	Exotic entertainers	Owner, entertainers
	Massage	Owner, attendants/ practitioners
Ottawa-Gatineau, ON/QC	Adult entertainment parlor	Owner, operator
	Body-rub parlor	Owner
Hamilton, ON	Adult entertainment establishment	Owner, operator, attendant
	Body-rub parlor	Owner, operator, attendant
Winnipeg, MB	Escort agency	Owner, escort
Kitchener, ON	Adult entertainment parlor—5 classes:	Owner
	Class A, Class B (books and videos)	Owner
	Class C (adult goods available)	Owner
	Class D (body-rub parlors)	Owner, attendant
	Class E (nudity and dancing services)	Owner
	Alternative massage centers	Owner
London, ON	Adult live entertainment parlors	Owners
	Adult entertainment body-rub parlors	Owners
Saint Catharines, ON	Adult entertainment parlor	Owner, operator
	Body-rub parlor	Owner, operator
Victoria, BC	Body painting studio	Owner, attendant

Figure 5.1. An overview of sex work licensing in fourteen Canadian cities.

Population data from Statistics Canada. 2006. "2006 Census of Population—Population and Dwelling Counts." http://www12.statcan.ca/english/census06/data/popdwell/Table .cfm?T=801&PR=0&SR=1&S=3&O=D.

FIGURE 5.1 (continued)		
CITY	LICENSING SCHEME	LICENSEE
	Body-rub parlor	Owner, attendant
	Encounter studio	Owner, attendant
	Escort agency, escorts	Owner, attendant
	Model studio	Owner, attendant
Windsor, ON	Adult entertainment parlor	Owner, operator
	Escort/ personal service agent	Owner, escort/ attendant
	Complimentary holistic massage	Practitioner/attendant
Oshawa, ON	Adult entertainment parlor	Owner, operator, attendant
	Body-rub parlor	Owner, operator, attendant
Barrie, ON	Adult entertainment establishment, *Class A* (novelty goods store)	Owner, attendant
	Adult entertainment establishment, *Class B* (erotic dance club)	Owner, attendant
	Escort service	Owner, attendant, driver

Data on municipal licensing schemes from licensing bylaws available on city websites and conversations with licensing officials; massage parlors in Toronto, Vancouver, Edmonton, and Windsor require attendants to have officially recognized training in massage or holistic practices; however, a number of the establishments licensed as holistic massage centers are actually body-rub parlors or "fronts for prostitution."

Antiprostitution licensing conditions help to reveal the ways in which municipal licensing bylaws both contradict and reinforce federal criminal sanctions against prostitution. The bylaws may contradict the federal law by providing licenses for businesses that likely operate in violation of the Criminal Code, like body-rub parlors. Yet they reinforce the Criminal Code by providing another prohibition against sex for sale. The municipal antiprostitution policies may help cities avoid overstepping their authority, but they create contradictions because the cities are quietly collecting licensing fees for these quasi-legal trades. Licensing bylaws, then, recognize and attempt to control undesirable activities while the criminal laws seek to eliminate them. The local and national laws reveal a tension between the need to include sex workers in order to maintain order and boundaries and the desire to exclude them from full political membership, punish their supposed transgressions, and deter others from transgressing the boundaries of respectability.

Municipal bylaws can make it difficult for sex workers to protect their health and safety. The no-touch and antiprostitution measures make it difficult for sex workers to negotiate and openly communicate with clients. Because operators are constantly wary of bawdy house charges, they are reluctant to discuss the true nature of their business with new employees, and new employees are left to figure out what the rules are and how the written rules differ from actual practices (Pivot Legal Society 2006, van der Meulen and Durisin 2008). Workers are afraid to report violent incidents because they worry the police will charge them or will use the incident as an excuse to close the parlor.

The sex workers' fears that municipal policies could be used to help police enforce the Criminal Code against them are not entirely unfounded. Jacqueline Lewis and Eleanor Maticka-Tyndale found that one reason for the introduction of sex trade licensing schemes in Calgary and Windsor was to assist the police with monitoring these industries. In fact, one police officer they interviewed noted, "Escort work is particularly difficult to police. You can't find it . . . When it's licensed we know who they are and where they are. We can keep tabs on it" (2000, 440). According to *Ottawa Citizen* reporter Dan Gardner, massage parlors are not generally closed because they violate federal prostitution laws but because they do not have licenses and frequently violate zoning regulations (2002, A1). The bylaws are a way to control prostitution and the sex trade without relying on the Criminal Code provisions, which are difficult and expensive to enforce (Edwards 2006, B2). The bylaws provide state authorities with a means of controlling sex workers rather than offering effective ways to make sex work safer.

Discussion: Ugly Bodies in Canada's Municipalities

Disorderly Conduct: Respectability and the Feminine Ideal

In addition to the no-touch provisions discussed previously, a number of Canada's municipal bylaws for sex businesses also contain provisions to ensure good conduct and good character. In Hamilton, Ontario, for example, body-rub attendants are to be "properly dressed, neat and clean in his or her person and civil and well-behaved to members of the public with whom he or she is dealing" (Bylaw 07-170, Schedule 4, 27 [1]) and additional provisions require attendants to wear a "light-colored, durable, hygienic uniform" (Bylaw 07-170, Schedule 4, 27 [2]). Similarly, in Toronto, body-rub attendants and erotic dancers are to be civil and well behaved to members of the public (545-357 and 545-389). In Kitchener, Ontario, it is possible to refuse a license if the applicant's past or present behavior causes the licensing manager to believe he or she will not carry out the business with honesty and integrity (Bylaw 88-100; Schedule A, 9 [f]).

In some cities, the provisions for good character and conduct are applied to all licensed work, although many cities only apply these provisions to sex workers. Toronto, for example, explicitly demands good behavior from pedicab drivers, horse-drawn vehicle drivers, and tow-truck drivers, in addition to dancers and body-rub attendants. In other cities, the proscription for good behavior only applies to licenses where sex work may occur, like massage parlors and holistic centers. In Windsor, Ontario, for example, holistic practitioners are the only category explicitly required to be properly dressed, neat, clean, and civil to members of the public.

The good character bylaws assume that sex workers are not honest, civil, or well behaved. The policies imply that those in the sex trade need to be regulated into orderly conduct, honesty, and integrity. Sex workers are constructed as being a threat to the city's more deserving citizens, their clients. Though research suggests most clients are not violent (Atchison 2010; Lowman and Atchison 2006), and that indoor work tends to be safer than outdoor work (O'Doherty 2011), the bylaws ignore the fact that sex work can be risky and that some clients are violent, rude, and disrespectful (Lowman 2000). The bylaws also fail to reflect the fact that more clients victimize sex workers than sex workers victimize clients (Atchison 2010). Placing the onus for good behavior on sex workers is unfair and reinforces a sexual double standard that makes women responsible for men's behavior.

The bylaws requiring good conduct treat sex workers of all genders as potential threats. However, most licensed sex workers are women, and it is revealing to consider how the bylaws are gendered. The good character bylaws attempt to reintegrate the female sex worker into respectable society by bringing her into the paternalistic care and control of the state. State regulation of sex work is based in part on the "permeability of the boundary between the sex worker and non–sex worker body and the reintegration of the prostitute into respectable society" (Bell 1994, 50). The bylaws contain the threat the sex worker supposedly poses to both citizens and the gender order by controlling these women's behavior. The bylaws attempt to establish respectable sex workers while also making the notion of a respectable sex worker something of an oxymoron by firmly locating sex work as unnatural and abnormal.

Unhealthy Sexuality, Sexual Deviance, and the Sex Worker's Threatening Body

One of the most illustrative ways the municipal bylaws render sex workers' bodies unnatural and abnormal is the inclusion of health testing in a number of cities including Hamilton (Bylaw 07-170, Schedule 4, 21 [2]), Oshawa (Schedule O, 4), Saint Catharines (Schedule B5, 14.c) and Toronto (545-333). In Oshawa, Saint Catharines, and Toronto body-rub attendants are required to present a certificate of health to the licensing authorities in order to obtain their licenses. In Hamilton, anyone suspected of having a communicable disease is not to be admitted to the parlor.

Health testing is an extremely controversial issue among legislators, public health officials, and even sex workers; however, I argue health testing is a way to survey and monitor sex workers but does little to protect people from disease. Health testing sex workers makes it seem as though the city is doing something to contain the threat sex workers supposedly pose. Sex workers are considered "vectors of disease" and must be regulated in order to control contagion throughout the city in the municipal licensing systems. Because policymakers and the public frequently consider them to be a group of diseased people, they are not full subjects in a society where "the natural" body is a young (and innocent?), healthy body. Their disease is also connected to their sexual moral failings, or their promiscuity (Young 1990, 128).[6]

While it is true that most establishments serving the public are subject to health codes, the laws and regulations apply to the establishment and not to individual workers, meaning the owner is responsible for ensuring a healthy establishment. For example, restaurants are licensed and subject to health codes; however, individual servers are not licensed. Sex workers tend to be one of the few groups where individual workers are licensed by the city and subject to a range of surveillance and control measures (while their clients, who are equally culpable regarding the potential health consequences of their actions, are not).

In Oshawa, Saint Catharines, and Toronto, the onus is on body-rub attendants to prove that they are free from communicable disease and fit for licensing; however, *clients are not subject to any form of testing* despite the fact that transmission of STIs is more likely to occur from men (the majority of clients) to women (the majority of body-rub attendants) and that sex workers in Canada regularly practice safer sex (Brock 1998, 87; Alexander 1997, 89). Before a body-rub attendant is issued a license, he or she must provide the city with a letter from a recognized doctor or health practitioner indicating he or she is free from communicable disease. The testing is directly connected to the issuance of the license and there is no required ongoing testing.

Testing sex workers in Canada does not seem to be the best way to reduce the harms associated with unsafe sexual practices. Instead, it raises questions about sex workers' human rights and the way the law helps to construct sex workers as deviants. While the sex worker remains diseased in the popular imagination, there are studies that suggest sex workers have better sexual health than the general population (Metzenrath 1999, 28). Research also suggests that sex workers in North America are not the "vectors of disease" they are frequently thought to be (Brock 1998; Jeffrey and MacDonald 2006). But the idea that sex workers are a threat to others, in part, because they are considered diseased and dirty, and thus deviant, continues. Testing a specific group or population while others are free from state intervention makes that group responsible for the city's sexual health. It is unfair in light of the fact that many people, not just sex workers, have multiple sexual partners and are not forced to undergo testing.

The health requirement thus shows how sex workers are simultaneously written into and excluded from full membership in the polity by punitive laws that establish the sex worker as the "other" and/or an outsider. In cities that require an initial health check, sex workers are assumed to be threatening to the body politic and must be controlled to protect citizens. Here, state authorities maintain boundaries between healthy citizens and unhealthy outsiders by simultaneously including and excluding "ugly" bodies from the polity. The state must recognize commercial sex in order to control it.

Public/Private Dichotomies

The body-rub and stripper licenses create a state record of a person's sex work involvement. The licenses make someone's work in the sex industries part of their public record and public knowledge and turn sex workers into a separate category of women who exist in and threaten the public sphere. A state record of someone's involvement in sex work is troubling because sex work is stigmatized and sex workers are frequently discriminated against on the basis of their work.

It is not entirely clear who has access to licensing files, and sex workers worry about who can access this info and how they might use it. As a result, many licensed body-rub attendants work in fear, constantly wondering if they are going to be fined or otherwise penalized for doing their job (van der Meulen and Durisin 2008, 300). The municipal licensing records could potentially be used by other state agencies, including taxation and social services. For example, these records can be used in legal proceedings and a woman's participation in prostitution can be used to deny her custody of her children (Lewis and Maticka-Tyndale 2000). A public record of participation in sex commerce could violate sex workers' right to privacy if these records are used to justify discrimination and rights abuses.

The bylaws are a form of surveillance and control that suggests a hierarchy of sex and sexual practices, one where monogamous sexual pleasure is considered a part of natural and normal sexuality as long as it takes place in private and behind closed doors. Sex workers fall on the lower rungs of this hierarchy because they have the audacity to make their disreputable sexual practices public by moving sex outside of the home and into the economic market (Young 1990, 137). They disrupt the separate spheres of public and private activities, suggesting that the boundaries between public and private are not rigid. Considering the bylaws mostly apply to women, they bring into relief the assumption that women's proper place is in the private sphere of the home, under the paternal control of men. The bylaws attempt to minimize the threat of corruption and disorder that sex workers symbolize by virtue of their public role. Licensing sex workers suggests that they are a group of people who need to be monitored and controlled for the public's interest. Municipal codes governing the sex trade are a relatively recent component in the larger history of policing "degenerate sexuality," which is central "to the policing of the 'dangerous classes'" (McClintock 1992, 71). Policing degenerate sexuality helps to maintain sexual boundaries while it simultaneously excludes sex workers from full membership in the polity.

Conclusion

My argument that many municipal licensing bylaws discursively construct sex workers as outsiders in Canadian communities raises empirical questions about how these bylaws are enforced, what impact they have on sex workers and their working conditions, and how sex workers understand and respond to them. Like Annie Hill's chapter in this volume (chapter 4), it also raises questions about how regulation could be used to make conditions in the sex industries better while also including sex workers as members in the polity.

Though many of the existing city bylaws construct sex workers as deviant outsiders and do little to protect sex workers' rights, these laws and policies can be used to make the sex trade safer and more equitable; however, it is extremely important to work with sex workers to develop policies that foster meaningful inclusion. Young argues that participatory democracy offers a way to ensure groups that are oppressed or disadvantaged have opportunities to influence policies that affect them (1990; 2000). She suggests that effective group representation requires three institutional mechanisms: self-organization of group members, group analysis and generation of policy proposals, and group veto power regarding policies that affect the group (1990, 184). Along these lines, both Alexandra Lutnick's and Raven Bowen and Tamara O'Doherty's chapters in this volume (chapters 2 and 3, respectively) make a number of suggestions about how to research sex work in inclusive and ethical ways, including involving sex workers in all aspects of the research enterprise, ensuring that research reflects the heterogeneity of sex workers, and being self-reflexive about researcher biases and prejudices.

In order to make sex work policymaking more inclusive, policymakers should include sex workers in all stages of the process, ensure that sex worker participants reflect a wide variety of experiences in the sex trades, and be more self-reflexive about their own biases and prejudices. Including marginalized groups, like sex workers, in the policymaking process could help to avoid policies that construct them as deviant, ugly bodies and could possibly result in policies that recognize sex workers as full members of their communities.

Some municipalities have started to open up the policymaking process to sex workers and their representatives. In Toronto, Municipal Licensing and Standards recently consulted with erotic dancers for the first time in at least twenty years (Godfrey 2011). The City of Vancouver concluded consultation with a variety of stakeholders, including some sex workers and their representatives, on how to end sexual exploitation, and it seems likely the city will adopt some of the sex workers' suggestions. Yet cities still have a long way to go in creating policy that recognizes sex workers as full members of their communities and responds to their health and safety concerns.

Notes

1. Three sex workers, Terri-Jean Bedford, Valerie Scott, and Amy Lebovitch, and their lawyer Alan Young challenged the constitutionality of Canada's criminal laws governing prostitution, including sections prohibiting operating a common bawdy house (brothel), living on the avails, and communicating for the purposes of prostitution in a public place. They argued that sex work is a legal occupation, yet Section 7 of the Charter of Rights and Freedoms makes it impossible for sex workers to work safely and thus violates sex workers' right to security of person (Bedford 2011). They also argued that Canada's main prostitution laws violate principles of fundamental justice, also Section 7 of the charter. In 2010, Justice Himel, ruling for the Ontario Superior Court, released her decision striking down the three main laws against prostitution: common bawdy house (Section 210), (living on the avails of prostitution [Section 212 (1) (j)]), and (communicating for prostitution in public [Section 213 (1) (c)]). The laws were only struck down in Ontario, but the decision set an important legal precedent nationally. In 2012, the Ontario Court of Appeal maintained the ruling that the bawdy house law and part of the living on the avails law are unconstitutional because they violate the principles of fundamental justice. However, the Court of Appeal found the communicating provisions constitutionally valid (Canada [Attorney General] v. Bedford, 2012 ONCA 186 20120326). The Supreme Court of Canada is scheduled to hear an appeal in the spring of 2013.

2. I use the term "sex work" broadly to include all sexual services exchanged for compensation. I include skin work, like exotic dance, as well as erotic massage, escort services, and street-based sex work. My examination, however, focuses on the sex trade sectors regulated by Canada's cities, including exotic dance, erotic massage, and escorts.

3. The City of Vancouver's action plan to end sexual exploitation generated debate about the role the cities can play in regulating commercial sex and how to make sex work safer (Gibson 2011; Jang 2011). In Saskatoon, Saskatchewan, the police chief is currently working on a law to regulate online advertising with an escort license (CTVNews.ca Staff 2011; Hutton 2011). Meanwhile, politicians in Edmonton are debating new rules for escorts that might include health testing; they also hope to create Canada's first enforcement team to ensure erotic businesses comply with immigration, labor, and health standards (Kent 2011).

4. Census metropolitan areas are geographic areas used by Statistics Canada that include both the urban core and the surrounding "fringes" integrated

or associated with the urban core. In cases where the census metropolitan area included the surrounding areas, I focused on whether or not the urban center had bylaws related to the sex trade. In the future, I would like to further examine how these suburban "fringes" regulate sex work.

5. The range of services offered varies among the parlors and also depends on the worker. In some parlors, workers offer nude massages usually followed by a hand job, though in some parlors fellatio and intercourse may be offered (*Constellation* 2009, 43–44). Parlors where workers regularly perform hand jobs, fellatio, and sex for pay likely violate the bawdy house laws. In some cities, public officials suggest that prostitution is a problem in massage parlors. In Toronto, for example, Bruce Robertson, head of licensing and standards, argues that illegal activity in both licensed and unlicensed premises is a growing problem and that the department is currently considering new approaches toward regulation (Kuitenbrouwer and Alcoba 2011).

6. While the bylaws seem to have been written with female sex workers in mind, male sex workers are also subject to health testing. Considering most of the men who work in body-rub parlors have male clients, the health testing bylaws also implicitly treat homosexual sex as threatening to social order.

References

Alcoba, Natalie. 2011. "City Should Set Toronto Island as Red Light District: Mammoliti." *National Post*, March 22. http://news.nationalpost.com/2011/03/22/city-should-set-toronto-island-as-red-light-district-mammoliti.

Alexander, Priscilla. 1997. "Feminism, Sex Workers, and Human Rights." In *Whores and Other Feminists*, ed. Jill Nagle, 83–97. New York: Routledge.

Atchison, Chris. 2010. *Report of the Preliminary Findings of John's Voice: A Study of Adult Canadian Sex Buyers.* http://www.johnsvoice.ca.

Bedford, Terri-Jean. 2011. *Dominatrix on Trial: Bedford v. Canada.* Bloomington, Ind.: iUniverse.

Bedford v. Canada. 2010. ONSC 4264.

Bell, Shannon. 1994. *Reading, Writing, and Rewriting the Prostitute Body.* Bloomington: Indiana University Press.

Benoit, Cecilia, and Frances M. Shaver. 2006. "Critical Issues and New Directions in Sex Work Research." *Canadian Review of Sociology and Anthropology* 43, no. 3: 243–64.

Brock, Deborah R. 1998. *Making Work, Making Trouble: Prostitution as a Social Problem.* Toronto, Ontario: University of Toronto Press.

Bruckert, Chris, and Martin Dufresne. 2002. "Re-Configuring the Margins: Tracing the Regulatory Context of Ottawa Strip Clubs, 1974–2000." *Canadian Journal of Law and Society* 17, no. 1: 69–87.

Chez Stella. 2009. "Pour Travailler en Sécurité Comme Masseuse/Working Safely as a Masseuse." *Constellation* April, 42–49.

Crawford, Neta C. 2004. "Understanding Discourse: A Method of Ethical Argument Analysis." *Qualitative Methods* 2, no. 1 (Spring): 22–25.

CTVNews.ca Staff. 2011. "License, Regulate Sex Workers Saskatoon's 'Top Cop' Says." CTVNews.ca. September 27. http://www.ctvnews.ca/license-regulate-sex-workers-saskatoon-s-top-cop-says-1.703498.

Edwards, Peter. 2006. "Massage Parlour Laws Cut Crime." *Toronto Star*, July 14, B2.

Gardner, Dan. 2002. "How Cities 'License' Off-Street Hookers." *Ottawa Citizen*, June 16, A1.

Gibson, Kate. 2011. "There's Much to Be Done to Ensure Sex Workers' Safety in Vancouver." *Georgia Straight*, September 29. http://www.straight.com/article-475366/vancouver/kate-gibson-theres-much-be-done-ensure-sex-workers-safety-vancouver.

Godfrey, Tom. 2011. "Strippers Want Status Redressed." *Toronto Sun*, June 3. http://www.torontosun.com/2011/06/03/strippers-want-status-redressed.

Goffman, Irving. 1963. *Stigma: Notes on the Management of a Spoiled Identity*. New York: Simon and Schuster.

Hardy, Cynthia, Bill Harley, and Nelson Phillips. 2004. "Discourse Analysis and Content Analysis: Two Solitudes?" *Qualitative Methods* 2, no. 1 (Spring): 19–22.

Hunt, Alan. 2002. "Regulating Heterosexual Space: Sexual Politics in the Early Twentieth Century." *Journal of Historical Sociology* 15, no. 1: 952–1909.

Hutton, David. 2011. "Police Propose Licensing Escorts." *StarPhoenix*, September 24. http://www2.canada.com/saskatoonstarphoenix/news/story.html?id=8946e3bc-d307-4215-abf4-7dceba6892f2&p=2.

Jang, Kerry. 2011. "Vancouver Taking Comprehensive Approach to Sex Trade Issues." *Vancouver Sun*, September 21. http://www2.canada.com/vancouversun/news/archives/story.html?id=185e7254-6f62-4551-9422-8ef22f03892e.

Jeffrey, Leslie Ann. 2004. "Prostitution as Public Nuisance: Prostitution Policy in Canada." In *The Politics of Prostitution: Women's Movements, Democratic States and the Globalisation of Sex Commerce*, ed. Joyce Outshoorn, 83–102. Cambridge, U.K.: Cambridge University Press.

Jeffrey, Leslie Ann, and Gayle MacDonald. 2006. *Sex Workers in the Maritimes Talk Back*. Vancouver: University of British Columbia Press.

Kent, Gordon. 2011. "New Bylaw Might Require Medical Certificates for Body-Rub Workers." *Edmonton Journal*, September 22, A5.

Knight, Dean. 2010. "The (Continuing) Regulation of Prostitution by Local Authorities." In *Taking the Crime Out of Sex Work: New Zealand Sex Workers' Fight for Decriminalisation*, ed. Gillian Abel, Lisa Fitzgerald, Catherine Healy, and Aline Taylor, 141–58. Bristol, U.K.: Polity Press.

Kuitenbrouwer, Peter, and Natalie Alcoba. 2011. "Behind the Sign: Investigating the Growing Number of Erotic Massage Centres in Toronto." *National Post*, May 7. http://news.nationalpost.com/2011/05/07/behind-the-sign -investigating-the-growing-number-of-erotic-massage-centres-in-toronto.

Lewis, Jacqueline, and Eleanor Maticka-Tyndale. 2000. "Licensing Sex Work: Public Policy and Women's Lives." *Canadian Public Policy* 26, no. 4: 437–49.

Lowman, John. 2000. "Violence and the Outlaw Status of (Street) Prostitution in Canada." *Violence against Women* 6, no. 9: 987–1011.

Lowman, John, and Chris Atchison. 2006. "Men Who Buy Sex: A Survey in the Greater Vancouver Regional District." *Canadian Review of Sociology* 43, no. 3: 281–96.

Maticka-Tyndale, Eleanor, Jacqueline Lewis, and Megan Street. 2005. "Making a Place for Escort Work: A Case Study." *Journal of Sex Research* 42, no. 1: 46–53.

McClintock, Anne. 1992. "Screwing the System: Sexwork, Race, and the Law." *Boundary* 2 19, no. 2: 70–95.

Metzenrath, Sue. 1999. "To Test or Not to Test?" *Social Alternatives* 18, no. 3: 25–30.

O'Doherty, Tamara. 2011. "Victimization in Off-Street Sex Industry Work." *Violence against Women* 17, no. 7: 944–63.

Pivot Legal Society. 2006. *Beyond Decriminalization: Sex Work, Human Rights, and a New Framework for Law Reform*. Vancouver: Pivot Legal Society. http:// www.pivotlegal.org/pdfs/BeyondDecrimLongReport.pdf.

Ross, Becki L. 2009. *Burlesque West: Showgirls, Sex, and Sin in Postwar Vancouver*. Toronto, Ontario: University of Toronto Press.

Sanchez, Lisa E. 2004. "The Global E-rotic Subject, the Ban, and the Prostitute Free Zone: Sex Work and the Theory of Differential Exclusion." *Environment and Planning* 22: 861–83.

Schneider, Anne, and Helen Ingram. 1993. "Social Construction of Target Populations: Implications for Politics and Policy." *American Political Science Review* 87, no. 2: 334–47.

Standing Committee on Justice and Human Rights. 2006. *The Challenge of Change: A Study of Canada's Prostitution Laws. Report of the Subcommittee on Solicitation*. Ottawa, Ontario: Department of Justice. http://www2.parl.gc.ca/ HousePublications/Publication.aspx?DocId=2599932&Language=E&Mode =1&Parl=39&Ses=1.

STAR. 2006. *Safety, Security and the Well-Being of Sex Workers, A Report Submitted to the House of Commons Subcommittee on Solicitation Laws (SSLR)*. Windsor, Ontario: Sex Trade Advocacy and Research (STAR). http://web2.uwindsor .ca/courses/sociology/maticka/star/pdfs/safety_and_security_report_final _version.pdf.

vander Meulen, Emily, and Elya Maria Durisin. 2008. "Why Decriminalize? How Canada's Municipal and Federal Regulations Increase Sex Workers' Vulnerability." *Canadian Journal of Women and the Law* 20, no. 2: 289–311.

van Dijk, Teun A. 1993. "Principles of Critical Discourse Analysis." *Discourse and Society* 4, no. 2: 249–83.

Young, Iris Marion. 1990. *Justice and the Politics of Difference*. Princeton, N.J.: Princeton University Press.

———. 2000. *Inclusion and Democracy*. Oxford: Oxford University Press.

Licensing Bylaws

Bylaw 07-170. City of Hamilton. 2009. Being a By-Law to License and Regulate Various Businesses.

Bylaw 32M98. City of Calgary. Being a Bylaw of the City of Calgary to License and Regulate Businesses.

Bylaw 88-100. City of Kitchener.2008.

Bylaw 91-2008. City of Winnipeg. 2009. Doing Business in Winnipeg.

Bylaw 120-2005 (consolidation of). City of Oshawa. 2010. Business Licensing.

Bylaw 395-2004. City of Windsor. 2005. Business Licensing.

Bylaw 545. City of Toronto. 2008. Toronto Municipal Code Licensing.

Bylaw 2002-189. City of Ottawa. 2002. Harmonized Licensing.

Bylaw 2005-318. City of Saint Catharines. 2005. Business Licensing.

Bylaw 2005-276. City of Barrie. 2005. To License and Regulate Various Businesses Particularly Related to the Adult Entertainment Industry.

Bylaw 4450. City of Vancouver. 2010. License.

Bylaw 10398. City of Edmonton. 2009. Exotic Entertainers.

Bylaw 12452. City of Edmonton. 2009. Escort Licensing.

Bylaw L-6. City of London. 2008. Business Licensing.

CHAPTER 6

Bad Girls and Vulnerable Women

An Anthropological Analysis of Narratives Regarding Prostitution and Human Trafficking in Brazil

Thaddeus Gregory Blanchette and Ana Paula da Silva

WHEN THE BRAZILIAN CONGRESS ratified the United Nations Protocol to Prevent, Suppress and Punish Trafficking in Persons (also known as the "Palermo Protocol") in 2004 and approved its National Plan to Combat Human Trafficking (PNETP) in 2008, the Brazilian federal government recognized the need to act against trafficking in persons. This development represents an advance in the fight against modern slavery in *terrasbrasilis*, a fight some say began with the Eusébio de Queirós law of 1850 and the prohibition of the transatlantic slave trade. However, the PNETP is by no means devoid of problems. In a country where laws are routinely ignored (not the least by the authorities charged with upholding them), the future of Brazil's antitrafficking policy will largely depend on the attitudes and ideologies of the political agents who create and implement antitrafficking initiatives. This chapter identifies some of these attitudes and, in doing so, warns of possible antidemocratic side effects that certain hegemonic narratives regarding gender and class could cause in the fight against so-called modern slavery.[1]

The data presented in the following pages come from our prolonged engagement with the political agents involved in the formulation of Brazil's National Plan during various meetings, seminars, and conferences that took place between 2004 and 2007. In collecting these data, we used the technique of observation–participation as described by anthropologist Bronislaw Malinowski (1961 [1922]), whereby the investigator takes part in the daily lives and rituals of the people he or she wishes to study and, through his or her observations, attempts to reveal the underlying structures of their collective life. Our investigation, however, did not presume the existence of any cohesive, clearly bounded "native tribe" whose rituals can be presented authentically and unequivocally. We understand the trafficking policy debate in Brazil to be one example of what Pierre Bourdieu calls a "political field," an arena in which political products, problems, programs, analysis, comments, concepts, and events are generated by competition among active political agents and between which the common citizen—reduced to the mere *status* of "consumer" in the process—is invited to choose (Bourdieu 1981, 3–4).

We applied Malinowski's ethnographic methods to the study of this political field, documenting the presence of a series of narratives regarding the trafficking of persons in Brazil—narratives that have become so omnipresent and naturalized that we can term them "hegemonic" (always remembering that hegemonies are never absolute or complete). Although our notion of hegemony is not exactly congruent with the one delineated by Antonio Gramsci (1971), it draws upon it. By "hegemonic" we understand an omnipresent ideology that is naturalized and imposed as a cultural norm, justifying the political, social, and economic status quo. Although the hegemonic narratives we discuss are far from being universally accepted, they have dominated public discussions about human trafficking to such an extent that those affirmations that appear to sustain them are generally accepted as self-evident, and assertions that cast any doubts upon them are rejected as esoteric or "crazy" and are subject to extremely rigorous inspection. Furthermore, these particular narratives appeared in discussions during the time period in question (2004–2007) with such a degree of frequency that they could almost be described as "memes" in the popular, Internet-related sense of the word: one couldn't escape them and they were repeated, ad nauseam, by almost all actors within the political field of Brazil's antitrafficking policymaking apparatus.

The hegemonic narratives in question point to a series of traditional beliefs regarding gender, class, and race/color that underpin the humanist debates of the antitrafficking movement. These prejudices determine which Brazilian women will be subject to increased state surveillance "for their own good" during their overseas travels and which women will be understood as beyond the purview of the country's new antitrafficking measures. As foundational beliefs motivating law enforcement practices and social interventions, the discourses that we describe in the pages that follow threaten to transform Brazil's federal antitrafficking program into yet another filter that will attempt to block the international migration of certain Brazilian citizens.[2]

The Palermo Protocol and Article 231
of the Brazilian Penal Code

Trafficking of persons first became an issue in Brazil in the late nineteenth and early twentieth centuries when young Jewish women, supposedly abducted from Eastern Europe, began appearing en masse in the brothels of Rio de Janeiro. At the time, this phenomenon was understood as a classic example of the *white slave trade*, although historians Beatriz Kushnir and Critiana Schettini have at least partially challenged this view by showing that the immigrant women involved in prostitution organized a series of mutual aid associations and were very much active agents— rather than passive victims—in the construction of their lives (Kushnir 1996; Schettini 2006).

With the precipitous drop in immigration from Europe in the decades following World War II, the human trafficking issue was largely forgotten in Brazil. However, in the last few years of the twentieth century and the beginning of the twenty-first, it has made a forceful return in Brazilian politics, this time presented as a threat to Brazilian immigrants, who were arriving in significant numbers during the years immediately prior to the terrorist attacks on the Pentagon and the World Trade Center in 2001. Following those attacks, increased surveillance of immigrant populations became the norm across the world, and in the United States and Western Europe, new legal measures were enacted to close countries' borders to immigration, particularly from Asia, Africa, and South America (GAATW 2007). It was in this general atmosphere of increased criminalization of racialized and class-defined immigrant "Others" that the Palermo Protocolcame into effect in late 2003.

Kamala Kempadoo has discussed how the Palermo Protocol originated in 2000 as an international response to the problems inherent in the United Nation's prior understanding of the trafficking of persons. Briefly put, earlier international agreements on trafficking exclusively focused on the movements of suspect (read single) women across state boundaries, with prostitution automatically understood as "sexual exploitation." The Protocol was an attempt to not only subsume trafficking under the heading of international criminal activity but also broaden and clarify the scope of trafficking so that it focused on the international movement of workers for slave labor of all kinds. It also opened the door to defining prostitution as a phenomenon separate from sexual exploitation. In other words, with the promulgation of the Protocol, a series of forced labor migrations became understood as the "trafficking of persons," while migration for sex work only became classifiable as such if it involved exploitation and work conditions that could be considered as "analogous to slavery" (Kempadoo 2005, 63–68).

Brazil ratified the Protocol in 2004 (UNODC 2006), and the political agents involved in the fight against human trafficking in Brazil like to describe the treaty as an international consensus regarding the issue. What the Protocol actually offers, however, is a vague guide to member countries' policies. The Protocol concretely prohibits "the recruitment, transportation, transfer, harboring or receipt of persons, by means of the threat or use of force or other forms of coercion, of abduction, of fraud, of deception, of the abuse of power or of a position of vulnerability or of the giving or receiving of payments or benefits to achieve the consent of a person having control over another person, for the purpose of exploitation" and specifically targets sexual exploitation within this definition (UNODC 2001, Article 3). Unlike earlier international agreements, the Protocol clearly indicates that sex work itself is neither a necessary nor a sufficient condition for human trafficking. According to its definitions, sexual exploitation or prostitution minimally must include a third person, an exploiter, to actually be classified as *trafficking of persons*.

Unfortunately, however, the Protocol does not clearly define the concrete forms this "exploitation of others" might take, leading to serious problems for policymakers when it comes to actually deciding which activities police are to qualify—and repress—as trafficking. For example, almost everyone would agree that the concept of "sexual exploitation of others" would certainly apply to a twelve-year-old girl who was kidnapped and prostituted against her will by the owner of a brothel. But is it still "sexual exploitation"—and thus trafficking—when an older woman (over the age of legal consent) voluntarily decides to engage in prostitution overseas, paying for her own travel expenses and not suffering conditions analogous to slavery in her work? The answer varies from nation to nation. The German government certainly would not consider such a woman to be "trafficked," but the U.S. government would.[3]

What actually constitutes "trafficking in persons" is even more confusing in Brazil. Although the country ratified the Palermo Protocol in 2004,

Article 231 of the Brazilian penal code (originally established in 1940 during the dictatorship of Getúlio Vargas, sixty-four years prior to the Palermo Protocol) is currently still the only legal instrument used to define the crime of human trafficking. Article 231 stipulates that prostitution is a sine qua non of trafficking, with the crime described solely as "promoting or facilitating the entry, into national territory, of a person to work as a prostitute or in other forms of sexual exploitation, or the departure of a person from the country for the same purpose abroad" (Brazilian Penal Code, Article 231). The concepts of *exploitation of others* and *violation of human rights*, which are necessary components of the definition of human trafficking according to the Palermo Protocol, are thus not included in the definition of trafficking promulgated by Brazilian federal law.

Moreover, a recent addition to the law (Article 231a) broadens the definition of human trafficking to include any person who moves about within national territory for the purposes of prostitution as well. In other words, according to the letter of the only extant Brazilian law regarding the trafficking of persons, a *trafficker* is any individual who helps a person move from Point A to Point B to engage in prostitution, whatever the circumstances, even in those cases in which a person is attempting to aid or succor said person. Under Articles 231 and 231a, it is possible to argue that a person who pays a taxi for a sex worker to go to her job safely is, in fact, a human trafficker. Brazil is therefore in an interesting situation; its Policy to Combat Human Trafficking is supposedly based on the Palermo Protocol, but its legal system continues to define the crime of trafficking as something exclusively involving the movement of prostitutes.

As the Global Alliance against Traffic in Women (GAATW—one of the world's most well-known and active antitrafficking organizations) warns, the contradictory definitions that exist in Brazilian laws and policies concerning human trafficking may result in "the closing of brothels [or other prostitution venues], making it impossible for the professional sex worker to make a living." Past experiences with such attempts to close brothels in Brazil also indicate that they can result in police officers demanding bribes from prostitutes in exchange for "protection," a situation that is made even more problematic by the fact that police officers are often involved in brothel ownership and management in Brazil (Nederstigt and Almeida 2007, 3–4). Given this situation, GAATW has classified Brazil's new National Plan to Combat Human Trafficking (PNETP) as a "policy open to interpretation"; the results of the policy will depend almost entirely on how it is put into practice and not on its formal declarations of intent.

A crucial question in the fight against trafficking in Brazil is thus how the country's laws will be applied in the PNETP. This, in turn, largely depends on how the political agents active in dealing with the issue in the national and local arena define these laws in practical, quotidian terms and, more specifically, how they define *sexual exploitation,* as this is still reported as the major reason for human trafficking both in Brazil and beyond its borders. It also matters *who* they understand to be potential trafficking victims (Nederstigt and Almeida 2007, 3; OIT 2005, 12).

In Brazil, discussions about the trafficking of persons in the media are replete with stories in which Brazilian innocents (generally presented as poor, dark skinned, or black) are lured by false promises made by foreigners (typically presented as, "false princes" who are seemingly well-to-do foreign men with "blond hair and blue eyes") who offer the opportunity for work and/or fame abroad. Tragically, in these narratives, as soon as the Brazilians arrive in the destination country, they discover that these "princes" are in fact their future pimps (a scenario that is depicted in Figure 6.1).

Figure 6.1. A pamphlet produced by the Rio de Janeiro–based antitrafficking organization Projeto TRAMA, which reproduces the most common Brazilian myth regarding trafficking. Here, a "blond Prince" seduces a Brazilian of African descent with stories of success abroad in order to trick her into forced prostitution.

Illustration courtesy of Projeto TRAMA.

As was the case during the white slavery panic in Rio de Janeiro at the beginning of the twentieth century, the current Brazilian trafficking narrative appears to be based more upon media-generated stereotypes than on realistic appraisals of migration and its perils. There is no proof that significant numbers of Brazilian women are being lured out of the country in the manner presented by the previous story, although individual cases of sexual slavery involving Brazilians obviously exist. However, studies among Brazilian emigrants and sex workers indicate that the majority of those labeled as "trafficking victims" by the Brazilian media and government are people who seek out sex work abroad, on their own volition, and who do not work under conditions "analogous to slavery."[4] The violations of human rights these emigrants suffer appear to be predominantly the result of their vulnerability as illegal or irregular immigrants; to seek justice or protection from the authorities, many need to identify themselves as "illegals" to the police and thus face deportation (Piscitelli 2007; Sect. Jus. and OIT 2007, 115–18).

As we and anthropologist Adriana Piscitelli have documented (Blanchette and da Silva 2013; Piscitelli 2004), concern regarding trafficking in persons began to coalesce in Brazil in the late 1990s. With Brazil's ratification of the Palermo Protocol, this concern was transformed into a federal mandate to produce a national policy and then a national plan to combat human trafficking. Between 2005 and 2008, a federal interministerial organization was set up to "mobilize civil society" to discuss and produce the policy and plan through a series of local and national meetings and seminars.

Most of the subsequent debate regarding trafficking was thus held within the confines of a nascent political field (in Pierre Bourdieu's sense of the term: 1981) whose agents were largely representatives of the executive institutions of the Brazilian state, powerful transnational organizations, and certain nongovernmental organizations (NGOs—which are often religious in nature). The number of organizations participating in the process is too large and their constituencies too diverse for us to do more than generally describe them here. State agents included representatives of the Human Rights Secretariat, the Ministry of Justice, the Women's Policy Secretariat, their associated state- and municipal-level counterparts, the federal police, the highway police, the National Force for Public Security, and the state and municipal police forces. At the transnational level, the U.S. Embassy and the United Nations Office on Drugs and Crime were also highly active in the Brazilian debate, as were the

International Labor Organization and the International Organization for Migration—all of which have helped fund Brazilian antitrafficking initiatives. NGOs included allies of international antitrafficking organizations, such as Projeto TRAMA (a Rio de Janeiro–based consortium of NGOs representing GAATW); religious groups (especially those linked to the Catholic Church, such as the Women's Pastoral); and women's and children's rights groups (especially those involved in the struggle against the sexual abuse of children). However, in spite of the almost universal identification of sex workers as "especially vulnerable" to trafficking, representatives of the Brazilian sex workers' and transsexuals' rights movements were not formally included in this discussion process until its very end, around October 2007, and even then their complaints and suggestions regarding the combating of trafficking were almost completely ignored.[5] The president of Brazil's largest sex workers' rights organization, the Rede Brasileira das Prostitutas, was only invited to participate in the discussions regarding the PNETP after the policy itself had already been ratified. Even then, she was limited to discussing the effects of trafficking on HIV prevention.

The political agents involved in discussing and formulating the PNETP were notably homogenous, both socially and culturally. The majority (90 percent or so) could be classified as white or "light brown" in terms of color/race.[6] They generally held a college degree, worked as professionals, had traveled internationally, and were drawn from the richest 20 percent of Brazilians. In short, this was a group composed of relative socioeconomic, ethnic, and cultural elites that was engaged in drawing up policies to "protect vulnerable groups" that were largely imagined as passive subjects of these policies. Going by their public proclamations, these agents were, for the most part, consciously aware that they were creating policies that would be enacted on "Other" Brazilians, generally classified as darker, poorer, and less educated than the agents themselves. In short, the process of discussing and implementing the PNETP was very much a "top-down" affair and not the response to grassroots demands from organized sectors of civil society.

By participating in and observing the seminars, debates, workshops, and roundtables that took place in this coalescing political field,[7] we perceived four general narratives that were widely repeated by a large portion of the political agents active in the antitrafficking policy debate. These narratives were, in fact, hegemonic in the sense that they were naturalized, normative, generally unquestioned, and repeated by almost all the agents involved in creating the PNETP. They can be summarized as follows:

1. The fight against trafficking reflects on the honor of Brazil in the community of nations. Antitrafficking measures must thus be taken immediately, even if there is not a clear consensus as to what trafficking actually involves.
2. Certain people are vulnerable to trafficking. There are thus two kinds of Brazilians: those who can freely move about internationally and those who should be discouraged—or even restricted—from doing so for their own good, due to their vulnerabilities.
3. Prostitution is inherently degrading and morally on a par with drug trafficking, even though it is not illegal in Brazil. Prostitutes are either victims without agency who need to be redeemed for society or fallen women who should be controlled for society's protection.
4. There are two kinds of Brazilian women: "family girls" and "street women." The first group should not be restricted in their travels overseas, while the second group should preferably be restricted to Brazil.

Four Narratives Regarding Human Trafficking

Taken together, the four hegemonic narratives that emerged in the process of defining the PNETP reveal little worry for the human or constitutional rights of Brazilians traveling abroad and a good deal more concern for the reformulation of a traditional morality that defines women as either "good" or "bad." These narratives affirm that two classes of Brazilian women exist—those who can travel and "those who should not travel, for their own good." The essentialized characteristics of these classes presented in the narratives reformulate traditional prejudices based on color, class, and sexual purity in humanist terms. This dichotic understanding of Brazilian femininity is then mobilized in the service of a project aimed at "rescuing the country's dignity and honor"[8] by prohibiting trafficking, thus creating a situation in which the harassment of Brazilian women traveling abroad (particularly those who are darker skinned and poor) is naturalized as a necessary collateral effect of the fight to build a better world.

Narrative 1: The Fight against Trafficking
Reflects on the Honor of Brazil

The first narrative emphasizes the need for Brazil to demonstrate that it is a responsible member of the community of nations by taking steps to enforce the Palermo Protocol. To be effective, international treaties of this sort must be defined within and translated into the terms of national jurisprudence. When a country agrees to abide by a human rights treaty, this should mark the beginning of a debate about the laws that will be implemented so that the country may move toward being in accordance with the treaty. However, this is not what happened during the few and short public discussions about the new National Policy, where the Palermo Protocol was presented as a fait accompli that bound Brazil's hands in terms of defining what was to be repressed.

Typically, representatives of the Brazilian state ministries (who were the most prominent formulators of the new National Policy) employed this narrative to explain why new antitrafficking measures must be adopted immediately, without prior studies as to what trafficking is in Brazil or how it is configured. Something must be done *right now*, the logic went, or Brazil will lose the respect of its international partners.

In one set of public meetings in Rio de Janeiro in 2006 between local human rights NGOs and the federal institutions charged with creating the new National Policy to combat trafficking, we asked why Brazil didn't first put its internal legal house in order before implementing new policies (by changing Article 231 so that it was congruent with the Palermo Protocol). The representative of the Ministry of Justice present at the meeting explained, "We are honor-bound to maintain our international commitments and cannot wait on the Brazilian Congress to change the Penal Code." The representative of the federal Women's Policy Secretariat then added, "Seeing as how the Palermo Protocol is what guides us, we don't need to change national law before acting on this issue. Besides, it's important that Brazil demonstrate a demonstration of good faith to the international community at this point."

As we've already shown, the claim that the Protocol offers concrete guidelines for law enforcement is erroneous. Thus the process of defining the PNETP, which has been characterized by its supporters as a grassroots, democratic human-rights initiative, became in reality a quasi-authoritarian process[9] that was implemented from the top down and sought popular legitimacy by appealing to the country's international responsibilities and honor. The need to combat the "trafficking of persons" was thus defined as a major problem for Brazil by the Brazilian Federal Government, in response to pressures from its European and North American allies and from the UN, long before there was any sort of national consensus as to what the trafficking of persons actually *was*. In the rush to implement policy to protect "the honor of Brazil," no workable legal definition of trafficking based on the Palermo Protocol was ever proposed and, in fact, none exists today. The absence of a wider debate as to what actually constitutes trafficking during the drafting of Brazil's National Policy has guaranteed that, for the foreseeable future, the effective legal definition of trafficking in our country will continue to be Article 231. This, in turn, ensures that repressive antitrafficking activities in Brazil continue to focus on preventing the migration of sex workers, without regard as to whether these people actually encounter situations "analogous to slavery." In other words, then, the rush to define Brazil's National Policy has created a situation in which antivice policing is considered to be—and reported as—"actions against trafficking in persons."

Narrative 2: Certain Demographics Are Vulnerable to Trafficking

The second narrative is particularly interesting because it names the parties concerned, namely, those who will be subject to increased surveillance and control under the new national policy "for their own good." The key word used most often in this narrative is *vulnerable*, and a large part of the fight against trafficking in Brazil can largely be summed up as a struggle to *identify vulnerabilities* and then create programs that discourage members of vulnerable groups from migrating.

In antitrafficking discourse in Brazil, vulnerability is summed up as a series of attributions, almost always presented in essentialist and reductionist forms. These include color and race (black or dark-skinned people being understood as more vulnerable than whites); class (poor people being more vulnerable than the rich); gender (women being more vulnerable than men); education (university students being less vulnerable than people who cannot read and write); age (children being more vulnerable than adults); and even the sociocultural position relative to the Brazilian metropolitan regions (people from the interior shanty towns and the suburbs being more vulnerable than those who live in urban areas and/or city centers). These *vulnerabilities* are almost never explored, explained, or even defined by antitrafficking agents; in most of the cases observed, they are simply cited, as if their epistemological and etymological contents were obvious. In this way, the explanatory power of *vulnerabilities* in the overall picture of human trafficking is highly subject to subjacent prejudices. Very often in antitrafficking discourse, presumably sociological descriptions of these supposedly *vulnerable* traits are promiscuously mixed and matched with exclusionary stereotypes.

We witnessed an excellent example of this during a June 2005 seminar at the headquarters of the State Council for Women's Rights (CEDIM) in Rio de Janeiro. On this occasion, an employee of the State Secretariat for Social Assistance and Human Rights described the victims of human trafficking in Rio de Janeiro as "highly vulnerable," being that they were "women of African descent living in the city's suburbs, economically excluded and with little formal education," under conditions that "make it difficult for them to travel abroad in safety." This speaker was immediately followed by a leader of the local antitrafficking division of the federal police, who stated that human trafficking had intensified since the end of the Brazilian military government because now, "having a passport has been legally defined as a citizen's right." He claimed that during the military dictatorship, passports were simply not issued to individuals understood to be "the type of people that should not travel overseas." According to this gentleman, "Often, you only have to take one look at the person to know that they will get into trouble if they leave Brazil, but we still have to issue a passport. This was not previously the case."

At this seminar, then, the politically correct terms describing vulnerabilities (i.e., African descent, economically disadvantaged, and uneducated) occupied the same semiotic and political space as their unspoken, socially excluding synonyms (black, poor, and stupid). Both sets of terms were united by the same political desire: to prohibit—or at least strongly discourage—individuals with certain characteristics from traveling abroad. As an employee of the Federal Ministry of Justice stated during the First National Seminar on Combating Human Trafficking in October 2007, "Nobody should leave Brazil until they are in a condition to do so with dignity."

Among the antitrafficking agents involved in the PNETP, the question of who should have the power to decide what "dignity" means and how this should be applied is almost never raised, let alone discussed. Agents' narratives, however, reveal a general belief that migration for sex work is "undignified" as is, indeed, any form of immigration involving the violation of the destination country's immigration laws. "Dignity" thus becomes a code word for styles of global mobility, which are typical of the middle class and—given long-standing structures of racially based economic and educational exclusion—typical of white or light brown Brazilians. Using one's credit card to purchase a ticket to Spain so that one may attend an academic conference is a "dignified" form of international movement. Borrowing money from a friend or employer to go to Spain to work illegally (i.e., without a visa) is "undignified." It is particularly undignified if such labor involves the sale of sexual services.

Narrative 3: Prostitution Is Inherently Degrading to Women

The third narrative situates prostitution as exceptionally dangerous, exploitive, illegal, and degrading labor that no informed, intelligent woman would ever choose over any other viable option. According to this view, sex work ipso facto must thus involve slavery. Clear examples of this position can be found in material published by the Sempreviva Feminist Organization (SOF), an NGO active in the trafficking debates, which defines any form of prostitution as synonymous with the trafficking of women, qualifies sex work as a "contemporary form of slavery," and affirms that prostitutes are routinely sold as slaves to prospective buyers (SOF 2003, 1). The Semprevivas' allegations, it should be noted, are sustained by no sources whatsoever, which is typical of instances where this narrative appears. However, what is relevant here is the argument that prostitution is essentially *coercive* (if not a form of slavery) and *illegal* (supposedly controlled by a *criminal mafia*; it should be noted here that prostitution is *not* illegal in Brazil, a fact often ignored by those who employ this narrative) and, most importantly, necessarily degrading to woman.

The best example we observed of this narrative occurred during the Seminar on Human Trafficking and Sexual Exploitation, held by the State Secretariat for Social Assistance and Human Rights in Rio de Janeiro at the Museum of Modern Art (MAM), on November 24, 2004. At this event, the then Rio de Janeiro State Secretary of Human Rights, Jorge da Silva, compared prostitution to drug dealing in terms of the threat it presented to the nation's youth. It should be noted in this context that while prostitution is not illegal in Brazil, drug dealing is. Comments such as those made by Secretary Da Silva to the effect that prostitution is the equivalent of drug dealing, thus raise disturbing questions about a state that, on the one hand, affirms its duty to serve society and support human rights and, on the other hand, is served by public employees who, counter to the laws of the land, understand prostitutes as criminals engaging in the destruction of society and the violation of human rights.

The roots of the "prostitution-as-degradation" narrative can be found in the Brazilian conservative social tradition described by anthropologist Roberto DaMatta, which situates the *house* and the *street* as two distinct moral regions defined by their own ethics and inhabited by different types of human beings (DaMatta 1997, 44–48). In this traditional logic, Brazilians are known *persons* at home, protected from the harsh realities of life by the depth of their social network and their specific position within it. In the streets, however, they are anonymous *individuals* at the mercy of a brutal system that is completely indifferent to their human needs. According to DaMatta, to be "individualized" in this way, in a semitraditional society such as Brazil, is not to be treated as a full-fledged citizen but to lose all respect and consideration. In this view, a prostitute is a degraded female individual. Lacking redeeming family ties, she falls away from the home and, as a consequence, becomes a streetwalker and a public woman. As such, she loses her rights to respect and consideration.

In the Brazilian antitrafficking debate, a certain variety of conservative feminism expresses views about prostitutes that align with this more conservative and traditional approach. These feminist activists see the redemption of the prostitute through increased professionalization and social inclusion (outside the sex trade, of course), while their conservative allies see family, marriage, and children as ways to retain potential prostitutes within the bounds of socially positive femininity. Both positions are supported by an a priori moral condemnation of prostitution as essentially degrading and socially detrimental. If the conservatives understand the prostitute as a *vagabunda* who needs to be repudiated or controlled, abolitionist feminists see her as "uma *fodida*" (in the words of DaMatta) who needs to be saved.[10] Both viewpoints deny the individual prostitute the consideration and respect extended to a "normal" person and situate her as "the kind of person who *has* to rigidly follow all the laws" (DaMatta 1997), an indistinct individual and, therefore, a proper subject for universalized (and universalizing) programs.

This narrative thus normalizes the absence of sex workers and their allies from the PNETP process. Either these individuals are "fallen women" and dangerous criminals or they are so brutalized by their circumstances that they have lost all potential for positive political agency. Both views situate prostitutes as passive targets of antitrafficking programs and not as architects of these programs or as allies engaged in their implementation. The most important contribution of this narrative, however, is that it naturalizes the idea that Article 231 of the Penal Code is, in fact, a necessary and perhaps even sufficient law for the repression of trafficking in Brazil.

Narrative 4: Family Girls vs. Street Women

The final narrative further reifies the division between "family" and "street" women that was postulated in the preceding narrative. It relates the story of a Brazilian "family girl"[11] who is confused with "a common prostitute" when crossing an international border. To better understand this narrative, we must first look at what has traditionally constituted the concept of female honor in Brazil.

Many authors have analyzed this system of beliefs and its intersections with categories of race, color, and class, as well as the transformations and continuities it has passed through with the advent of modernity (for further discussion of this, see Bassanezi 1997; Besse 1996; Caulfield 2000a; 2000b; Esteves 1989; Fonseca 1997; Graham 1989; Pedro 1994; Pereira 2006; Soihet 1997). Almost all of these authors emphasize that Brazilian culture has reproduced, over time, an ideology that divides women into two groups, following the double standard of *home* and *street* as outlined by DaMatta (1997). On the one hand, there is the *honest* or *family girl*, whose purity is essentially measured by her sexual behavior: virginity in the case of young women and chastity and loyalty in the case of older women (Fonseca, 1997, 528). On the other hand, there are *dishonest* or *street women*, who are seen as corrupted or suspect and whose classification, once again, is based on their promiscuous sexual behavior, unfaithfulness, and/or mercenary attitudes towards sexual relations.

Certainly, relatively few Brazilians today expect that a woman should maintain her virginity until she marries or that she should passively accept masculine infidelities in the name of preserving the sacred institution of marriage. However, many Brazilians still believe in the existence of *honest* and *dishonest* women and still think of this classification in terms of women's sexual behavior. What a *family girl* is, exactly, today is widely debated, but one thing remains certain: she is definitely not a *prostitute*. In fact, in a country where the expected behavior of an *honest woman* is subject to multiple and conflicting definitions, *prostitute* still serves as a unifying ideological point by providing an example of the ultimate female dishonesty.

It is from this viewpoint that we should understand the stories told by antitrafficking agents, in which "family girls" are confused with prostitutes when going through customs in a foreign country. These stories abound in the social spaces surrounding antitrafficking events. A typical example of this narrative can be found in the words of a thirty-year-old sociologist, an employee of an antitrafficking NGO: "I am tired of having to prove to European officials that I am not a prostitute. It happens every time I go to France or Spain: I always experience the shame of being wrongly identified as a prostitute. On one of my last trips [in 2006], I was detained by customs officials for almost an hour while the official asked me all kinds of questions! It was obvious he thought that I was going to Europe to work as a whore. All Brazilian women are alike for these men. We really have to do something to reduce the number of Brazilian prostitutes in Europe, as this is turning into a national embarrassment."

The outrage of the woman who told this story resides in the concern about European men's perception that "all Brazilian women are alike [i.e., prostitutes]" and that this perception was applied to her, an *honest woman*. A personal embarrassment is thus transformed into a national one, and the proposed remedy is not to correct European prejudices but to reduce the number of *dishonest* Brazilian women who are supposedly infesting Europe.

Being identified as a prostitute can be an unpleasant experience, given existing prejudices regarding sex work. However, describing this experience as *embarrassing* necessarily implies internalization of the idea that prostitution should, in fact, be stigmatized. Many of the women involved with the antitrafficking movement object to the constant association of Brazilians with sex in the global media, claiming that this objectifies and degrades women. However, as the late Gabriela Leite of the Brazilian Prostitutes' Network observed after a national seminar regarding the PNETP in 2007, "Up to now, nobody has managed to explain to me why the association between Brazilian women and sex is necessarily so awful."

Everyone is saying that the international reputation of Brazilian women as sexy is horrible. Horrible? Internationally, Brazilian women are considered to be beautiful, sexy, good in bed and free of hang-ups. Since when has this been considered such a horrible thing? [. . .] But there it is: these adjectives are only considered problematic when they are associated with prostitution. The "embarrassment" about which these women talk has nothing to do with the identification of Brazilian women and sex. No anti-trafficking militant would ever suggest, for example, that Adriana Galisteu, Luciana Jimenez, or Xuxa[12] should be taken off air in the name of combating "the blight on our national honor." The problem only arises when this stereotype is linked to prostitution. But once this has been admitted, then we'd have to accept that there are really not that many rational reasons to hate prostitution, nor is it all that different from things we daily see in so-called "normal" relationships. We, as Brazilian women, would have to take a good, long look at our own sexual activities and values. It is thus easier and more comfortable to pretend that we do not like Brazilian women being portrayed as sex objects. Right. We women spend a fortune on beauty products, plastic surgery, skintight clothes, breast implants, Botox and God knows what else; we dance and sway like crazy during Carnival, we do the bottle dance and the Creu,[13] but what we Brazilian women are *really* concerned about is our association with sex in the eyes of the world. (Interview with author, December 13, 2007)

The "sexual objectification of the Brazilian woman," then, doesn't seem to be a personal problem for many—if not most—Brazilian women, as long as it does not come attached to the stigma of prostitution. According to Leite, the logical way to react to this situation would be to destigmatize sex work. However, because many Brazilian women maintain (consciously or not) traditional distinctions between "good girls" and "bad women," many of these women end up directing their anger regarding the stigma attached to female promiscuity toward women perceived as prostitutes. The prejudices of foreign immigration officials that Brazilian "family girls" often encounter when they cross an international border thus inspire anger among these women toward migrant sex workers who are seen as having destroyed their reputation in Europe. Unfortunately, these same

Brazilians rarely ask why immigration officials should judge women based on their "reputation" in the first place. One effect of this narrative is thus to naturalize steps taken by the PNETP to reduce the number of Brazilian women overseas who are perceived as sex workers (again, often according to racialized class stereotypes). Alternative antitrafficking tactics—such as empowering Brazilian sex workers to see themselves as citizens and enjoining Brazilian consulates and embassies to treat them as such whenever these women encounter difficulties overseas—are not contemplated.

Do Bad Girls Go Everywhere . . .?

In the Daspú clothing line, produced by and for prostitutes and managed by the late Gabriela Leite, there is a T-shirt with the phrase "Good girls go to Heaven: bad girls go everywhere." It is precisely this affirmation that appears to frighten many members of the Brazilian antitrafficking movement. Although the movement's rhetoric demonstrates a superficial concern with human rights, the practices of repression formulated by the Brazilian state—supposedly guided by the Palermo Protocol, but generally following the legal mandate defined by Articles 231 and 231a of the Penal Code—continue to situate prostitution as a necessary and sufficient characteristic of *human trafficking*. Antivice activities are thus routinely cast as integral parts of the PNETP while other forms of state intervention—such as the repression of slave labor in Brazil's agricultural sector, a notorious and long-standing problem—are rarely counted as part of antitrafficking policy.

As researcher Marina Pereira Pires de Oliveira has shown in her analysis of how justice is administered in cases involving the violation of Article 231, on a concrete and daily level, the antitrafficking repression conducted by the country's various police forces still seems to be driven by a concern with limiting the movement of prostitutes and not by the desire to eliminate recruitment for practices that are similar to slavery. In fact, in the cases studied by Oliveira, such things as the use of violence, the abuse of a situation of vulnerability, or exploitation analogous to slavery—all necessary and defining elements of trafficking, according to the Palermo Protocol—rarely appear (Oliveira 2008, 138). As the late Gabriela Leite observed at the end of the First National Seminar on Combating Human Trafficking, "A lot has been said here about fighting trafficking, but . . . what is actually going to happen is that prostitutes will be locked up and labeled as trafficking victims. And this [happens] in a country where prostitution is not illegal."

Leite's point was illustrated to us once again in August 2011 when our local cadre of antitrafficking agents was convened in Rio de Janeiro for yet another congressional fact-finding mission regarding human trafficking. On this occasion, the federal police agent responsible for directing antitrafficking activities in the state[14] openly admitted that his organization could only understand "trafficking" as the aided movement of prostitutes because this, after all, was how Brazilian Law defined the crime, according to Article 231 of the Penal Code. He then admitted that his unit was largely acting in a "preventive" fashion—actually catching traffickers was extremely difficult due to the fact that witnesses to the alleged crimes rarely wished to cooperate with the police. Finally, he gave us a detailed example of what such "preventive measures" entailed.

Earlier in the year, the federal police in Rio had received an anonymous denunciation, via the Federal Anti-Trafficking Hotline (publicized on all the government's antitrafficking posters), that a group of thirteen women was embarking for Turkey in order to work as "dancers." These women were thus stopped at the Rio de Janeiro International Airport and directed into a secluded room without the benefit of legal counsel. There federal police agents told the women that they "were leaving Brazil to engage in an illegal activity" and that the police "strongly advised" them to desist in their travel plans. The women were then held in the room until their plane had taken off. This procedure was later revealed in a subsequent congressional report as standard practice for Brazil's federal police in cases where suspected prostitutes were found to be attempting to migrate overseas (Senado Federal 2012).

In other words, according to the Brazilian Federal Police, the most effective current strategy for policing trafficking involves using anonymous denunciations to identify migratory sex workers and prevent them from leaving the country. This identification is carried out by the members of Brazilian society in general, who are increasingly informed, via official trafficking education campaigns, that "trafficking victims" have a class (working or poor), gender (female), color (black or brown), and profession (prostitute). In strictly legal terms, this strategy involves the attribution of victimization before a crime has even taken place and the curtailment of the right of the "victims" to free movement, which is guaranteed to all citizens by the Brazilian Constitution, in the name of preventing a hypothetical future crime overseas. In other words, unable to crack down on the so-called criminals who are supposedly instigating women to migrate for sex work, the federal police has decided that the best thing to do is to crack down on the women themselves "for their own good."

Many of the political agents involved in the construction of Brazil's antitrafficking policy are social scientists, social workers, feminists, socialists, religious activists, and antiracists—whatever their official attributions. One would thus expect a certain sensitivity among these individuals to the contradictions displayed by the strategy that has been outlined. However, almost no discussion has yet been held about these contradictions and presumptions at the government-subsidized conferences and seminars where antitrafficking policy is discussed and formulated. The narratives we have analyzed allow us to perceive that this is due, at least in part, to the fact that many of the antitrafficking movement's political agents are guided by conservative and traditional values, which give emotional reinforcement to their assertions in favor of human rights. These values perpetuate, in a liberal and humanist language, the old notion that "two Brazils"[15] exist and that only one should receive all the consideration and respect that its position deserves; the other must be managed by universal and inflexible laws for its own good.

Notes

1. "So-called" because we agree with Kamala Kempadoo that it is important to distinguish between work regimes that presume the legal ownership of workers (or slaves) and those based on servitude for debt, *indentureship*, and forced work for contracted salaries (even if unjust) that are nominally based on free work principles and market exchange value (Kempadoo 2005, 63, note 14).

2. There is not enough space in the present article to discuss *how* and *why* these narratives have become hegemonic. Blanchette and da Silva (2012) and Blanchette, Bento, and da Silva (2013) go into further depth regarding these points.

3. According to Dr. Mohamed Y. Mattar, the first antitrafficking case in the United States involved six Russians employed in a striptease joint in the state of Alaska. Although only two of the women were under the age of legal consent, all were considered to be "trafficked" according to the stipulations of the Palermo Protocol as far as the "sexual exploitation of another" is concerned. At the same time, during the World Cup of 2006, many German cities invested in providing for the safe sale of sexual services by foreigners (even when this involved brothels), clearly differentiating this type of commerce from trafficking activities (GAATW, 2011).

4. See, for example, our work on Copacabana (2005) or Piscitelli's work on the Northeast Brazil, Spain, and deported immigrants (2004; 2006; 2007; 2008).

5. The following experience of Davida, a sex workers' rights NGO, is just one example. On at least four occasions—at local and national conferences and by means of a mailed letter and the Internet—during the process of formulating the policies to combat human trafficking, representatives of Davida asked those heading the interministerial antitrafficking task force for a clear definition of the concept of "sexual exploitation." Not only was this request ignored, but Davida never received any acknowledgment that it had been received and contemplated.

6. It's important to note here that Brazilians generally do not classify by race according to hypodescendent rules, as is done in the United States, but contextually by color and appearance. A person with light brown skin might classify themselves as white, "morena/o" (brown), or black, depending on the circumstances.

7. More specifically, the First National Seminar on Combating Human Trafficking in Brasília on October 3 and 4, 2007, but also various local conferences, meetings, and seminars in Rio de Janeiro, organized by CEDIM, the State Secretariat for Human Rights, the NGO TRAMA, and the Federal Ministry of Justice Federal between 2004 and 2007.

8. As stated by an employee of the Ministry of Justice at the First National Seminar about the Combat of Human Trafficking.

9. By "quasi-authoritarian," we mean a process wherein self-proclaimed authorities in trafficking, generally representatives of the Justice Ministry (and other components of the interministerial group set up to create the PNETP), picked which social agents were to be integral parts of the debate. In doing so, the appearance of "democratic social inclusion" was maintained without actually creating a democratic process.

10. Literally "fucked."

11. "Moça de família," or literally "family maiden"(with virginity implied in the term "maiden").

12. Brazilian female television personalities who are renowned for their use of sexualized imagery in their presentations of self.

13. Notoriously sexual Brazilian popular dances.

14. Not the same man referenced in Narrative #2 but his successor to the same position, six years later.

15. The concept that "two Brazils" exist is founded on observations by Brazilian social scientists such as DaMatta and Gilberto Freyre. One "Brazil" is understood to be composed of generally white, generally middle-class persons who should be treated as individuals. The other is made up of mostly black and brown, mostly poor individuals who need to be managed as a mass.

References

Bassanezi, Carla. 1997. "Mulheres dos Anos Dourados." In *História das Mulheres no Brasil*, ed. Mary Del Piore, 607–39. São Paulo, Brazil: Contexto.

Besse, S. K. 1996. *Restructuring Patriarchy: The Modernization of Gender Inequality in Brazil, 1914–1940*. Chapel Hill: University of North Carolina Press.

Blanchette, Thaddeus, Andressa Bento, and Ana Paula da Silva. 2013. "The Myth of Maria and the Imagining of Sexual Trafficking in Brazil." *Dialectical Anthropology* 37, no. 2 (June): 195–227.

Blanchette, Thaddeus, and Ana Paula da Silva. 2005. "'Nossa Senhora da Help': Sexo, turismo e deslocamento transnacional em Copacabana." *Cadernos Pagú* 25: 249–80.

———. 2012. "On Bullshit and the Trafficking of Women: Moral Entrepreneurs and the Invention of Trafficking in Persons in Brazil." *Dialectical Anthropology* 36, no. 3: 107–25.

Bourdieu, Pierre. 1981. "La representation politique. Elements pour unethéorie du champ politique." *Actes de la Rechercheem Sciences Sociales* 36: 3–24.

Brazilian Penal Code (Código Penal Brasileiro). 2004. Articles 231 and 231a. http://www.planalto.gov.br/ccivil_03/decreto-lei/del2848compilado.htm.

Caulfield, Sueann. 2000a. *Em Defesa da Honra: Moralidade, modernidade e nação no Rio de Janeiro (1918–1940)*. Campinas, Brazil: Editora da UNICAMP.

———. 2000b. "Onascimento do Mangue: Naçãoe controle da prostituição no Rio de Janeiro." *Tempo* 9: 43–63.

DaMatta, Roberto. 1997. *A Casa e a Rua: Espaço, cidadania, mulher e morte no Brasil*. Rio de Janeiro, Brazil: Rocco.

Esteves, Martha de Abreu. 1989. *Meninas Perdidas: O cotidiano do amor no Rio de Janeiro da "Belle Epoque."* São Paulo: Paz e Terra.

Fonseca, Cláudia. 1997. "Ser mulher, mãe e pobre." In *História das Mulheres no Brasil*, ed. Mary Del Piore, 510–53. São Paulo, Brazil: Contexto.

Global Alliance against Trafficking in Women (GAATW). 2007. *Collateral Damage: The Impact of Anti-Trafficking Measures on Human Rights around the World*. Bangkok, Thailand: GAATW.

———. 2011. *What's the Cost of a Rumor? A Guide to Sorting Out the Myths and the Facts about Sporting Events and Trafficking*. Bangkok, Thailand: GAATW.

Graham, S. L. 1989. *House and Street: The Domestic World of Servants and Masters in 19th Century Rio de Janeiro*. Stanford: Stanford University Press.

Gramsci, Antonio. 1971. *Selections from the Prison Notebooks*. International Publishers.

Kempadoo, Kamala. 2005. "From Moral Panic to Global Justice: Changing Perspectives on Trafficking." In *Trafficking and Prostitution Reconsidered: New Perspectives on Migration, Sex Work and Human Rights*, ed. Kamala Kempadoo, Jyoti Sanghera, and Barbara Pattanaik, i–xxix. London: Paradigm.

Kushnir, Beatriz. 1996. *Baile de máscaras: Mulheresjudias e prostituição. As polacas e suasassociações de ajudamútua.* Rio de Janeiro, Brazil: Imago.

Malinowski, Bronislaw. 1961 [1922]. *Argonauts of the Western Pacific.* New York: Dutton.

Mattar, Mohamed Y. n.d. "A Regional Comparative Legal Analysis of Sex Trafficking and Sex Tourism." http://www.protectionproject.org/wp-content/uploads/2010/09/Regional-Comparative-Legal-Analysis.pdf.

Nederstigt, Frans, and Luciana C. R. Almeida. 2007. "Brazil." In *Collateral Damage: The Impact of Anti-Trafficking Measures on Human Rights around the World,* ed. Global Alliance Against Traffic in Women, 87–113. Bangkok, Thailand: Amarin Printing and Publishing.

Oliveira, Marina Pereira Pires de. 2008. "Sobre armadilhas e cascas de banana: Uma análise crítica da administração de Justiça em temas associados as Direitos Humanos." *Cadernos Pagú* 31: 125–49.

Organização Internacional de Trabalho (OIT). 2005. *Tráfico de Pessoaspara Fins de Exploração Sexual.* Brasília, Brazil: OIT.

Pedro, Joana Maria. 1994. *Mulheres Honestas e Mulheres Faladas: Uma questão de classe.* Florianópolis, Brazil: Editora da UFSC.

Piscitelli, Adriana. 2004. "Entre a praia de Iracema e a União Européia: Turismo sexual e a migraçãofeminina." In *Sexualidades e Saberes: Convenções e Fronteiras,* ed. Adrianna Piscitelli, Maria Filomena Gregori, and Sérgio Carrara, 283–318. Rio de Janeiro, Brazil: Garamond.

———. 2006. "Sujeição ou subversão? Migrantes brasileiras na indústria do sexo na Espanha." *Revista História e Perspectiva* 35: 17–32.

———. 2007. *Tráfico Internacional de Pessoas e Trafico de Migrantes entre os Deportados(as) não Admitidos(as) que Regressam ao Brasil via o Aeroporto Internacional de São Paulo.* Brasília, Brazil: Secretária Nacional de Justiça, Ministério da Justiça.

———. 2008. "Entre 'mafias' e 'ajuda': Visões de migrantes brasileiros." 26th Meeting of the Brazilian Anthropology Association (ABA), June 1–4, 2008, Porto Seguro, Brazil.

Presidência da República. 2006. *Política Nacional de Enfrentamento ao Tráfico de Pessoas.* Decreto nº 5.948 de 26/10/2006. Brasília, Brazil: Federal Government.

———. 2008. *Plano Nacional de Enfrentamento ao Tráfico de Pessoas.* Decreto nº 6.347 de 08/01/2008. Brasília, Brazil: Federal Government.

Schettini, Cristina. 2006. *Que tenhas teu corpo: Uma história social da prostituição no Rio de Janeiro das primeiras décadas republicanas.* Rio de Janeiro, Brazil: Arquivo Nacional.

Sempreviva Organização Feminista (SOF). 2003. "O Cruel Negócio da Prostituição." *Folha Feminista* 43: 2–3.

Senado Federal. 2012. *Relatório Final da Comissão de Juristas para a Elaboração de Anteprojeto de Código Penal, criada pelo Requerimento nº 756, de 2011.* Brasília, Brazil: Senado Federal, June 26.

Soihet, Rachel. 1997. "Poor Women and Violence in Urban Brazil." In *A History of Women in Brazil*, ed. Mary Del Piore, 362–400. São Paulo, Brazil: Contexto.

United Nations Office on Drugs and Crime (UNODC). 2001. *Protocol to Prevent, Suppress and Punish Trafficking in Persons, Especially Women and Children, Supplementing the United Nations Convention against Transnational Organized Crime (Palermo Protocol)*. New York: United Nations.

———. 2006. *Trafficking in Persons: Global Patterns*. New York: UNODC.

U.S. Department of State. 2005. *Trafficking in Persons Report: June 2005*. Washington, D.C.: U.S. Department of State.

CHAPTER 7

Raids, Rescues, and Resistance

Women's Rights and Thailand's Response to Human Trafficking

Edith Kinney

Raids, Rescues, and Rights

Streams of men came and went throughout the night. Former police investigators and legal professionals from the International Justice Mission (IJM), a faith-based American nongovernmental organization (NGO), surveilled the brothel, looking for evidence of sex trafficking.[1] IJM hired a local man to go undercover, posing as a customer to gain access to the brothel's interior.[2] He counted the condoms in the trash, mapped the facility, and made recordings of women working in the brothel without their knowledge or consent. IJM reported their findings to a local antitrafficking task force, including evidence suggesting that some women in the brothel were trafficked migrants and others were minors. The task force was a "multidisciplinary" effort that included social workers, legal advocates, activists from a local antitrafficking NGO, and police, who agreed to raid the brothel with IJM's help.

Late one night, the raid team approached the brothel. A zealous American operative kicked down the door "John Wayne–style."[3] Agents swarmed the property with sirens blaring and guns drawn. Police rounded up all the women they encountered, handcuffing "rescued victims" and allowing journalists to photograph the women without protecting their identities. Unable to communicate with many of the terrified Burmese and Shan women, the panicked rescue team called local NGOs for translation assistance. Officials attempted to separate minors from adults. They also distinguished Thai women from undocumented Burmese and ethnic minorities. By doing so, the rescuers hoped to identify which women were "willing victims" (voluntary sex workers) and which were "unwilling victims" of trafficking who might be persuaded to cooperate with investigators.[4]

The "rescued" women thought they were being arrested for prostitution and immigration offenses. Social welfare officials detained the women against their will in a locked shelter facility "for their own protection." Some women escaped by stringing sheets out the window, running away from their rescuers. The detained women were "subjected to continual interrogation and coercion" by investigators who warned that "refusing to be witnesses against their traffickers would further delay their release" (EMPOWER 2003). But many "rescued" women had voluntarily migrated to Thailand intending to work in the sex trade. Although some women had been exploited during their journeys, they did not self-identify as trafficking victims and had little incentive to assist investigators.

Many women were reluctant to cooperate with police based on prior experiences of corruption, harassment, or rape. Others refused to provide information for fear of being exposed as sex workers. Some migrant women worried they would be charged as traffickers because they had helped others migrate to Thailand to work in the sex industry. Ultimately, the undocumented adult women were deported. The underage girls languished in government rehabilitation shelters for over a year until they were finally repatriated. Both groups returned to the grim circumstances of poverty, violence, and oppression they had attempted to escape in the first place. Many intended to return to Thailand and resume sex work as soon as possible, albeit with increased debt, which put them at greater risk of exploitation and trafficking. With few "rescued" women willing to testify, the prosecutor could not build a strong case against the alleged trafficker. The raid did not deter the brothel owner, who soon had his business running again with more migrant women.[5] And so it continued: one woman is "rescued" and another takes her place.

The ineffective brothel raid that was described exemplifies the problematic relationship between crime-control and rights-based approaches to human trafficking and exploitation in the sex industry. Like many other fronts in the global "war on trafficking," the rescue paradigm that has animated antitrafficking campaigns in Thailand reflects a tension between competing interests: law enforcement, which is focused on policing crime and borders, and human rights advocates, who emphasize the need to protect individuals from exploitation and discrimination. But even well-intentioned antitrafficking interventions have wrought significant "collateral damage"—much of it borne by the very groups most vulnerable to trafficking and exploitation (GAATW 2007).

Over the past three decades, Thailand's sex industry has been targeted in domestic government crackdowns and advocacy campaigns by anti-prostitution, sex workers' rights, public health, and international faith-based organizations attempting to address trafficking and commercial sexual exploitation. The Thai women's movement in the 1980s was stimulated by advocates and academics, many of whom focused on the exploitation of Thai women in the sex trade. While some activists sought to abolish prostitution because they saw it as an expression of patriarchy and women's subordination, others aimed to address exploitation by improving working conditions in the sex trade and legitimating sex work as work. Activists of all stripes engaged the discourse of human rights, to both identify harms and develop "rights-based" approaches to trafficking and commercial sexual exploitation. Such approaches emphasize legal protection for exploited persons, nondiscriminatory treatment, access to just legal institutions, adequate health and social services, and safe repatriation or immigration relief. These reform efforts expanded in the 1990s, and campaigns to raise awareness about trafficking by Thai and international advocacy networks converged with politicians' concerns about exploding rates of global migration and new forms of transnational organized crime, sharpening the domestic and international focus on sex trafficking in Thailand.

Increased attention to (and funding for) countertrafficking measures—shaped in large part by the global reach of U.S. antitrafficking policies—created a political opportunity structure with open windows for action and advocacy. What my research shows, however, is that these windows were not just openings but also constraints on the changes that movement actors were able to secure. The windows of opportunity were set in a structure historically characterized by state-led antitrafficking campaigns that emphasized border control, "crackdowns" on prostitution, and the prosecution of traffickers. The question for activists seizing the opportunity for pragmatic reform is whether they can advance rights-based, gender-conscious efforts within such institutional confines.

This chapter examines the progress, problems, and collateral damage of Thailand's "war on human trafficking." It analyzes how legal and policy reforms initially championed by women's rights organizations (to protect and assist trafficked victims) were implemented by the criminal justice and social welfare officials charged with executing antitrafficking interventions. The chapter draws on field research in Thailand from 2004 to 2005 and 2007, including visits to official rehabilitation centers and NGO shelters, as well as interviews with antitrafficking task force members, criminal justice officials, social workers, NGO activists, policymakers, and United Nations (UN) personnel. I explore how advocates mobilized rights discourses in domestic and international campaigns for the reform of laws and enforcement practices regarding trafficking and commercial sexual exploitation. I also examine how the implementation of rights-based antitrafficking reforms by state institutions geared to suppress crime and prostitution diluted much of the transformative potential of those reforms. The following analysis explores some of the unintended consequences of antitrafficking campaigns in Thailand, revealing how efforts to end "modern day slavery" enacted within a crime-control framework can paradoxically operate to undermine the rights and security of the very groups such interventions aim to empower and protect.

Sex, Suffering, and Saviors: The Historical Construction of (Sex) Trafficking in Thailand

Human trafficking is a global phenomenon. The crime of trafficking involves the recruitment or movement of persons within or across borders, by means such as fraud or coercion, for the purpose of exploitation.[6] The International Labour Organization (ILO) estimates that nearly twenty-one million people—more than half of whom reside in the Asia-Pacific region—are victims of forced labor, including those who are trafficked and trapped in slavery-like conditions of labor exploitation, domestic servitude, forced begging, or commercial sexual exploitation (ILO 2012). But although the causes and effects of trafficking are diverse, Thailand's antitrafficking campaigns historically adopted a myopic focus on combating "sex trafficking" by "rescuing" women from the commercial sex industry.[7] As such, the tactics used to police prostitution have informed the tactics employed to police trafficking.

The modern eroticization of Thailand as a "sexual paradise" and the "brothel of Asia" in many Westerners' minds is somewhat anachronistic. The country had regulated and taxed brothels under the Contagious Disease Act of 1908, but prostitution was criminalized in 1960 during a moral cleansing and social order campaign. The 1960 Prostitution Suppression Act prohibited selling sex and procuring and profiting from prostitution. The main thrust of the law, however, was the reform of sex workers. Women convicted of prostitution—even those forced into the sex trade— were fined and sent by court order to serve a year in "rehabilitation centers" for "socially handicapped women." Attempts to escape state shelters were penalized by fines and additional periods of imprisonment. Women engaged in sex work were deemed deviants in need of discipline, behavioral modification, and moral rehabilitation.

Despite the criminalization of prostitution, however, a highly visible, diversified, and profitable sex trade flourished throughout Thailand under the guise of "entertainment places." The 1966 Entertainment Place Act allows establishments such as karaoke clubs, massage parlors, and go-go bars to register venues and employees with the police. Women employed as "service employees" in entertainment venues may also sell sexual services indirectly or go off-site with clients. Still, prostitution remains illegal, and entertainment workers are excluded from the protection of Thai labor laws and migrant-worker registration programs (Pollack 2007; Puckmai 2010). This legal ambiguity facilitates highly discretionary and selective enforcement of Thailand's antiprostitution and antitrafficking laws, creating opportunities for police corruption and abuse of sex workers.

Although many sex establishments in Thailand cater to local clientele, the "prostitution problem" in Thailand is internationally notorious in significant part because of its association with Vietnam War–era prostitution around American military bases and "Rest and Relaxation" centers, government-promoted sex tourism, and the HIV/AIDS epidemic in the 1980s and 1990s (Boonchalaski and Guest 1994). These international connections—as well as deliberate awareness-raising efforts by women's rights advocates—have contributed to the notoriety of Thailand in sex trafficking discourses. The plight of the trafficked and sexually exploited Thai prostitute galvanized domestic and international women's rights organizing, becoming a focal point of transnational advocacy networks of feminists from both antiprostitution and sex workers' rights movements in the 1980s.[8]

Among these groups, some cast sex workers as individuals subject to the same socioeconomic forces that affected the rest of the region—and who deserved to have their human rights respected regardless of their trade. Moving away from earlier charity- or behavior modification–oriented approaches to prostitution-as-deviance, some middle-class women's advocates in Thailand formed NGOs in the mid-1980s in order to develop pragmatic strategies to promote the rights of women working in the sex industry and to decrease migrant women's vulnerability to exploitation (Tantiwiramanond and Pandey 1991). The EMPOWER Foundation (Education Means Protection of Women Engaged in Recreation), for example, provides sex workers with Thai and English lessons, nonformal education, HIV/AIDS prevention outreach, and rights-awareness programs. Championing the view that "sex work is work," EMPOWER lobbies all levels of government to extend labor protections and employment rights to entertainment industry workers to reduce exploitation.

Other activists formed organizations to assist female migrants. Thai activists and academics worked to raise awareness about the socioeconomic conditions and inequitable development policies that motivated migrant "peasant girls" to become "Bangkok masseuses," as well as the transnational "sexploitation" of Thai women in foreign sex and "mail-order bride" industries (Phongpaichit 1982; Skrobanek 1983; Skrobanek, Boonpakdi, and Janthakeero 1997). Siriporn Skrobanek formed the Foundation for Women (FFW) in 1987 to prepare women for safer migration and to support repatriated trafficking survivors. These advocates for women's rights and migrants' rights were also central to the 1994 formation of one of the largest and most influential migrant and sex workers' rights networks, the Global Alliance against Traffic in Women (GAATW). GAATW aims to "empower women rather than treat them as victims" by including those directly affected by trafficking in research and advocacy projects, and by promoting laws and policies respecting freedom of movement, choice of occupation, and safe working conditions.[9]

But research and activism by Thai women's rights organizations regarding the sexual exploitation of Thai women also provided ammunition for Western feminists opposed to prostitution and the globalizing sex industry (such as the Coalition against Trafficking in Women [CATW]). The icon of the trafficked, sexually exploited, "suffering third world prostitute" was invoked repeatedly in efforts to proclaim women's rights as human rights in the 1990s (Doezema 2001). The trafficked "sex slave" provocatively embodied intersecting forms of violence against women and exemplified diverse feminist critiques regarding the patriarchal roots of women's social, economic, and sexual subordination. Consequently, Thailand's "prostitution problem"—variously constructed as a consequence of women's low status, cultural norms regarding "dutiful daughters" and male sexual privilege, a legacy of American military presence, or uneven global and national development facilitating sex tourism—has contributed to the overrepresentation of Thailand in sex trafficking discourses.

A combination of domestic advocacy and international shaming campaigns provoked the Thai government to address trafficking, as well as forced and child prostitution, in the early 1990s. But although officials assisted Thai women trafficked *abroad* by working with foreign embassies and facilitating repatriation, the criminal justice response to trafficking and commercial sexual exploitation *within* Thailand resulted in the increased harassment, arrest, and abuse of migrant sex workers.[10] A 1993 Human Rights Watch report on Burmese women and girls trafficked into Thai brothels found "the main target of [Thailand's] highly publicized crackdown on forced and child prostitution has been the victims themselves," in a punitive campaign that "contrasts sharply with [Thai officials'] efforts on behalf of Thai women trafficked into Japan and subsequently arrested as illegal immigrants" (Human Rights Watch 1993).[11] While migrant sex workers were arrested and deported under the rubric of trafficking—a response fueled in part by fears about the spread of HIV—Thai officials attempted to "protect" Thai women from trafficking by curtailing their freedom of movement, requiring married women to obtain their husband's permission to travel outside the country and interviewing single women applying for passports to assess their motivations for migration.

Frustrated by these unintended consequences, in the mid-1990s Thai activists began to reassess the risks of appealing to politicians and criminal justice officials to address trafficking. Thai activists and elite allies turned their attention to reforming laws to target enforcement on forced and child prostitution and to minimize exploitation in the sex industry. Spurred by the work of the National Commission on Women's Affairs to combat the commercial sexual exploitation of children, many NGOs, including sex workers' rights organizations, pressed for a less punitive approach to prostitution that was attentive to the different needs of women and children. In 1996, Thailand repealed its punitive 1960 antiprostitution legislation and promulgated a new law, the Prevention and Suppression of Prostitution Act.[12] While sex work was not decriminalized, the law focused on combating child prostitution by penalizing customers and punishing parents involved in the "sale" of their children into the sex industry. Minors convicted of prostitution were, and still are, subject to compulsory rehabilitation. Sex work by adults generally is considered an offense against public morality and is only subject to a fine, although advertising and association for prostitution are subject to jail terms. The act retained provisions authorizing court officials to send those convicted for prostitution-related offenses to stints in vocational training where the offender "wishes to receive the protection and occupational development" in a rehabilitation center.

Despite these progressive reforms, police continued to raid brothels under the auspices of immigration laws, arresting and deporting migrant women for illegal entry (Pollack 2007, 187). Thailand replaced its rarely used 1928 antitrafficking law in 1997 to reform the processing of trafficking cases and the treatment of victims. The 1997 Measures in Prevention and Suppression of Trafficking in Women and Children Act prohibited the trafficking of women and children of both sexes, providing protections for women and children of other nationalities who are trafficked into the country.[13] Rather than jailing victims, they were placed in government shelters—but these were often the same institutions where sex workers were sent for "retraining" under the 1960 Act.

In addition to expanding the range of persons covered by its antitrafficking statutes, Thailand increased the range of actors involved in their implementation. The Ministry of Social Development and Human Security (MSDHS), which houses the Bureau of Anti-Trafficking in Women and Children, serves as the lead government agency responsible for coordinating antitrafficking activities and providing support to trafficked persons. However, the network of actors working to address trafficking and exploitation in Thailand is much broader than that single agency. Over the past decade, Thailand has developed "multidisciplinary" antitrafficking task forces at the national and provincial levels that include criminal justice officials, social service agencies, legal advocates, and NGOs. These teams aim to better identify potential cases of trafficking, plan interventions, and assist victims, promoting the successful prosecution of traffickers (Kinney 2006). Women's and children's rights NGOs contributed to the more effective processing of trafficking cases by providing shelter and rehabilitative services for victims (and potential witnesses). A series of domestic Memoranda of Understanding (MOU) between government organizations, police, and NGOs formalized these relationships, detailing special procedures to treat trafficked persons as victims rather than criminals by providing legal protection, shelter outside jails or immigration detention centers, and rehabilitative services.

Trafficking became a centerpiece of the national agenda in 2004 when Thailand's Prime Minister Thaksin Shinawatra declared "war on trafficking"—soon after the U.S. placed Thailand on a "Watchlist" in the 2004 Trafficking in Persons Report. Thaksin pledged to create a special task force dedicated to trafficking, reforming laws, rooting out corruption among enforcement agencies, and boosting prevention and protection efforts by establishing a $12.5 million fund to care for victims and support anti-trafficking projects. A new national action plan institutionalized collaborative partnerships between state agencies and domestic and international NGOs. Meanwhile, Thailand signed bilateral and multilateral agreements with neighboring countries to facilitate mutual legal assistance, victim repatriation, and cross-border coordination between antitrafficking stakeholders. A 2005 Cabinet resolution established antitrafficking operation centers at the provincial, national, and international levels, with MSDHS serving as the focal point for interagency coordination. Further, specialized law enforcement, investigation, and prosecution units were created in the Royal Thai Police, Ministry of Justice, and Office of the Attorney General to tackle trafficking. Yet despite the spate of new divisions, institutions, training programs, and countertrafficking agreements, reforms were slow to take root. For example, frontline actors and immigration officials continued to employ inadequate vetting procedures, resulting in the incarceration of trafficked persons in immigration centers. Law enforcement agents charged with identifying and rescuing victims of trafficking were simultaneously engaging in "crackdowns" on illegal immigration. Furthermore, Thailand's 1997 antitrafficking law did not prohibit forced or bonded labor, nor did it address the trafficking of men, thus disincentivizing the investigation of trafficking outside the sex sector.

Increased attention to the trafficking issue through the mid-2000s—and the significant funds allocated to combat it—have created new political opportunities for advocates. These include promoting rights-based reforms of antitrafficking law, policy, and practice and positioning themselves as necessary partners for the effective governance of trafficking. However, resistance to the incorporation of rights-respecting practices into the criminal justice response to trafficking—exacerbated in part by the persistence of the "victim" paradigm and the raid-rescue-repatriate response it entails—reveals how antitrafficking laws can function as a pretext for crackdowns on undocumented migrants. Paradoxically, such interventions can perpetuate abuse and exacerbate vulnerability to exploitation, particularly in the sex industry.

Sex Trafficking Interventions and the Violation of Trafficked Persons' and Voluntary Workers' Rights

Despite the efforts of a diverse group of actors, the activists and officials I interviewed in the mid-2000s revealed that reforms intended to protect the rights of trafficked persons were not fully institutionalized. Enforcement officials' prioritization of border-security and crime-control concerns over victims' needs presents a significant obstacle to implementation of rights-based responses to trafficking by undermining victims' freedom of movement and rights to legal assistance. Reports from activists in the field suggest that rather than improving the situation of those vulnerable to trafficking and exploitation, Thailand's "war on trafficking" has legitimized the police abuse of sex workers, increased marginalization of migrants, and subjected trafficked persons to involuntary detention and repatriation practices that raise the risk of retrafficking and exploitation (EMPOWER 2003; EMPOWER 2005; Jones 2003; Pollack 2007; Puckmai 2010; Skrobanek 2003; Thrupkaew 2009).

The following discussion analyzes field research that culminated in 2007 and illustrates how the cultural and institutional context of enforcement slowed reform and obstructed recognition of victims' rights in trafficking cases. Antitrafficking interventions in Thailand through the middle of the last decade often proceeded in three stages: rescue, rehabilitation, and repatriation. Each stage of implementation exposes the obstacles to rights-based, gender-conscious reform posed by working through institutions dedicated to crime control and permeated by a masculinized, militarized culture.

Repressive Rescues: The Sociolegal Context of Enforcement and the Infantilization of Female Migrants

As evidenced in the botched brothel raid described at the outset of this chapter, women "rescued" from commercial sex establishments often have difficulty differentiating antitrafficking interventions from periodic raids intended to crack down on prostitution and illegal immigration. Raid-and-rescue operations enacted in a crime-control context ultimately look more like arrest than liberation. As migrant sex workers from EMPOWER Thailand indicate in the art installation presented in Figure 7.1, women are taken into custody, their property is confiscated, and they are detained in government facilities with strict restrictions on communication and movement.

Figure 7.1. Sex workers from EMPOWER create art projects to raise awareness about the rights violations that migrant sex workers experience as effects of anti-trafficking raids and rescues: "We are locked up," "They force us to be witnesses," "We are forced re-training," "Our family must borrow money to survive while we wait," "Military abuses + no work continues at home," "We must find a way back to Thailand to start again." Photograph by the author.

Trafficking interventions by Thai law enforcement officials—most notably "raids and rescues" by police—foster mistrust and resentment among sex workers, especially given the prevalence of police complicity in the sex trade. Police officials of all ranks are known to patronize brothels, and several activists informed me that women detained in raids often recognize their "rescuers" as former clients.[14] Sex workers' rights advocates argue that antitrafficking policies empower police to raid businesses under the pretext of trafficking investigations, affording officers opportunities to demand bribes and extort money (GAATW 2009, 50). Another antitrafficking activist observes that the pressure to crack down on trafficking in combination with the continued criminalization of prostitution "provides a loophole for corrupt officials to abuse their [authority] and thus [helps] keep the sex industry flourish[ing]" (Skrobanek 2003). Indeed, as one NGO advocate explained, many raids are "just for show and media attention so the police can say they are 'doing something' about prostitution, since they usually tip off the owner for a bribe."[15]

Unfortunately, trafficking interventions relying on "rescues" rather than addressing exploitative work conditions may actually promote trafficking since rescued workers are quickly replaced, particularly in brothel prostitution. By treating all sex workers as victims rather than potential "anti-trafficking workers and human rights defenders" in their own right, brothel raids inadvertently remove voluntary workers who may have developed strategies that can assist trafficked persons, as well as those who want to leave an establishment or find that the work conditions were not what they expected (EMPOWER 2003). As one sex worker advocate explained to me, "[Women] are much better off in a brothel than [working alone as a domestic worker] in a house. In a brothel if you've been trafficked . . . you've got eight other women telling you when to run away, and where to run, how to run away and how to keep safe in the meantime . . . Women already have a whole lot of strategies they use with each other and for each other. And when those women get 'rescued,' there's no one in that brothel who's got those strategies anymore."[16]

Furthermore, the procedures police employ to identify trafficked persons often focus more on crime and immigration control rather than the rights of potential trafficking victims. Victim identification procedures reenact exclusionary and discriminatory policies. Thai police continue to identify trafficking victims based on their documentation status, applying different laws to different groups of women—Thai women arrested during raids are fined under prostitution laws, whereas migrant women without documents are detained as witnesses in trafficking prosecutions (GAATW 2009, 50–51). Although Thailand has a long history of internal trafficking—particularly of ethnic minorities lacking Thai citizenship—the focus on illicit border crossing by law enforcement leads officials to assume that foreign women are trafficked while local women are "willing victims." Such selective enforcement practices violate rights-based principles of nondiscriminatory application and interpretation of law, potentially denying trafficked or exploited persons the protections and services to which they are legally entitled while subjecting others to arbitrary arrest and detention.

Without effective planning for the needs of suspected victims, rescue operations can further harm the rights and dignity of trafficked persons. Exasperated informants from sex workers' and migrants' rights groups reported that police and rescue-based NGOs repeatedly failed to plan for and provide interpretive services for migrant women detained in raids.[17] Ethnic minority activists explained that they often received phone calls in the middle of the night requesting translators for groups of confused and frightened Ahka, Shan, and Lahu women imprisoned after raids.[18] One activist who had served as an "emergency translator" explained that interpreters are rarely screened or trained to explain legal terms, potentially biasing investigations and neglecting the rights of victims.[19] Failure to provide adequate interpretive services violates victims' rights to be given legal information and assistance in a language they can understand.

Instrumental Justice and Rehabilitative Interventions: Controlling Victims through Shelter Detention and "Retraining"

After "rescue" by antitrafficking enforcement officials, women are often held in custody for extended periods of time, detained either in immigration centers as illegal aliens awaiting deportation or in shelters as victims (and sometimes witnesses) in need of protection. In both cases, women's rights are often subordinated to law enforcement officials' interests in building effective prosecutions against criminal traffickers and exploiters. Even when women are held in one of the government's rehabilitation and occupational training centers run by MSDHS or in a private NGO shelter, their interests are often lost in efforts to inculcate elite and middle-class Thai notions of female sexual propriety.

In the early 1990s, Thai women's advocacy organizations, such as FFW, championed reforms to provide protection to women trafficked into Thailand by ensuring they were treated as victims and housed in shelters rather than imprisoned like criminals in jails or detention centers. However, many of the "rescued" women were detained indefinitely in closed shelters that prohibited detainees from leaving or receiving visitors, providing another example of the repressive consequences of well-intentioned interventions.[20] Involuntary detention of victims violates international legal principles protecting rights to liberty and security of person and freedom of movement.[21] Thailand's 1997 antitrafficking law provided that women suspected of being trafficked must not be detained for longer than ten days in an "appropriate place" that is not a detention cell or prison. Nevertheless, "rescued" victims were regularly confined for indefinite periods in NGO shelters, rehabilitation centers, or safe houses and forbidden from leaving the shelter grounds "beyond the occasional supervised excursion or trip to court" (Gallagher and Pearson 2010, 77). It is now widely recognized by policymakers as "bad practice" to confine victims of trafficking in prisons or immigration detention facilities, in part because successful prosecutions rely on victim cooperation (see, for example, U.S. Dept. of State 2008, 35).

In 2004, MSDHS operated ninety-seven shelters throughout the country for abused women and children, as well as six regional shelters for foreign victims of trafficking and a central shelter outside Bangkok to house up to five hundred foreign trafficking victims, minors caught in prostitution, and other "socially disadvantaged" women. In remote regions of the country where no government centers exist, victims are held in private NGO shelters.[22] The majority of trafficked persons placed in shelter detention are women and girls in "closed shelters" that use restrictive practices to monitor detainees and prevent escape. Closed shelters, such as the one in Figure 7.2, are not subject to external evaluation, and there are no mechanisms by which detained women and children can challenge their detention (Gallagher and Pearson 2010, 78).

Authorities defend detention as necessary to protect women from pimps, traffickers, and often from the women themselves. One shelter operator in Northern Thailand explained that surveillance and detention of trafficking victims was important to prevent "flights of freedom," estimating that over half of the escaped "victims" immediately returned to work in the sex trade—often at the same brothel from which they were rescued.[23] Another social welfare official explained that isolating adult women in a government facility—even self-identified voluntary sex workers—was vital to their safety and "to help the women understand that they are victims."[24] Such efforts to disabuse women of their "false consciousness" regarding sex work infantilize women and fail to respect their rights to privacy and self-determination.

Law enforcement officials also explained that detention in closed shelters was necessary to ensure victims would be available to testify against traffickers.[25] However, legal advocates for victims reported that lengthy shelter confinement due to repeated court delays frustrated trafficking victims' desire to pursue formal "justice" by cooperating with prosecutors.[26] In my own observations of government and private NGO shelters in Thailand from 2004 to 2005, shelter workers estimated that trafficked women were detained for "support and protection" from two months to four years.[27] Ethnic minorities who lacked citizenship or identity papers suffered especially lengthy detentions, waiting until Thai social workers were able to convince foreign officials to accept them back into their native countries.

Figure 7.2. A "closed" government shelter. Barred windows "protect" victims of trafficking by inhibiting escape. Photograph by the author.

One shelter worker explained her efforts to convince victims that detention was in their best interest, despite the wait: "The girls get increasingly discouraged waiting for something to happen in their case. After about one month, they complain, 'It's boring here—I want to leave the shelter or go home.' We tell them they have to wait for the case and they can't leave, because they wouldn't be safe and the trafficker could find them and make them go back to the brothel."[28]

Migrants' rights advocates informed me that many exploited migrants realize that engaging in the legal process will delay their return to work, threatening the security of families who rely on remittances to survive.[29] The invasive and exhausting legal process required to develop a criminal trafficking case encourages many trafficked persons lacking legal status to conceal experiences of exploitation in order to be classified as illegal migrants and deported, thereby hastening their opportunity for remigration. This undermines efforts to convict traffickers and inhibits access to justice for victims.

When not held as witnesses for the prosecution, many rescued women languished in shelters for other reasons. Women in shelter detention are subjected to rehabilitation programs that aim to steer them away from the sex trade and into alternative labor sectors. Although voluntary adult sex workers are no longer subject to compulsory rehabilitation under Thai antiprostitution laws, those deemed to be trafficking victims are sent to the very institutions that subjected prostitutes to punitive moral reeducation programs in the 1960s. Sex worker advocates explained, "All the girls get scared when they hear about 'Baan Kredtrakarn,'" the main government shelter, "because they don't want to go through 'rehabilitation training'— there is no end to that sentence."[30] Some private NGO shelter operators leveraged this fear to control victims and reduce escape attempts.

I visited Baan Kredtrakarn in 2005. The facility is on an island, accessible only by a ferry sent from the shelter. Residents are required to take classes about sewing, cooking, or beauty services to discourage them from returning to "immoral" but relatively lucrative work in the sex industry. Other residents, particularly migrant and ethnic minority women and children, are assigned to programs making "traditional ethnic handicrafts" that are popular with foreign tourists. The social workers I met explained that occupational training programs aim to prevent trafficking by teaching women work skills they can employ "back home," simultaneously reasserting sexual propriety and preventing women's migration in the first place.[31]

Shelter detention and rehabilitation programs extend the power of the carceral state.[32] Despite the good intentions of social workers and shelter advocates, "rescued" women are confined in facilities that demonstrate little respect for trafficked women or voluntary sex workers as autonomous, rights-bearing subjects. Instead, such values are displaced by traditional concerns regarding crime control, prostitution suppression, and the policing of sexual impropriety.

Repatriation and Retrafficking: Policing National Security and Ignoring Risks to Victims

The tension between victims' rights and security-oriented priorities in Thailand's antitrafficking campaign is most evident in the repatriation process. Like the remand of women into shelter detention, repatriation of foreign women trafficked into Thailand in the mid-2000s was enacted in ways that do not protect women's rights.

Women's rights advocates seek safe repatriation of trafficked persons, as victims often lack the funds or travel documents to return to their home country. However, repatriation often returns "victims" to the same circumstances of poverty, violence, and insecurity that they left voluntarily and leads to a cycle of remigration. One social worker, clearly bothered by the persistent remigration of a teenaged Cambodian girl who had already been sent to Baan Kredtrakarn four times, stated that the girl defiantly informed her that "she intended to return to the same brothel just as soon as she was sent back to Cambodia—there is nothing for her there—no job, no real family—so she just keeps coming back, no matter how many times I tell her it is wrong to sell her body. She says she would rather do that than make baskets here all day, despite the risk of [contracting] HIV."[33]

Many adult migrants deemed trafficking victims do not want to be repatriated (particularly those from Myanmar) and intend to remigrate immediately upon their return. A women's advocate who facilitated the repatriation of Lao women "rescued" from a Thai brothel explained that she helped reduce both trafficking and "illegal immigration" by "blindfolding victims so they don't learn the roads and try to come back into Thailand."[34] By inhibiting informed, independent, and legal migration, such interventions drive would-be migrants into illicit channels that can put them at risk for trafficking. Even official repatriation processes can violate victims' rights to confidentiality, privacy, and security. Social welfare officials and NGO advocates who attempt family tracing to ensure victims' safe repatriation can inadvertently expose women as sex workers (and failed migrants), thereby creating barriers to community reintegration upon their return.

Repatriation can also place victims at increased risk of abuse by officials in their country of origin. Activists reported that shortly after the 2004 U.S. *Trafficking in Persons Report* lowered Thailand's ranking on efforts to combat trafficking (U.S. Dept. of State 2004), Prime Minister Thaksin "oversaw the deportation of 20 'sex trafficking victims' from Burma, who were handed over to the military—*unarmed* women handed over to the *armed* Burmese military at the border. And it was to show, 'yes we will comply with U.S. [antiprostitution and antitrafficking] policies.'"[35] Given that Burmese officials are implicated in forced labor and trafficking schemes, repatriating women—particularly ethnic minorities—back to Myanmar appears to violate the principle of *non-refoulement*, which prohibits the expulsion of persons who have the right to be recognized as refugees back into situations where they are at risk of persecution. In this context, rather than realizing the right of trafficked victims to return home safely or seek asylum in Thailand, repatriation simply becomes "deportation with a smile."

Conclusion

Many advocacy organizations in Thailand promote reforms designed to ensure trafficked persons will be treated as victims rather than criminals. Activists have achieved significant success in raising awareness about trafficking and pressuring the state for legal reforms that provide shelter and rehabilitation for victims. They have also secured substantial operational reforms and MOUs that institutionalize collaboration between NGOs and state agencies addressing cases of trafficking and exploitation. For the government, these campaigns to combat trafficking and "sexual slavery" demonstrate to the international community Thailand's commitment to women's rights, and human rights in general.

But new laws against trafficking not only protect exploited migrants recognized as trafficking victims. Antitrafficking campaigns also legitimate the crime-control agendas that have long dominated the institutions charged with implementing these campaigns. As a result, those campaigns actually may not advance the rights of sex workers or migrants vulnerable to exploitation. Repressive rescues, enforced shelter detention and rehabilitation, and poorly conceived repatriation practices can have the perverse effect of increasing survivors' risk of being retrafficked. Such unintended consequences demonstrate that even well-intentioned reforms can lose their liberatory character when implemented through traditional criminal justice institutions.

Although Thailand's 2006 military coup d'état temporarily impeded reform efforts, NGOs, the UN, and other international sources, including the U.S. Department of State's annual *Trafficking in Persons Report* rankings, maintained pressure on the ever-evolving Thai government to continue its efforts to combat trafficking. In 2007, after my fieldwork concluded, Thai authorities developed a new MOU with state and international agencies. This MOU included guidelines instructing officials to protect all trafficking victims regardless of gender or nationality. This advancement also led to Thailand's new Anti-Trafficking in Persons Act, which came into force in June 2008.

The 2008 Act addressed some of the critiques activists previously shared with me regarding inadequate or inhumane antitrafficking interventions. It also sought to remedy some of the problematic institutional responses to exploitation that I witnessed. The 2008 Act is more inclusive than the 1997 Act, criminalizing a broad range of exploitative situations beyond sex trafficking and protecting trafficked men in addition to women and children.[36] This comprehensive definition of "trafficking" protects the rights of workers in all sectors and encourages officials to investigate exploitation outside the sex industry. Expanding the definition of victims to include trafficked men helps to counter the gendered assumption that women are trafficked whereas men are smuggled, which simultaneously infantilizes women and minimizes human rights violations against men. The 2008 Act calls for specialized law enforcement units to deal with the gender issues and victim sensitivities involved in many trafficking cases. Importantly, the law provides opportunities for victims to pursue legal claims against their exploiters. The 2008 Act, once again, seems well-intentioned.

Unfortunately, though, there are reasons to be skeptical about these changes. Even after completing antitrafficking training programs, many officials continue to lack awareness that victim–survivors are entitled to long-term rights (Pollack 2007). High turnover among enforcement officials limits awareness of new antitrafficking laws, while corruption of police and immigration officials undermines investigations. Thai authorities continue to fail to identify victims, and "aggressive efforts to arrest and deport immigration violators led to some victims being punished" (U.S. Dept. of State 2012, 341). Although the 2008 law and 2011 regulations issued by the Ministries of Labor and Interior ostensibly allow some foreign victims temporary residence and work permits while awaiting the conclusion of legal processes, benefits are granted on a case-by-case basis for labor trafficking victims, and only thirty permits have been issued (U.S. Dept. of State 2012). Long-term government shelters serve adult male victims and their families, but no such facilities exist for female victims. In fact, many women "rescued" in sex trafficking raids continue to be mandatorily detained—both as victims and as witnesses—in government shelters that lack adequate health care and educational programs; they are not provided with identity documents or legal aid, nor are they informed if they are free to leave (EMPOWER 2012; Gallagher 2010). And although periodic crackdowns on the sex industry produce arrests of undocumented workers and the detention of some victims, few convictions of traffickers result (GAATW 2007; U.S. Dept. of State 2011; U.S. Dept. of State 2013). Indeed, in a research project assessing the impact of the 2008 Act, EMPOWER concluded, "We have now reached a point in history where there are more women in the Thai sex industry who are being abused by anti-trafficking practices than there are women being exploited by traffickers" (EMPOWER 2012, vi).

Thai citizenship and immigration policies also compound many ethnic minorities' and migrants' vulnerability to trafficking and exploitation. For example, an estimated two million "hill tribe" minorities born and residing within Thailand's borders lack citizenship status, without which they cannot own land, travel freely between districts, or access social welfare services; all of these increase their vulnerability to trafficking and exploitation. Recent efforts to enforce Thailand's migrant nationality verification campaign have resulted in crackdowns on unregistered migrants and mass deportations. Some Thai authorities reportedly extort sex and money from unregistered Burmese migrants detained in Thailand for immigration offenses, selling those unable to pay labor brokers to traffickers (Human Rights Watch 2010).

Corruption, conflicting enforcement mandates, institutional inertia, and social discrimination against migrants, ethnic minorities, and sex workers have stymied the realization of reforms designed to promote trafficking victims' rights. The collateral damage from even well-intentioned, rights-conscious antitrafficking interventions includes not only the repression of rescued victims but also the failure of systemic reforms that could more effectively tackle the root causes of trafficking and labor exploitation. Against this backdrop, it remains to be seen whether the 2008 Act will produce durable reform in Thailand.

Activists, scholars, and policymakers would be well advised to revisit the Thai antitrafficking campaign as an empirical case in the future. Although the success of the 2008 reforms is uncertain, any successes that do manifest can provide valuable lessons in effective advocacy for interested parties. Moreover, even research regarding unsuccessful efforts at reform can provide cautionary tales for advocates of legal change as an instrument of social reform. Antitrafficking actors must be aware that the historical legacies of implementing institutions may dilute or disrupt reforms. Hopefully this chapter contributes to such transformative ends.

Notes

1. Quotations in this chapter are drawn from 50 one- to two-hour semistructured interviews with NGO activists, legal advocates, UN program coordinators, local police, regional and international law enforcement officials, prosecutors, social workers, and public welfare bureaucrats. Due to the sensitive nature of many interviewees' comments and critiques, interviews were confidential and conducted on the condition of anonymity. Quotes are attributed to each interviewee's role with respect to antitrafficking and/or advocacy work. Where necessary to preserve the anonymity of my interviewees, I have withheld the identity of the organization or agency with which the interviewee was involved.

2. Interview with George, American faith-based NGO activist, July 2005.

3. Interview with Banyat, Thai antitrafficking NGO director, March 2005.

4. Interview with Solada, Thai antitrafficking task force, victim assistance, February 2005.

5. Interview with Banyat, Thai antitrafficking NGO director, March 2005.

6. See the United Nations Protocol to Prevent, Suppress and Punish Trafficking in Persons, Especially Women and Children, supplementing the Convention against Transnational Organized Crime, 15 November 2000, Article 3(a). The definition notes that exploitation includes "the exploitation of the prostitution of others or other forms of sexual exploitation," but it leaves these terms undefined, reflecting the heated debates that took place during the drafting process between competing factions of antiprostitution, sex workers' rights, and human rights lobbying blocs (Jordan 2002).

7. Thailand is a country of origin, transit, and destination for victims of trafficking and labor exploitation in a variety of sectors. Though males may be exploited in the sex industry, this chapter focuses on "sex trafficking" of women, as Thailand's antitrafficking laws, enforcement interventions, and advocacy campaigns have historically targeted the sex trade (Pollack 2007).

8. Activists from Thai women's NGOs participated in the 1983 Global Feminist Workshop to Organize against Trafficking in Women, which framed prostitution in terms of "female sexual slavery" (Barry, Bunch, and Castley 1983), as well as the Second World Whores' Congress in Brussels in 1986, a key moment in the burgeoning sex workers' rights movement (Pheterson 1989).

9. Interview with Prabha, international antitrafficking organization advocate, April 2005. Today, GAATW involves a transnational network of over ninety organizations, addressing trafficking as both a cause and a consequence of human rights violations.

10. As Thai women's economic opportunities have improved, recruiters increasingly have sought out Burmese and ethnic highland women to work in the lower rungs of Thailand's sex industry (Feingold 2000).

11. After the Japanese government announced a crackdown on illegal immigrants, Thai officials urged Japan not to jail undocumented Thai migrants and to protect Thai women from "Japanese gangster bosses" (Human Rights Watch 1993).

12. Prevention and Suppression of Prostitution Act BE 2539 (1996). Sex workers' rights organizations were consulted in the drafting of the 1996 Act, and some drafters supported the principle that adult sex work should not be criminalized, focusing instead on eliminating child prostitution (Pollack 2007, 179).

13. Thailand's Measures in Prevention and Suppression of Trafficking in Women and Children Act, B.E. 2540 (1997) included fines up to $6,700 and six to twelve years in jail for trafficking, with stiffer penalties if victims were underage. The law did not cover male trafficking victims.

14. Interview with Val, sex worker NGO activist, July 2005; Interview with Michele, international women's organization activist, May 2005; Interview with Pii Moo, ethnic minorities' rights and women's rights activist, March 2005.

15. Interview with Walter, activist at an international NGO, March 2005.

16. Interview with Val, sex worker NGO activist, July 2005.

17. Interview with Ellen, sex workers' rights advocate, March 2005; interview with Ma Su, migrants' rights activist, April 2005.

18. Interview with Naang Aye, Shan women's rights activist, July 2005; Interview with Apple, Lahu women's activist, February 2005.

19. Interview with Mee, ethnic minority NGO activist, April 2005.

20. See, for example, Human Rights Watch (1993, 95), which describes the primary government shelter for foreign victims of trafficking. See also Gallagher and Pearson (2010).

21. The International Covenant on Civil and Political Rights (ICCPR) recognizes the right to freedom of movement for persons lawfully within the territory of a relevant state, though this right may be constrained for trafficked persons without regular migration status or refugee status. Still, arbitrary or discriminatory detention violates international law, and the ICCPR requires states to observe procedural guarantees of judicial or administrative review of the lawfulness of the detention (ICCPR Art. 9[4]). See Gallagher (2010) for an overview of the international legal framework regarding trafficking.

22. According to Thailand's Department of Social Development and Welfare, 1,633 foreign victims of trafficking were housed in government shelters between 1999 and August 2004 (UNESCAP 2005). The U.S. Department of State noted that despite a network of over ninety government shelters, coverage was uneven and the northernmost shelter was "too far to provide rapid and adequate victim services to key northern provinces such as Chiang Mai, Chiang Rai, and Phayao" (2005). Instead, victims were detained in private NGO shelters.

23. Interview with Malee, NGO activist and private shelter operator, February 2005. Jones (2003), Soderlund (2005), and Thrupkaew (2009) provide similar reports documenting alleged trafficking victims "running from the rescuers."

24. Interview with Baan, NGO activist and private shelter operator, March 2005.

25. Interview with Phu, provincial prosecutor, June 2005; interview with Wichit, provincial police chief, June 2005; interview with Sompop, district police chief, July 2005.

26. Interview with Sumalee, legal advocate, Thai antitrafficking task force, March 2005; interview with Virada, legal advocate, Thai antitrafficking NGO, July 2005.

27. Confidentiality clauses in my interview consent forms prohibit naming specific institutions.

28. Interview with Nancy, director of faith-based NGO/shelter, March 2005.

29. Interview with Bai, migrants' rights activist, April 2005.

30. Interview with Val, sex workers' rights activist, July 2005.

31. Interview with Ban, social worker at government shelter, rehabilitation, and vocational training facility, April 2005; interview with Oraphan, government social worker and social welfare bureaucrat, May 2005.

32. The expanding criminal justice system and increasing citizen contact with disciplinary institutions typify the ascendancy of a "carceral state" that shapes government and political identity, action, and attitudes (Weaver and Lerman 2010). Reflecting the broader phenomenon of "governing through crime" (Simon 2007), antitrafficking efforts are animated by an innocent "victim subject" and a turn to the criminal justice system to address social problems and police the poor. Feminist reforms addressing sexual violence, exploitation, and trafficking have also contributed to the expansion of the carceral state; for a provocative analysis of the ascendancy of "carceral feminism" in the U.S. antitrafficking movement and the international women's movement, see Bernstein (2007, 2010, 2012).

33. Interview with Ban, social worker at government shelter, rehabilitation, and vocational training facility, April 2005.

34. Interview with Jeeb, local women's rights and antitrafficking advocate, April 2005.

35. Interview with Val, sex workers' rights activist, July 2005.

36. Section 4 of Thailand's 2008 Anti-Trafficking in Persons Act defines "exploitation" as "seeking benefits from the prostitution, production or distribution of pornographic materials, other forms of sexual exploitation, slavery, causing another person to be a beggar, forced labour or service, coerced removal of organs for the purpose of trade, or any other similar practices resulting in forced extortion, regardless of such person's consent."

References

Barry, Kathleen, Charlotte Bunch, and Shirley Castley, eds. 1984. *International Feminism: Networking against Female Sexual Slavery: Report of the Global Feminist Workshop to Organize against Traffic in Women, Rotterdam, the Netherlands, April 6–15, 1983*. New York: International Women's Tribune Centre.

Bernstein, Elizabeth. 2007. "The Sexual Politics of the 'New Abolitionism.'" *Differences* 18, no. 3: 128–51.

———. 2010. "Militarized Humanitarianism Meets Carceral Feminism: The Politics of Sex, Rights, and Freedom in Contemporary Antitrafficking Campaigns." *Signs: Journal of Women in Culture and Society* 36, no. 1: 45–71.

———. 2012. "Carceral Politics as Gender Justice? The 'Traffic in Women' and Neoliberal Circuits of Crime, Sex, and Rights." *Theory and Society* 41, no. 3: 233–59.

Boonchalaksi, Wathinee, and Phillip Guest. 1994. *Prostitution in Thailand*. Nakhon Pathom, Thailand: Institute for Population and Social Research, Mahidol University.

Doezema, Jo. 2001. "Ouch! Western Feminists' 'Wounded Attachment' to the 'Third World Prostitute.'" *Feminist Review* 67 (Spring): 16–38.

EMPOWER Chiang Mai. 2003. *A Report by EMPOWER Chiang Mai on the Human Rights Violations Women Are Subjected to When "Rescued" by Anti-Trafficking Groups Who Employ Methods Using Deception, Force and Coercion*. Chiang Mai, Thailand: EMPOWER Foundation.

———. 2005. "U.S. Sponsored Entrapment." *Research for Sex Work* 8 (June): 25–27. http://www.nswp.org/sites/nswp.org/files/research-for-sex-work-8-english.pdf.

———. 2012. *Hit and Run: Sex Workers' Research on Anti-Trafficking in Thailand*. Chiang Mai, Thailand: EMPOWER Foundation.

Feingold, David. 2000. "The Hell of Good Intentions: Some Preliminary Thoughts on Opium in the Political Ecology of the Trade in Girls and Women." In *Where China Meets Southeast Asia: Social and Cultural Change in the Border Regions*, ed. Grant Evans, Christopher Hutton, and Kuah Khun Eng, 183–203. New York: St. Martin's.

Gallagher, Anne. 2010. *The International Law of Human Trafficking*. Cambridge, U.K.: Cambridge University Press.

Gallagher, Anne, and Elaine Pearson. 2010. "The High Cost of Freedom: A Legal and Policy Analysis of Shelter Detention for Victims of Trafficking." *Human Rights Quarterly* 32, no. 1: 73–114.

Global Alliance against Traffic in Women (GAATW). 2007. *Collateral Damage: The Impact of Anti-Trafficking Measures on Human Rights around the World*. Bangkok, Thailand: Amarin Printing and Publishing.

———. 2009. "Asia Regional Consultation Report." Paper presented at Asia Regional Consultation, Godavari Village Resort, Kathmandu, Nepal, August 29–September 4.

Human Rights Watch. 1993. *A Modern Form of Slavery: Trafficking of Burmese Women and Girls into Brothels in Thailand*, ed. Dorothy Thomas, Asia Watch Committee (U.S.), and Women's Rights Project (Human Rights Watch). New York: Human Rights Watch.

———. 2010. "Open Letter Requesting Investigation of Claims Migrants Deported from Thailand Facing Human Rights Abuses by DKBA," July 19. http://www .hrw.org/en/news/2010/07/19/open-letter-requesting-investigation-claims -migrants-deported-thailand-facing-human-.

International Covenant on Civil and Political Rights (ICCPR Art. 9[4]), *adopted* Dec. 16, 1966, G.A. Res. 2200 (XXI), U.N. GAOR, 21st Sess., art. 12, U.N. Doc. A/6316 (1966), 999 U.N.T.S. 171 (*entered into force* Mar. 23, 1976).

International Labour Organization (ILO). 2012. *ILO Global Estimate of Forced Labour: Results and Methodology*. Geneva, Switzerland: International Labour Office.

Jones, Maggie. 2003. "Thailand's Brothel Busters." *Mother Jones 28*, November/ December, 19.

Jordan, Ann. 2002. *Annotated Guide to the Complete UN Trafficking Protocol*. Global Rights (formerly International Human Rights Law Group), Washington, D.C.

Kinney, Edi. 2006. "Appropriations for the Abolitionists: Undermining Effects of the U.S. Mandatory Anti-Prostitution Pledge in the Fight against Human Trafficking and HIV/AIDS." *Berkeley Journal of Gender, Law and Justice* 21, no. 1: 158–94.

Pheterson, Gail. 1989. *A Vindication of the Rights of Whores*. Seattle, Wash.: Seal Press.

Phongpaichit, Pasuk. 1982. *From Peasant Girls to Bangkok Masseuses*. Women, Work and Development 2. Geneva, Switzerland: International Labour Office.

Pollack, Jackie. 2007. "Thailand." In *Collateral Damage: The Impact of Anti-Trafficking Measures on Human Rights around the World*, ed. Global Alliance against Traffic in Women, 171–202. Bangkok, Thailand: Amarin Printing and Publishing.

Puckmai, Pornpit. 2010. "Raids . . . Who Wins, Who Loses . . . or Is It All for Show?" Asia Pacific Network of Sex Worker$. February 10. http://apnsw.wordpress .com/2010/02/23/raids-%E2%80%A6-who-wins-who-loses%E2%80%A6or-is -it-all-for-show/.

Simon, Jonathan. 2007. *Governing through Crime: How the War on Crime Transformed American Democracy and Created a Culture of Fear*. New York: Oxford University Press.

Skrobanek, Siriporn. 1983. "The Transnational Sex-Exploitation of Thai Women." The Hague, the Netherlands: Institute of Social Sciences.

———. 2003. "Human Trafficking: From Vertical to Horizontal Journey." *Voices of Thai Women* 20 (May): 2–5.

Skrobanek, Siriporn, Nattaya Boonpakdi, and Chutima Janthakeero. 1997. *The Traffic in Women: Human Realities of the International Sex Trade.* New York: Zed Books.

Soderlund, Gretchen. 2005. "Running from the Rescuers: New U.S. Crusades against Sex Trafficking and the Rhetoric of Abolition." *Feminist Formations* 17, no. 3: 64–87.

Tantiwiramanod, Darunee, and Shashi Ranian Pandey. 1991. *By Women, for Women: A Study of Women's Organization in Thailand.* Singapore: ISEAS.

Thrupkaew, Noy. 2009. "The Crusade against Sex Trafficking." *The Nation*, September 16. http://www.thenation.com/article/crusade-against-sex-trafficking?page=full.

UNESCAP Social Development Division. 2005. *Report on the Post-Yokohama Mid-Term Review of the East Asia and the Pacific Regional Commitment and Action Plan against Commercial Sexual Exploitation of Children, 8–10 November 2004, Bangkok.* ST/ESCAP/2368.

U.S. Department of State. 2004. *Trafficking in Persons Report.* Washington, D.C.: Office of the Under Secretary for Global Affairs.

———. 2005. *Trafficking in Persons Report.* Washington, D.C.: Office of the Under Secretary for Global Affairs.

———. 2008. *Trafficking in Persons Report.* Washington, D.C.: Office of the Under Secretary for Global Affairs.

———. 2011. *Trafficking in Persons Report.* Washington, D.C.: Office of the Under Secretary for Global Affairs.

———. 2012. *Trafficking in Persons Report.* Washington, D.C.: Office of the Under Secretary for Global Affairs.

———. 2013. *Trafficking in Persons Report.* Washington, D.C.: Office of the Under Secretary for Global Affairs.

Weaver, Vesla M., and Amy E. Lerman. 2010. "Political Consequences of the Carceral State." *American Political Science Review* 104, no. 4: 817–33.

CHAPTER 8

The Contested Citizenship of Sex Workers

The Case of the Netherlands

Joyce Outshoorn

THE NETHERLANDS decriminalized prostitution in 1999 by lifting the ban on brothels and allowing for regulation of the sex industry. Prostitution was recognized as work and prostitutes as regular workers who are entitled to the social and legal rights accompanying that status.[1] Fundamental to the new act lifting the ban (*Wet Opheffing bordeelverbod*, Staatsblad 1999, 464, 9 November 1999) is the distinction between voluntary sex work, which is legal, and forced prostitution, which is illegal. Human trafficking is regarded as a fundamental component of the latter. However, in the past decade it has become evident that women working in the sex industry have not been able to achieve all the usual social rights of other workers, and they are often victims of exploitation and violence (Dekker, Tap, and Homburg 2006; KLPD 2008). Migrant sex workers face additional barriers.[2] As only European Union (EU) citizens can work legally as sex workers,[3] those from outside the EU cannot obtain work permits and thus become undocumented workers without rights and protection once their temporary visas expire. The diversity among sex workers leads to contradictory discourses. Dutch sex workers are constructed legally as modern, assertive sex workers, but those from elsewhere are constructed as victims of trafficking, enterprising migrants, or profiteers of the welfare state.

This chapter addresses the following two questions: (1) To what extent has the 1999 Act improved sex workers' rights and (2), given the categories of sex workers created by the new law and its implementation, what are its differential effects on these categories of workers? I contend that with the construction of the categories of legal and illegal prostitutes, the new policy actually opened opportunities for the deprivation of rights instead of guaranteeing these. I shall also examine the recent attempts to restrict the 1999 Act, which aimed to fight human trafficking and crime in the sex industry (TK 2009–2010, 32211 [*Wet regulering prostitutie en bestrijding misstanden sex branche*], nr 1–3, 11 November 2009)[4] by establishing a new system for regulating the registration of sex workers, the criminalization of clients who employ the services of an undocumented or nonregistered prostitute, and the licensing of escort services. I argue that these measures will neither dismantle the various categories of sex workers nor seriously address the frequently deplorable working conditions and the lack of rights sex workers still face. In fact they will weaken the position of sex workers in new ways.

Examining the course of the decriminalization and its consequences in the Netherlands is important for scholars of prostitution. Proponents of decriminalizing prostitution generally regard this as the driving force for improving the position of sex workers and fighting forced prostitution. Academic research on the effects of the 1999 Act brings to light the persistent problems in prostitution and shows that these negative outcomes result from poor implementation of legislation rather than legalization itself (Biesma et al. 2006; Bovenkerk et al. 2006; Daalder 2007a; 2007b; Dekker, Tap, and Homburg 2006; Wagenaar 2006; Wagenaar, Altink, and Amesberger 2013; Weitzer 2012). Examining the Dutch experience lets us see that decriminalization alone is not a sufficient condition for improving the position of sex workers and eliminating forced prostitution. My analysis of prostitution policy also offers more insight into the classification processes inherent to policymaking: the continual creation of categories of citizens to whom certain benefits or penalties accrue. As scholars working in the social constructionist tradition in sociology (e.g., Gusfield 1981; Schur 1980; Spector and Kitsuse 1977) and the construction of policy definitions in political science (e.g., Cobb and Elder 1972; Dery 1984; Schattschneider 1960; Schneider and Ingram 1993; 1995; 1997) have long since recognized, classification is an exercise of power by policymakers that determines policy outcomes and has real consequences for groups of citizens. My analysis to follow intends to make an empirical contribution to feminist policy analysis, while at the same time reminding practitioners of its forgotten roots in the social constructionist tradition and the conviction that the tradition can still be fruitful for gaining insight into the gendered effects of policymaking.

The 1999 Act

The Netherlands regulated prostitution in the nineteenth century, but brothels and living off the earnings of the prostitution of others were criminalized under the Morality Acts of 1911. Prostitutes themselves were never criminalized (De Vries 1997). Despite the ban on brothels and pimping, prostitution continued to thrive and authorities condoned its practice as long as it did not disturb public order. With the globalization of the sex industry in the 1970s, prostitution spread beyond the traditional red-light districts of the major cities, but the ban made it impossible for municipalities, notably in Rotterdam, to deal with the accompanying nuisance. There were also indications of the trafficking of women from abroad (Acker and Rawie 1982, 130). This issue was first raised by the Working Group on Sex Tourism during the 1982 Hague Conference on sexual violence, organized by the women's policy agency (Outshoorn 2004, 186). This agency later funded the Foundation against Trafficking of Women (*Stichting tegen Vrouwenhandel*), a feminist organization that provided services for trafficked women and lobbied the government for higher penalties for trafficking as well as for residence permits for victims of trafficking.

With these developments, in the 1980s the National Association of Municipalities started lobbying for a repeal of the ban on brothels and demanding new regulation (Outshoorn 2004). Feminist activists in favor of sex workers' rights supported the repeal and in addition demanded the recognition of prostitution as sex work to improve the position of prostitutes.[5] Given the strong position of the religious parties in government and Parliament, who were opposed to prostitution on religiously inspired moral grounds, it took nearly twenty years to enact new legislation (Outshoorn 2004). In 1994, a new secular majority was elected to Parliament, and the "Purple" cabinets Kok I and Kok II (consisting of the Liberals, Social Liberals, and the Social Democrats but without the Christian Democrat party that had been in power since 1918), finally paved the way for the repeal.

The new act (*Wet Opheffing Bordeelverbod*) was passed in 1999 and took effect in 2000. It lifted the ban on brothels in order to regulate prostitution, protect minors from sexual abuse (by raising the age of consent from sixteen to eighteen years old), and "protect" (not improve) the position of prostitutes (Outshoorn 2004, 197–99). It also aimed at ridding the sex industry of criminal elements by introducing the licensing of sex clubs.

Forcing a person into prostitution remained a criminal offense (force includes the use of deceit, coercion or abuse of authority). Although the religious political parties opposed the act for allowing immoral practices, all the other parties saw it as a realistic solution to a social problem (Outshoorn 2004, 185). The implementation of the act was delegated to the municipalities who were to set up the licensing system, ensure compliance with fire and safety regulations and labor and social security laws, and cooperate with the local health authorities (Wagenaar 2006). Meanwhile the police were responsible for verifying the age of sex workers and migrant sex workers' residence permits. This delegation is in line with the traditional autonomy of the municipalities, which resent interference by the central government. In the case of prostitution, this autonomy was defended by the argument that the municipality is more able to tailor the law to local needs.

While the act granted sex workers full civil rights (in contrast to countries where they were regarded as vagrants and lost their citizenship rights, including the right to vote) and did not exclude them from the basic welfare benefits of social assistance and the statutory old-age pension, they now stood to gain full social rights, including the right to do work of their own choosing, the right to social insurance, and the recognition of their right to sexual self-determination. There were obligations on the part of sex workers as well: they would have to pay taxes and make social insurance contributions.[6]

In the debates leading up to the repeal, trafficking was regularly linked to prostitution. The articles in the Penal Code on human trafficking were revised in 1993, with a more precise definition of the offense and higher penalties for traffickers so they could be remanded in custody (Outshoorn 2004, 193–95). The articles were framed in a gender-neutral way and defined trafficking as forcing a person into prostitution. Since 1988 there has been an administrative provision allowing trafficked women from other countries to obtain a temporary residence permit so that they can testify against their traffickers in court (ibid.).[7] In the parliamentary debates on trafficking, many members of Parliament (MPs) portrayed foreign women as victims of deceit by traffickers who, in the words of the Christian Democrat spokesperson "operate from coldblooded profit motives" (TK 1987–88, UCV 32 [*Vrouwenhandel*], 1 February 1988, p. 3) This framing was tied to a discourse about the divide between rich and poor countries: victims were driven by poverty, which made them gullible to tales about a better life in wealthy Western Europe. Against the background of mounting public concern about illegal migration, a more insidious edge crept into this discourse. The Christian Democrat parliamentary spokesperson talked about "an uncontrollable stream of foreign prostitutes" entering the country and the minister of justice, Ernst Hirsch Ballin, from the same party, framed this as the "open flank" of Dutch immigration policy (TK 1991–1992, 21027 [*Opheffing Bordeelverbod*], 21 May 1992, p. 4994, 5001). This framing opened a discursive space for "false" victims, who used the loopholes in the law to work illegally as prostitutes in the Netherlands. Consequently, in the 1990s the Christian political parties that opposed lifting the ban on brothels started to argue that *all* women from non-EU countries working in the sex industry were victims of forced prostitution, corresponding with the broader international debates on prostitution (Outshoorn 2005). They argued that the best way to stop trafficking was to prevent non-EU women from coming into the country to work in the sex industry in the first place. This ignored women migrants who consciously decided to work as sex workers in the West and those who might make use of intermediaries to enter the country (Outshoorn 2001, 480) and thus were liable to deportation as "illegals."

Successive cabinets all refused measures allowing work permits for non-EU sex workers for fear of trafficking and illegal migration and also argued there was no national interest at stake for importing sex workers, a ground normally used for justifying extending work permits to non-EU citizens. They were backed by a solid majority in Parliament, where records show many references to the fear of foreign prostitutes entering the country, which would subvert restrictive immigration policies. The fear also surfaced in the Memorandum to the 2000 Act, as demonstrated by one of the aims of the bill: to halt "the stream of foreign prostitutes" (TK 1996–97, 25437 [*Opheffing Algemeen Bordeelverbod*], nr 3 [*Memorie van Toelichting*], 1 July 1997, p. 13). In later debates on trafficking, right-wing parties worried that undocumented workers could pretend to have been trafficked in order to obtain a temporary residency permit (e.g., TK 2008–2009, 28638 [*Mensenhandel*], nr 44 [*Verslag van een algemeen overleg*], 13 July 2009). Granting permits was also regarded as subverting national immigration policy.

The voting on the Act split neatly along the religious/secular divide of the political party system, with the religious parties strongly opposed (Outshoorn 2004, 200). This opposition continued when municipalities had to implement the act, with religious parties bent on limiting its impact and lobbying for the funding of religious NGOs to enable prostitutes to exit the sex industry.

The Categories of Sex Workers

One major consequence of connecting the act to immigration policy was that it led to a fourfold classification of prostitutes in its implementation. Given the widely diverging estimates of the number of sex workers in the Netherlands, and the fluid nature of their origins over the past decade, it is not possible to estimate how large each category is. First, there is the Dutch sex worker (ethnically undefined—parliamentary debates were surprisingly color-blind) who willingly chooses to work in prostitution and is the bearer of civil and social rights. This is the modern "assertive and emancipated prostitute" constructed in the various bills (e.g., TK 1988–89, 21207 [Mensenhandel], nr 3 [Memorie van Toelichting], 11 February 1989, p. 4). This modern sex worker can be from another EU country whose nationals have the right to work in the Netherlands and are eligible for the same social and civil rights (save for the right to vote in national and provincial elections and to stand as a candidate in these elections); these EU citizens compose a second category of prostitutes.

However, the Dutch government constructed a third category during the negotiations about the EU enlargement of 2004, when the Baltic states, Poland, Hungary, the Czech Republic, and Slovakia joined the EU. Fearing the influx of cheap labor, the government decided that workers from these countries can only work in the Netherlands if they are self-employed. These measures were also supported by the more traditional socialists and many in the trade unions. The self-employment criterion also applies to sex workers; they can work independently but cannot be employees with social rights, distinguishing them from their Western European counterparts. The government also worried that EU enlargement would increase the trafficking of women to work in brothels. Since the fall of the Berlin Wall in 1989, many women from Central and Eastern Europe had been working as prostitutes in the Netherlands. In 2007, Central and Eastern European citizens were accorded working rights equal to other EU citizens. But this third category remained in order to categorize citizens from the newly acceding states of Bulgaria and Romania who, as EU citizens, can travel freely to the Netherlands but are only allowed to work as independent contractors. If caught working as "employees" in brothels, they (and their employers) are fined.

Finally, following the refusal of successive cabinets to grant working permits to non-EU sex workers, a fourth category of sex workers— non-EU women working illegally without any rights—was created.[8] These sex workers can be victims of trafficking or "enterprising migrants"— either the clients of human smugglers or anyone entering the country on a tourist visa who becomes an "illegal migrant" once the visa expires. In contrast to the third category, they run the risk of being deported. In Parliament, the Green Left party has been the only party to point out the implicit racial character of the dichotomy between legal and illegal prostitutes: white, EU citizens are protected by legal rights while black, Latino, or Asian non-EU prostitutes have no legal protection (TK 1998–99, 25437 [*Opheffing Algemeen Bordeelverbod*], 27 January 1999; TK 44, p. 3038; TK 45, p. 3135). This dichotomy has persisted over time.

The Debates after the 1999 Act

The Construction of the Legal and Illegal Sector

At the request of Parliament, a first evaluation of the lifted ban was conducted from 2001 to 2002. In the report commissioned by the Ministry of Justice, Annelies Daalder (2002) showed that in an effort to stop the spread of prostitution, local councils "froze" the number of brothels in their precincts by not allowing new competitors to the market. Some municipalities with an orthodox Protestant majority refused to license any sex business. Many prostitutes had little knowledge of their rights, and attempts by the Red Thread or social and health care workers to reach them were inadequate. The licensing system was not yet in place in all municipalities, leading to more mobility by criminalized prostitutes such as underage or undocumented prostitutes. In the nonlicensed sector, incidents of human trafficking and coercion were reported, but the most frequent infringement of the law was prostitutes working without a permit, making them the most vulnerable to exploitation (Goderie, Woerds, and Spierings 2002; Daalder 2002, 41). Daalder also reported a shift to nonregulated locations for sex work, such as in saunas, camper cars, and bars (Daalder 2002, 44). Although the report does document the countries of origin of the prostitutes, it does not note their ethnicity.

In the same report, Ine Vanwesenbeeck, Mechtild Hoïng, and Paul Vennix (2002) analyzed a representative sample of sex workers on their social position after the change in the law. The authors reported that the autonomy of prostitutes was quite high but wondered if their interviewees' responses were influenced by their interest in passing as independent sex workers. If they tell the state that they work independently and not as employees, the brothel owners do not have to deal with income tax or social insurance contributions for disability and unemployment. There was abundant evidence of control of prostitutes by managers (e.g., dictating dress, working hours, and the percentage of earnings going to the managers). In general, the researchers concluded it was too early to say whether criminality, violence, and coercion had declined since legalization. The annual reports of the National Reporter on Human Trafficking showed some increase in trafficking, but this can be ascribed partly to better reporting by victims and to a new definition of trafficking in 2006 that included forced labor in other industries.[9]

A second Ministry of Justice evaluation in 2006 concluded that the licensing system was operative and regularly monitored; there was little indication that the trade had moved to nonlicensed premises (Daalder 2007a, 11; Daalder 2007b). Daalder did not rule out that prostitution was shifting to the Internet or that brothels were in decline because of the weaker economy. She reported that underage prostitutes and undocumented workers in the licensed part of the sex industry had more or less disappeared. Sasha Biesma et al. (2006, 103) found little evidence of a larger underground illegal sector or any large contingent of minors working in the sex industry (ibid., 100–101).

However, in the same evaluation Helga Dekker, Ruud Tap, and Ger Homburg (2006) noted that the rights of sex workers had not improved; forced prostitution and pimping were still recurring phenomena despite the fact that trafficking had become more difficult because of improved law enforcement. Prostitutes had not become independent workers, although the majority of them maintained they were (Dekker, Tap, and Homburg 2006, 42, 82). The existence of shady businesses such as massage parlors, swingers clubs, and sauna clubs was difficult for local authorities to tackle. Dekker, Tap, and Homburg concluded that although prostitution had not become "normal work," the quality of labor conditions in the licensed trade was not "structurally bad," despite the power relations between workers and the operators (ibid., 80).

The second evaluation commissioned by the Ministry of Justice also showed a major loophole in the new regulations. There were indications that prostitution had shifted to escort services and the Internet. The non-licensed sex clubs and escort services could easily move to municipalities with no or lenient licensing requirements, and there were no impediments to selling sex on the Internet. As in the 2002 evaluation, the second evaluation noted the countries of origin of prostitutes but did not report on the racial or ethnic composition of the "work force."

Although the evaluations showed there were still many doubtful practices in the prostitution branch, they contributed to the informed public's liberal understanding that the decriminalization of the sex industry had led to the emergence of two prostitution sectors. First, there was the licensed sector, where, because of the licensing system and inspection by police or the local authorities, no underage prostitutes and undocumented workers were found. The prostitutes working here were mainly white Dutch citizens and "traditional" EU citizens. Second, there was the nonlicensed sector, consisting of a variety of sexual service providers, where pimping and coercion still occurred and many prostitutes were "illegal" or minors. The women working here were understood to be mainly "foreign," coming from Eastern Europe and West Africa, taking the place of Latin American or Asian women of earlier decades.

The New Counternarrative

It was this liberal understanding of the state of affairs in the mid-2000s that came under attack, and not just from the religious political parties and organizations who continued to oppose decriminalization. Public opinion was increasingly influenced by a steady stream of popular books and documentaries highlighting the plight of victims of prostitution and the violence of their exploiters.[10] Karina Schaapman's 2004 book, *Zonder moeder*, where she came out as an ex-prostitute, received widespread publicity because she was a Social Democrat member of the Amsterdam City Council. She argued that most prostitutes do not choose to become prostitutes but are pressured into it because of drug addiction, debts, or past (sexual) abuse. With her colleague Councilor Amma Asante, she later wrote a policy paper in which they declared the 1999 law to be "bankrupt," although they maintained they did not want to repeal it (Asante and Schaapman 2005, 3). Based on interviews with stakeholders in the field and disparate secondary sources, they argued that the position of prostitutes had not improved. Since 2000, many prostitutes had moved to "invisible types" of prostitution, such as escort services, and violence and pimping were still rife in window and escort prostitution (ibid., 5). Half of the prostitutes are of "foreign" descent (ibid., 10) and the majority are "illegal," working under bad conditions and for low wages. Moreover, they claimed, trafficking abounds and "loverboys" (pimps) recruit Dutch girls for prostitution. Exiting prostitution is hard, as many prostitutes have debts or do not speak Dutch; there is widespread drug abuse; and many prostitutes have no health insurance and run the risk of STDs and unwanted pregnancies. Asante and Schaapman recommended licensing escort services, criminalizing pimps, and raising the age of consent for sex work from eighteen to twenty-one years old.

Two members of the Red Thread, an interest group for sex workers in the Netherlands, provided a more evidence-based report. Sietske Altink and Sylvia Bokelman (2006) visited licensed brothels and irregular sex businesses (such as Thai massage parlors and escort agencies) to see if the working conditions of sex workers had improved in recent years. They found that sex workers were not independent workers but rather dependent employees of club owners and managers, whose authority was omnipresent. (Many of the sex workers could not talk to the researchers without permission from their boss.) Many, mainly Eastern European women, lived on the work premises, making them totally dependent on the owner/manager. Their illegal status made them vulnerable to coercion and blackmail by their employers. The only improvement in work conditions they found was in the regulation of working hours. Despite the "alarming" situation (2006, 12), Altink and Bokelman were in favor of decriminalization but only under stricter conditions. They argued labor laws should be applied to guarantee better work conditions and to protect the integrity of the sex worker. The state should deal with human trafficking and exploitation, and the local authorities should prevent criminals from investing in the sex industry and encourage innovation in the sex industry by stopping the freeze on the number of sex clubs and allowing new competitors into the market.

Two figures dominated the new counternarrative generated by the media. First, there was the figure of the "loverboy" who forced young girls into prostitution and, second, the figure of the trafficked young woman. Criminologist Frank Bovenkerk and his team, puzzled by two conflicting narratives—one of social workers who saw "loverboys" as a growing social problem and one of experienced Amsterdam police officers who held that they hardly encountered "loverboys" (2006, 9–10)—studied the phenomenon in a field study in Amsterdam and some smaller cities. They found few "loverboys" but plenty of good old-fashioned pimping. Deconstructing the framing of "loverboys" as a romantic creation of young girls and social workers (ibid., 15), they showed how "loverboys" are portrayed as Moroccan or Antillean young men who lure young white girls into prostitution. Pimping is no longer the preserve of white Dutch men, who have moved on to more profitable criminal activities such as the trafficking of drugs, but has become a niche for deprived young migrants making a career in crime. Bovenkerk et al. (ibid., 57–61) classify the "loverboy" phenomenon as a typical moral panic constructed by the popular press and Christian social workers. Nevertheless, Bovenkerk et al. also show that the aims of the 1999 enactment, such as ridding prostitution of crime and creating decent working conditions, have not been achieved.

The second major figure in the counternarrative was the victim of trafficking who ended up in prostitution. Stories about young girls from Eastern Europe and the Balkans, lured by unscrupulous traffickers into the sex industry, figured regularly in the media, including the quality press (e.g., *NRC Handelsblad, M Maandblad,* September 2003; October 2005). Journalist Ruth Hopkins published her book *Ik laat je nooit meer gaan* (*I Will Never Let You Go*) in 2005, but although she was critical of the moralist discourse on trafficking and the exaggeration of the numbers of victims, her interviews with victims of trafficking tended to affirm the familiar trafficking narrative. Her major indictment is the "indifference" of government toward trafficking; despite trafficking laws and a national reporter on the crime, she argues that the authorities do far too little to stop "modern slavery" in prostitution. In her view, the illegal status of non-EU sex workers in the Netherlands and EU antimigration policies preclude the solution. Work permits for migrants who want to work in prostitution are the best way of stopping the trafficking of women. Her call for action is only partly heard by politicians, who back the cause of fighting the trafficking of women for prostitution but not the remedy of legalizing the status of illegal sex workers.

The Deconstruction of the Two Sectors

The division of the licensed sector, with its legal Dutch and "traditional" EU workers, and the nonlicensed sector, with its illegal non-EU workers, was thoroughly undermined when the investigative unit of the national police force (KLPD)[11] published a report about the widely publicized Sneep[12] case of a gang of traffickers running a major prostitution network in three cities, including Amsterdam (KLPD 2008). The report showed that the majority of the seventy-eight reported victims came from the Netherlands and Germany, while others were from EU countries such as Ireland, Bulgaria, and the Czech Republic. The traffickers had operated quite openly in the licensed sector for several years. To analyze how this had been possible, the KLPD team examined how picking up the signals of forced prostitution was likely to be thwarted in many cases. The first opportunity for identifying forced prostitution is often when a prostitute is interacting with a social welfare or health care worker or a client or when local authorities grant licenses and residence permits to workers. These contacts all have the ability to report problems to the police. Street-level cops can also identify trafficking and report it to their superiors, who in turn take the case to the public prosecutor and the courts. However, the report shows that there are barriers to identifying abuse at each stage of the process. A potential explanation offered by the KLPD team for the failure to identify forced prostitution is that any possible observer can be pressured by conflicting interests and turn a blind eye (ibid., 104–10). Prostitutes want the coercion to stop but will not report it for fear of deportation; clients might want to help, but they also want to have sex; club owners' and managers' overriding concern is turnover, and they profit from low labor costs despite the risk of contravening regulations; social workers are torn between reporting and maintaining their contact with the victim; local authorities work under pressure and want to avoid fuss; police faced with performance measurement are tempted to take up cases that are less time-consuming and easier to charge; the public prosecutor worries whether the witnesses will turn up and the case will hold in court and may abstain from prosecuting. The KLPD concluded that legalization has not ended abuse in the prostitution sector and that present monitoring is no guarantee that women are not working under the threat of coercion. It regards the idea of a "cleansed prostitution branch" in the sex industry as an illusion (ibid., 8, 10).

The KLPD report was important not just for its factual contribution to the public debate and for undoing the accepted division between the licensed and nonlicensed sector, one supposedly clean and the other criminal. It also overturned the distinction between the modern emancipated prostitute from the Netherlands or the older EU countries, and the helpless victims of trafficking from non-EU countries. In the Sneep case, most of the trafficked women turned out to be Western EU citizens, notably from the Netherlands and Germany and not the stereotypical young girls from Eastern Europe.

The Political Response

The Parliamentary Debate

In the first years after legalization, successive cabinets and Parliament awaited the results of the various evaluations, but prostitution returned to the parliamentary agenda when the Christian parties seized on the moral panic about "loverboys" in the mid-2000s. The results of the second evaluation (Daalder 2007a) and the continuing media attention also convinced the other political parties that the purposes of the act were not being achieved. The discourse about the assertive modern sex worker began to be overshadowed by the return of the older framing about victims of forced prostitution and the role of organized crime. In 2007, a new cabinet of Christian Democrats, Social Democrats, and the Christian Union (Balkenende IV) came into power and announced amendments to the act, framing prostitution as a "breeding place for crime" (Regeerakkoord 2007, 35).

In Parliament, the depiction of the sex worker shifted to the image of the prostitute as victim, with a new emphasis on child prostitution,[13] including "slightly mentally handicapped girls."[14] There was continual reference to "thousands" of women coerced into prostitution in the Netherlands each year; even the Social Democrats, who had always been in favor of the decriminalization, went along with this idea.[15] The discourse about forced prostitution challenged the new definition of trafficking in the Penal Code that was adopted in 2005 to comply with international antitrafficking measures,[16] which equated forced prostitution with exploitation, along with other types of forced labor, and no longer singled out trafficking for the purposes of prostitution or the crossing of borders.

The new emphasis on victims and organized crime focused heavily on Eastern European victims, given the unease in the Netherlands about the EU's enlargement. It made the victim—previously from the "Third World"—change color, while at the same time "coloring" the traffickers by emphasizing their Turkish or Balkan roots, as in the Sneep case. In short, while the new Penal Code article obliterated boundaries, nationalities, ethnicities, and gender (it talks about "persons") and did away with classifications, many members of the public and politicians continued to see "(white) girls and young women" and "foreign mafiosi." The exception to these perceptions was the group of Nigerian female refugees in the mid-2000s who disappeared, however, they gained media attention because they were under eighteen and reputedly coerced into prostitution by "voodoo" rituals in Nigeria.[17]

The New Proposal to Regulate the Sex Industry

A new proposal to redress the perceived problems of the 1999 Act was introduced in Parliament in 2009 (TK 2009–2010, 32211) with the main purpose of reducing trafficking. The new bill proposed a licensing regime for all forms of prostitution (including the highly mobile escort services) with uniform regulation across all communities (but keeping the option of a local ban open),[18] and the registration of prostitutes. If clients use the services of nondocumented or nonregistered workers, they will be liable for a fine. Non-EU residents would not be allowed to work in the sex industry, on the familiar grounds that it would increase trafficking. The registration of prostitutes—an unprecedented shift in Dutch prostitution policy—and several measures to clarify the difference between self-employment and wage work were intended to enable them to work independently. After an amendment from the populist Freedom Party, the bill also included raising the age of consent to work as a prostitute from eighteen to twenty-one years old (TK 2009–2010, 32211). As the minister of justice summarized his aims during the parliamentary debate, "By the introduction of a compulsory licensing system in combination with compulsory registration and the national register of escort services, an almost closed administrative system is erected that can improve the fight against abuses in the sex industry and the judicial suppression of forced prostitution" (TK 2010–2011, 51-8-60 [*Bestrijding misstanden sex branche*], 10 February 2011).

The bill (*Regulering prostitutie en bestrijding misstanden sex branche*) was passed in March 2011 by the Second Chamber, receiving a generous majority that cut across the religious-secular divide in Parliament (contrary to the voting pattern in 1999). The Social Democrats and the Socialists supported the bill, although they had been in favor of decriminalization before. The newly represented populist Freedom Party perpetuated the discourse of vulnerable young girls and their "loverboys," proposing an amendment to raise the age for prostitution from eighteen to twenty-one, and turned against the decriminalization of prostitution (TK 2009–2010, 32211, nr 7 [*Amendement Agema*], 15 April 2010). Parties differed in their judgments of the 1999 Act; the orthodox religious parties regarded it as a failure, while the secular parties ascribed the current abuses to insufficient implementation. As a Socialist Party MP stated, there are sufficient laws and regulation to deal with the abuses, "but it needs to be done properly: more capacity for the police, the public prosecution and social work, and better cooperation" (TK 2010–2011, 46-20-46 [*Bestrijding misstanden prostitutie*], 1 February 2011). The major points of contention were the registration of prostitutes (held to be in contravention of the right of privacy by the secular MPs) and the criminalization of the client if he uses the services of an unregistered prostitute.[19] The idea behind registration was ostensibly to forge a new contact between a prostitute and the local authority in order to establish if she is working out of free will, but the subtext is the will to control. As the minister said during the debate, "Compulsory registration increases the visibility and the grip on the sex sector and retrieves prostitutes from anonymity" (TK 2010–2011, 51-8-59 [*Bestrijding misstanden prostitutie*], 10 February 2011). A client was supposed to check the registration pass of the sex worker when buying her services, but the minister retracted the pass.

The licensing of escort services and the new age of consent were not controversial. MPs generally suspected escort services were harboring and exploiting the illegal sex workers and the MPs expected that twenty-one-year-olds would be less likely to believe "loverboys" than eighteen-year-olds. The social rights of prostitutes only came to the fore during the closing stages of the debate, with the minister of justice promising to take measures to protect the health and security of prostitutes and their right to self-determination. But he also stated that issues concerning the right to work were best left to the sex sector itself, as the state should not take over but only facilitate (TK 2010–2011, 51-8-73 [*Bestrijding misstanden seksbranche*], 10 February 2011).

The First Chamber, however, had serious doubts about the bill. The registration of prostitutes proved to be the major point of contention, with nearly all parties critical about the lack of guarantees for the privacy of sex workers. There was a potential majority for the more uniform nationwide system of licensing (to control the escort services) and for raising the age of consent for sex work to twenty-one years old. Some hilarity in the normally staid Senate arose during the debate on the requirements of the client, who has to check whether the sex worker of his choice is registered, otherwise he is also criminalized. The minister's suggestion was that the client should check the national register on his cell phone before proceeding. This led the Christian Union spokesman to hold that the "psychology of the moment" is at odds with this bureaucratic action, and the Independent member's proposal contradicted "all biological realities" (EK 2011–2012, 32211 [*Bestrijding misstanden seksbranche*], 5-7-23, 5-7-25, 30 October 2012).

The First Chamber does not have the right of amendment, so it offered a motion to split the bill to save the licensing of the escort services and the higher age for sex work. By dropping the criminalization of the client if he buys the services of an unregistered sex worker, the First Chamber could count on a large majority. If the minister did not agree with this solution, the majority would vote against the whole bill. In response, the minister promised to revamp the bill and introduce it to the Second Chamber in the coming fall (EK, 2012–2013, 32211, 8 July). The First Chamber then passed the motion splitting the bill but refrained from voting on the whole proposal.

Conclusion

There is some controversy over the question of whether the position of sex workers has improved since the decriminalization of prostitution in 2000. Most researchers and the Red Thread have shown there is still abuse, but few argue this is a reason to repeal the decriminalization in the 1999 Act. In the licensed sector, underage prostitution and undocumented sex workers have more or less disappeared, but there has been a shift "underground," where forced prostitution occurs and migrant workers are exploited. Despite these improvements, after the KLPD (2008) it became more difficult to maintain that there was a cleansed legal sector and a grubby illegal sector. Furthermore, in the legal sector forced prostitution is still common. Along with the widely publicized "loverboy" scare and media coverage of trafficking, the report strengthened opposition to decriminalization. The framing of the issue has shifted from creating normal working conditions and sex workers' rights to the necessity of strict regulation, including the registration of sex workers, to fight human trafficking and attack organized crime. This framing was the foundation of the new bill, which failed in the

First Chamber of Parliament. As has been noted in the recent First Chamber debate, there was a shift from fighting abusive practices to securing total surveillance and control.[20]

The thrust toward a more restrictive policy will not change two basic issues. First, the classification underlying prostitution policy will remain intact. The major dichotomy will still be between legal and illegal sex workers, although the definitions of these categories have changed over time: they now have different nationalities and ethnicities than in the 1990s. This is mainly a consequence of the Dutch policy response to the enlargement of the EU, which has facilitated legal work for EU sex workers, allowing for more white (Central and Eastern European) sex workers. Undocumented workers are also more likely to be non-EU Eastern Europeans and West Africans, with fewer women coming from Latin America and South East Asia. From the research evidence, one can conclude that not granting work permits to non-EU women leaves them at risk for blackmail and coercion into poor working conditions and bad pay. In this way, *policy actually creates these working conditions.* Moreover, the hegemonic discourse on trafficking, with its focus on vulnerable young women, distracts attention from the working conditions of prostitutes, which are essential for ensuring their social rights. The power of policy classification has generally had pernicious effects on the position of sex workers. The failed bill actually created a new classification of registered and nonregistered sex workers that cuts across the already existing categories.

Second, it is unlikely that access to social rights will improve, even for legal sex workers. The construction of the "independent" worker allows her boss to get away with subverting tax and social security laws but leaves her without sickness and unemployment benefits, while at the same time requiring her to comply with dress codes and work hours, which indicate that she is in fact an employee. If she does decide to become a true independent worker, she has trouble getting bank loans, and if she wants to set up a brothel, she runs into resistance from the local authority, which often refuses licenses to new brothels. Moreover, the stigma of sex work is still present, so that many sex workers prefer to remain anonymous and not claim their rights. A pimp still takes his percentage of a prostitute's earnings; he may offer her protection in return or be her lover, but when is he coercing her?

In actual fact, the registration of prostitutes is likely to be conducted by the municipalities instead of the central state. Along with the new higher age restrictions for work, this will further infringe on sex workers' civil and social rights. The right to work is normally granted at age of sixteen in the Netherlands, and registration with the (local) state is not required for other professions (beyond the customary registration at the Chamber of Commerce for tax purposes, which is not compulsory but not uncommon among sex workers). With registration, sex workers' privacy is at stake, even more so because the Dutch administrative state has a poor record on guarding citizen's rights to privacy (Kagie 2010). Undocumented workers are still at risk for blackmail because of their illegal status. New restrictive legislation will make it harder for them to find work, as the client will also run a risk in hiring their services. One can conclude that to improve the position of sex workers, decriminalization is a necessary condition but is not sufficient on its own; the issues outlined require a range of different remedies, not the totalizing system of control outlined by the pending regulation.

Notes

1. The research presented here is based on data from the research project "Sexual and Bodily Citizenship and Feminist Body Politics in a Multicultural Europe," a subtheme of the Feminism and Citizenship (FEMCIT) project "Gendered Citizenship in Multicultural Europe: The Impact of the Contemporary Women's Movements," financed by the Sixth Framework Programme of the European Union, Priority 7, Networks of Excellence and Integrated Projects: Citizens and Governance in a Knowledge-Based Society, 2007–2011.

2. Estimates of the number of prostitutes in the Netherlands vary widely. In the 1990s, a number of over 30,000 was quoted in Parliament, half of which were of "foreign" origin. Today the numbers are more modest; most studies estimate that there are 15,000 to 25,000 sex workers, with half of "foreign" origin. Estimating is difficult given the difficulties of defining what a prostitute is. Ine Vanwesenbeeck (1994) estimates 20,000–25,000 nationally, while Amma Asante and Karina Schaapman (2005) estimate 15,000–20,000. Van Wijk et al. (2010) estimate there are between 5,150 and 7,660 in Amsterdam but give no national estimate.

3. In the majority of Dutch discourses, women who sell sexual services are usually called "prostitutes"; the Dutch equivalent of "sex workers"—*sex werkers*—is not prevalent. Prostitutes do not identify with the term "sex worker," preferring to call themselves prostitutes. In this chapter I will follow the terminology of the sources I examine.

4. TK stands for Tweede Kamer, the Second Chamber of Parliament; EK stands for Eerste Kamer, the First Chamber or Senate of Parliament.

5. Both the Red Thread (*Rode Draad*), founded in 1986 as a trade union and lobby group, and the Foundation against Trafficking of Women (*Stichting tegen Vrouwenhandel-STV*), established in 1987, lobbied for the recognition of prostitution as sex work and were in favor of lifting the ban on brothels. Both were feminist initiatives and received government funding over the years. STV became part of *CoMensha*, a service and expertise center for combating human trafficking, in 2006.

6. In fact the Dutch revenue service already taxed a prostitute if it knew of her work, often charging the maximum rate, with the burden of proof reversed: she would have to prove she earned much less.

7. The *Vreemdelingen circulaire* B 9.

8. This includes the right to health care. Undocumented migrants cannot insure themselves for health care, as this requires a residence permit. By law, medical professionals and hospitals have to check if patients are insured before providing services (insurance is compulsory for citizens). It is by no means clear if this law is in contravention with EU directives about the right to health care, as individual member states have considerable leeway in implementing these; moreover, states can opt out of certain measures, as the Netherlands did on labor migration from the Central and Eastern European states (CEES) after the EU enlargement. There is, however, civil disobedience by health care providers for ethical reasons: many in the health sector provide services for those with life-threatening conditions, using hidden sources of funding, and there is a more-or-less secret network of health workers who provide services to undocumented workers regardless of the severity.

9. Figures on trafficking are hard to come by because of underreporting and the varying definitions of the offense (Mensenhandel 2007, 15–25, 285). The *National Reporter on Human Trafficking* provides yearly figures based on those of the Foundation against Trafficking of Women (*CoMensha* since 2006) and police records. It notes an increase in reported cases from 284 in 2001 to 1222 in 2011 (Mensenhandel 2012, 51). The higher figures are partly due the broader definition of the offense since 2005, which now includes the incidence of forced labor in sectors such as horticulture and the restaurant business, but also point to the increase in trafficking for sex work. The new Article 237a of the Penal Code reworded forced prostitution as human trafficking, regardless of whether national borders had been crossed. It is therefore not surprising that in the last report (2008), the most frequent country of origin for victims of trafficking was the Netherlands itself, with 39 percent of all cases (a "share" steadily rising over recent years) consisting mainly of women residing in the Netherlands who are forced into prostitution by local (not necessarily Dutch nationals) entrepreneurs (Mensenhandel 2009, 114–15).

10. Bovenkerk and Pronk (2007) counted no fewer than thirty-two television programs on the topic since 2000, in particular from the Evangelical Broadcasting Company (*Evangelische Omroeporganisatie*; EO).

11. *Korps Landelijke Politiediensten* (National Force of Police Services).

12. Sneep was the police code name used in the press. It was also known as the "Saban B." case—named after the leader of the gang, who was convicted in 2009 but escaped to Turkey in 2010 during a compassionate leave from jail.

13. Age limits for "youth" or "child" vary. The minister of justice always used eighteen years as the legal age for defining minors. The age of consent for sex work was also eighteen (for sex in general it is sixteen years). But some social workers use "very young prostitutes" to describe any sex worker under twenty-three years old (TK 2002–2003, 25437, nr 31, *Brief Minister*, 13 May 2003, p. 12). The spokespersons for the Liberal Party and the Christian Democrats also used twenty-three years old to define "youth prostitution" (TK 2008–2009, 28638, nr 39 [*Verslag Algemeen Overleg Vaste Kamercommissie Justitie*], 22 December 2008, p. 7, 13).

14. See the spokespersons of the Liberal Party and the Christian Union (TK 2008–2009, 28638, nr 39 [*Verslag Algemeen Overleg Vaste Commissie Justitie*], 22 December 2008, p. 7, 13). Investigation turned up no such cases.

15. TK 2007–2008, *Verslag Algemeen Overleg Vaste Commissie BZK en Justitie*, 4 September 2008, p. 2; TK 2008–2009, 28638 (*Mensenhandel*), nr 44 (*Verslag Algemeen Overleg Vaste Commissie Justitie*), 13 July 2009, p. 2.

16. The UN Protocol to Prevent, Suppress and Punish Trafficking in Persons, Especially Women and Children (Palermo Protocol), 2000.

17. For a serious discussion of Nigerian trafficking into the Netherlands and the Koolvis trial against the offenders, see Mensenhandel (2009, 389–399).

18. This had been a contested point during the parliamentary debates in 1999 when the Christian Democrat Party (CDA) tried to circumvent the Dutch constitution, stating that the Penal Code applies to the entire state territory, thus excluding local opt-outs (Outshoorn 2004).

19. Clients were supposed to ask the prostitute for her pass, but that would disclose her identity to the client. The minister then retracted the pass (not the registration), which doesn't solve the matter of how the client is supposed to check her registration (TK 2010–2011, 32211, nr 30 [*Derde Nota van Wijziging*], 10 February 2011).

20. Pauline van Meurs (Labour Party), EK 2011–2012, 32211 (*Wet regulering prostitutie en bestrijding misstanden seksbranche*), 57-10, 30 October 2012.

References

Acker, Hanneke, and Marijke Rawie, eds. 1982. *Seksueel geweld tegen vrouwen en meisjes.* The Hague, the Netherlands: Ministerie van Sociale Zaken en Werkgelegenheid.

Altink, Saskia, and Sylvia Bokelman. 2006. *Rechten van prostituees. Evaluatie Opheffing Bordeelverbod. De sociale positie van prostituees.* Amsterdam, the Netherlands: De Rode Draad.

Asante, Amma, and Karina Schaapman. 2005. *Het onzichtbare zichtbaar gemaakt. Prostitutie in Amsterdam.* Amsterdam, the Netherlands: Nota Partij van de Arbeid.

Biesma, S., R. van der Stoep, H. Naayer, B. Bieleman. 2006. *Verboden bordelen. Evaluatie Opheffing bordeelverbod niet-legale prostitutie.* Groningen, the Netherlands: Intraval.

Bovenkerk, Frank, and G. J. Pronk. 2007. "Over de bestrijding van loverboymethoden." *Justitiële Verkenningen* 7, no. 7: 82–94. Themanummer Mensenhandel.

Bovenkerk, Frank, Marion San, Miranda Boone, Tim Boekhout van Solinge, and Dick Korf. 2006. *Loverboys of Modern Pooierschap.* Amsterdam, the Netherlands: Augustus.

Cobb, Roger W., and Charles D. Elder. 1972. *Participation in American Politics: The Dynamics of Agenda-Building.* Boston: Allyn and Bacon.

Daalder, Annelies L. 2002. *Het bordeelverbod opgeheven: Prostitutie in 2000–2001.* The Hague, the Netherlands: Wetenschappelijk Onderzoeks- en Ducumentatie Centrum (WODC).

———. 2007a. *Prostitutie in Nederland na opheffing van het bordeelverbod.* The Hague, the Netherlands: Wetenschappelijk Onderzoeks- en Documentatie Centrum (WODC). Onderzoek en Beleid, nr. 249.

———. 2007b. "De opheffing van het bordeelverbod. Gevolgen voor mensenhandel?" *Justitiële Verkenningen* 33, no. 7: 64–77.

Dekker, Helga, Ruud Tap, and Ger Homburg. 2006. *De sociale positie van prostituees. Eindrapport.* Amsterdam, the Netherlands: Regioplan.

Dery, David. 1984. *Problem Definition in Policy Analysis.* Lawrence: University Press of Kansas.

De Vries, Petra. 1997. *Kuisheid voor mannen, vrijheid voor vrouwen. De reglementering en de bestrijding van prostitutie in Nederland in de tweede helft van de negentiende eeuw.* Hilversum, the Netherlands: Verloren.

Goderie, Marjolein, Sandra ter Woerds, and Frans Spierings. 2002. *Illegaliteit, onvrijwilligheid en minderjarigheid in de prostitutie een jaar na de opheffing van het bordeelverbod.* Utrecht: Verwey-Jonker Instituut.

Gusfield, Joseph. 1981. *The Culture of Public Problems.* Chicago: University of Chicago Press.

Hopkins, Ruth. 2005. *Ik laat je nooit meer los. Het meisje, de vrouw, de handelaar en de agent.* Breda, the Netherlands: De Geus.

Kagie, Rudie. 2010. *Privacy. Hoe Nederland verandert in een controlestaat.* Amsterdam, the Netherlands: Uitgeverij Contact.

KLPD. 2008. *Schone schijn. De signalering van mensenhandel in de vergunde prostitutiesector.* Driebergen, the Netherlands: Report Dienst Nationale Recherche KLPD.

Mensenhandel. 2007. *Vijfde rapportage van de Nationaal Rapporteur.* The Hague, the Netherlands: Bureau NRM.

———. 2009. *Zevende rapportage van de Nationaal Rapporteur.* The Hague, the Netherlands: Bureau NRM.

———. 2012. *Mensenhandel in en uit beeld. Cijfermatige reportage 2007–2011.* The Hague, the Netherlands: Bureau NRM.

Outshoorn, Joyce. 2001. "Debating Prostitution in Parliament. A Feminist Analysis." *European Journal of Women's Studies* 8, no. 4: 472–91.

———. 2004. "Voluntary and Forced Prostitution: The 'Realistic Approach' of the Netherlands." In *The Politics of Prostitution: Women's Movements, Democratic States and the Globalization of Sex Commerce,* ed. Joyce Outshoorn, 185–205. Cambridge, U.K.: Cambridge University Press.

———. 2005. "The Political Debates on Prostitution and Trafficking." *Social Politics* 12, no. 1 (Spring): 141–55.

Regeerakkoord. 2007. *Coalitieakkoord tussen de Tweede Kamerfracties van CDA PvdA en Christen Unie.* February 7.

Schaapman, Karina. 2004. *Zonder moeder.* Amsterdam, the Netherlands: Balans.

Schattschneider, E. E. 1960. *The Semi-Sovereign People: A Realist's View of Democracy in America.* New York: Holt, Rinehart, and Winston.

Schneider, A., and H. Ingram. 1993. "Social Construction of Target Populations: Implications for Politics and Policy." *American Political Science Review* 87, no. 2: 334–47.

———. 1995. "Social Construction (Continued): Response." *American Political Science Review* 89, no. 2: 441–46.

———. 1997. *Policy Design for Democracy.* Lawrence: University Press of Kansas.

Schur, Edward M. 1980. *The Politics of Deviance: Stigma Contests and the Uses of Power.* Englewood Cliffs, N.J.: Prentice Hall.

Spector, Malcolm, and John D. Kitsuse. 1977. *Constructing Social Problems.* Menlo Park, Calif.: Cummings.

Vanwesenbeeck, Ine. 1994. *Prostitutes' Well-Being and Risk.* Amsterdam, the Netherlands: Free University Press.

Vanwesenbeeck, Ine, Mechtild Hoïng, and Paul Vennix. 2002. *De sociale positie van prostituees in de gereguleerde bedrijven, een jaar na wetswijziging.* Utrecht/Den Haag, the Netherlands: Rutgers Nisso Groep/WODC, Ministerie van Justitie.

Van Wijk, Anton, Annemiek Nieuwenhuis, Denise van Tuyn, Tom van Ham, Jos Kuppens, and Henk Ferwerda. 2010. *Kwetsbaar* beroep. *Een onderzoek naar de prostitutiebranche in Amsterdam*. Arnhem, the Netherlands: Bureau Beke.

Wagenaar, Hendrik. 2006. "Democracy and Prostitution: Deliberating the Legalization of Brothels in the Netherlands." *Administration and Society* 38, no. 3: 198–235.

Wagenaar, Hendrik, Sietske Altink, and Helga Amesberger. 2013. *Final Report of the International Comparative Study of Prostitution Policy: Austria and the Netherlands*. The Hague, the Netherlands: Platform 31.

Weitzer, Ron. 2012. *Legalizing Prostitution: From Illicit Vice to Lawful Business*. New York: New York University Press.

CHAPTER 9

Comrades, Push the Red Button!

Prohibiting the Purchase of Sexual Services
in Sweden but Not in Finland

Gregg Bucken-Knapp, Johan Karlsson Schaffer, and Pia Levin

FOR SCHOLARS OF SEX WORK, Sweden's decision to criminalize the purchase, albeit not the sale, of sexual services in 1999 represents a legislative development that has been the subject of considerable analysis. Scholars have presented many explanations as to why Sweden, under the governing Social Democratic Party, became the first state to regard prosecuting the buyer as an effective policy for reducing prostitution. Some accounts stress the importance of feminist policymakers and elites (Ekberg 2004; Östergren 2006), others highlight the significance of Sweden's membership in the European Union (Gould 2001), and still others emphasize the long-term residual impact of Swedish religious traditions in conjunction with a contemporary emergence of feminist ideas (Dodillet 2009). Regardless of one's preferred explanation, there is a deep-seated consensus that Sweden's prostitution model merits considerable attention, not least because of the degree to which it is invoked in other states considering prostitution policy reform.

However, scholars have directed comparatively less effort toward analyzing similar reform processes in neighboring Nordic countries, where prostitution policy reform has also been a subject of great public debate in recent years. Beyond similar contentious debates over prostitution policy, neighboring Nordic states share a consensus-oriented political culture, a historically dominant evangelical Lutheran state-church, high levels of gender equality, strong women's organizations, a high or very high percentage of female legislators, and an advanced social-democratic welfare state. Yet despite these similarities among Nordic states, no overarching Nordic prostitution policy model exists. In 1999, Denmark opted to decriminalize prostitution, stopping short of fully legalizing sex work and granting it legal protection in line with all other professions. In 2006, Finland tightened its laws governing prostitution, making it illegal to purchase sexual services from a knowingly trafficked individual or a victim of pandering. In 2008, Norway criminalized the purchase of sexual services (CPSS) similar to Sweden, yet also featured an extraterritorial component prohibiting Norwegian citizens from purchasing sexual services abroad.

Alongside the Swedish experience, Finland's 2006 revision of its prostitution policies stands out as particularly intriguing. On the face of it, the Finnish reform represented an expanded use of criminalization as a policy tool, with the ban on purchasing sex from trafficked individuals joining existing legislation prohibiting buying or selling sexual services in public places. Yet what makes the Finnish case analytically tantalizing is that Finnish legislators rejected the Swedish prostitution model. Such an outcome was far from a given, particularly with the strong support for CPSS among Finnish policymakers in the early 2000s.

Against this backdrop, this chapter examines the paths leading to divergent prostitution policy reform in Sweden and Finland in the 1990s and 2000s. Why did Sweden wind up with CPSS but not Finland? Drawing from literature in comparative politics that examines "ideational turns," our argument is as follows: In the case of Sweden, feminist actors across the political spectrum who supported the ban successfully deployed gender equality ideas as well as causal stories (Stone 1989) characterizing female prostitutes as having abusive life histories in a number of crucial settings, including party congresses, parliamentary debates, official documents, and statements to the press. Pro-ban actors benefited from the degree to which gender equality ideas were more broadly embedded in Swedish political institutions by the early and mid-1990s, the result of long-term efforts by Swedish feminists. No such pervasive discourse involving gender equality ideas existed in Finnish society or its political institutions. While some feminists there pushed for CPSS from the 1990s onward, they were confronted with interest groups, epistemic actors, and policymakers who successfully mobilized ideas concerning the rights of individuals to make decisions regarding their own body and sphere of economic activity without state interference. Of equal importance, the Finnish reform process took place against the backdrop of specific concerns that trafficking in human beings for sexual purposes to Finland was growing rapidly and required a firm policy response. As such, the legislative outcome became centered on the need to ensure Finnish compliance with the 2000 United Nations (UN) Protocol to Prevent, Suppress and Punish Trafficking in Persons, especially Women and Children (also known as the Palermo Protocol).

We draw on multimethod qualitative research to document the differing ideational terrains underpinning the Swedish and Finnish reform processes. Our analysis relies on official documents in the form of parliamentary debate minutes, committee reports, and legislative proposals, as well as minutes from party congress debates, NGO and academic reports, and media statements by key actors. By constructing a narrative based on relevant documents and statements, we demonstrate that gender equality ideas played an unequivocal role in the emergence of the Swedish ban, whereas Finnish policy reflected a sharply more competitive ideational climate with different underlying conditions.

Theoretical Frame

Our analysis is informed by the ideational turn in comparative politics (Béland and Cox 2011; Berman 2001; Blyth 2002; Gofas and Hay 2010), as well as the empirical constructivist literature in international relations (Checkel 1998; Keck and Sikkink 1998; Price 1998; Towns 2010). Broadly, these related approaches have demonstrated how ideas are central to the agenda-setting process, the definition of policy challenges, and the shape of interpretive frameworks held by actors. As such, a focus on the role of ideas allows scholars to highlight an important variable in the policymaking process, one overlooked by literatures chiefly emphasizing actors' interests or institutions. In keeping with the ideational literature, we focus attention on both the ideas that were relevant in each setting and the extent to which actors were able to draw upon these ideas in pushing for policy reform, or the extent to which competing ideas blocked legislative success (Bucken-Knapp and Karlsson 2008). A central component of this ideational approach is the contention that actors must take into account broader ideational frameworks when seeking to mobilize support on behalf of their policy preferences (Gourevitch 1989; Hansen and King 2001; Kingdon 1995). This is not to argue that ideas are highlighted at the exclusion of other explanatory factors in this chapter. As Thomas Risse-Kappen (1994) has noted, ideas cannot float freely—if they are to "matter," they require actors embedded in institutions. Thus we share the explicit conviction of scholars such as Vivien Schmidt (2002) that ideas must be nested alongside "institutional and/or interest-based variables" when analyzing the politics of reform.

The idea of gender equality is especially important to the prostitution policy reform processes in both Finland and Sweden. However, gender equality as an idea can vary substantially from setting to setting (as well as over time) and does not reflect one universally shared analysis of social and political problems requiring action. Indeed, even within individual states where gender equality has become broadly supported by elites, political parties differ in their conceptualizations of gender equality goals and the necessary instruments for achieving those goals (Magnusson 2000; Eduards 1991). As such, prior to examining the Swedish and Finnish prostitution policy reform process, it is necessary to detail briefly the contemporary role of gender equality as an idea in both Sweden and Finland.

In Sweden, the dominant contemporary understanding of gender equality reflects a mix of liberal, socialist/reformist, and radical ideational influences (Sainsbury 2004). Reformist feminism shaped ideas about gender equality by emphasizing equality of result (i.e., policy outcomes intended to eradicate gender inequality by focusing on "sameness" in outcomes rather than "equal differences"), by privileging state intervention into more private spheres of life, and by subsuming liberal concerns about equal rights and status. A comparatively weaker radical feminist movement has also shaped contemporary Swedish ideas about gender equality, partially through its emphasis on the personal as political (Sainsbury 2004) and by calling attention to structural violence against women. Moreover, the contemporary Swedish gender equality discourse can, to some extent, be characterized by distinguishing it from that of the other Scandinavian states. As Trude Langvasbråten (2008) notes, the Swedish discourse "understand[s] and articulate[s] gendered inequalities as a societal problem, deeply embedded in social structures, more specifically a 'gender-power system.'" This is in sharp contrast to neighboring Scandinavian states, where gender inequality is framed as stemming from individual choices and where policy measures such as affirmative action have been heavily contested (Langvasbråten 2008). Thus the influence of gender equality ideas in the case of Swedish prostitution policy reform will be seen chiefly in policy entrepreneurs' emphasis on using state policy to alter unequal power/gender relations and to bring about an end to structural violence against women within Swedish society.

Since the 1950s in Finland, gender equality has been pursued within the frame of welfare state policies that aim to create social equality. Rather than gender equality being an ideological value in and of itself, women's political and economic participation is closely linked to nation building and to social and economic progress. As a result, the Finnish gender equality debate has emphasized policies that are intended to improve women's opportunities without explicitly acknowledging the role of structural (male) oppression. Thus in the Finnish debate, many assume that feminism—as a political movement that privileges and promotes gender equality through gender-specific political and social action—is unnecessary. Furthermore, feminism is assumed to create discord because gender equality in Finland is generally interpreted as part of the pursuit of social justice; policymaking to this end has de-emphasized conflict between the genders and placed a premium on developing consensus-oriented solutions (Holli 2003; 1991).

Especially since the late 1980s, Finnish gender equality has become increasingly cast in neoliberal terms, emphasizing individual rights and interpreting the concept of gender equality as one of nondiscrimination. This move toward formal equality accentuates that regulations and guidelines apply equally to men and women and stresses individuals' freedom of choice and protecting private lives from interference (Kantola, Nousiainen, and Saari 2012; Pylkkänen 2012). As we detail in the next section, these diverging notions of gender equality in Sweden and Finland regarding where it is acceptable for the state to interfere legislatively in people's private lives had a significant impact in shaping the debate on the criminalization of the purchase of sexual services in these countries.

Sweden: Gender Equality and Victimhood

The adoption of the CPSS ban by the Swedish Parliament in 1998 was a substantial shift beyond existing policy that had criminalized procurement. Yet it was not the first time that prostitution had been on the legislative agenda during the postwar era (Dodillet 2009; Östergren 2006). In 1972, Swedish Social Democratic Labor Party (SAP) Justice Minister Lennart

Geijer established the Sexual Crime Investigation in order to address what he saw as the need for a greater correspondence between existing laws and shifting sexual norms. The Investigation's final report was released in 1976, and while not focusing exclusively on prostitution, the report highlighted procuring and brothels as features of the commercial sex industry that must be prohibited in order to uphold societal morals. The report was subject to strong criticism from many actors who submitted written statements during the subsequent remiss procedure. The youth wing of the ruling SAP called the investigation to task for not emphasizing the relationship between capitalist society and sexual crimes. The National Federation of Social Democratic Women (SSKF), under the leadership of Göteborg member of Parliament (MP) Lisa Mattsson—who, as president, is formally empowered to speak, but not vote, at party congresses and board meetings—argued that the Riksdag needed to advocate a "societal view of sexuality" and argued on behalf of "contact between equal people" as the precursor for a healthy sexuality (Dodillet 2009, 80; McBride and Mazur 2010). On the basis of the substantial protests voiced during the remiss period, the report was shelved. However, it did lead to the convening of the 1977 Prostitution Investigation by the recently elected nonsocialist coalition.

No less controversial than its predecessor, the work of the 1977 Investigation was marred by sharp internal divisions. Chief investigator Inger Lindquist, whose own analysis focused on individual rather than gender structures, opposed attempts by chief secretary Hanna Olsson and other experts to portray prostitution as stemming from patriarchal society. Following the decision by Lindquist to remove these critical voices, her 1981 report dismissed criminalization as having undesirable consequences, including pushing the sex trade underground, placing female prostitutes at risk, creating enforcement difficulties, and being unlikely to act as a meaningful deterrent (SOU 1981:71).[1] Instead, the report proposed the prohibition of public pornographic performances (the only measure enacted), criminalizing the purchase of sexual services from a prostitute under the influence of narcotics, a broader application of existing legal measures against procurement, and prosecuting landlords with knowledge that a property had been let to those involved in procurement.

While no comprehensive prostitution policy emerged, this period did coincide with a broader ideational development among Swedish political elites, epistemic actors, and relevant advocacy groups that contributed directly to the adoption of CPSS. A gradual process unfolded from the late 1960s to the mid-1990s in which the broad Swedish women's movement recategorized women's issues as matters of *gender equality*. While women's issues as a focus of political activity were sometimes constructed so as to formulate cross-class alliances of women, men as potential allies were not targeted. Yet according to Diane Sainsbury (2004, 70), gender equality broadened the possibilities for political mobilization, facilitating the inclusion of like-minded men, irrespective of class or party identification. This "discursive turn" was strategically crucial, in that the Swedish women's movement's goals were no longer regarded as particularistic to women when advanced under the mantle of more general societal norms central to democratic societies—namely, equality and democracy (Sainsbury 2004). Epistemic actors in Sweden contributed conceptual tools that facilitated a gendered analysis of existing conditions preventing the attainment of gender equality. Most prominent among these was historian Yvonne Hirdmann (1988), who in the late 1980s popularized the term *genussystem*, characterized by a dichotomy that keeps male and female attributes distinct and by a logic of hierarchy in which men are considered the societal norm. Governmental activity focusing on gender equality during this period included the appointment of several investigative committees, leading to several major reports, including "Women in State Service" (*Kvinnor i statlig tjänst* [SOU 1975:43]), examining the working conditions of women working within the state; "Steps on the Way" (*Steg på väg* [SOU 1979:56]), , resulting from the 1975 UN Women's Conference in Mexico City; and "Every Other Seat for a Woman" (*Varannan damernas* [SOU 1987:19]), charged with identifying strategies for increasing women's political representation.

The impact of gender equality ideas on public policy was certainly slowed (if not halted) as a result of the 1991 parliamentary elections, when the number of female MPs fell from 38 percent to 34 percent. For those campaigning for full numeric equality in the Riksdag, such a reversal was deemed catastrophic. As a result, a broad feminist network of female politicians, academics, and other public figures formed *Stödstrumporna* (Support Stockings), threatening to run candidates in the 1994 election if established parties did not place greater emphasis on gender equality and if female candidates were not more actively promoted. Parliamentary parties took this challenge to the party system seriously: in 1994, 40 percent of elected MPs were women. Moreover, the Social Democrats, returning to their regular role as the governing party, stressed their commitment to integrating gender issues into the mainstream of party concerns.

Even before the election, the then minister of gender equality, Liberal Bengt Westerberg, announced two measures placing prostitution front and center on the political stage, reflecting the degree to which the party viewed pursuing gender equality policies as politically important. First, in December 1992, Westerberg announced that, given the decade that had lapsed since the 1981 parliamentary report on prostitution, a new investigative committee would be formed to examine the need for policy reform, with the question of "criminalizing the john's activity" falling under the report's remit (*Expressen* 1992). Inga-Britt Törnell, the former (and Sweden's first) ombudsman for gender equality and a then-serving justice on the Supreme Court of Sweden, was appointed as sole investigator for the report. Shortly thereafter, Westerberg also established the Women's Violence Commission (*Kvinnovåldskommissionen*), the mandate of which was "from a women's perspective, to conduct an overview of questions that have to do with violence against women and propose remedies for counteracting such violence" (Regeringens proposition 1997/98:55).

Similar to the preceding investigation, the work of the Törnell committee was marked by internal divisions among staff members and media leaks prior to the publication of the final report. Professor Sven Axel Månsson, one of the academic experts appointed to the report, resigned in protest following public comments from Törnell questioning the wisdom of criminalization, while he simultaneously declared his support for CPSS (*TT Nyhe*tsbanken 1994). However, when released, the Törnell report proposed a policy in sharp contrast to that of earlier prostitution investigations: criminalization of both the buyer and seller of sexual services. Törnell maintained that criminalizing both parties would serve an important normative function, bringing about increased gender equality and signaling societal opposition to the sex trade. She argued criminalization would deter both buyers and sellers and saw it as a device for women to resist efforts to get them to enter the sex trade (SOU 2010:49, 70–71). Reflecting the contentious nature of the investigation's work, two of the assigned experts produced separate dissenting opinions, one calling for no criminalization and the other advocating for CPSS (SOU 1995:15).

However, Törnell's attempt to portray criminalization of both buyers and sellers as a logical consequence of the desire to achieve gender equality squared poorly with broadly held societal views of women entering the sex trade as the result of abusive life experiences and dependency on drugs and alcohol. To criminalize those who were already oppressed would amount to additional punishment, as the SSKF, then under the leadership of Stockholm MP Inger Segelström, argued:

> The majority of prostitutes find themselves in a very vulnerable position. This is reflected in, among other things, the injuries of a physical, psychological and social character that impact female prostitutes to a great extent. Therefore, it should only be the customers' actions that are criminalized. An additional reason [is that] in a situation where both parties are criminal, the police will direct their activities against prostitutes. The risk, in practice, is apparent that it would just be the one party, that is the women, who would be charged and punished. In that sense, an unequal situation would only be reinforced. (SSKF 1995)

Similarly, the National Organization of Women's Shelters in Sweden (ROKS) submitted a written response to the Törnell report arguing, "We propose a criminalization of only the purchaser. [It] is clearly confirmed as to the power relation between the parties: the 'seller's' powerlessness, resulting from drugs and alcohol, sexual assault in childhood—80% to 90% according to research, low self-esteem, etc. If one these adds a gender equality perspective to the discussion, the logic stops abruptly" (National Organization of Women's Shelters in Sweden 1995).

Indeed, not only pro-CPSS proponents argued that criminalization of both parties would negatively impact the well-being of female sex workers. At the 1997 SAP congress, party leadership, seeking to block four pro-CPSS resolutions, declared its opposition to the conclusions reached in the Törnell report: "[Prostitution] involves women being exploited and degraded and it counteracts our striving towards equality between men and women . . . The party central committee considers it out of the question to criminalize prostitutes. That would be inhumane and lead to the women being put on par with her exploiter. Prostitution is one of the most extreme consequences of man's domination and women's subordination" (Socialdemokraterna 1997a, 33).

Despite efforts by then Minister of Gender Equality Laila Freivalds to block the congress from overruling the party leadership, nearly all speakers stressed the symbolic importance of the ban in addition to its expected outcome of reducing prostitution. Delegate Carina Brandt implored her fellow members to vote in favor of criminalizing purchasers: "If [this vote] goes so far as to a roll call, you should know that the green button stands for continued exploitation of society's daughters and the red button for stop! Comrades, push the red button!" (Socialdemokraterna 1997b, 202).

Similarly, one of the key architects of the pro-CPSS strategy in the SAP, Inger Segelström, stressed that backing CPSS would show that "the world's most gender equal party in the world's most gender equal society . . . can no longer accept that men can use money to buy women" (Socialdemokraterna 1997b, 196). While such arguments may have overlapped with those of transnational feminist networks opposing prostitution, Gunilla Ekberg, who has served as coexecutive director for the Coalition Against Trafficking in Women (one of the leading NGOs mobilizing against legalized prostitution) stresses that the initiative to see CPSS adopted stemmed from the Swedish feminist movement (2004, 1191).

When the ban came to a vote in the Riksdag in 1998, it did so as one of a series of broader measures designed to counteract violence against women, known as the Women's Peace Bill, which had its origins in the Women's Violence Commission of 1992. The SAP, the Left Party, the Greens, and the Center Party supported the proposed CPSS, while the Moderates and the Liberals opposed any form of criminalization. The Christian Democrats backed Törnell's proposal, wherein both parties would be criminalized. Some critics, such as Liberal MP Lennart Rohdin, questioned whether the desire to implement the ban had simply become symbolic politics, noting, "I have a feeling that even if we were in agreement that criminalization was of no help to prostitutes, that the need by many for this moral condemnation is so great that it would still determine the outcome" (Riksdagens snabbprotokoll 1998).

The SAP Labor Market Minister Ulrica Messing admitted the normative components of the legislation but stressed that these would bring about changed attitudes in Swedish society: "We think that prostitution is one of the worst expressions of the uneven division of power between men and women, and that it doesn't just impact prostitutes or those who purchase their services, but all of society. That's why we propose a criminalization of the purchaser. We are convinced that this will result in changed attitudes and decrease violence in society. We are also convinced that this will reduce prostitution" (Riksdagens snabbprotokoll 1998).

When the votes were cast, only the Moderate Party and the bulk of the Liberals voted against the bill, with the Christian Democrats abstaining. Based on salient ideas regarding gender equality, coupled with a narrative of female prostitutes as victims of abuse, feminist actors were able to mobilize support for a policy that made Sweden the first state to criminalize the purchase, albeit not the sale, of sexual services through the Prohibition of Purchase of Sexual Services Act (Swedish Ministry of Justice 1998).

Finland: Competing Ideas and Compromise Policy

For much of the twentieth century, prostitution received little attention in Finland; historically, it was viewed as a problem of morality, health, law and order, youth, or gender equality (Järvinen 1990). In the 1980s, street prostitution was invisible and considered highly unusual (Häkkinen 1995; Varsa 1986). Police in Helsinki knew of only a few dozen prostitutes, who were believed to work independently. Consequently, when the Vagrancy Act of 1936 controlling prostitutes was repealed in 1986 (Järvinen 1990), only sanctions against pimping remained.

It was not until the early 1990s that Finnish prostitution discourse shifted decisively, when Russian and Estonian women selling sex on the streets, in restaurants, and in hotels increased the visibility of commercial sex and directed the public focus toward transnational sex work (Marttila 2009). Observers viewed the causes of prostitution to be a result of political and economic changes in the former Soviet Union, improved possibilities for crossing borders, and notable wealth disparities between Finland and its neighbors to the east and south (Jyrkinen 2005). Yet the economic recession of the 1990s also increased the number of Finnish women involved in sex work, normalizing commercial sex and increasing the overall number of sex workers (Kauppinen 2000). Such structural factors were far less central in the Swedish case, where pro-ban actors were driven by a general conviction that a sex purchase ban represented an effective practical response to Sweden's rather limited prostitution market, as well as an important symbolic statement about unequal power relations between men and women.

At this time, Finnish public debate on prostitution centered largely on nuisances associated with commercial sex—its connection to violence and international crime and public order disturbances. Helsinki residents demanded parliamentary action against street prostitution and disturbing the neighborhood peace (Koskela, Tani, and Tuominen 2000). Yet lacking legislation, law enforcement officials attempted to control prostitution with ad hoc measures, such as restricting night traffic on certain streets.

In response, female MPs throughout the 1990s submitted private member bills demanding the restriction of procurement (KK 590/1993, KK 9/1994, KK 594/1997, KK 868/1997, TA 26/1995). In 1996, MP Paula Kokkonen (National Coalition), together with sixty-two male and female cosignatories, demanded criminalization of attempts to purchase sex in public places (LA 31/1996). According to political scientist Anne Maria Holli, the initiative was a compromise agreed upon by the Network of Women MPs in Parliament (Holli 2004, 111).[2] The use of criminal law was intended to decrease harassment of ordinary women. In fact, Kokkonen pointed out that prostitution was a large-scale social problem that could not be eliminated by criminal law alone but with social policy measures. The initiative received a mixed response in the initial hearing, as some male MPs preferred criminalizing both customer and seller or reinforcing the Vagrant Act, which also criminalized prostitutes (PTK 93/1996). The initiative was sent to the Legal Affairs Committee where it was later merged with the revisions of the Sex Crime Act (HE 6/1997) in which the government proposed criminalizing the purchase of sexual services from a minor. The Legal Affairs Committee decided in the end not to include criminalization of attempts to purchase sexual services in public places in its revision of the Sex Crime Act (LaVM 3/1998). Consequently, Left Alliance MP Annika Lapintie proposed a Swedish-style CPSS in the final stages of the legislative process, just weeks after the Swedish Riksdag had passed its bill. At the time, most MPs shared the opinion of the Legal Affairs Committee that street prostitution was a question of public ordinance regulation rather than a topic for the Penal Code. MPs who were against the proposition feared that the Swedish legislation would remain only symbolic, and several of them quoted fellow MP Kokkonen's initiative from 1996 that prostitution could not be erased by criminal law alone (PTK 77/1998). As a result, Lapintie's arguments that a general CPSS was important to Finnish gender equality fell short by eighty-three votes against sixty-two, keeping the initial governmental proposal and making it a crime to purchase sex from a minor only.

Prostitution remained a hot topic and efforts to diminish street prostitution continued in the municipal arena when the Helsinki city council passed a municipal ordinance that criminalized the purchase and sale of sexual services in public places in 1999. While Lapintie's efforts to enact CPSS had not been supported by the government in the 1990s, she tried again in 2002, receiving considerable backing from her fellow legislators. Disturbed by law enforcement's interpretation of the ban to apply to prostitutes only (Holli 2004), Lapintie collected one hundred signatories in the two hundred–person Eduskunta to support her call for the government to adopt CPSS (TPA 178/2002), and a newspaper poll showed that as many as 137 MPs actually supported the call (Helsingin Sanomat 2002). Simultaneously, Minister of Justice Johannes Koskinen (Social Democrat) appointed a working group to suggest changes to the Penal Code in order to comply with the Palermo Protocol, adopted by the UN in 2000. Among other tasks, the group was commissioned to assess whether CPSS was necessary.

The working group presented its opinion in July 2003, proposing CPSS by a one-person majority (Oikeusministeriö 2003, 5). While advocating CPSS, gender equality ideas did not chiefly guide the working group's analysis. Rather, the report proclaimed prostitution to be socially problematic and connected to mental and physical health problems and drug abuse among prostitutes. The report assumed prostitutes to be highly susceptible to violence, which potentially worsened their already vulnerable social positions. The working group also argued that prostitution was mainly under the control of organized crime and that CPSS would send a powerful signal that prostitution is not accepted in Finnish society.

However, the report also included two dissenting opinions. In the first, Jukka Lindstedt, chairman and senior adviser for legislative affairs at the Ministry of Justice; Counsellor Jaakko Haltunen at the Ministry for Foreign Affairs; and Judge Ulla Lahtinen at the Helsinki District Court were opposed to criminalization. They proposed new legislation on pandering and trafficking, which, if required, would be limited to cases where the seller is a victim of human trafficking or pandering. In a second dissenting opinion, Haltunen and Lahtinen argued that solely criminalizing the purchase of sexual services was unnatural and artificial, whereas a more efficient and equitable way to combat prostitution would be to criminalize both buying and selling.

In the initial hearing round that followed the report, seventy-two statements from legal experts, law enforcement, feminist actors, and interest groups focused on prostitution in relation to international crime.

Regardless of the policy advocated, these actors stressed that their concern was for victims of trafficking and procuring (Oikeusministeriö 2004, 3). For instance, the Helsinki district court stated that neither social nor gender equality would increase by criminalizing the purchase of sexual services. Rather, the court suspected that criminalizing the customers would complicate investigating and ruling on procuring and human trafficking for sexual exploitation (Helsingin käräjäoikeus 2003). Conversely, the National Council of Women of Finland argued that criminalizing the purchase of sex (rather than sexual services) would have an immediate effect in preventing human trafficking and sex tourism to Finland (Naisjärjestöjen Keskusliitto 2003).

Consultative bodies that submitted statements during the initial hearing round seem to have been influenced by a report from the National Bureau of Investigation (NBI), whose statements estimated that the annual number of people engaged in prostitution was between ten thousand and fifteen thousand and controlled by organized crime in Russia and Estonia (Aaltio 2009). Yet the NBI report, and the statements that cited it, regarded foreign prostitutes as voluntarily and consciously having chosen the sex industry, given their lack of other realistic choices due to the socioeconomic situation in their home country (Leskinen 2003). Therefore, while considered victims, sex workers were simultaneously considered responsible for their actions (Roth 2010).

In April 2004, Minister of Justice Koskinen presented the first part of the working group's proposals on measures to combat human trafficking, pandering, and prostitution (HE 34/2004) to the Eduskunta. CPSS was not included since the government decided to evaluate the effects of an earlier Public Order Act (HE 20/2002), one that addressed a much broader range of activities thought to constitute a public nuisance, including instances where the sale of sexual services resulted in a disturbance of the peace. Further, the government chose to wait for guidelines to emerge from the Council of Europe Convention on Action against Human Trafficking in Human Beings and for more data to emerge as to the impact of the Swedish ban. Once it became clear that the Ministry of Justice planned to leave out CPSS from the 2004 proposal, Lapintie opted to bring forth her own initiative, calling for CPSS as requested in the working group's majority proposal (LA 22/2004). Lapintie, together with eight female cosignatories across party lines, argued that the CPSS would improve both gender and social equality as the ban would work preventively and reinforce the tools to combat trafficking. Several MPs contested Lapintie's proposal, claiming it lacked pragmatism and ignored principles of fairness and sex workers' rights. Social Democrat MP Esa Lahtela stated that he could not understand how it would be possible to criminalize the buying of something but not the selling. He also feared that a one-sided CPSS could be used to extort men, viewing criminalization of both the selling and buying as a logical sign of true equality (PTK 32/2004).

Therefore, the prostitution policy debate reveals a striking contrast in the depth of ideas about gender equality that had permeated among MPs in the Finnish and Swedish parliaments. In Sweden, an increasingly hegemonic discourse in favor of CPSS spread throughout society, though not without resistance. Many law enforcement officials, administrative agencies, and some policymakers were skeptical of whether CPSS would decrease prostitution. However, an emerging sense among Swedish political elites that gender equality ought to inform policy as a whole provided a supportive and crucial ideational climate, strengthening the hand of those supporting CPSS. Pro-ban actors in Finland also put forward gender and social equality ideas, but these were neither the sole weapon of choice among CPSS proponents nor widely shared by Finnish political elites.

In the next two years, members of the Eduskunta went even further in questioning the assumption that CPSS would increase gender equality in Finland. Lapintie's motion from 2004 had been sent to the Legal Affairs Committee and merged with a government bill (HE 221/2005) put forward by newly appointed Minister of Justice Leena Luhtanen in December 2005, in one of her first official acts. In contrast to the Swedish case, Luhtanen's decision to do so appears to have been poorly anchored within the coalition government, as only the Swedish People's Party had formally decided (in 1999) to support CPSS. MPs in the Eduskunta underlined enforcement difficulties, claiming that a CPSS would push the sex trade underground. Several MPs contested whether CPSS really was a question of gender equality, and a few male MPs declared the bill to be insulting toward Finnish men as it portrayed them as exploiters of female victims (PTK 3/2006). Particularly notable is the fact that gender, and not party lines, structured the debate, with many male MPs opposing CPSS. This is in contrast to Sweden, where with only limited exceptions, the parliamentary debate was structured much more along party lines, with only Liberals, Moderates, and one

Christian Democrat MP speaking in opposition to CPSS. Female and male MPs were roughly equally represented in terms of speakers opposing CPSS.

And so by 2006, policymakers' support for CPSS had turned sharply more critical than it was in 2002. This shift was further accelerated by the presence of an epistemic actor who successfully called into question the assumed victim status of sex workers that had guided the initial call for CPSS. Anna Kontula, a prominent prostitution researcher, challenged claims about the number of sex workers in Finland, while also stressing that it was incorrect to portray all sex workers as unwilling participants in the sex trade. The assumed victim status of prostitutes that had previously guided the logic of the proponents of the ban was now under attack from a well-regarded epistemic actor. The Finnish sex workers' interest organization Salli, founded in 2002 to give sex workers a voice in the CPSS debate, largely shared Kontula's opinions, emphasizing sex workers' rights to decide over their own bodies (Kontula 2005). Salli participated actively in commenting on legislation concerning prostitution and was successful in defining prostitution as sex work and comparable to any other profession. According to Salli, government policy should aim to focus on guaranteeing sex workers rights, improving working conditions, and ending the stigma of sex work rather than abolishing sex work (Seksialan Liitto SALLI 2003). Unsurprisingly, Salli portrayed CPSS as bringing more harm to sex workers than good, an opinion also shared by Pro-Tukipiste, a well-regarded civic organization providing assistance to Finnish and foreign sex workers (Oikeusministeriö 2004).

Increasingly substantial opposition to CPSS and a fear that the bill would not pass led the chair of Parliament's Legal Affairs Committee Tuija Brax (Greens) to redraft an alternative compromise bill that strongly resembled the first dissenting opinion in the 2003 working group report. In this new bill, it would be illegal only to purchase sexual services from a knowingly trafficked victim, reflecting the consensus in Parliament on combatting trafficking. Although the compromise proposal was furiously criticized from both proponents and opponents of CPSS, it was passed in June 2006. Even though resistance against the original CPSS was articulated around sex workers' rights, MP Heidi Hautala (Greens) suspected another underlying motive behind the opposition: the male right to purchase sex (Hufvudstadsbladet 2006).

Conclusion

For scholars of comparative politics, the Swedish and Finnish cases of prostitution policy reform not only shed light on two intriguing instances of policy reform but also have value for debates as to the importance of "fit" and "national mood" when considering why policy entrepreneurs succeed in some settings yet fail in others (Kingdon 1995). Central to the broad literature stressing "fit" is the belief that policy entrepreneurs stand the greatest chance of success when arguments and proposals can be embedded in "persuasive ideational frameworks" (Hansen and King 2001). The two cases reviewed in this chapter shed light on this claim. In Sweden, an increasingly powerful discourse in favor of CPSS spread throughout society. While this did not occur without resistance, it nonetheless facilitated the attempt by pro-ban actors to establish a broader "fit" for their desired policy.

Certainly, many Swedish law enforcement officials, administrative agencies, and some policymakers were skeptical of whether CPSS would decrease prostitution. However, an emerging sense among Swedish political elites that a specific variant of gender equality, one in which state policy could be used to alter power relations and reduce structural violence against women, provided a supportive and crucial ideational climate, strengthening the hand of those supporting CPSS. By grafting the call for CPSS to ideas about gender equality that were broadly resonant in most Swedish political parties, pro-ban actors rendered powerless those arguments put forward by opponents, thus securing a decisive legislative victory.

In Finland, prevailing gender equality ideas prevented ban proponents from being able to establish the type of fit between idea and policy proposal that existed in the Swedish case. The notion that commercial sex is violence against women and an expression of inequality between genders (in which the state should intervene with the use of the penal code) was not widely shared by Finnish political elites. Consequently, gender equality was not the sole weapon of choice among CPSS proponents, many of whom identified themselves as feminists. Rather, the Finnish debate over prostitution policy reform was partially driven by concerns over trafficking in women from post-Communist states. Pro-ban actors advanced gender and social equality ideas, but instrumental arguments stressing the need to adopt CPSS as a means for combating trafficking were especially prevalent. Unlike Sweden, the proposed ban faced a strong challenge within Parliament, as well as from NGOs and epistemic actors. Opponents of the ban emphasized the incompatibility of CPSS with equality norms and the difficulties of enforcement, and they questioned whether women in prostitution were victims. Faced with a climate in which no one set of ideas could be invoked to guarantee victory for CPSS, the trafficking compromise emerged.

The notion of fit also has relevance for those following prostitution policy reform debates in other European states such as Denmark, France, Ireland, and the United Kingdom. Our findings suggest that local agents (Acharya 2004) seeking to import the Swedish prostitution model to new settings must be familiar with the relevant ideational frameworks in those states if they are to succeed. Gender equality ideas may have resonated in Sweden, but this does not imply they will have similar influence in all settings, as the power of these ideas is partially conditional on a successful fit. Indeed, Norway's 2008 sex purchase ban confirms this point. There, the key ideas that carried the day did not have to do only with gender equality but with law and order and concerns over the visibility of foreign sex workers in city centers (Bucken-Knapp and Karlsson Schaffer 2011).

Of course, an awareness of the ideational terrain in various states is not exclusive to those seeking adoption of CPSS. Actors looking to block the Swedish model or those seeking to build support for more liberal prostitution policies also need to consider how best to embed their policy proposals in persuasive ideas if they are to add that state to their column on the tote board. To no small extent then, the outcome of the ongoing battle over prostitution policy reform across Europe may reflect how well competing actors can properly read local ideational conditions and whether those can be harnessed in support of one's policy aims.

Notes

1. A subsequent parliamentary report on sexual crime was released in 1982. Here too, CPSS was rejected in favor of further measures to combat procurement. See *Våldtäkt och andra sexuella övergrepp* (SOU 1982, 61).

2. The Network of Women MPs was founded in 1991 in order to better influence legislative work. The network works across party lines and includes all female MPs. It has no official duties, gives no official statements or reports, and holds no votes but agrees on issues unanimously after discussion within the group (Helsingin Sanomat 2001).

References

Aaltio, Elina. 2009. *Vapaaksi marginaalista—marginaalista vapautta. Naisliikkeen ja prostituoitujen etuliikkeen kamppailu seksin oston kriminalisoinnista 2002–2006, TANE-julkaisuja nro 12.* Helsinki, Finland: Sosiaali-ja terveysministeriö, Tasa-arvoasiain neuvottelukunta.

Acharya, Amitav. 2004. "How Ideas Spread: Whose Norms Matter? Norm Localization and Institutional Change in Asian Regionalism." *International Organization* 58 (Spring): 239–75.

Béland, Daniel, and Robert Henry Cox, eds. 2011. *Ideas and Politics in Social Science Research.* New York: Oxford University Press.

Berman, Sheri. 2001. "Ideas, Norms and Culture in Political Analysis." *Comparative Politics* 33, no. 2: 231–50.

Blyth, Mark. 2002. *Great Transformations.* New York: Cambridge University Press.

Bucken-Knapp, Gregg, and Johan Karlsson. 2008. "Prostitution Policy Reform and the Causal Role of Ideas: A Comparative Study of Policymaking in the Nordic Countries." *Statsvetenskaplig Tidskrift* 110, no. 1: 59–65.

Bucken-Knapp, Gregg, and Johan Karlsson Schaffer. 2011. "The Same Policy, but Different Ideas: The Ideational Underpinnings of the Norwegian and Swedish Bans on the Purchase of Sexual Services." Paper presented at the Second European Conference on Politics and Gender, Central European University, Budapest, Hungary, January 13–15.

Checkel, Jeffrey. 1998. "The Constructivist Turn in International Relations Theory." *World Politics* 50, no. 2: 324–48.

Dodillet, Susanne. 2009. *Är sex arbete? Svensk och tysk prostitutionspolitik sedan 1970-talet.* Stockholm, Sweden: Vertigo Förlag.

Eduards, Maud L. 1991. "The Swedish Gender Model: Productivity, Pragmatism and Paternalism." *West European Politics* 14, no 3: 166–81.

Ekberg, Gunilla. 2004. "The Swedish Law That Prohibits the Purchase of Sexual Services." *Violence Against Women* 10, no. 10: 1187–218.

Expressen. 1992. "Westerberg till attack mot könshandeln." December 12.

Gofas, Andreas, and Colin Hay, eds. 2010. *The Role of Ideas in Political Analysis.* London: Routledge.

Gould, Arthur. 2001. "The Criminalization of Buying Sex: The Politics of Prostitution in Sweden." *Journal of Social Policy* 30, no. 3: 437–56.

Gourevitch, Peter. 1989. "Keynesian Politics: The Political Sources of Economic Policy Choices." In *The Political Power of Economic Ideas,* ed. Peter Hall, 87–106. Princeton, N.J.: Princeton University Press.

Häkkinen, Antti. 1995. *Rahasta vaan ei rakkaudesta.* Helsinki, Finland: Otava.

Hallituksen esitys Eduskunnalle kansainvälisen järjestäytyneen rikollisuuden vastaisen Yhdistyneiden Kansakuntien yleissopimuksen ihmiskauppaa ja maahanmuuttajien salakuljetusta koskevien lisäpöytäkirjojen hyväksymisestä ja niiden lainsäädännön alaan kuuluvien määräysten voimaansaattamisesta sekä laeiksi rikoslain 20 luvun ja järjestyslain 7 ja 16 §:n muuttamisesta (HE 221/2005).

Hallituksen esitys Eduskunnalle laiksi rikoslain muuttamisesta ja eräiksi siihen liittyviksi laeiksi (HE 34/2004).

Hallituksen esitys Eduskunnalle oikeudenkäyttöä, viranomaisia ja yleistä järjestystä vastaan kohdistuvia rikoksia sekä seksuaalirikoksia koskevien säännösten uudistamiseksi (HE 6/1997).

Hallituksen esitys laiksi turvallisuuden edistämistä yleisillä paikoilla koskevien säännösten uudistamiseksi (HE 20/2002).

Hansen, Randall, and Desmond King. 2001. "Eugenic Ideas, Political Interests and Policy Variance: Immigration and Sterilization Policy in Britain and the U.S." *World Politics* 53, no. 2: 237–63.

Hassi, Satu. *Seksiravintoloiden toiminnan rajoittamisesta* (KK 9/1994).

Hassi, Satu, et al. 1993. *Prostituutioon liittyvän liiketoiminnan vähentämiseksi tarvittavista toimenpiteistä* (KK 590/1993).

Helsingin käräjäoikeus. Helsingin käräjäoikeuden lausunto työryhmän osamietinnöstä "Ihmiskauppa, paritus ja prostituutio" (21.8.2003).

Helsingin Sanomat. "Oikeusministeriö ei lämpene seksipalvelujen ostokiellolle" (19.11.2002).

Hirdmann, Yvonne. 1988. "Genussytemet—reflexioner kring kvinnors sociala underordning." *Kvinnovetenskaplig tidskrift*, no. 3: 49–63.

Holli, Anne Maria. 1991. *Miehisestä tasa-arvosta kohti naisten käsitteellistä tilaa. Tasa-arvoasiain neuvottelukunnan tasa-arvopoliittinen diskurssi vv. 1972–86.* Helsinki, Finland: Helsingin yliopisto.

———. 2003. *Discourse and Politics for Gender Equality in Late Twentieth Century Finland.* Helsinki, Finland: University of Helsinki.

———. 2004. "Towards a New Prohibitionism? State Feminism, Women's Movements and Prostitution Policies in Finland." In *The Politics of Prostitution: Women's Movements, Democratic States and the Globalization of Sex Commerce*, ed. Joyce Outshoorn, 103–22. Cambridge, U.K.: Cambridge University Press.

Hufvudstadsbladet, *Sexköpslagen, Värdekonservatism i riksdagen "Det är som på 1950-eller 60-talet,"* 21.6.2006.

Järvinen, Margaretha. 1990. *Prostitution i Helsingfors—en studie i kvinnokontroll.* Åbo, Finland: Åbo Akademis förlag.

Jyrkinen, Marjut. 2005. *The Organisation of Policy Meets the Commercialisation of Sex: Global Linkages, Policies, Technologies.* Economy and Society 146. Helsinki, Finland: Hanken, Swedish School of Economics and Business Administration.

Kantola, Johanna, Kevät Nousiainen, and Milja Saari. 2012. "Johdanto." In *Tasa-arvo toisin nähtynä. Oikeuden ja politiikan näkökulmia tasa-arvoon ja yhden-vertaisuuteen*, ed. Johanna Kantola, Kevät Nousiainen, and Milja Saari, 7–30. Helsinki, Finland: Gaudeamus.

Kauppinen, Jaana. 2000. "Kansainvälinen ihmiskauppa ja suomalaisten suhtau-tuminen ulkomaalaisiin prostituoituihin." *Naistutkimus—Kvinnoforskning* 2: 60–64.

Keck, Margaret, and Kathryn Sikkink. 1998. *Activists beyond Borders*. New York: Cornell University Press.

Kingdon, John W. 1995. *Agendas, Alternatives, and Public Policies*. New York: Longman.

Kokkonen, Paula, et al. 1996. *Laiksi rikoslain 20 luvun 8 §:n muuttamisesta* (LA 31/1996 vp).

———. 1997. *Ilotalojen toimintaan puuttumisesta* (KK 594/1997 vp).

———. 1997. *Ilotalojen toimintaa tutkivien viranomaisten puolueettomuudesta* (KK 868/1997 vp).

Kontula, Anna. 2005. *Prostituutio Suomessa*. Helsinki, Finland: Sexpo säätiö.

Koskela, Hille, Sirpa Tani, and Martti Tuominen. 2005. *"Sen näköinen tyttö"— tutkimus katuprostituution vaikutuksista helsinkiläisten naisten arkielämään*. Helsinki, Finland: Helsingin kaupungin tietokeskuksen tutkimuksia.

Lakivaliokunnan mietintö. 1998. *Hallituksen esitys oikeudenkäyttöä, viranomaisia ja yleistä järjestystä vastaan kohdistuvia rikoksia sekä seksuaalirikoksia koskevien säännösten uudistamiseksi* (LaVM 3/1998).

Lapintie, Annika, et al. 2004. *Laki rikoslain 20 ja 25 luvun muuttamisesta* (LA 22/2004).

———. 2002. *Seksipalvelujen ostamisen kriminalisointi* (TPA 178/2002).

Langvasbråten, Trude. 2008. "A Scandinavian Model? Gender Equality Dis-courses on Multiculturalism." *Social Politics* 15, no. 1: 32–52.

Leskinen, Jari. 2003. *Organisoitu paritus ja prostituutio Suomessa. Keskusrikospoli-isin Rikostutkimus 2002*. Keskusrikospoliisi, Vantaa, Finland.

Magnusson, Eva. 2000. "Party-Political Rhetoric on Gender Equality in Sweden: The Uses of Uniformity and Heterogeneity." *NORA—Nordic Journal of Femi-nist and Gender Research* 8, no. 2: 78–92.

Marttila, Anne-Maria. 2009. *Tavoitteena tasa-arvo. Suomalainen keskustelu rajat ylittävästä prostituutiosta*. Helsinki, Finland: Sosiaali- ja terveysministeriö.

McBride, Dorothy E., and Amy Mazur. 2010. *The Politics of State Feminism: Innova-tion in Comparative Research*. Philadelphia: Temple University Press.

Naisjärjestöjen Keskusliitto. *Lausunto ihmiskauppatyöryhmän osamietinnöstä Ihmiskauppa, paritus ja prostituutio*, 9.10.2003.

National Federation of Social Democratic Women (SSKF). 1995. *S-kvinnors yttrande över prostitutionsutredningens betänkande* (SOU 1995: 15).

National Organization of Women's Shelters in Sweden (ROKS). 1995. *Betänkande av 1993 års prostitutionsutredning "Könshandel."*

Oikeusministeriö. 2003:5. *Ihmiskauppa, paritus ja prostituutio. Työryhmän osamietintö.*

————. 2004:3. *Ihmiskauppa, paritus ja prostituutio. Tiivistelmä lausunnoista.*

Östergren, Petra. 2006. *Porr, horor och feminister.* Stockholm, Sweden: Natur och kultur.

Price, Richard. 1998. "Reversing the Gun Sights: Transnational Civil Society Targets Land Mines." *International Organization* 52, no. 3: 613–44.

Pylkkänen, Anu. 2012. "Muodollisen tasa-arvon pitkä historia ja sen sisäänrakennetut erot." In *Tasa-arvo toisin nähtynä. Oikeuden ja politiikan näkökulmia tasa-arvoon ja yhdenvertaisuuteen*, ed. Johanna Kantola, Kevät Nousiainen, and Milla Saari, 57–72. Helsinki, Finland: Gaudeamus.

Räsänen, Päivi, et al. *Seksibisneksen rajoittamiseksi tarvittavista toimenpiteistä* (TA 26/1995).

Regeringens proposition. 1997/98:55. *Kvinnofrid.*

Riksdagens snabbprotokoll. Protokoll 1997/98:114, 1998-05-28.

Risse-Kappen, Thomas. 1994. "Ideas Do Not Float Freely: Transnational Coalitions, Domestic Structures, and the End of the Cold War." *International Organization*, 48, no. 2: 185–214.

Roth, Venla. 2010. *Defining Human Trafficking, Identifying Its Victims: A Study on the Impact and Future Challenges of the International, European and Finnish Legal Responses to Prostitution-Related Trafficking in Human Beings.* Turku, Finland: Turun Yliopisto.

Sainsbury, Diane. 2004. "Women's Political Representation in Sweden: Discursive Politics and Institutional Presence." *Scandinavian Political Studies* 27, no. 1: 65–87.

Schmidt, Vivien A. 2002. *The Futures of European Capitalism.* Oxford: Oxford University Press.

Seksialan liitto SALLI. *Lausunto OM:n työryhmämietinnöstä 2003:5 "Ihmiskauppa, paritus ja prostituutio,"* 8.10.2003.

Socialdemokraterna. 1997a. *Partistyrelsens utlåtande over motionerna om "Strategi för välfärd: Framtidskongressen Sundsvall 1997."* Stokholm: Socialdemokraterna.

————. 1997b. *Protokoll: Framtidskongressen, Sundsvall 8–14 September 1997 (del 3).* Stockholm: Socialdemokraterna.

Statens offentliga utredningar (SOU). 1975. *Kvinnor i statlig tjänst.* (SOU 1975:43).

————. 1979. *Steg på väg.* (SOU 1979:56).

————. 1981. *Prostitutionen i Sverige, bakgrund och åtgärder.* (SOU 1981:71).

————. 1982. *Våldtäkt och andra sexuella övergrepp.* (SOU 1982:61).

————. 1987. *Varannan damernas.* (SOU 1987:19).

————. 1995. *Könshandeln.* (SOU 1995:15).

———. 2010. *Förbud mot köp av sexuell tjänst En utvärdering 1999–2008.* (SOU 2010:49).

Stone, Deborah. 1989. "Causal Stories and the Formation of Policy Agendas." *Political Science Quarterly* 104, no. 2: 281–300.

Swedish Ministry of Justice. 1998. *Lag (1998:408) om förbud mot köp av sexuella tjänster.*

Towns, Ann. 2010. *Women and States.* Cambridge, U.K.: Cambridge University Press.

TT Nyhetsbanken. 1994. "Expert hoppar av prostitutionsutredning i protest." November 29.

Täysistunnon pöytäkirjojen puheenvuorot. 1996. (PTK 93/1996).

———. 1998. (PTK 77/1998).

———. 2004. (PTK 32/2004).

———. 2006. (PTK 3/2006).

Varsa, Hannele. 1986. *Prostituution näkymätön osa: Miesasiakkaat. Lehti-ilmoitteluprostituution asiakkaista.* Helsinki, Finland: Tasa-arvoasiain neuvottelukunta.

· III ·

Negotiating Status

The Promises and Limits of
Sex Worker Organizing

CHAPTER 10

Collective Interest Organization among Sex Workers

Gregor Gall

THE "SEX WORK" DISCOURSE posits that the act of carrying out sexual services is an act of labor and work on par with others forms of "conventional" labor and work in the service sector. Some forms of labor have often been denoted as "erotic" and "emotional," where the "heart" is managed and commercialized (Hochschild 2003). Consequently, those who provide sexual services are workers, and more specifically *sex workers.* And among sex workers, commentators, and social scientists, the sex work discourse has now been sufficiently established and accepted, and one of the significant issues emanating from it concerns the representation of sex workers' interests at work.

Within the sex work discourse, there is a justified assumption that sex workers have interests that contrast and conflict with those of sex industry operators (like club or brothel owners). As a result, sex workers cannot rely on sex industry operators to either represent their interests or provide a means of doing so. Rather, sex workers require independent means of interest representation—namely, *by* sex workers, *of* sex workers, and *for* sex workers. Because of the power imbalance between individual sex workers and sex industry operators, sex workers are compelled to band together and form collective organizations that seek to offset this asymmetry in power.

Therefore, this chapter holds that sex workers *as workers* require the means by which to engage in the processes and outcomes of collective interest representation within both their site of work and their working lives. To consider these processes and outcomes, I examine three examples of *nonunion* collective forms of self-organization in Australia, Canada, and the United States. The decision to study nonunion forms arises because of the difficulties that sex worker unionization projects have experienced to date (see Gall 2012). Therefore, I considered it important to study alternative forms of collective interest representation. Doing so can help in evaluating the generalized challenges facing sex-workers' collective self-organization, including providing insights into types of sex worker interest representation that are based upon the labor union form.

The generic context of studying any form of sex worker collective self-organization is that the conditions of sex workers' labor is different from those of other workers in two key aspects. First, this labor is not regulated by the state in the same way as other work; instead, it is more heavily regulated, often through criminal codes and hostile public policies that are rooted in value systems that view it as a form of deviancy and as a social problem (see, for example, Cheryl Auger's chapter in this volume). In many Australian states, prostitution is lawful but heavily regulated, while in Canada prostitution has been technically decriminalized since the 1970s but almost any activity associated with prostitution is illegal (e.g., living off the income of prostitution, soliciting clients, and running brothels). In California, strip shows and exotic dancing are lawful while prostitution is not. Second, this labor is also *socially* regulated by citizens; with the exception of loan sharks or those workers who produce nuclear weapons, sex workers face a level of public opprobrium that is unrivaled. The resulting stigmatization reinforces the criminalization of, and hostile public policies toward, sex workers. Given all of this, any form of sex worker organization for collective interest representation cannot solely focus on the site of work if it is to be effective.

Labor unionism is the most obvious way for workers—including sex workers—to create appropriate and independent forms of interest representation. Of course, for sex workers, their labor unions need to be more than conventional labor unions that concentrate mainly on interest representation concerning work and employment in the workplace, especially given the aforementioned extra-workplace forms of sex work regulation. Sex workers' labor unionism also needs to take into account that, for the most part, sex workers are not *employed*: they often have no contracts of employment and do not work together in large numbers. Instead, they often work alone and do not have a fixed place of work. In other words, the characteristics of sex workers' places of work seldom conform to those other workplaces (such as factories) where unionization has been relatively easy. So it is not particularly surprising to find that projects to unionize sex workers have been slow, fitful, fragile, and uneven despite many notable, heroic, and continuing attempts in Australia, Britain, Canada, Germany, the Netherlands, and the United States (Gall 2006; 2007; 2009; 2010).

However, sex workers have made further attempts at unionization since these initial efforts in other countries of both the global north (e.g., France, Hungary, Sweden, and Turkey) and the global south (e.g., Argentina, Bolivia, India, Peru, and South Africa).[1] Nonetheless, these later attempts in the global north and south have also been met with obstacles and challenges of a similar nature and scale to those of the initial attempts. Consequently, there is still no shining exemplar of "regular" unionization to guide and inspire sex workers in their quest for social, political, and economic justice. Moreover, in surveying these attempts and efforts, it is evident that while sex workers often view the idea of unionization as a "good" one in principle, they find it less than appropriate in practice. However, others are antagonistic toward unionization because they see themselves as businesswomen (and men), hoping to make their fortunes and gain access to better lives through sex work. Indeed, some aspire to become operators of brothels, saunas, and the like. Consequently, their "right to do business" as entrepreneurs and their view of themselves as individuals does not sit easily with the solidaristic and collectivist underpinnings of unionization.

Nevertheless, these concerns about the efficacy of labor unionism do not necessarily rule out other means of collective representation. This is because sex workers generally recognize that, individually, few of them hold positions of strength when it comes to dealing with the clients, operators, or regulators who help determine and shape their working lives. Therefore, many sex workers view different forms of collective self-help and self-reliance, and the accompanying collective organization, as critical to leveling the playing field on which they work and operate. Indeed, the culture and politics of collectivism are not necessarily seen as being in contradiction to or incompatible with individualism, for the former can support the right to exercise the latter. Many sex workers believe the utility of collective interest representation is all the more salient because sex work remains regulated by the state (through criminalization) in a way that is not true for most other forms of work and many segments of society see it as a form of social and moral deviancy.

Therefore, given sex workers' limited prospects for unionization as a means for delivering economic and social justice, let alone emancipation and liberation, it is useful to examine how sex workers have sought alternate collective means for defining and creating their own communities within their worksites. Doing so requires examining the contending pressures constructing and mobilizing these communities for the protection and advancement of their interests. Thus this chapter provides a complement to those by Valeria Feldman (chapter 11) and Yasmin Lalani (chapter 12) because they also consider nonunion forms of collective action that focus on improving sex workers' working conditions and working lives on a number of different issues and in a number of different arenas.

In some ways this chapter then returns to the promise and portent of the pressure-group form of sex workers' rights organizations that preceded sex workers' attempts at unionization (see Gall 2006; Jenness 1993; Weitzer 1991). Among the leading exemplars of the former are Call Off Your Old Tired Ethics (COYOTE) in the United States, the English Collective of Prostitutes (ECP), and the Red Thread in the Netherlands. These groundbreaking organizations concentrated on civil, political, and human rights rather than economic and labor rights, which is where subsequent sex worker unions have focused. Essentially, COYOTE and other similar organizations sought to gain legitimacy for sex work and sex workers through legal reform and political discourse (Jenness 1993).

Indeed, because of difficulties and obstacles facing all sex worker organizations (including unions) and the need for any sex worker organization to confront the extra-workplace political and legal regimes that regulate sex work, both union and nonunion forms of sex worker collective self-organization in the workplace have coalesced around a form and modus operandi of extra-workplace pressure-group activity that I call "independent collectivism" (Gall 2010). A key aspect of independent collectivism is that it is independent of operators, employers, the state, and any other third parties. Thus it is an organization composed of, by, and for sex workers only. This organizational form is new, as even COYOTE, for example, was composed of sex worker supporters who were not sex workers.

To examine independent collectivism of a nonunion kind, I consider the Scarlet Alliance in Australia, the Lusty Lady workers' cooperative in San Francisco, and the West Coast Cooperative of Sex Industry Professionals in Canada as exemplars of sex workers' independent collective interest representation at—and for—work. I selected these because they represent an array of different types of self-organization at different stages in their development. The Scarlet Alliance is a long-standing form of more general, extra-workplace sex worker self-organization, while the Lusty Lady cooperative emerged more recently and is wholly based within a single workplace. Finally, the West Coast Cooperative is a nascent attempt to create a network of self-determined, self-supporting sex worker businesses. Although their spatial locations (in terms of country and state) have ramifications for how they operate and what successes they have had, the three locations were not chosen to represent different variables of the types of regulation (i.e., federal, state, or hybrid) in this regard.

I therefore begin this chapter by outlining labor unionism to contextualize the study of these organizations. I then summarize sex workers' independent collectivism projects in their respective geographical spaces. My purpose here is to furnish an understanding of the vacuum in collective representation and self-determination that these three organizations have sought to fill and the roles that they have sought to play, particularly in contrast to the existence and fate of similar sex worker organizations. The activities of the three examples are then examined.

Studying these nonunion forms of sex worker collective interest representation indicates that there is more than one way to achieve the goal of reducing the power of clients, operators, and regulators. Thus this chapter demonstrates how sex workers are imaginatively thinking through and experimenting with multiple forms of independent collectivism and interest representation, working to determine which are the most efficient and effective for building their capacity to create leverage over clients, operators, and regulators. The contribution to wider knowledge is then twofold. First, the study of sex worker self-agency has tended to focus on interventions in the political arena with little regard to those in the economic arena (see Weitzer 1991). To help fill this gap, this chapter examines the pursuit of economic justice by sex workers for sex workers and begins to allow a more rounded assessment of sex worker agency in toto. Second, this study is situated within a political economy perspective, which understands that the totality of sex workers' struggle for justice per se requires an interconnected analysis of the struggles for political and economic justice. Consequently, this chapter portrays the study of the struggle for justice in and at work as part of the wider struggle to influence the extra-work regimes (i.e., judicial, public policy, or morality) that regulate sex workers' working lives. Both confirm the existence of sex worker self-agency.

Methods

The data for studying the Scarlet Alliance are derived from face-to-face interviews I conducted in 2009 and 2010 with its lead officers and affiliates (the Crimson Coalition in Queensland and the Sex Workers' Union). The data for studying the Lusty Lady are derived from face-to-face interviews I conducted in 2008 and 2009 with leading officers of the cooperative and sex worker groups in San Francisco (like the Erotic Service Providers' Union [ESPU]). Both sets of data were supported by primary sources, such as the websites and publications of the organizations and secondary sources—namely, newspaper reporting accessed through the Lexis-Nexis database. The research materials for studying the West Coast Cooperative of Sex Industry Professionals were derived from similar primary and secondary source documentation, although this involved e-mail correspondence rather than face-to-face interviews.

Labor Unionism

A union is a voluntary association of citizens with many and varied purposes throughout civil society. However, a union of workers—a labor union—is a collective organization *of workers in the workplace* that focuses on economic and workplace justice through negotiating improved terms for the wage–effort bargain and the organization of work by creating collective leverage over the employer. As such, a labor union is a relatively tight form of organization compared to a more general union of citizens because it is based on the principle of solidarity. Its key resource is the collective power of its members—when mobilized through industrial action—at the points of production (i.e., workplaces), distribution, and exchange in the economy. However, because workers are the weaker party in the employment relationship with capital, all labor unions also seek to influence the state to regulate employers and capital and, thus, intervene in the political arena (Hyman 1975).

Labor union projects for sex workers in countries of the global north and south were developed by sex worker activists because existing sex workers' rights organizations (like COYOTE, the ECP, and the Red Thread) focused on the civil, political, and human rights of sex workers, with little to no attention on their economic, labor, and workers' rights. Indeed, sex worker–union activists believed that labor unions could provide them the agency to represent their interests in the economic and political arenas. But as they sought to do this, it became apparent that their employment status (i.e., being self-employed, independent contractors, or lone workers), the absence of employers as bargaining partners, the paucity of fixed work sites for organizing, and their tendency to negotiate directly with clients presented potent obstacles to unionization. Yet labor unionism is an option for freelance or independent workers,[2] as well as transient and migratory workers where there is an identifiable professional occupation, or other form of identity, and a structured labor market. Thus labor unionism is not necessarily inappropriate for all sex workers. Yet because sex work is not viewed by society as work (i.e., legitimate, valued, or skilled) and because sex workers exist on the margins of legality, they rarely have occupational or professional control or structured labor markets. Consequently, sex worker labor unionism has become the antithesis of what it professes to be—namely, sex worker advocacy groups that concentrate on the civil, political, and human rights claims of sex workers rather than their economic rights.

Australia

By virtue of their names, many sex worker groups in Australia since the 1970s have appeared as quasi-labor unions: the Private Workers' Association, Prostitutes' Collective of Victoria (PCV), Queer and Esoteric Workers' Union, and Workers in Sex Employment (WISE). Yet they are (or were) pressure or rights groups, not labor unions. Thus they concentrated their activities on providing personalized and tailored health service provision and peer education. Only the odd exception, like the PWA, has attempted to also deal with economic and worksite issues (Gall 2009). However, realizing the inadequacy of political rights alone, some rights groups moved toward unionization to gain economic justice by being either its advocates or its facilitators. For example, WISE and the PCV joined the Liquor, Hospitality and Miscellaneous Workers' Union (LHMWU) in 1995 in an effort to recruit prostitutes in Victoria state.[3] Yet the initial momentum in the LHMWU was lost after internal and external hostilities toward sex worker organizing collided, and so the LHMWU only carried out low-key, behind-the-scenes recruitment through sex work support projects like peer education and health service provision. The prime hostility was from different sections within the LHMWU to provide further resources, following a short period of support for this to gain members. This led to the effective ending of this unionization project.

The rolling back of the menu of workers' rights (which had been established in 1906) by conservative federal (and state) governments between 1996 and 2007 also meant that attempts to attain labor rights for sex workers fell on increasingly barren ground. But two further attempts were made to establish unions for sex workers. First, the Striptease Artists of Australia (SAA) for exotic dancers earned an industrial award from the Australian Industrial Relations Commission (AIRC), a state agency, for determining wages and working conditions under the former system of arbitration and conciliation in Australia in the early 2000s. Yet SAA petered out after this success provoked a backlash from sex industry operators (Gall 2010). Second, the Sex Workers' Union (SWU) tried from its base in Sydney (where its key activists lived and worked) to organize any and all sex workers. But according to a prominent SWU activist (interview with author, June 2009), the conservative government's abolition of many of the country's systems of arbitration and conciliation in the form of the AIRC did not help these efforts. In essence, the SWU remains an idea and not a real entity.

The salience of this sketch is twofold. First, the existing geographically state-based sex worker groups have not been able to influence federal policy or associate with each other, in order to aggregate influence and resources, to any great extent. Second, unionization has not been able to deliver on its promise to provide more effective collective interest representation in either the economic or political arena any more than the pressure or rights groups have. This helps provide the basis for understanding the purchase of the Scarlet Alliance.[4]

The Scarlet Alliance

Midway through a long period of a Labor-controlled federal government, activists in the geographically state-based sex workers' rights groups wanted to provide a stronger voice and network for their rights-oriented groups. Therefore, in 1989 they formed the Scarlet Alliance, which aims to "achieve equality, social, legal, political, cultural and economic justice for past and present workers in the sex industry, in order for sex workers to be self-determining agents, building their own alliances and choosing where and how they work" (Scarlet Alliance n.d.). Over the years, it has become more than just the collective federal voice of its affiliates, acting as the main driver and leader of sex workers and sex workers' rights groups in Australia.

Oftentimes, though, the media has incorrectly identified the Scarlet Alliance as a labor union. The misconception arises as a result of its affiliation with the Australian Council of Trade Unions, the introduction of its subtitle of "the Australian Sex Workers' Association" in 2004, its bar on membership for sex industry business owners and operators, and because it promotes sex workers' rights in terms of the discourse of labor rights. Indeed, showing that it is not a labor union, in an internal debate on how to organize sex workers in the mid- to late 2000s, the initiative from some Scarlet Alliance activists to establish the SWU was given little support from the Scarlet Alliance because labor unionism was seen as being inappropriate in principle and practice (author interviews with SA and SWU, June 2009, August 2010).

Despite these challenges, the Scarlet Alliance has become the most developed, embedded, and long-lasting example of a nonunion form of collective sex worker organization focused on both economic and political rights in equal measure. It is constituted and operates as a campaigning group focused on attaining rights and representation, and it is active in policy, regulation, service provision, and support work. The Scarlet Alliance premises its work on the idea that sex workers are self-determining agents, building their own alliances and choosing where and how they work. The Scarlet Alliance's strength can be gauged from a number of its characteristics and actions.

First, it is primarily composed of affiliated geographically state-based sex workers' rights groups. These groups are the lead bodies for sex workers in each of their respective eight states. Accordingly, each is focused on the particular issues affecting sex workers in its state. The importance of this can be seen in the determination of the regulation of sex work on a state-by-state (and not federal) basis and in the differing complexion of the political process in each state, which decides on the form of regulation. It is the combination of the local embeddedness of these affiliated organizations and the guiding and coordinating work of the Scarlet Alliance (which gives it a high profile) that allows the Scarlet Alliance to exist as *the* national body that both assists the state-based affiliates and lobbies and influences the federal government. In other words, there is a happy and productive marriage of different scales of sex worker organization. But specifically, the Scarlet Alliance is much more than just the sum of its constituent parts. It provides strong, proactive, and vibrant leadership in sex workers' campaigns for economic and political justice rather than just reflecting in a reactive manner the wishes of its affiliates.

Second, federal and state governments have accorded the Scarlet Alliance—after much struggle to prove itself as a bona fide representative body of sex workers—the status of the recognized body of and for sex workers in Australia. In this sense, it is seen as a social partner in the European corporatist mold. Although it is not uncontested by others concerned with the sex industry (like the operators and police), and it is not uniformly influential across all Australian states, this is a major achievement because it allows the Scarlet Alliance to play a major role in determining policy, enforcement, and regulation. The roots of this achievement result from a combination of the Scarlet Alliance's expertise on sex work, its representative status among sex workers, and the efforts of a core of dedicated activists.

Third, and linked to the second point, the Scarlet Alliance has cleverly and strategically colonized (and almost monopolized) the state's provision of health and education services to sex workers by, in effect, being subcontracted to do so. This has meant not only that these services exist and will continue to do so but that they are provided in a way that is suitable and appropriate for sex workers. Fourth, the Scarlet Alliance has operated extensive education and training programs for sex worker activists and sex workers in general; as a result, it has helped build up a cadre of activists to conduct its work and campaigns. Since 2004, the Alliance has procured government funding to support its programs and staff; this funding has been a key component in achieving its programming and staffing success. To add to these characteristics, the Alliance has adopted an internationalist position by supporting sister organizations in Southeast Asia, particularly those in Thailand, Papua New Guinea, and Hong Kong. Finally, in 2005 individual sex workers were permitted to join the Alliance in order to strengthen relationships between the Alliance and individual members of its affiliates.

But this description does not explain why the Scarlet Alliance has become such a powerful and legitimate collective voice of—and for— sex workers. This is the result of four factors: (1) its characteristics of being a long-standing federated, democratic, participative, and relatively well-resourced organization; (2) the longevity of the sex work discourse and the activism of sex workers within Australia, dating from the late 1970s and giving these a greater reach than elsewhere (see Gall 2006); (3) the left-of-center political climate in urban Australian society providing a relatively more hospitable environment in which to work for sex workers' rights; and (4) the fact that for the majority of sex workers in Australia, sex work takes place in a brothel, which means that rights and conditions in the workplace are more important and that organizing on this terrain is relatively easier. The first factor concerning the Alliance's organizational nature is no mean feat given the distance between urban areas.[5] In this sense, sex workers in Australia seem to have overcome some of the challenges faced by their counterparts in North America, which largely remain as city- and state-based organizations without the same degree of interorganizational integration and cooperation, much less a central federation. That the majority of sex workers are located in a very small number of large urban areas in Australia compared to the far more numerous metropolises of the United States has also helped.

California

Call Off Your Old Tired Ethics (COYOTE) was founded in 1973 in San Francisco as the first ever advocacy group for prostitutes, subsequently operating with the subtitle "The Sex Workers' Rights Organization." It then helped found similar groups in other cities so that the structure of most sex worker groups in the United States is largely city-based rather than state-based. However, from the early 1990s onward, individuals active in COYOTE in San Francisco created the St. James Infirmary (an occupational health and safety clinic run for and by sex workers); the Sex Workers Outreach Project (SWOP—an advocacy rights and education group); the Exotic Dancers' Alliance (EDA—an advocacy group for dancers): the Cyprian Guild (an escorts' support group); Sex Workers Organized for Labor, Human, and Civil Rights (SWOLHCR); and the Erotic Service Providers' Union (ESPU) (see Jenness 1993; Majic 2011; Weitzer 1991). Although there has been a crossover of memberships, it is also true that significant differences have emerged between many of the lead activists in each organization over strategic orientation and tactical methods (author interviews with members of COYOTE, ESPU, and SWOP in January 2008 and January 2009).

Composed primarily of former prostitutes and their supporters, COYOTE deployed a strategy of politically campaigning for statewide decriminalization and resources for prostitutes' well-being and also against police harassment stemming from the criminalized status of prostitution (and its attendant social stigma). Its activists believed that labor unionism and campaigning for economic and workplace justice were impractical at the current moment because organizing prostitutes would constitute an unlawful activity (as prostitution itself remained illegal).

With the rise of the "moral majority" and the AIDS backlash in the United States during the 1980s, many COYOTE activists concentrated their efforts on creating and sustaining organizations that would more immediately meet their occupational health and safety needs, such as the California Prostitutes Education Project (CAL-PEP) and the St. James Infirmary (Lutnick 2006). However, with the rise of exotic dancing, the EDA emerged to provide interest representation for dancers, playing an instrumental role in campaigning against stage fees and better working conditions by deploying class action lawsuits. The highpoint of the EDA's activities for economic justice was the unionization of the Lusty Lady peepshow in San Francisco, where the dancers gained union recognition in 1996 with the help of the Service Employees' International Union (SEIU) (Gall 2006, 72–78; Funari and Query 2000). Meanwhile, the Cyprian Guild was established to deal with the issues facing escorts (rather than street-based or brothel/massage parlor sex workers), but it did not develop much beyond a mutual help group that held meetings, and it was unclear about whether its focus should be on escorts' rights as workers or businesses (author interview, January 2008). Nonetheless, that such numerous developments took place in San Francisco—as opposed to other U.S. cities—indicates how the city's culture of progressive politics has influenced its sexual politics.[6]

Frustration with the inward-looking orientation of Lusty Lady union members—concerning themselves only with Lusty Lady issues—and a lack of SEIU help and resources in unionizing other sex workers led a number of activists to establish Sex Workers Organizing for Labour, Civil and Human Rights (SWOLCHR). SWOLCHR campaigned against stage fees and pressure to prostitute in strip clubs, helped file class action lawsuits to recoup stage fees, and made presentations to the California Labor Commission with some SEIU assistance. The victimization of the lead

SWOLCHR activist—a working dancer—by the clubs led to SWOL-CHR's disintegration,[7] and the subsequent demise of the EDA in 2004 led to the creation of the ESPU. The ESPU's activities have included collecting signatures in support of a ballot measure to decriminalize prostitution in San Francisco, giving testimony to the San Francisco Entertainment Commission in 2006 on a proposed amendment to the police code for the regulation of live adult-entertainment businesses, and submitting evidence to the Commission on the Status of Women. The ESPU also works in conjunction with the San Francisco Labor Council to proselytize among sex workers for labor unionism and train sex worker activists in labor union skills.

This brief account serves to highlight that both union and nonunion forms of collective representation have remained relatively weak and ineffectual in spite of the high point of the Lusty Lady's achievement.[8] Success in gaining economic justice has been poor. Moreover, the sex worker groups remain fragmented among themselves and confined to the city level. Consequently, like other sex workers' rights groups across the United States, those in California are not part of, or affiliated with, an influential national organization comparable to the Scarlet Alliance in Australia.

The Lusty Lady

The case of the Lusty Lady shows how the search for economic justice has taken a new turn. Following the club's closure by the owner, the dancers and staff bought the business, turning it into a workers' cooperative in 2003. The principle of the cooperative is that only workers at the Lusty Lady could be members (although membership was not compulsory), and so the cooperative was owned and run only by its members and not by any outside interests. The hope was that, on the one hand, the constant conflict experienced with the previous conventional management and owners could be ended. Meanwhile, on other hand, workers could exercise more control over their working lives and, in doing so, contribute to a more successful collective enterprise and achieve more job satisfaction. The way to do this was for the workers themselves to own the "means of production" so that no conventional management was needed. But shortly after becoming a cooperative, the Lusty Lady came under pressure to make financial cost savings. Revenue dropped due to an economic downturn with the bursting of the "dot-com bubble" and they needed to repay the loan used to buy the business (Friend 2004). On top of this, the amount of time and energy required to operate a cooperative became abundantly clear. Thus staff turnover—especially among the dancers—meant that there was a loss of the requisite technical and social capital, and the voluntary effort needed from members to run the cooperative infringed on their leisure time (Lusty Lady 2004). As a result, many cooperative members with both the willingness and technical skills to manage a business left, and attending cooperative meetings each Sunday morning became something of a "drag" for many members (author interviews January 2008, January 2009).

These difficulties were compounded and extended by a bitter internal feud. In 2006, a number of male support (i.e., nondancer) workers tried to derecognize the SEIU Local 790 union against a backdrop of internal strife, ranging from inflammatory e-mails and verbal communications, suspensions, firings, and competing allegations from dancers and support staff of sexual harassment and unfair labor practices (Clark-Flory 2006; Matier and Ross 2006). The feud began when some male support workers began arguing that the co-op was losing money (which affected wage levels and job security) because, they claimed, the dancers were too fat, too big, and unsexy and that the union contract was invalid because the co-op makes no distinction between management and labor. This outraged the dancers, who regarded the views of these male workers as discriminatory and rolling back the gains of a hard-fought battle to unionize the Lusty Lady. In the process, a considerable divide opened up between the co-op's board of directors, which generally supported the business case of the male workers, and the SEIU Local 790 union, which supported the dancers. However, these tensions eventually eased, aided by dancer initiatives to increase revenue that improved the cooperative's financial position and by the departure of nondancer staff that were critical of the dancers.

The experience of the Lusty Lady indicates not only some of the benefits of worker-owned businesses but also the problems and challenges of raising capital and self-management (with the consequence that the dancers maintained union representation as an insurance policy [Koopman 2003; Steinberg 2003]).

Canada

By 2004, two separate sex workers' rights groups, the Exotic Dancers' Association and the Exotic Dancers' Association Canada, had folded, adding to the impasse created by the previous inability of both the Canadian

Association for Burlesque Entertainers and the Association for Burlesque Entertainers to make any substantial headway in the 1980s and early 1990s in organizing dancers and strippers for economic and workplace justice (see Gall 2010). The Strippers United Association, formed in 2004, was stillborn, while the Canadian Guild for Erotic Labour (CGEL), also established that year as a "national organization of workers and allies who have come together to support and promote labour rights and labour organizing for . . . workers engaged in erotic labour" (CGEL, n.d.), has sought to convince other unions to help it organize sex workers. Although the CGEL gained support from the Canadian Union of Public Employees (CUPE) and the Canadian Labour Congress (CLC—the Canadian union movement's top union organization), as well as the support of legal reformers known as the Pivot Legal Society, this has not led to unionization itself. For example, the CUPE made clear its intention to support, not lead, unionization, and both the CUPE and the CLC are equally supportive of pursuing public policy and regulatory change vis-à-vis decriminalizing sex work through political party means. Thus the overall situation in Canada has not progressed for unionized sex workers (see Bruckert 2002; Gall 2006; Ross 2000; 2006) despite the lawful and unrestricted nature of exotic dancing in Canada (compared to prostitution).

Meanwhile, the long-standing Sex Professionals of Canada (formerly, the Canadian Organisation for the Rights of Prostitutes) lobbied for the legalization of prostitution—albeit unsuccessfully for many years until 2010.[9] In common with other Canadian sex workers' rights group, it has organized conferences, public meetings, lobbies of public authorities, and demonstrations. Activity on sex workers' rights by sex workers continues to be organized on a province-by-province and city-by-city basis, so that a plethora of poorly resourced and often competing organizations exist. Neither the creation of the Sex Trade Workers of Canada, an advocacy group, nor the CGEL has changed this situation. Finally, in 2008, two sex worker activists from Prostitutes' Empowerment Education and Resource Society (PEERS) in Victoria, British Columbia, attempted to open a cooperative brothel, where cooperative members would be paid wages and receive medical leave, vacation pay, and workers' compensation. Any surplus from the cooperative (called Victoria Independent Providers and marketed as "an escort agency with a difference") was to be donated to street-based sex workers. However, the project was shelved because of the Sex Professionals of Canada's inability to gain legal changes that would make prostitution and brothel prostitution lawful. Prostitution's illegality also made gaining capital and financial services extremely difficult.

This brief sketch shows that because neither union nor nonunion collective interest representation—as so far constituted—provided sufficient efficacy for sex workers, some sex workers in Vancouver tried again to work toward establishing a sex workers' brothel cooperative. In doing so, they indicated that sex workers trying to own their own "means of production" is a recurring theme in the pursuit of economic justice. This is because the task of reforming the whole of society is so great that attempting to establish an organization of its own seems more realistic.

West Coast Cooperative of Sex Industry Professionals

The British Columbia Coalition of Experiential Women (BCCEW) was established in 2005 as the result of a series of meetings between 2002 and 2004 involving sex workers and sympathetic academics from Simon Fraser University. The BCCEW initiated a social action research project called the Developing Capacity for Change Project in 2006.[10] During this time, and in discussions over sex worker cooperatives in India, a number of Vancouver sex workers expressed their desire to explore a cooperative business model as "a way to generate alternative sources of income, increase health and safety, build community capacity and begin to take control of our collective destiny" (BCCEW n.d.). As a result the West Coast Cooperative of Sex Industry Professionals was founded and incorporated in 2007, and in 2008 it began raising capital and developing business skills.

With a similar agenda to the Scarlet Alliance and Lusty Lady of empowering sex workers to control their own working lives, the West Coast Cooperative sought in particular to create decent labor standards to improve the occupational health, safety, and capacities of sex industry professionals as employees and contractors within a legitimized profession. The West Coast Cooperative's key objective was to open a cooperative brothel in order to take sex workers off the streets, where they have been subject to violence and murder, and to allow them to work together for their own protection and in furtherance of their labor rights. In order to create such a cooperative brothel, the West Coast Cooperative of Sex Industry Professionals has established a number of social enterprises, working in the arts, publishing, catering, and consulting in order to raise the necessary capital. The aim was to have the brothel up and running for the 2010 Winter Olympics in Vancouver.

However, the inability to change legislation so that a legal brothel could be established (as is the case in New Zealand and the Netherlands), as well as difficulties in raising sufficient capital, have meant that the project has not yet come to fruition, although efforts remain ongoing. Indeed, the landmark ruling in the Bedford v. Canada case in September 2010, where the three leaders of the Sex Professionals of Canada successfully challenged federal and provincial (Ontario) laws on procuring sexual services (see Makin 2010), gives some hope that the laws governing sex work continue to progress toward legality. However, a higher court interceded to maintain the current position of unlawfulness until an appeal against the ruling is heard. A similar attempt at legalizing prostitution in British Columbia (which includes Vancouver) is pending.

Conclusion

My argument in this chapter has been that the turn to unionization among sex workers has yet to develop a definitively more effective form of collective interest representation for sex workers and their pursuit of economic and workplace justice than the civil and political rights–based approach of earlier organizing efforts. This lack of success has been heavily influenced by the existing unions' attitudes toward sex workers. Consequently, a renewed focus on prior and alternate nonunion organizational forms of independent collectivism is then warranted. The Scarlet Alliance demonstrates that there is more than one way to organize collectively in order to deal effectively with clients, operators, and regulators *contra* labor unions for, as a particular nonunion form of organization, it has attained an influential role in constructing a more sympathetic form of regulation governing sex work. Part of its purchase is based on its construction as a national organization composed of state affiliates.

That is not to say that these alternate (nonunion) organizational forms have achieved sex workers self-regulation, for attempts at unionization still persist and much work still remains to be done. Elsewhere, the Lusty Lady and West Coast Cooperative represent a more total (but also more microscale) approach to controlling what goes on in the workplace and in doing so obviate the need for conventional management and, in many regards, unions as well, because sex workers collectively own and manage the enterprise they work in. They have sought to own their own "means of production" on a scale that is far greater than a few sex workers working together in a commonly owned apartment for their safety. The idea of a sex workers' cooperative speaks to the adjoining concerns that many sex workers find themselves in—namely, of being simultaneously wage laborers and entrepreneurs. However, it is difficult—as the saying goes—to have "islands of socialism in seas of capitalism" because of the challenge of raising sufficient capital, which when gained means ceding control to an outside nonworker party, thus negating the point of a worker-owned and worker-controlled cooperative.

For sex worker activists, the broad lesson to emerge from this chapter is that in constructing organizational forms of self-agency in pursuit of social justice, it is necessary to construct forms of self-organization that can pursue economic and workplace justice without eschewing action in the broader political arena. This is because the economic and political are two sides of the same coin. This dual focus requires more activism and more activists as well as strategic thinking and acting, but it does, nonetheless, ensure that the totality of the regimes and forces that regulate sex work are confronted. That said, the formidable internal and external challenges to the creation of any form of sex worker self-organized interest representation requires that different models will be used by different groups of sex workers across space and time. There is no "one size fits all" solution to the challenge of creating and sustaining robust and effective forms of self-representation, especially given differing national and subnational cultures, institutional frameworks, and regimes of regulation.

Nonetheless, the answer to the question of which organizational form is most appropriate depends on the scale and nature of the task being undertaken, the resources at hand, and the nuanced analysis of the specific, multilayered environment in which the sex workers operate. In the case of the most long-standing and effective organization, the Scarlet Alliance has operated in a system of overlying, concurrent jurisdictions for the regulation of sex work and employment at the federal and state levels. By having a countrywide body comprising different affiliates from each state, it has helped ensure a productive balancing of centrifugal and centripetal dynamics so that Australia's two great metropolises have not overly dominated the organization. In this way, and appropriate to is national context, the Scarlet Alliance has constructed considerable influence for itself and for sex workers in Australia. While it speaks and acts with political authority on behalf of its affiliates, it has also become a significant player itself. This is all the more remarkable an achievement because federal and many state attitudes have been hostile to sex workers as citizens and workers.

Postscript

The Lusty Lady closed on Labor Day, September 2, 2013, after a dispute with the building's landlord over unpaid rent. Some of the Lusty Lady dancers believed that ending the lease over this issue was a subterfuge to close a competitor down, as the landlord was the largest operator of strip clubs in northern California. The landlord disputed this.

Notes

1. See Gall (2012) for a survey of these countries, where—as in the case of India—what are seen by many as unions are not. Rather, they are pressure-group organizations.

2. See the many cases of varied groups of immigrant and insecure workers in the United States (Milkman, Bloom, and Narro 2010).

3. The LHMWU is now known as United Voice. The approach of WISE and the PCV to the LHMWU in Melbourne reflected the strength of those groups in adjoining states (Australian Capital Territory, Victoria), their orientation on workers' rights, and the critical mass of the sex industry in Melbourne. The two approached the union in Melbourne rather than its headquarters in Sydney, where no other similarly orientated sex worker rights group existed.

4. It is a moot point whether the Scarlet Alliance could then be said to have impeded, directly or indirectly, the development of the other aforementioned union and nonunion means of organization.

5. The SA operates through its Annual National Forum, teleconferences, e-lists, and electronic member forums. It is headquartered in Sydney, the largest city in Australia.

6. In 1998, San Francisco became the first and only city in the United States to pass an ordinance that complied with the United Nations' Convention for the Elimination of Discrimination against Women. However, the tradition of progressiveness and radicalism dates much further back (see Castells 1983; Lutnick 2006, 58, 63–65; and Majic 2011).

7. The victimization of this activist, Daisy Anarchy, took a number of forms, including her being "blacklisted" from clubs for work and subjected to violence and intimidation.

8. For example, the union, the Las Vegas Dancers' Alliance (LVDA), was established in 2002 but folded in 2005 and the Sin City Alternative Professionals' Association, founded in 2004, is not a successor union to the LVDA but a chapter of the Sex Workers Outreach Project (SWOP) USA (see Gall 2012, 27).

9. However, on October 25, 2012, the Supreme Court of Canada granted leave to appeal and cross-appeal the 2010 Ontario Court of Appeal decision on a test case concerning activities associated with prostitution. The Ontario decision was a huge step forward in the striking down of many of the Criminal Code sections, which made unlawful the organizing of prostitution (such as maintaining a brothel). The Supreme Court also granted the motion to put the Ontario decision on hold until judgment is passed so that the Criminal Code sections are still in force in Ontario. The ramifications for the lawful status of activities associated with prostitution in other provinces and the federal system are thus unclear as the situation is one of stasis.

10. THE BCCEW become the BC Coalition of Experiential Communities in order to include members representing male and transgender sex workers. Before and after this change, it has been an affiliate of the Canadian National Coalition of Experiential Women, a national sex workers' rights group (run by sex workers).

References

British Columbia. n.d. "Leading the Way: Strategic Planning toward Sex Worker Cooperative Development." http://bccec.files.wordpress.com/2008/03/leading _the_way.pdf.

Bruckert, Chris. 2002. *Taking It Off, Putting It On: Women in the Strip Trade*. Toronto, Ontario: Women's Press.

Canadian Guild for Erotic Labour. n.d. "About Us—Who We Are." http://cgelo .tripod.com/index.html.

Castells, Manuel. 1983. *The City and the Grassroots: A Cross Cultural Theory of Urban Social Movement*. Berkeley: University of California Press.

Clark-Flory, Tracy. 2006. "Larger Ladies Stir Up Storm at Strip Club." *Salon*, October 3. http://www.salon.com/mwt/broadsheet/2006/10/03/lusty_lady/index .html.

Friend, Tad. 2004. "Naked Profits." *New Yorker*, July 12.

Funari, Vicki, and Query, Julia. 2000. *Live Nude Girls Unite!* DVD documentary. Brooklyn, NY: First Run/Icarus Films.

Gall, Gregor. 2006. *Sex Worker Union Organizing: An International Study*. New York: Palgrave Macmillan.

———. 2007. "Sex Worker Unionisation: An Exploratory Study of Emerging Collective Organisation." *Industrial Relations Journal* 38, no. 1: 70–88.

———. 2009. "Union Organising with 'Old' and 'New' Industrial Relations Actors: The Cases of Sex Workers in Australia and the United States." In *The Future of Union Organising: Building for Tomorrow*, ed. Gregor Gall, 173–84. New York: Palgrave Macmillan.

———. 2010. "Sex Worker Collective Organisation: Between Advocacy Group and Labour Union?" *Equality, Diversity and Inclusion* 29, no. 3: 289–304.

———. 2012. *An Agency of Their Own: Sex Worker Union Organising*. London: Zero Books.

Hochschild, Arlie. 2003. *The Managed Heart: The Commercialisation of Human Feeling*. Berkeley: University of California Press.

Hyman, Richard. 1975. *Industrial Relations: A Marxist Introduction*. London: Macmillan.

Jenness, Valerie. 1993. *Making It Work: The Prostitutes' Rights Movement in Perspective*. New York: Aldine de Gruyter.

Koopman, John. 2003. "Lusty Lady Becomes First Worker-Owned Strip Club." *San Francisco Chronicle*, June 26.

Lusty Lady. n.d. "A Brief History of the Lusty Lady Theater." http://www.lustyladysf.com/history.

Lutnick, Alexandra. 2006. "The St. James Infirmary: A History." *Sexuality and Culture* 10, no. 2: 56–75.

Majic, Samantha. 2011. "Serving Sex Workers and Promoting Democratic Engagement: Rethinking Nonprofits' Role in American Civic and Political Life." *Perspectives on Politics* 9, no. 4: 821–39.

Makin, Kirk. 2010. "Judge Decriminalizes Prostitution in Ontario, but Ottawa Mulls Appeal." *Globe and Mail*, September 28.

Matier, Phillip, and Andrew Ross. 2006. "S.F. Strip Club's Hefty Lady Show Sparks Tempest." *San Francisco Chronicle*, October 2.

Milkman, Ruth, Joshua Bloom, and Victor Narro. 2010. *Working for Justice: The LA Model of Organizing and Advocacy*. Ithaca, N.Y.: ILR Press.

Ross, Beckie. 2000. "Bumping and Grinding on the Line: Making Nudity Pay." *Labour/le Travail* 46: 221–50.

———. 2006. "Troublemakers in Tassels and G-Strings: Striptease Dancers and the Union Question in Vancouver, 1965–1980." *Canadian Review of Sociology and Anthropology* 43, no. 3: 307–22.

Scarlet Alliance. n.d. "Review of the 4th National HIV/AIDS Strategy." http://www.scarletalliance.org.au/library/review-4th02.

Steinberg, David. 2003. "Under Nude Management." *Clean Sheets*, September 17.

Weitzer, Ronald. 1991. "Prostitutes' Rights in the United States: Failure of a Movement." *Sociological Quarterly* 32, no. 1: 23–41.

CHAPTER 11

Sex Work Politics and the Internet

Carving Out Political Space in the Blogosphere

Valerie Feldman

"Nothing about us, without us."

—Stacy Swimme, *Bound, Not Gagged*, blog post, May 23, 2007

I N THE THREE YEARS that I conducted participant observation with U.S.-based sex workers' rights activists (2007–10),[1] I heard this line many times, both as a warning to be open and reflexive about my own research and also as a criticism of historical trends in cultural and intellectual productions about sex work. Though a few sex workers have published popular books about their experiences in the industry, sex workers' rights activists in the United States bemoan the vast production and consumption of scholarly and journalistic information on sex work that neither benefits their political efforts for the recognition of sex work as a legitimate form of labor and collective identity, nor takes into account the diversity of their perspectives and experiences.[2] A common concern is that most scholarly and popular writing on sex work focuses on individuals who are perceived to be the most marginalized: women working in street prostitution (Weitzer 2005, 214–15) or, more recently, those who have been trafficked for sex. Despite this focus, studies estimate that street-based sex workers make up a minority of the contemporary industry (Bernstein 2007, 30; Vanwesenbeeck 2001, 279; Weitzer 2005, 215), meaning that common understandings of sex work exclude the majority of the industry.

Contemporary sex workers' rights activists are well aware of these inconsistencies and contend that they often occur because sex workers themselves are rarely included in the process of knowledge production about their work and industry. In an effort to publicly present their own take on issues relevant to their work and industry, some sex workers' rights activists in the United States have been writing about their ideas on the community sex-worker activist blog *Bound, Not Gagged (BnG)*.[3] *BnG* is one of very few multiauthored blogs run by and for sex workers and, to my knowledge, it is the only blog of this variety with explicitly activist origins and goals.[4] Individual sex worker blogs are numerous, and some of these are focused on generating business while others tell stories from within the industry. While experience-based sex worker blogs may occasionally touch on political issues, the development of a specifically activist sex worker blog like *BnG* raises two broader questions that I address in this chapter. First, how are sex workers' rights activists using this blog as a tool to organize collectively for the purpose of challenging limited public and political perceptions of their work? Second, as a political tool, how effective is *BnG* at facilitating this collective organization? This chapter examines how sex workers' rights activists in the United States have utilized *BnG* as a tool for political mobilization, as a space for internal and external political dialogue, and as an outspoken "mouthpiece for [the] movement"[5] that challenges conventional understandings of sex work.

Specifically, I contend that in addition to standard techniques of political organization such as local meet-ups and staged protests, blogs offer powerful tools for socially and legally marginalized groups to engage in public political discourse about the issues facing their communities. Although the political usefulness of blogs may be limited by political opportunities (Lynch 2007) and the ways they are used, blogs may lay foundations for the collective mobilization of marginalized communities by offering safe spaces for anonymous status disclosure and platforms for distributing event and industry information to isolated communities. They also provide space for activists to define and debate the boundaries of their experiences and how they relate to movement goals. Finally, blogs offer a way for sex workers to contest stereotypical understandings of their work by providing a space where they can anonymously, but publicly, comment on sex work–related news, politics, and policies.

In the following sections, I provide an overview of relevant literature and the background and intended purpose of *Bound, Not Gagged*. Based on a qualitative analysis of *BnG* blog entries from 2008, as well as ethnographic data collected from national sex worker activist conferences (Desiree Alliance Conference 2007 and 2008)[6] and sex workers' rights organizations, I examine trends in the type of posts and comment section interactions of *BnG*. I conclude with a discussion of the possibilities and limitations of the use of blogs by sex workers' rights activists for political purposes.

New Social Media and Activism

Activism *by* and *for* sex workers has been ongoing to various degrees in the United States since at least the 1970s (Jenness 1993, 2), but the movement has achieved few criminal justice policy changes or "spaces at the table" in decision-making processes regarding prostitution.[7] Yet these limited gains have not discouraged sex workers' rights activists in their work—since the early 2000s, the number of sex worker social movement organizations and the visibility of their activities across the nation appears to be growing.[8] As the spatial organization of the sex industry has changed, with many workers moving online and indoors due to demographic shifts in urban residency and changing patterns of law enforcement (Bernstein 2007, 29–39; Murphy and Venkatesh 2006, 129), the sex worker movement has seen a similar shift in spatial organization, manifesting as changes in the kinds of tools and strategies they use for mobilizing, framing, and addressing the public with their messages. The Internet's communicative capacities provide a new range of possibilities for sex worker organizing, but interactive social media has been especially important here. As Clay Shirky has observed, "Access to information is far less important, politically, than access to conversation" (2011, 5). Significantly, blogs host extensive informational posts while providing relatively anonymous access to political conversation in comment sections.

Since the web went public in the 1990s, early research about the Internet focused on its impacts on civil society and democracy, rather than the specific use and effects of different web-based media. Some hailed the web as an opportunity to build a "cyberdemocracy" in which individuals could engage and interact as equals online despite differences in age, race, gender, nationality, or religion that might hinder equal interaction in the real-time world (Ogden 1994; Poster 2001). Others pointed to the dangerous isolating effects of supplanting conventional face-to-face association with computer-mediated communications (Kraut et al. 1998; Nie and Erbring 2000). A number of scholars have also pointed to the potential reproduction of class inequalities in access to information services. For example, Jorge Schement (2001) points out that information services like the Internet, cable, and phone services produce ongoing costs, whereas traditional information goods such as radios and televisions require one-time purchases.

With regard to political activism, however, several scholars argue that Internet communication and networking may provide lower cost alternatives for social movements to mass-distribute their messages and calls to action than print media (Kidd 2003; Lynch 2011; Stein 2009). Web 2.0 applications specifically allow users to create and distribute their own content on the web, including video and audio, which partially mitigates the problem of uneven access to mainstream media outlets. However, Evgeny Morozov (2011) has demonstrated how states may use such media to suppress political activism, for example, through the surveillance and profiling of protesters on sites like Twitter. Despite such concerns, the Arab Spring uprisings of 2010–11 clearly demonstrated the importance of social media and technology for grassroots political action. In observing these revolutionary actions, Marc Lynch posits that the "stylized debates between optimists and skeptics has reached its limit" and that we must now turn to examining the causal mechanisms and systemic effects of social media (2011, 303).

Surprisingly few academic studies have been conducted on *how* social movements use the web to supplement conventional collective action (Calhoun 1998, 379; DiMaggio et al. 2001, 319).[9] A notable exception to this is Laura Stein's (2009) comprehensive content analysis of established U.S. social movement organization (SMO) websites.[10] While demonstrating that SMOs frequently use their websites to provide information, call constituents to action, make requests for funds and connect with the websites of coalitional groups and allies, she finds that very few of these sites contained spaces for interaction and dialogue or creative expression (2009). As she acknowledges, part of this dearth of interaction and expression on websites may be due to her focus on established movement organizations rather than emerging or developing movement groups. Another factor in the patterns Stein observed may have simply been the type of web media on which she focused; different forms have particular strengths and weaknesses. For example, Twitter can provide real-time moment-to-moment information and updates, but individual Tweets are limited to 140 characters or fewer. Alternatively, blogs typically archive older posts, and informational websites may hold information as long as sites are active. Therefore, examining a blog as one form of social media used by sex workers' rights activists offers a partial corrective to overly general statements about computer-mediated communications as liberating and democratizing, or as tools of isolation or political suppression, as well as insight into how specific forms of social media are useful to activists for specific purposes.

We Are Bound, Not Gagged

Cofounded by two sex worker activists, Stacey Swimme and Melissa Gira, *BnG* was launched in May 2007 in the midst of the political scandal involving the so-called D.C. Madam, Deborah Jean Palfrey.[11] In response to sex workers' frequent exclusion from media coverage in favor of credentialed "experts," *BnG* was conceived as a space for sex worker voices to be asserted and heard. *BnG* still serves primarily as a site for sex worker surveillance and analysis of media coverage on sex work and sex work–related issues. However, as I will demonstrate, it clearly functions as more than just a filter for sex work news.

As a community blog, *BnG* hosts sixteen featured authors for blog posts, though at the time of this writing, *BnG* had fifty-three contributors.[12] Of these fifty-three authors, I personally know eighteen; all are current or former sex workers affiliated with movement organizations across the United States. While the blog is not open for public posting, featured bloggers have occasionally posted information and statements on behalf of other advocates for sex workers' rights and, in other instances, on behalf of oppositional advocates in order to generate discussions. Any registered user of WordPress, a free open-source blogging tool, may contribute to discussions within the comments section. My analysis revealed that while just four *BnG* authors created 75 percent of eighty-eight posts in March 2008, seventy-six different WordPress users posted in the comment sections, indicating that the blog draws at least a modest readership.[13]

Many of the *BnG* authors are prominent members of the Desiree Alliance, a national network of sex workers' rights activists and allies in other professional fields—public health, social science, sex education, and others. The group's primary aim is to build support networks for local and regional activism that advocates for sex workers' human, labor, and civil rights. In the past, Desiree Alliance conferences—where activists and allies share ideas and information, train new leaders, and collaborate on projects—have taken place annually in different locations across the United States. Recently, however, organizers decided to make the event biannual to reduce organizing and traveling costs. In addition to listservs and national conference calls for organizations like Desiree and Sex Workers Outreach Project (SWOP), a national sex worker advocacy organization, blogs like *BnG* provide a comparatively low-cost alternative for sex workers' rights activists and affiliates to keep in touch and communicate over space and time.

However, organizational listservs, conferences, and meetings are not open to the general public or antiprostitution activists. Organizing committees carefully screen listserv and conference applicants; only those supporting a sex workers' rights platform are invited to participate. As Stacey Swimme, cofounder of *BnG* and the Desiree Alliance comments, "Melissa Farley [a prominent anti-prostitution activist] and people like her are not in anyway [*sic*] invited to join us in Chicago [at Desiree]. It is a closed event for our trusted friends and allies only. We don't create events to give people like Farley access to abuse, manipulate and harm sex workers."[14] The public accessibility of *BnG* implies a clearly different function targeted at a wider, more diverse audience than listservs and private face-to-face meetings.

How Are Activists Using *BnG*?

Safe Spaces

Bound, Not Gagged was initially created as a public platform for sex workers to analyze and comment on sex work–related news, scholarship, and events, but more than this, *BnG* provides a safe space for sex workers to come out, a foundational step for further collective action. In the face of very real (and sometimes violent) legal and social sanctions faced by sex workers, the Internet's anonymity allows them to safely claim their status in the industry. Virtual anonymity allows sex workers to "come out" online and speak *as* sex workers on issues of interest to them in rational deliberation with political and moral opponents, the general non–sex worker public, and each other, while still safeguarding their off-line identities. This collective coming-out-via-blogging provides a potent tool for validating the authenticity of sex workers' experiential knowledge. This online anonymity is not limited to sex worker blogs, but the power of a collective sex worker blog like *BnG* lies in its potential to provide support and a sense of community to sex workers who read and write on the blog.

Similar to Stein's (2009) findings on established SMO websites, *BnG* posts are also used for mobilizing and informing the current and potential movement base. Information regarding local organization or chapter events is circulated on *BnG*, serving as a reminder to local activists or potential activists who may want to attend and also offering a way to keep the broader network of activists across the United States in touch with what local groups are doing in places as far apart as Tucson, Arizona, and New York City. For example, chapters of SWOP typically post videos and photos of local events and activities that they have organized on December 17th, which they have designated as the International Day to End Violence against Sex Workers. News of international sex worker activist events may also be posted in a show of solidarity and support. Though less frequent than other types of posts, fundraising information and posts requesting donations for specific sex work SMOs have also been circulated through *BnG*.

More than simply providing information to sex workers' rights activists and the broader public, *BnG* provides a means for activists to support each other in their political and industry work. Many posts circulate media stories, audio, and video featuring sex workers' rights activists in action or activist-generated videos. The most frequent comments in response to featured bloggers' posts are supportive statements and encouragement from other movement actors. For instance, when a *BnG* author posted about her presentation with another activist at San Francisco State University for "Sex::Tech," an HIV Prevention Conference focused on youth and technology, activist friends of the presenters filled the comments section with congratulations and resounding support for a job well done.[15] Another commenter, who appears not to have been previously affiliated with *BnG* or the ongoing movement, writes, "Thank you so much for this site and helping us all have a voice! i wish i had been there for you all's talk."[16]

Related to this, some posts and comments on *BnG* have followed up on discussions from Desiree Alliance conferences that provide explicit information and tips on how sex workers should address and respond to the media to avoid identity exposure and make sure that their interactions with members of the press are mutually beneficial. In one such post, sadielune recaps two ideas generated by activists at a conference panel on movement-media relations: the production of a sex worker–activist speakers' bureau that would be trained to speak and present in front of the media and a "black and white" list of media contacts that would flag some journalists for unfair representations of sex workers, while marking others as fair and respectable contacts.[17] Such posts have been met with comments of gratitude from other activists in the comments section, along with additional tips from similarly media-savvy activists.

Good and Bad Experiences

One of the primary aims of the sex workers' rights movement is to achieve recognition from policymakers and the broader public of the diversity of sex worker perspectives and experiences. As such, some of the posts on *BnG* were devoted to the personal stories of sex workers regarding their work in the industry, similar to posts found on individual sex worker blogs. However, the potential strength of a multiauthored blog is that a diversity of stories may be presented on a single site for easy public consumption. On *BnG*, many of these posts were construed as "typical-day-in-the-life-of" stories and painted positive pictures of interactions with clients and significant others in order to provide counter-representations of sex workers that reveal their experiences as not so different from other members of society, or at least not always steeped in violence and exploitation.

Though most of these posts drew positive support from like-minded activists, others, particularly those that illustrated negative experiences in the industry, inspired concerns about the public presentation of the sex workers on and linked to *BnG*, despite the movement's emphasis on respect for diversity. In one instance, two independent escorts who were active members in the sex workers' rights movement had written posts on their personal blogs as well as on *BnG* about the negative experiences they had while temporarily working at a Nevada brothel. One of these escorts criticized brothels for waving their "legal status as their carrot so that you feel like you NEED them to make that money."[18] In other words, she believed that legal brothels exploit the fact that they are the only legal route to prostitution by paying lower wages to their workers than could be made through illegal independent work. However, in a *BnG* post that has since been deleted, this same author also criticized brothel workers for continuing to work under conditions of lower autonomy because they "didn't know any better."[19] Another *BnG* author and activist read these posts and objected to the other author's criticism of brothel workers, recognizing them as a violation of the nonjudgmental respect for diversity in sex work that the movement touts. In response, she wrote a warning post about not silencing other types of sex workers in the movement: "I can't even imagine what would happen in this movement if the tables were turned: a sex worker from a much different background with much different experiences coming into our community and telling us what is wrong with the way we work, and then blogging about it? What *would* that look like? PLEASE THINK ABOUT THIS. Cuz I know that we DO know how this feels, we just have yet to make the correlation."[20]

These posts spawned a good deal of heated discussion among sex workers' rights activists in the comment section of *BnG* regarding *how much* and *what kind* of information about sex workers should be disclosed *publicly*. Nearly all agreed that criticizing others for working in their part of the sex industry was unacceptable (hence the removal of the original post), but the conversation about what types of sex work experiences were acceptable to share in public spaces continued. While some commenters continued to press for the disclosure of diverse sex worker experiences in all spaces—whether good, bad, or mundane—it was clear that activists were concerned that the public presentation of some experiences might overshadow others or fall into conventional tropes about the harms and dangers of working in the industry. The escort bloggers who initially wrote about their brothel experiences expressed hurt and resentment in their comments at being sanctioned for describing their personal experiences online. In response, one self-identified sex worker, lisaroellig, states that she has worked in all varieties of sex work, including street-based work, work under the management of pimps and madams, and as an independent escort, but that she carefully excludes some stories from her public presentation in order to ensure that her negative stories are not twisted for use against movement goals like decriminalization, destigmatization, and civil and labor rights. She writes, "Believe me I have stories. After twenty years, you bet your ass I do. I choose to keep those stories away from the public. We have many enemies and although at times it could be cathartic for me personally, any of those stories will only further the oppression against us. That is how it goes for us."[21] In response, another sex work activist comments, "If people can't speak their truth about their own experiences, then what kind of 'movement' is it, anyway?"[22] In support of maintaining the diversity of perspectives within the movement, many other commenters echoed this sentiment, urging lisaroellig to share her stories despite concerns that they would be used against the cause of sex workers' rights.

Like many movements, the sex workers' rights movement captures a diversity of opinions and experiences. While many discussions in the comment sections of *BnG* revolved around articulating which perspectives were clearly *outside* of a sex workers' rights movement perspective (which I address in the following section), discussions and disagreements between sex workers' rights activists over the specific goals and appropriate actions of the movement, such as those mentioned earlier, were relatively rare.

Re-Presenting Sex Work in Media and Research

The majority of *BnG* posts fall in line with the founders' initial intents, featuring commentary on and links to mainstream media coverage and representations of sex work. Favorite past topics have included the blog's foundational media coverage of the D.C. Madam scandal and suicide, New York Governor Eliot Spitzer's tryst with an escort, and coverage of the Long Island serial killer.[23] Information, quotes, and videos from news stories are often posted alongside scathing critiques of media portrayals of sex workers, analysis and articulation of sex worker perspectives on current events and, when warranted, support for particular media coverage. Posts most often critique these media stories for including only antiprostitution perspectives or for reproducing stereotypes about sex workers (i.e., that all sex workers are self-interested, drug-addicted, street-based workers who are pimped or trafficked).

For example, one *BnG* post tears apart an article in *SF Weekly* (Smith 2008) that sardonically critiqued a UCSF study (which Alexandra Lutnick describes in chapter 3) finding that police were extorting sex from prostitutes (Lutnick and Cohan 2008). The article mocked the UCSF study and questioned its credibility on the grounds that the first author is a self-proclaimed sex worker who would benefit at least partially from the decriminalization of sex work that the study supports. Because of the author's identity, combined with the then current campaign for Proposition K, a 2008 ballot measure to decriminalize prostitution in San Francisco, the author curtly dismissed the study's findings. In response, the author of the *BnG* post argues for adding the *SF Weekly* author to the sex workers' rights activists' media blacklist: "Not because it was an article that doesn't support Prop K or sex workers' rights per se, but because of the use of ridiculously sensationalized phrases like 'blowjobs-for-badges' and his general tone of discrediting sex workers, their self-reported hardships, and any research conducted by people who have worked in the sex industry about sex work."[24] In another instance, *BnG* critiqued media stories for only addressing the opinions of academic or media "experts" while overlooking the experiential knowledge of sex workers in the activist community. One post roundly took Diane Sawyer to task for a *20/20* report on "Prostitution in America" that did not incorporate any sex worker perspectives on prostitution policy but focused solely on the perspectives of Nicholas Kristof, a well-known antiprostitution reporter from the *New York Times*.

However, not all informational posts on *BnG* revolve around media representations and coverage. Some posts directly tackle research on prostitution, providing clear analyses of what is "good" or "bad" about particular studies for sex workers as a group. For example, *BnG* authors and commenters were largely critical of a preliminary study conducted by economist Steve Levitt and sociologist Sudhir Venkatesh (2007) on street-based sex workers in Chicago that had been receiving press due to the authors' notoriety. Because of the economic focus of that study on topics like pay rates and work relations with pimps, some critiqued it for asking the wrong questions about sex work.[25] Others were critical of the study's inclusion of former prostitutes for data collection, without actually incorporating them into the research process where they may have had leverage in producing research relevant to sex workers.[26] In contrast, community-based research like the Move Along Report (Alliance for a Safe and Diverse D.C. 2008), produced by the D.C. organization Different Avenues to document prostitution law enforcement in D.C., received overwhelmingly positive support on *BnG* for its rigor and for incorporating affected community members in the research process.[27]

Other *BnG* posts have followed and analyzed how political or legislative policies impact sex workers, rather than directly analyzing media coverage. These analyses are not limited to the United States, although U.S. policies have often been placed under the greatest scrutiny. For example, the antiprostitution pledge[28] of the President's Emergency Plan for AIDS Relief (PEPFAR)—drafted by Randall Tobias, the USAID Administrator who was later accused of hiring escorts through Madam Deborah Jean Palfrey's agency—drew heat from *BnG* authors and commenters for its negative impact on international sex worker organizations.[29]

A Place to Be Publicly Heard

While undoubtedly cathartic for individual activists and other sex workers who read them, many of the posts and analyses already described appear intended for broader public consumption in an effort to combat stereotypes about sex workers, to offer perspectives and cases that run counter to dominant narratives that frame all prostitutes as women or children victimized at the hands of violent men (pimps or clients), and, most fundamentally, to present sex worker perspectives without mainstream media distortion. As the very first *BnG* post demonstrates, as a group, the original *BnG* authors were not representative of all sex workers, but they certainly had something to say about sex work that wasn't being captured by mainstream discussions:

> In the story of alleged DC Madam, Deborah Jean Palfrey, one voice is conspicuously absent: ours, and our lips are, despite what you may have heard, hardly sealed. We're a group of educated, Internet-savvy, politically game escorts, and we aren't for hire. (Not here, anyway.) We're apparently the exception to the rule, but for us, this is just business as usual. Of course, rich and powerful men want access to erotic companionship. Of course, Washington is a hotbed of hypocrisy. We know this not because we've been privy to really fantastic pillowtalk, which some of us have, but because we work the halls of government by day, as well. We want to talk to you, but we might have to do it in private. We might have to do it in the dark. We might not be able to tell you our real names, but that doesn't mean we have to be quiet about it, either.
> We're Deepthroated, bound, maybe, but certainly not gagged. And here, we're going to go down, and dirty, on Washington.[30]

BnG offer a lens into how some sex workers interpret current events, knowledge production, and media portrayals of sex workers. In the face of stereotypes about sex workers as uneducated, divided by the competitive nature of their profession, or victims of trafficking, posts on *BnG* stand to demonstrate that sex workers can be articulate, intelligent, and thoughtful about issues that affect them, that they can be engaged in collective enterprises, and that their experiences are not simply reducible to victimization. *BnG*'s tendency to tackle sex work–related issues and provide counternarratives also speaks to its public nature; in comparison, sex work activist e-mail listservs to which I belong do not contain the same level of issue-tackling as *BnG* posts and comment discussions.[31]

Another important public function of *BnG* is to provide a space for sex workers to present unfiltered and often complex experiences and perspectives on sex work as *valid*. This is quite important to activists, as negative stereotypes of and dominant cultural expectations for sex workers can facilitate an easy dismissal of their statements. When sex workers are perceived primarily as victims, they may be expected to fulfill a victim role by not complicating their status with contradictory experiences or sentiments. In other instances, cultural portrayals of sex workers as self-interested professional "gold-diggers" may similarly discredit their ability to present complex accounts of their work and lives.

To illustrate, in a particularly evocative post on *BnG*, author karlykirchner expressed her rage and frustration at having one of her *BnG* posts—and really, much of the blog—misinterpreted and dismissed in a post on the popular feminist blog *Jezebel*. This author, karlykirchner, had written a thoughtful *BnG* post describing her internal struggles over coming out as a sex worker to her mother; ultimately, she revealed that coming out to her mother ended up being a positive and relatively nondisruptive experience.[32] In response to this *BnG* post, a Jezebel author quoted and supported the sentiments of a non–sex worker "expert" who states, "There seems [*sic*] to be two basic motivations for writing about one's tenure as a hooker, neither educational. The prostitute either wants to glorify or vilify the industry and its consumers. Either of these seems simplistic and disingenuous."[33] This Jezebel article was frustrating to activists on *BnG* for its dismissal of *BnG*'s intentions as shallow and one-dimensional and for legitimating a non–sex workers' expertise over the experiential knowledge of actual sex workers.

Debating and Deliberating Opposition

Comment sections for posts on news, research, policies, and relevant current events have also provided a space for deliberative discussion, disagreement, and consensus on individuals' interpretations of issues. For these more publicly oriented posts, "outside" commenters—those not affiliated with the sex workers' rights movement—have frequently posted their oppositional sentiments, generating heated discussion and debate between those who support a sex workers' rights platform (which entails full labor and civil rights for those currently engaged in the industry) and those who support the abolition of prostitution and the removal of all prostitutes (consenting or not) from the sex industry.

In these discussions, sex workers' rights activists in the comment sections actively sought to argue their case against abolitionist posts and, in the process, provide greater clarity for public readers about the movement's emphasis on harm reduction and rights for sex workers, whether they remain in the industry or not. For example, in response to a *BnG* post that both lambasted Randall Tobias (the now-former U.S. Deputy Secretary of State) for his hypocritical solicitation of sex workers *and* called on sex workers' rights advocates and allies to support the rights of sex workers around the world, one abolitionist commenter mockingly quoted part of this *BnG* post to write,

> "We in the US—sex worker rights advocates and our networks of supporters—all have a role to play in ensuring the wellbeing [*sic*] of sex workers around the world,"
>
> I can only assume you are kidding. Sex work is slavery my friend. People are being bought and sold and used. Trying to legitimize the fact that poor women have to have a dozen strangers' penises down their throat to survive for another day is not a legitimate moral position. The way to end the abuse is to end the prostitution.
>
> Yeah, Tobias is a creep and a hypocrite. Yes, abstinence has no place in any public policy. But don't try to tie that all up in some pro-prostitution, "sex work" nonsense.
>
> Prostitution hurts people. Period.[34]

The post's author responded by asserting that she had never heard a realistic plan to end prostitution, but that jailing prostitutes and removing their rights to health care, food, clothing, and shelter—for which international groups have criticized Tobias's USAID antiprostitution pledge—were morally indefensible because they also hurt people.[35] In contrast, other comment discussions between movement insiders (authors) and presumable outsiders were less heated, despite outsiders criticizing some of the statements on *BnG*. For example, commenter Marianne wrote that she felt *BnG* authors were too hard on abolitionist Melissa Farley's criticisms of Eliot Spitzer.[36] The blog post author disagreed and listed several reasons why, but the tone of the exchange was calm and open. In some instances, oppositional commenters on *BnG* even attempted to outline ways that abolitionists and sex workers' rights advocates could possibly work together, indicating a conciliatory complexity that is often lost in strictly dichotomous portrayals of abolitionist and sex workers' rights perspectives.

Who's In and Who's Out?

As noted, *BnG* provides a safe space for sex workers to speak anonymously and openly online as current or former sex workers. However, the cover of anonymity provided by the Internet can be a double-edged sword. How do *BnG* commenters distinguish between sex workers' rights movement "outsiders" (abolitionists) and "insiders" (those who agree with and support the goals of the movement)? Comments suggesting that prostitution should be abolished, that all clients and pimps are violent men, or that consensual prostitution is the exception rather than the rule are easily identified by both posters and readers of *BnG* as "outside" the movement, even if they come from individuals self-identifying as former sex industry workers. Often, "insider" contributors to *BnG* already know each other through real-time interactions that they have had at Desiree Alliance and other meetings, and so they are able to identify each other online via personal histories and knowledge of each other's virtual pseudonyms.

Despite this, some comments are not easily identified on their own merits as outside or inside the movement. For example, in the midst of a comment section discussion over what the movement should focus action on, one commenter claimed to be an independent escort but stated that he or she did not support Proposition K, a ballot measure that would have decriminalized prostitution in the city and county of San Francisco and defunded the prostitution diversion programs of SAGE, an antitrafficking organization. This commenter was immediately sanctioned by known insiders as a "hater with a really bad undercover disguise," implying that this commenter was an abolitionist posing as a sex workers' rights advocate.[37] It appeared that no one had had face-to-face experience with this poster, nor were his or her comments convincingly presented as authentically supportive of "sex workers' rights." Yet it was far from clear to a casual outside reader that this person was definitely an antiprostitution advocate.

Clues from another post on *BnG*, however, indicate that the outsider status of some commenters is far from ambiguous for blog authors, despite unfamiliar pseudonyms and a lack of face-to-face interaction. Amid a heated exchange between blog authors and a commenter who accused the authors of sounding more like pimps than sex workers, one of the *BnG* authors stated that the offending commenter "has the same IP address as the other trolls,"[38] and so she or he should be ignored. It is clear then that authors have access to less visible clues to identify "posers" from insiders or potential movement recruits. In this case, multiple inflammatory comments under different user names were being posted from the same Internet Protocol (IP) address, a red flag to authors that this commenter was not an ally and may not have been a sex worker at all.

Discussion

Although it is difficult to assess the impact of *BnG* on public and policymaker perceptions of sex work, it is clear that *BnG* performs some important functions for the sex workers' rights movement. It provides a safe, anonymous space for sex workers to publicly come out and collectively deliberate issues and events relevant to them. As such, it can be used to mobilize new sex worker and allied movement constituents. Blogs further provide a space for sharing diverse sex worker experiences and perspectives, as well as a space for challenging dominant public and political understandings of their work and industry.

However, examining the content of *BnG* reveals some limitations for the blog's potential to politically mobilize constituents and challenge common perceptions about prostitution and sex work. Namely, concerns over the authenticity of anonymous claims to sex worker identity, and portrayals of sex work, are at the heart of many of the blog's limitations. These issues are not limited to activist blogs such as *BnG* but they illustrate how the sometimes opaque operation of blogs, combined with the policing that goes along within them, may result in significant limitations for activists wishing to use blogs as political tools. For example, the intense policing of "outside" perspectives in *BnG* posts, but especially in the comment sections, poses a barrier to recruiting new sex workers or allies to the movement. Part of this policing is no doubt intended to maintain a safe space to air perspectives common to the movement, since so little space is offered to them in traditional media. In some ways, the blog is simply a public place for activists to express frustration with their social statuses and the dominant portrayals of their work. However, if commenters express that they do not agree with all sex worker–movement perspectives and are not already known by activist authors on *BnG* from face-to-face interactions, they risk online ridicule (many of the posts and comments, from both sex workers' rights advocates and abolitionists, are derisive) or accusations of being unenlightened abolitionists, an ironic form of censorship given the blog title's reference to free expression for a socially and legally constrained population. And so while *BnG* authors have access to nonpublic information like commenter IP addresses, allowing for a backstage distinction between "posers" and genuinely curious commenters, this fact is far from obvious to casual *BnG* readers. It stands to reason that this tenor on *BnG* may limit its possibilities for mobilizing new movement constituents, as it may deter some readers from joining comment discussions, let alone off-line movement activities and events.

Another limitation encountered on *BnG* is the issue of diversity in the statuses, experiences, and perspectives of sex workers. Like many other movements, the sex workers' rights movement actively struggles with issues of diversity. While conducting fieldwork, I frequently heard accusations that the movement failed to represent all sex workers in terms of race, class, and gender. Because of this, blog post authors are careful to note that their claims are not representative of all sex worker perspectives. This phenomenon echoes concerns over the digital divide in Internet access (see DiMaggio et al. 2001). Lower income and particular ethnic, immigrant, and racial groups within the sex worker community may have limited access to the Internet and therefore less opportunity to engage in conversations like those on *BnG*. Although organizers of *BnG* have little power to close the broader digital divide, the movement has made concerted efforts to diversify its off-line activities and membership. For example, Desiree Alliance offers scholarships for low-income and minority sex workers to offset the costs of conference attendance and encourage diverse participation.[39] Although the comment function of *BnG* is open to all, from what I observed, little effort has been made to actively recruit diverse online participation in terms of comments or authorship.

Finally, due to both the opacity of blog operation and the tensions between values and apprehensions within the movement, the messaging on *BnG* is not always clear to outside readers. Blog posts may be altered after their initial posting without any indication of changes, which means that interpreting comments and posts outside of real-time posting may be difficult for future readers. For example, I encountered some difficulty in accurately interpreting the *BnG* conversation about brothel work due to the deletion and alteration of certain comments and posts. Without personal communication with contributing activists, my original interpretations of these conversations were far from accurate. This limitation may produce confusing messaging for outside readers of blogs, whether they are potential new activists, policymakers, or the general public.

Moreover, the movement's value for publicly displaying diverse sex worker experiences stood in tension with concerns that publicly presented stories of *negative* sex industry experiences would be distorted. Positive or mundane sex work experiences seemed to be promoted over others on *BnG*, and from lisaroellig's comments, it seems that this preferential representation is rooted in concerns that negative sex work experiences will surely eclipse any discussion of positive or routine elements in sex work. The experience of *BnG* authors writing about their everyday work and life routines and their sometimes positive encounters with clients are clearly valid. But contrary to some activists' concerns, without counter-representations of negative sex work experiences on *BnG*, it may be easier for movement opponents and an uncertain public to dismiss *BnG* stories as representing only the "happy hooker" myth.

Conclusion

There are various explanations of why the sex workers' rights movement has thus far failed to make significant political headway in the United States.[40] Based on an international comparison of Australian and U.S.-based sex worker collective organizing, Gregor Gall's chapter in this volume (chapter 10) argues that the tendency toward less integrated city- and statewide sex worker organizations in the United States has partially impeded the progress of a sex workers' rights discourse in public policy. Blogs like *Bound, Not Gagged* demonstrate that the integration and concerted cooperation of local sex workers' rights groups in the United States is certainly possible, even if it currently takes place on a modest scale. While blogs and other social media are limited in their political capacity when appropriate political opportunity structures—such as elections, national scandals, and elite debates that may draw attention to and make blogs relevant in the public eye—are lacking (Lynch 2011; 2007), they still play political roles. As *BnG* demonstrates, blogs can serve important consciousness-raising functions, laying the groundwork for political mobilization. Future studies comparing the ways that different social media platforms—including Twitter, Tumblr, Facebook, and

Google Plus—are used by various movements may tell us even more about the specific limitations and opportunities for social change provided by different types of social media.

Social media have radically transformed the possibilities for political engagement and social activism. Despite facing a multitude of political and social barriers, through dedication and cooperation, the sex workers' rights movement in the United States continues to grow by utilizing innovative tools and tactics both on- and off-line. However, in order to realize the full political potential of blogs for recruiting movement constituents and challenging dominant perceptions about sex work, *BnG* might consider enhancing the transparency of community membership on the blog, creating some formal rules for authorship, and actively recruiting authors to increase the diversity of their authorship. *Tits and Sass*, a less political multiauthor sex worker blog that offers "witty commentary" on public depictions of the sex industry, provides an excellent model for this, with clear guidelines for writing contributions and active calls for diverse commentary.[41] By offering rules or applications for blog authorship, *BnG* could sincerely open the doors for greater discussion and diversity in their statements. This would still allow blog moderators to screen potential contributors in order to maintain *BnG* as a safe space, but it could enhance *BnG*'s potential for publicly displayed collaboration, cooperation, and discussion with groups and individuals that might not have otherwise been included. Additionally, a system for comment-section participants to flag "trolls" for an author or moderator to check would demystify and formalize the policing of participants who abuse their anonymity on the site. Finally, actively using on- and off-line means to recruit more diverse sex worker authorship and participation on *BnG* would further support movement goals of diversity in membership and presentation and may spur the movement to generate new ideas while sharpening older ones. Such changes may enhance the blog's potential as a critical movement tool when the next key political opportunity arises.

Notes

1. From 2007 to 2009, I conducted fieldwork and interviews with sex workers' rights activists from the Northern California chapter of Sex Workers Outreach Project (SWOP). In the process, I met members of other chapters, including SWOP-Chicago, SWOP-NYC, SWOP-East, and activists from other

organizations, national and international. I followed up with intermittent visits to the field in 2010.

2. For examples, see Monet (2005), Oakley (2007), and Brooks (2006; 2009). The majority of contemporary sex workers' rights activists in the United States are current or former sex workers. However, the movement also has allies in the field of public health, academia, and sex-positive feminism. The movement is the site of multiple and contested aims, including the destigmatization of sex work, the decriminalization of sex work, and the empowerment of sex workers to act on their own behalf in political and cultural arenas. For an excellent account of sex worker activism outside the U.S., see Yasmin Lalani's chapter in this volume.

3. *Bound, not Gagged* (blog), http://deepthroated.wordpress.com.

4. There is at least one other multiauthored sex worker blog that I know of, Tits and Sass (http://www.titsandsass.com), and it provides "witty commentary" on public depictions of the sex industry. However, it differs significantly from *BnG* because it does not appear to have any goals of motivating or mobilizing political action.

5. *Bound, Not Gagged* (blog post), August 29, 2008.

6. I chose to focus on 2008 *BnG* posts because this year contained the highest volume of posts. This was important for capturing the greatest variety of blog posts and discussions in a limited interpretive analysis. Field notes, blog posts, and comments were analyzed using HyperRESEARCH qualitative analysis software. First open coding and then more focused coding were used to inductively develop themes and patterns in the data.

7. One notable exception would be the appointment of the San Francisco Task Force on Prostitution, which resulted in funds for the St. James Infirmary. Recent work has demonstrated that sex workers' rights activists have also made some gains in influencing the field of HIV/AIDS prevention in the United States and internationally (see Majic 2011).

8. Some notable up-and-coming organizations include the Sex Workers Outreach Project (SWOP) (http://www.swopusa.org), the Desiree Alliance (http://www.desireealliance.org), and the Global Network of Sex Work Projects (http://www.nswp.org).

9. By this, I mean to distinguish online forms of membership activism—e-mail campaigns such as those promoted by MoveOn.org or Change.org—from activism that still incorporates face-to-face modes of collective organizing.

10. Stein's (2009) is not the only scholarship addressing activism and the web, of course. Castells (1996) discusses contemporary social movements to illustrate the importance of web-based informational exchanges, but he does not examine how social movements actually use the web to supplement real-time, face-to-face activism. The Chiapas Rebellion of 1994 is generally regarded as the first Internet-based revolution, and several scholars have addressed the importance of

Internet communication in these uprisings (see Froehling 1997; Knudson 1998) without necessarily examining how these web communications were limited or enhanced by specific web-based platforms.

11. Palfrey was charged and later convicted of prostitution-related racketeering for her D.C.-based escort agency, Pamela Martin and Associates (Duggan 2008).

12. Personal communication with Amanda Brooks, January 22, 2013. The discrepancy between featured and actual authors may be due to a lag in updating the featured author list as new members were authorized to make blog posts. In the future, I hope to conduct more extensive quantitative measures of participation and comment traffic on *BnG*.

13. This is a low number, given that high-volume mainstream sites may receive upwards of fifty thousand site visitors per day. I do not have access to the daily number of site visitors for *BnG*, so it is not clear what sort of site traffic the blog actually receives. However, the number of registered comment users does indicate that the site receives some form of regular readership; assuming that there are some readers who visit and read the site but choose not to comment (myself included), it is likely that the actual number of readers for *BnG* is higher.

14. *Bound, Not Gagged* (blog post), March 29, 2008, staceyswimme.

15. *Bound, Not Gagged* (blog post), January 24, 2008, staceyswimme.

16. *Bound, Not Gagged* (blog post), January 24, 2008, julie.

17. *Bound, Not Gagged* (blog post), July 19, 2008, sadielune.

18. Mario Passion, "Cautionary Words from a Brothel Survivor: But Still a Sex Worker Activist." *Mariko Passion: Educated Whore, Urban Geisha* (blog), August 25, 2008, http://marikopassion.wordpress.com/2008/08/25/cautionary-words-from-a-brothel-survivor/.

19. Personal communication with kittenINFINITE, January 25, 2013, and Naomi Akers, January 26, 2013.

20. *Bound, Not Gagged* (blog post), August 29, 2008, kittenINFINITE.

21. *Bound, Not Gagged* (blog post), August 29, 2008, lisaroellig.

22. *Bound, Not Gagged* (blog post), August 29, 2008, AmberRhea.

23. In March 2008, Spitzer resigned as governor of New York when he was found to have frequented a high-end escort service (*NPR* 2008). In separate news, from 2010 to 2011, New York police found the remains of at least ten women, many of whom were identified as sex workers, hidden along a southern beach of Long Island in New York. The killings were portrayed as the work of a serial killer (*New York Times* 2011).

24. *Bound, Not Gagged* (blog post), September 12, 2008, sadielune.

25. *Bound, Not Gagged* (blog post), January 7, 2008, Amanda Brooks.

26. *Bound, Not Gagged* (blog post), January 10, 2008, Melissa Gira.

27. *Bound, Not Gagged* (blog post), June 2, 2008, Jessica Land.

28. The pledge required that any organization accepting PEPFAR funds must not support prostitution in any way. This put many organizations that aid working prostitutes without encouraging them to exit the industry in a bind, as they could be interpreted as supporting prostitution.

29. *Bound, Not Gagged* (blog post), May 4, 2007, Melissa Gira.

30. *Bound, Not Gagged* (blog post), May 4, 2007, deepthroated.

31. I had initially intended to include sex worker–movement listservs as a comparative case of social media to blogs. However, when I sent a request to my listserv of interest (of which I am a member), members very clearly and vocally agreed that the listserv was too private to be laid bare in research. As a result, I have excluded any detailed discussion of it here.

32. *Bound, Not Gagged* (blog post), April 21, 2008, karlykirchner.

33. *Bound, Not Gagged* (blog post), April 22, 2008, karlykirchner. *Jezebel* (blog post), April 22, 2008, Jessica G.

34. *Bound, Not Gagged* (blog post), May 4, 2007, ohyeah.

35. *Bound, Not Gagged* (blog post), May 4, 2007, Melissa Gira.

36. *Bound, Not Gagged* (blog post), March 12, 2008, Marianne. At this commenter's request, I have used a pseudonym.

37. *Bound, Not Gagged* (blog post), March 1, 2008, jillbrenneman.

38. *Bound, Not Gagged* (blog post), March 12, 2008_k, jillbrenneman.

39. Here, I refer to not only sex workers of color but other groups that may not be represented by the majority of sex workers' rights activists, including male sex workers, transgender sex workers, and porn performers.

40. See Mathieu (2003), Jenness (1993), and Weitzer (1991).

41. *Tits and Sass* (blog), "Contribute," http://titsandsass.com/tag/contribute.

References

Alliance for a Safe and Diverse D.C. 2008. *Move Along: Policing Sex Work in Washington, DC.* Washington, D.C.: Different Avenues.

Bernstein, Elizabeth. 2007. *Temporarily Yours: Intimacy, Authenticity, and the Commerce of Sex.* Chicago: University of Chicago Press.

Brooks, Amanda. 2006. *The Internet Escort's Handbook 1: The Foundation.* Reno, Nev.: Golden Girl Press.

———. 2009. *The Internet Escort's Handbook 2: Advertising and Marketing.* Reno, Nev.: Golden Girl Press.

Calhoun, Craig. 1998. "Community without Propinquity Revisited: Communications Technology and the Transformation of the Urban Public Sphere." *Social Inquiry* 68, no. 3: 373–97.

Castells, Manuel. 1996. *The Rise of the Network Society: The Information Age: Economy, Society, and Culture, Volume 1.* Malden, MA: Blackwell Publishing.

DiMaggio, Paul, Eszter Hargittai, Russell Neuman, and John P. Robinson. 2001. "Social Implications of the Internet." *Annual Review of Sociology* 27: 307–36.

Duggan, Paul. 2008. "Trial Starts in Case of Upscale Escort Service; Court Testimony May Prove 'Embarrassing.'" *Washington Post*, April 8, B1.

Froehling, Oliver. 1997. "The Cyberspace 'War of Ink and Internet' in Chiapas, Mexico." *Geographical Review* 87, no. 2: 291–307.

Jenness, Valerie. 1993. *Making It Work: The Prostitutes' Rights Movement in Perspective.* New York: Aldine de Gruyter.

Kidd, Dorothy. 2003. "Indymedia.org: A New Communications Commons." In *Cyberactivism: Critical Theories and Practices of On-line Activism,* ed. Martha McGaughey and Michael Ayers, 47–69. New York: Routledge.

Knudson, Jerry W. 1998. "Rebellion in Chiapas: Insurrection by Internet and Public Relations." *Media, Culture & Society* 20: 507–18.

Kraut, Robert, Michael Patterson, Vicki Lundmark, Sara Kiesler, Tridas Mkophadhyay, and William Scherlis. 1998. "Internet Paradox: A Social Technology That Reduces Social Involvement and Psychological Well-Being?" *American Psychologist* 53, no. 9: 1017–31.

Levitt, Steven, and Sudhir Venkatesh. 2007. "An Empirical Analysis of Street Level Prostitution." Unpublished work, University of Chicago, September. http://economics.uchicago.edu/pdf/Prostitution%205.pdf.

Lutnick, Alexandra, and Deborah Cohan. 2008. "Working Conditions, HIV, STIs and Hepatitis C Among Female Sex Workers in San Francisco, CA." Presentation at the International AIDS Conference, Mexico City, Mexico, August 3–8.

Lynch, Marc. 2007. "Blogging the New Arab Public." *Arab Media and Society*, February, 1–30.

———. 2011. "After Egypt: The Limits and Promise of Online Challenges to the Authoritarian Arab State." *Perspectives on Politics* 9, no. 2: 301–10.

Majic, Samantha. 2011. "Serving Sex Workers and Promoting Democratic Engagement: Rethinking Nonprofits' Role in American Civic and Political Life." *Perspectives on Politics* 9, no. 4: 821–39.

Mathieu, Lilian. 2003. "The Emergence and Uncertain Outcomes of Prostitutes; Social Movements." *European Journal of Women's Studies* 10, no. 1: 29–50.

Monet, Veronica. 2005. *Sex Secrets of Escorts: Tips from a Pro.* New York: Alpha Books.

Morozov, Evgeny. 2011. *The Net Delusion: The Dark Side of Internet Freedom.* New York: Public Affairs.

Murphy, Alexandra K., and Sudhir Venkatesh. 2006. "Vice Careers: The Changing Contours of Sex Work in New York City." *Qualitative Sociology* 26: 129–54.

New York Times. 2011. "Bright, Careful, and Sadistic: Profiling Long Island's Mystery Serial Killer." April 21. http://www.nytimes.com/2011/04/22/nyregion/long -island-serial-killer-gets-a-personality-profile.html?pagewanted=all&_r=0.

Nie, Norman H., and Lutz Erbring. 2000. *Internet and Society: A Preliminary Report.* Stanford, Calif.: Institute for the Quantitative Study of Society.

NPR. 2008. "Spitzer Has Little Support in Albany," March 12. http://www.npr .org/templates/story/story.php?storyId=88132232.

Oakley, Annie, ed. 2007. *Working Sex: Sex Workers Write about a Changing Industry.* Emeryville, Calif.: Seal Press.

Ogden, Michael R. 1994. "Politics in a Parallel Universe: Is There a Future for Cyberdemocracy?" *Futures* 26, no. 7: 713–29.

Poster, Mark. 2011. "Cyberdemocracy: The Internet and the Public Sphere." In *Reading Digital Culture,* ed. David Trend, 259–71. Malden, Mass.: Blackwell.

Schement, Jorge Reina. 2001. "Of Gaps by Which Democracy We Measure." In *The Digital Divide: Facing a Crisis or Creating a Myth,* ed. Benjamin M. Compaine, 303–8. Cambridge, Mass.: MIT Press.

Shirky, Clay. 2011. "The Political Power of Social Media." *Foreign Affairs,* January/February. http://www.foreignaffairs.com/print/66987.

Smith, Matt. 2008. "Dubious UCSF Study Claims Cops Extort Sex." *SF Weekly,* September 10. http://www.sfweekly.com/2008-09-10/news/dubious-ucsf-study -claims-cops-extort-sex/1.

Stein, Laura. 2009. "Social Movement Web Use in Theory and Practice: A Content Analysis of U.S. Movement Websites." *New Media Society* 11, no. 5: 749–70.

Vanwesenbeeck, Ine. 2001. "Another Decade of Social Scientific Work on Prostitution." *Annual Review of Sex Research* 12: 242–89.

Weitzer, Ronald. 1991. "Prostitutes' Rights in the United States: The Failure of a Movement." *Sociological Quarterly* 32, no. 1: 23–41.

———. 2005. "New Directions in Research on Prostitution." *Crime, Law and Social Change* 43: 211–35.

CHAPTER 12

Gender Relations and HIV/AIDS Education in the Peruvian Amazon

Female Sex Worker Activists Creating Community

Yasmin Lalani

R ECENT SCHOLARSHIP ON SEX WORK has recognized the power of sex workers' political organizing and activism as integral to the development of women's social, sexual, and political agency (Biradavolu et al. 2009; Kempadoo and Dozema 1998). Tied to this, numerous studies have shown that some sex worker organizations have made formidable efforts to increase sex workers' HIV-related knowledge and strategies for condom use (Ghose, Swenderman, George, and Chowdhury 2008; Sanders 2006; Wahab 2004). While sex worker organizations are steadily gaining momentum internationally, there is still a need to investigate more deeply the gendered social relations that surround and influence sex worker organizations' collective, yet diverse, concerns and challenges. As Alison Murray (1998) and Kamala Kempadoo (2001) suggest, local-level research with sex worker organizations themselves is the only way to arrive at more sophisticated understandings about how female sex workers interpret their own lives, their health needs, and their work and how they choose to advocate for themselves in predominantly male mainstream political arenas.

In light of this, drawing on findings from a qualitative study conducted in the Amazon jungle city of Iquitos, Peru, my priority in this chapter is to theorize sex worker activists' social relations with the state, with male clients, and among each other using a gender relations framework. I apply Raewyn Connell's (2012) understanding of gender relations as a multidimensional "varied body of thought" (Connell 2012, 1677) in which gender is theorized as a complex set of relations that involve a range of bodies, institutions, and social processes at both the micro and macro levels (Connell 2012). In this vein, I argue that a gender relations analysis is essential for uncovering the nuances of female collective and individual agency and its relevance to sex worker identity, particularly within the social context of HIV/AIDS prevention education. A second benefit of using a gender relations framework is that it provides a way to challenge conventional discourses that portray sex workers as nonagentic in the company of "dominant" male clients or as a uniformly downtrodden group in the face of patriarchal social systems.

While AIDS cases in Latin America are typically confined to gay men and men who have sex with men (MSM), some areas such as the Amazon region of Peru are now showing an increase in the number of women who are affected or at risk (Bastos et al. 2008; Cáceres and Mendoza 2009). Given this increase, the purpose of this qualitative study was to gain a sharper insight into the social and gendered elements of women's vulnerability to HIV in Iquitos. Over a period of three months I conducted a qualitative interview study with female activists and their stakeholders (N = 13) from two community-based organizations (CBOs). The first CBO is Lazos de Vida, which is run by women and men living with HIV. The second is Sarita Colonia, which is run by and for female sex workers in Iquitos. Both organizations engage in political advocacy for sexual minorities and health promotion for HIV/AIDS prevention. In this chapter, I focus on the interview data from three female sex worker activists from Sarita Colonia. While I did interview a total of six female sex workers from Sarita Colonia, the three participants whose narratives I include in this chapter best highlight the organization's collective outcomes and future challenges and indicate how women's involvement in the organization positively affects how they and their peers reduce their own risk of HIV.

This chapter first briefly highlights how these activists have negotiated with the state to carry out health education initiatives and reduce the stigma associated with sex work. The second section offers a compelling illustration of sex worker agency "in action"—that is, how sex workers negotiate safer sex with clients. The third section draws our attention to the conflict and tensions that sex worker organizations face in their educational outreach work.

Research Context

The Amazon region of Peru makes up 60 percent of the country (Hunefeldt 2004). With a population reaching close to four hundred thousand, Iquitos is the administrative capital of the region of Loreto and is the largest city in the world that cannot be reached by road; access is limited to air or to the complex network of river systems (Maki, Kalliola, and Vourinen 2001). Iquitos was originally founded as a Jesuit mission in 1757, and European rubber barons occupied it in the late 1800s in swift pursuit of the Amazon's rubber trees and other natural resources for export (Fuller 2004; Galeano 1973; Hunefeldt 2004). The ethnic population of Iquitos and surrounding rural areas can be classified as *ribereño*—detribalized, rural, and Spanish speaking (Chibnik 1991). Since the 1940s, Iquitos has functioned as a hub for military bases, oil extraction and mining projects, and scientific research, all of which contribute to a partly transient population that consequently increases the demand for sex workers (Fuller 2004; Isla 2009).

The Amazon region of Peru is one of the poorest and most underserved regions of the country. Despite the succession of economic "booms" since the late 1800s, inhabitants of Iquitos and the surrounding area experience poverty varying from extreme to moderate (Espinoza 2009; Fuller 2004; Gyorkos et al. 2010). The health status of many people in the Amazon is therefore largely shaped by the combination of poverty and low population density in this large geographic region, where access to Western health care services is only possible by long river journeys (Casapía, Joseph, and Gyorkos 2007; Martínez, Villarroel, Seoane, and del Pozo 2004; Nawaz et al. 2001). There are, however, health centers and hospitals located in the urban centers of Iquitos and Pucallpa and the smaller towns of Yurimaguas and Tarapoto.

Unemployment in Iquitos is a major social problem because of the scarcity of well-paid and stable job opportunities (Cáceres et al. 2002). Iquitos' remote location therefore intensifies the burden of unemployment, as most people cannot afford to travel to other parts of Peru to find work or health care. Consequently, many Iquiteños create their own sources of income generation such as selling food in the markets or from their homes, performing manual labor, marketing themselves as tour guides, or by driving *motocarros* (three-wheeled motorized taxis). Eduardo Galeano (1973), in his seminal work on the processes of colonialism in Latin

America, captures the dynamic of the "self-employed" in resource-poor urban centers. He states that many people "get an occasional nibble at a job, or perform sordid or illegal tasks; they become servants, sell lemonade or what have you, get pick-and-shovel or bricklaying or electrical or sanitary or wall-painting odd jobs, beg, steal, mind parked cars—available hands for whatever turns up" (Galeano 1973, 271).

Prostitution is no exception to the list Galeano (1973) recites in the preceding quote. In the past fifteen years, this bustling Amazon urban center is now a popular destination for tourism, including sexual tourism (Cáceres et al. 2002; Smallman 2007). Prostitution is legal in Peru for persons over the age of eighteen (Nencel 2001), and there is a high prevalence of sex work practiced by women, young men, and transgender people in Iquitos (Amaya et al. 2007; Paris et al. 1999; 2001; Zavaleta et al. 2007) and in the nearby towns and villages of Nauta, Requena, and Pevas. Child prostitution and trafficking are also serious concerns (Smallman 2007). In recent years in Iquitos, a large official-looking painted sign has gone up on the wall of the main tourist promenade warning tourists of a jail sentence if they are caught purchasing sexual services with children. Additionally, the highly contested practice of human trafficking has been documented by ecofeminist scholar Ana Isla (2009), who reports that indigenous-identified women and girls compose a large part of the sexual labor in the region to cater to the employees in the Amazon's many "extractive" industries such as oil, logging, and mining. Based on in-depth qualitative interviews with six female sex workers, participants in this study reported that most female sex workers choose to engage in both full- and part-time sex work to supplement their income from other jobs. Sex work venues in Iquitos range from outdoor street areas and *plazas* (main squares) to indoor brothels and nightclubs.

Given the prevalence of poverty and sex work, Peru is considered one of the leading countries in Latin America for HIV research and has produced studies about sex workers' condom use practices and the prevalence of sexually transmitted infections and health service use (Paris et al. 1999). One innovative study conducted in Iquitos examined the relationships between *motocarro* drivers and sex workers, suggesting that sexually transmitted infections were high among *motocarro* drivers because many of their passengers were female sex workers who offered their services in return for transport (Paris et al. 2001). Despite the isolated location of Iquitos, female sex worker activists have made significant gains in HIV/AIDS educational outreach and political advocacy for and with their *compañeras* (peers) over the last ten years. These accomplishments will be discussed later in the chapter.

Applying a Gender Relations Framework to Sex Worker Activism and Health Education in Iquitos

Gender has long been identified as a key structural factor affecting HIV risk and prevention strategies (Campbell 1995; Rao-Gupta and Weiss 2009; UNAIDS 2009). For example, in many cultures, risk-taking behavior (such as unprotected sex) or acquiring multiple sexual partners outside primary relationships are revered expressions of hegemonic masculinity. By contrast, sexual naïveté and submissiveness in sexual encounters and courtship are considered traditionally feminine. These culturally driven expressions of gender (often referred to as "gender roles") shape both women's and men's risk of contracting HIV (Rao-Gupta and Weiss 2009). Yet only recently has the attention shifted away from past theories of gender "roles" to gender relations (Bottorff et al. 2012; Connell 2002; 2012; Scholfield et al. 2000) in order to better understand the gendered effects of health behavior practices and attitudes.

My discussion in this chapter thus draws on theorists who conceive of gender as *relational* and therefore "active," multilayered, and dynamic as opposed to static and role delimited. A gender relations analysis offers new ways to conceptualize and address gender in its broadest sense and in health research specifically (Bottorff, Oliffe, Kelly, and Chambers 2012; Connell 2002; 2012; Howson 2006; Scholfield et al. 2000). To further this claim, Bottorff et al. (2012) assert that a gender relations analysis can "examine men's and women's interactions and the means by which these interactions influence health opportunities and constraints" (Bottorff et al. 2012, 178). As Bottorff et al. (2012) claim, close attention to interactions lays bare the many contradictions in how gender is enacted and allows us to challenge essentializing assumptions about the attitudes and behaviors of men and women.

Another benefit of gender relations theory is that it invites further theorizing about the varying expressions of gender *within* the categories of "masculine" and "feminine." For example, Richard Howson (2006) offers a pragmatic conceptualization of gender diversity within genders. He argues that the category "femininity" can be subdivided into "emphasized," "ambivalent," and "protest" femininities. Each of these categories is described in relation to its proximity to upholding hegemonic masculinity (Howson 2006). For sex worker activists, I argue that "protest femininity" aptly characterizes the way they conduct their relationships with male clients. I take up this point later in the chapter.

Altogether, this shift away from "role theories" disrupts the essentializing discourses in some sex work and prostitution literature where women are assumed to be innocent victims that require immediate rescue from men. In this study in particular, sex worker activists often talked about the culture of *machismo* that defines relationships between men and women in the Amazon region of Loreto. Like most of Latin America, Peru is largely a patriarchal society marked by men's monopoly of public and political spaces, while women's activities are confined to the domestic sphere and low-wage jobs (Fuller 2001; 2004). However, there are regional differences that show a greater openness in the Amazon with respect to homosexuality and expressions of gender nonconformity (Salazar, Sandoval Figueroa, Maziel Giron, and Cáceres 2009). For instance, Iquitos has a vibrant and rapidly growing gay, lesbian, and transgender community. Activists have successfully run annual gay pride parades since 2005 and are routinely involved in antihomophobia and HIV awareness campaigns to sensitize and educate the general public. That said, the heterosexual majority is still largely constrained by heteronormative attitudes, behaviors, and beliefs, especially concerning men's health practices such as inconsistent condom use and infidelity outside primary romantic relationships (Cáceres et al. 2002; Fuller 2004). Sex worker activists are acutely aware of the systemic power differential between heterosexual men and women in Iquitos and the stigma associated with sex work; these are two central issues that drive sex worker organizations' political and educational agendas.

Using the State for Self-Help Activism

Despite having left sex work eight years ago, Silvia Torres still chooses to identify as a *trabajadora sexual* (sex worker). She currently holds five job titles: coordinator of the Centro Referencial de las Comunidades Gay, Trans, Lésbica y Trabajadoras Sexuales de Loreto (Reference Center for the Gay, Trans, Lesbian Communities and Sex Workers of Loreto), chair of the *trabajadora sexual* (TS) organization Sarita Colonia, a health promoter and peer educator for the Peruvian Ministry of Health, a representative of RedTraSex

(Network of Sex Workers of Latin America and Caribbean), and she is on the community advisory committee in the community education department of the largest local health nongovernmental organization (NGO) in Iquitos, Selva Amazónica. Apart from her job with the Ministry of Health, all her other positions of responsibility are voluntary. In this section, I use Silvia's narratives to outline the impetus and elements of TS self-organization in Iquitos that occurred with state support.

The most pressing issue that ultimately led TSes in Iquitos to self-organize was the threat of HIV infection. Prior to 1997, TSes were not politically organized and did not use condoms with their clients; condoms were not readily available and it was not customary for clients or TSes to suggest or insist on their use. This norm was later disrupted when the Monitoring Program for Sexually Transmitted Infections (hereafter referred to as the Monitoring Program), an independent unit of the Peruvian Ministry of Health in Lima, made contact with sex workers in Iquitos with some pressure from VIALIBRE, an NGO in Lima that is considered to be "the granddaddy of AIDS work in Peru" (Frasca 2005, 51).

For the most part, social movements for sexual minorities in Peru are tolerated, if not well-regarded by the state (in comparison to other countries) and some continue to be supported by the state, especially in response to the AIDS epidemic (Cáceres and Mendoza 2009). The Monitoring Unit catalyzed HIV/AIDS and sexually transmitted infection (STI) workshops and training with about two hundred TSes in Iquitos from which twenty were selected to learn how to be *Promotoras Educadoras de Pares* (PEPs)—peer health promoters for other *compañeras*. Silvia Torres was selected as one of the twenty. PEPs were meant to attend sex work venues to give talks and workshops about correct condom use, HIV and STI symptoms and treatment, and valuable information about sex workers' human rights. Initially however, other *compañeras* did not receive the peer educators very well. According to Silvia, they would tell the PEPs: "Que me vas a enseñar si eres una puta como yo?" (What can you teach me if you're just a whore like me?). But with repeated attempts at reaching out to their *compañeras*, their hesitation soon turned into acceptance of the PEPs' commitment to their *compañeras*' health and path to empowerment. Silvia stated, "We try to reach them [*compañeras*] more and more. Since 1997 until now, the 9th of June, things have changed so much. Now the *compañeras* take care of themselves more and we can tell from the studies that have been done recently in 2009 because since 2010 we don't know of any case of HIV . . . As *trabajadoras sexuales* I think that we have come a long way and the *compañeras* are taking care of themselves and there are very few cases of HIV in *trabajadoras sexuales*" (author interview, June 9, 2010).

The new trend of introducing condoms into sex work was, not surprisingly, met with considerable resistance from male clients. Maria, a TS in her fifties and a stakeholder in one of the sex worker organizations in Iquitos remembers, "We practically couldn't eat because of the work that we do. Why? Because the clients weren't coming! But why weren't they coming? Because we wanted people to get used to the idea of using a condom . . . but people didn't even want to enter the brothels! The brothels were empty!" (author interview, August 13, 2010).

Despite clients' temporary disapproval of condoms, TSes in Iquitos continued to make their voices heard about the importance of condoms to reduce the risk of HIV and about the need to reduce the stigma of sex work. In 2005, TSes formally organized and created three groups: Sarita Colonia, Las Loretanas, and Las Amazonas. Sarita Colonia is the only one of the three that receives legal support from the state and was created with the assistance of VIALIBRE. The two other splinter organizations, Las Loretanas and Las Amazonas, make up a sex workers "collective"; however Sarita Colonia is the only one so far that has legal backing as a community-based organization and is recognized at the regional and national levels.

During my fieldwork, I quickly learned that the LGBT community, HIV positive activist community, and sex worker activists all self-identify as *poblaciónes vulnerables* (vulnerable populations) and they all know each other. They sometimes attend the same meetings with other organizations or government and health officials voicing similar concerns about stigma and discrimination. For instance, all were involved in organizing and participating in the Sixth Annual *Marcha del Orgullo* (gay pride parade) in 2010. When Silvia recounted the story of Sarita Colonia's inception, she remembers being inspired by her peers in the LGBT and people living with HIV (PLWH) communities. They encouraged her to start an organization for *trabajadoras sexuales* in Iquitos because "a sex worker organization was the only one missing [from the group of other sexual minorities in Iquitos]" (author interview, June 9, 2010).

The first meeting of what later became the first sex worker organization, Sarita Colonia, was held in a beauty salon, and shortly after, members of VIALIBRE in Lima went to Iquitos to train Silvia in a series of workshops about human rights, labor rights, and clinical knowledge about HIV and STI transmission, symptoms and treatment. Silvia was then chosen to be a spokesperson for VIALIBRE's HIV/AIDS advocacy for key populations along with one other TS. They were both flown to Lima to participate in more workshops. In Lima, Silvia learned how to use the Internet for the first time, create an e-mail account, influence decision makers, and formulate proposals and work plans. It was also her first time having to speak to government ministry officials. Silvia says that she experienced discrimination by some government officials in Lima mainly in the form of "cold shoulder" dismissals of her presence or a refusal to speak with her. These initial moments of rejection did eventually evolve into collaborative relationships to work toward sex worker organizations' rights and recognition but only with continued persistence and commitment. Silvia explained, "So it was a lot of hard work that now we are harvesting the work that we have sown. Now, with the regional government, we work alongside them with the ombudsman. The girls here [in Iquitos] do not suffer *batidas* (raids). They now know that if there is a *batida* to call me" (author interview, June 9, 2010).

An important structural outcome of TS organizing and building relations with the regional government was the near cessation of *batidas* (police raids) in Iquitos. Police raids were commonplace in sex work locales, but through support from the local ombudsman and regional and municipal government officials, TSes have experienced a significant drop in raids. Silvia explained that TSes initiated and ran workshops with the police themselves to sensitize them around TSes labor and human rights. Now police in Iquitos, for the most part, know better than to descend into brothels or nightclubs to punish and arrest. TSes relations with a male-dominated institution are, for now, calm. Interestingly, Silvia pointed out with a bit of tongue-in-cheek humor that she wishes there was a *batida* so that more *compañeras* would attend her weekly meetings to discuss other issues.

TS organizations have engaged in both frontline peer education work and behind-the-scenes work with government officials in Lima and Iquitos. Both of these endeavors culminated in stronger public recognition for sex workers' rights to work and to optimal health. Although TSes interactions with the state were initially punctuated by stigma, discrimination, and a refusal to engage with them politically, these relations changed over time and became essential for TS organizations' survival and legitimacy for self-help activism. As Barbara Risman (2004) argues, "Gendered institutions depend on our willingness to do gender, and when we rebel, we can sometimes change the institutions themselves" (Risman 2004, 434). This is clearly shown in TSes' workshops with police in Iquitos; however, these peaceful conditions are not felt in other places in the Amazon. In Tarapoto, another jungle city about an hour's flight away, TSes regularly experience police raids and violence and have not had access to PEP training. Carlos Cáceres and Walter Mendoza (2009) state that Peru receives a robust amount of funding from the Global Fund to Fight AIDS, Tuberculosis, and Malaria (GFATM) and thus financial support to eradicate the violence experienced by TSes in Tarapoto is a possibility. One of Silvia's many tasks is to put together proposals for the GFATM; to forge relationships with government officials in other towns, such as Tarapoto; to strengthen solidarity among TSes in Loreto; and to initiate PEP training.

Sex workers' pleas to work *with* institutions such as the police can aid in reducing discrimination toward sex workers, and reducing this discrimination is a step toward gender equality. Sex worker activists have also worked hard to win the approval of government officials in charge of TSes' educational agendas (such as those in public health and education); these efforts also signify public officials' growing awareness and commitment to *all* women's health concerns and their access to health education. While hardly a complete project, Sarita Colonia continues to grow and evolve with the hopes of widening access to its education and human rights programs to TSes outside of Iquitos. State support is essential for this to occur.

Gender Relations at Work: Teachable Moments with Male Clients

As noted earlier, Howson (2006) asserts that enacting protest femininities shows how gender boundaries are negotiated (or literally "protested") and can bring about instructive and positive health outcomes. Data from this study suggest that sex workers who are involved in peer education as either stakeholders or peer educators are guided toward pushing gender boundaries for health and self-esteem. Silvia Torres believes that as a result of the consistent HIV/AIDS education outreach and organizing, many TSes are now much more confident and knowledgeable about the impact that sex work has on their bodies and the bodies of their clients. They are also better equipped to respond to male clients' preferences for unprotected sex. In this section, I introduce an experience of Rosi, a *trabajadora sexual* and peer health promoter for Sarita Colonia. What was most memorable about my interviews with Rosi was how proud she was about the progress she has made in her life. In her past, she describes herself as *mala* (bad) because she used to drink too much, get into fights, and generally be aggressive and argumentative with people. Her aunt introduced her to sex work and her preferred venue was the *Plaza de Armas*—the main square in the center of town, one block from the River Itaya. During the time when the Monitoring Program was recruiting PEPs, Rosi was chosen and this new position of responsibility made her feel valued and successful. The knowledge that Rosi acquired and the passion that she developed for her job as a health promoter for other TSes in Iquitos directly impacted her male clients, as I outline in the following paragraphs.

In our interviews, Rosi described to me a "teachable moment"—that is, an interaction with a client in which she intended to impart her knowledge about STIs or HIV to collaborate in safer sex. In the incident, she told me that her client agreed to use a condom but that he insisted that the bedroom lights be kept off. Rosi did not agree to his request, as part of her routine with her clients is to "check" them for any visual signs of sexually transmitted infections. Thus with the lights on, Rosi discovered that her client was covered in genital sores. She was immediately concerned and gently explained to him that she could not provide him any sexual services. She went on to explain the reasons why even if he used a condom, any skin-to-skin contact would be risky. The client then confessed to her that he had had these lesions for about a month but had not taken any action to seek medical attention. At this point, Rosi offered to take him to the doctor herself. She reenacts the conversation:

> I sent him. "If you want, tomorrow I'll wait for you at the clinic to get your diagnosis." "Ok señora, thank you." "Tomorrow I'll wait for you and I'm going to give you my cell number. Go there and I'll wait for you there." And the guy also gave me his cell number. And the next day I told him that I would give him his money back, the fifty soles. "No, don't worry, keep it for yourself," he says. "Thank you for your advice." I talked to him about STIs and about a bunch of other things. Seriously, the guy was waiting for me at the clinic door very early! He showed up, they did his analyses. He had syphilis, chancroid and gonorrhea. (author interview, July 6, 2010)

A gender relations analysis indicates how Rosi steered her interactions with her male client in a direction that would result in positive health outcomes for both parties. Judith Gerson and Kathy Peiss (1985) emphasize the relational nature of gender because it allows us to identify sites where individual agency is expressed through the negotiation of boundaries. In other words, they put forward the claim that while women are systemically oppressed in most cultures, oppressive social forces are not always acting on women at all times; there are many sites of resistance (individual, cultural, and institutional) where women harness their agency and steer cultural norms and social practices in other directions that would best serve them (Gerson and Peiss 1985). It is clear that Rosi exercised her agency to make the interaction with her client a site of resistance and health promotion.

We can also mobilize Howson's (2006) theorizing of femininities and "name" Rosi's work with her client as "protest femininity"; she chose to "take on" masculinity in her intimate encounters with a male client who, while he did agree to use a condom, tried to hide his sexually transmitted infection. In the interviews with other sex worker participants, they also reported using gentle but assertive conversations with their male clients to challenge their masculine beliefs about condom use.

Other sex workers in this study relied on their own knowledge and experiences of *machismo* in the Amazon province of Loreto to successfully negotiate the use of condoms. Very often, participants expressed their discontent with how men in their culture conduct themselves and manage their relationships with women. In general, they said they yearn for a different kind of Loretano man. As the interviewer, I was able to capture the disapproval and disappointment in their voices about men in Loreto who womanize, drink, incite domestic violence, and dismiss health issues. In stating this, I am not characterizing all men in Loreto the same way but rather exposing how the female participants in this study were discontented. Furthermore, perhaps because of their stigmatized identities as sex workers, this also indicates how they want to learn, help, and heal themselves and others while changing the masculine and feminine ideals that reinforce a range of gender and health inequities.

Talking openly about sexual health and insisting on condom use are not cultural norms that govern attitudes, beliefs, and practices surrounding female sexuality in Loreto (Fuller 2004). Some women in this study did report that women seem to be more concerned than men about using condoms to prevent STIs; however, prevailing attitudes that women ought to defer to men in sexual encounters (Fuller 2004) would likely outshine their health concerns. Sex worker activists, on the other hand, have learned from their *compañeras* how to navigate their interactions with their male clients by participating in and running health workshops that include strategies for condom negotiation. Thus enacting "protest femininities" while attempting to enlighten and teach men about the value of their own health (and the health of their wives or girlfriends) is indeed instructive and necessary to further develop women's agency and to even invite discussions about men's health.

Sex Worker Organizations' "Relational" Difficulties in Tourism Spaces

Amalia Cabezas's (2009) ethonography *Economies of Desire: Sex and Tourism in Cuba and the Dominican Republic* explores the ambiguity of "exchange" between tourists and locals, arguing that spaces where locals and tourists interact give rise to a range of relationships that could be classified as intimate romantic encounters, clearly delineated sex-for-cash transactions, or a nebulous hybrid of both scenarios. In Iquitos, although clearly not the destination of choice of many westerners for a Caribbean beach getaway, similar relations between tourists and locals exist in tourist areas. Some of the local women in Iquitos are popularly known as *gringueras*. Shawn Smallman (2007) references the similarity between the *jineteras* in Cuba (described in depth in Cabezas's [2009] ethnography) and the *gringueras* in Iquitos. As quoted in Smallman (2007), *gringueras* are "young women who look for the company of tourists in order to receive invitations, money, and in the best of all cases to leave the country. They also call themselves 'the gringuerillas' and a type of youth—which frequents the bars that they inhabit—calls them 'hamburgers' in the sense that they are fast food for gringos" (Smallman 2007, 180).

Most tourists in Iquitos, when they are not on scheduled jungle expeditions or Amazon river cruises, spend much of their leisure time in the evenings eating and drinking on the *malecón*, commonly known as the "boulevard"—a promenade overlooking the Itaya River where local families, street vendors, and entertainers gather and circulate alongside the bars and restaurants. Among the crowd are the alleged *gringueras*. Having spent considerable time on the boulevard myself as a former resident of

Iquitos in the late 1990s, and as a researcher more recently, I have absorbed the boulevard culture and can confirm that it is common to see the young local girls and women in the bars and restaurants paired up with male tourists young and old.

Yet, what is not known is what kinds of relationships these women have, or would like to have, with foreign men. Nor is the casual observer always able to determine what foreign men really want from Iquitos women. I say this because while it is almost too easy to draw conclusions about a sex worker–client dyad at play, the boulevard is a public space that brings together casual interactions between tourists and locals in a way that could allow for a range of relationships to unfold and develop, similar to Cabezas's illustrations of foreigners and locals interacting in hotel resorts and beaches. However, Cabezas (2009) asks, "Who is considered a sex worker? Who identifies as one? When is it a productive category for instigating social change?" (Cabezas 2009, 10).

What is critical to point out at this juncture is how sex workers who have self-organized in Iquitos define "sex work." In my interviews with Silvia, I asked her what she thought of the girls and women on the boulevard who seek out tourists. She told me that she and other PEPs have tried many times to approach them and to gather them for HIV/AIDS prevention talks and information about their rights. However, she laments, "I think that there [on the boulevard] there are some *compañeras* who don't accept the information. They don't accept themselves because we here define sex work from the moment that you receive a piece of clothing, a shoe, in exchange for sex. You are doing sex work" (author interview, June 9, 2010).

Magnolia, another TS activist concurs with Silvia's definition and says, "But they [girls and women on the boulevard] can't understand that from the moment they go with a man in exchange for something, they are providing a service, they are doing sex work but they don't identify that way. They do it [sex work] but they don't identify and that is where the risk is. A sex worker who self-identifies has high self-esteem and is going to protect herself" (author interview, July 7, 2010).

Silvia goes on to say that the common response from women on the boulevard is *"Yo no hago eso. Es mi amigo"* (I don't do that [sex work]. He's my friend). What is interesting here is that some of these foreign men may very well be "just a friend" and could simply be looking for companionship with or without sex. Romance, blossoming affections, and the potential for a short- or long-term relationship are very real possibilities in these spaces. While I was living in Iquitos, I was invited to a wedding of a forty-something-year-old American man and a nineteen-year-old Iquitos woman. Neither spoke each other's language, but both seemed to benefit from the arrangement.

It is evident from my conversations with Silvia and Magnolia that they take issue with the fact that the women on the boulevard do not identify as *trabajadora sexuales*. Identifying as a TS and belonging to any of the TS organizations in Iquitos can only be a good thing in the eyes of Silvia and Magnolia. As Magnolia stated previously, "A sex worker who identifies has high self-esteem and is going to protect herself." TS organizations in Iquitos have had positive effects for the activists themselves and their *compañeras*, such as opportunities to teach and inspire others about sexual health and human rights and the feeling of belonging to something constructive and life changing. Thus choosing to identify as a TS *is* a productive category for locals interacting with tourists in touristic spaces such as the boulevard in Iquitos.

However, per Howson (2006), these tense social relations among the two types of women could be theorized as the clashing of two expressions of femininities: protest femininity and emphasized femininity (Howson 2006). For example, Magnolia claims that foreign men prefer to seek out local women who look young and conventionally attractive. According to Howson (2006), a key characteristic of emphasized femininity is "publicly objectified beauty," and the boulevard is a public venue in Iquitos where "pretty girls" and foreign men meet. Howson (2006) argues further that coupled with the emphasis on conventional beauty in emphasized femininity is "a soft and docile personality that expresses such things as sociability rather than technical competence" (Howson 2006) and "fragility in mating scenes" (Howson 2006). Put another way, dominant expressions of heterosexuality may be more likely to play out in these relationships between local women and foreign men that could ultimately leave women more vulnerable to HIV and STIs. By contrast, female sex worker activists, through their peer education initiatives that challenge masculine beliefs about condom use (protest femininity), aim to steer heterosexual relations in a direction that best serves both women and men to reduce HIV risk.

How can sex worker activists achieve their goals for self-determination, solidarity, and health education without policing or excluding women who do not identify as sex workers? Using Howson's (2006) categories of emphasized femininity and protest femininity, this study has illustrated how the tense relations among the two categories of femininity can obscure important health promotion messages; women who do not identify as sex workers may not believe that sex workers' health curriculum applies to them, and sex worker activists strongly believe that women on the boulevard *should* identify as sex workers, "for their own good." I make the argument that because claiming the sex worker identity is linked to positive health outcomes (through enacting protest femininity), women who do not identify as sex workers are therefore left navigating likely risky traditional heterosexual relations with male tourists (emphasized femininity and hegemonic masculinity) because of the discrepancies with the sex worker label. Therefore, part of sex worker organizations' future contribution to women's empowerment could be to recognize the varying expressions of femininity that Howson (2006) describes—even women who do frequent the boulevard may simply be expressing their femininity in a particular way, and this does not have to be associated with taking health risks, having low self-esteem, or with being a sex worker. Sex worker organizations in Iquitos do approach the women and girls on the boulevard from time to time and should continue to do so in a way that allows for a range of women to feel they still have access to the health information, even if they choose not to publicly (or privately) identify as a sex worker.

Conclusion

The Peruvian Amazon is known among Latin American health scholars and practitioners as an area where many individuals are at high risk for HIV (Zavaleta et al. 2007), and this has concerned sex worker activists. This chapter has outlined the motivations and structural and intimate outcomes of sex worker organizations in Iquitos, and it has also introduced a key contemporary challenge for their future work. This study has shown that *trabajadoras sexuales* in Iquitos are vocal and are beginning to be supported by municipal, regional, and national government officials and other NGOs. Tied to this fact is the recognition that a constant part of their work involves advocacy to increase funding so that TSes in rural communities and other cities in the Amazon can also reap the benefits of membership and, more importantly, not suffer violence and discrimination from police or the general public.

I have highlighted TS–client relations to call attention to the ways that TSes can exercise their agency to avoid HIV risk, alter prevailing gender norms and expectations, and also provide a space where meaningful dialogue about sexual health and relationships can occur between TSes and clients. From a theoretical perspective, sex workers enacting protest femininity have advanced their collective agendas and have seen positive health outcomes for individual women and men. However, protest femininity need not be limited to sex workers and the same principles of steering gender norms in health-positive directions would benefit women without stigmatized identities. It is well documented in quantitative studies that the AIDS epidemic in Latin America is maturing, meaning that the number of AIDS cases in women is on the rise (Rao Gupta and Weiss 2009; UNAIDS, 2009). As such, public health responses could include the strategies and philosophical orientations that sex worker activists employ in order to place women's health and self-esteem as high-priority issues. Given that much of both the financial support for and the research on HIV/AIDS in Peru has been directed at men, the knowledge and experiences of female sex workers are prime starting points for beginning to understand how the AIDS epidemic is affecting all women.

Currently, TS organizations in Iquitos are confident about their priorities—health education, and human and labor rights. However, what is less clear is how they will move forward given the influx of tourism and the wider range of social relations involving ambiguous forms of (sexual) exchange. This is a timely and critical issue for sex workers and gender and health scholars to explore, preferably in tandem. Further research using a gender relations framework is needed in order to capture the interactional and varied expressions of gender as well as the temporal and changing cultural contexts in which agentic behaviors can be learned through peer education and/or state support.

References

Amaya, Guerra O., et al. 2007. "Seroprevalencia de anticuerpos contra el virus de hepatitis C (VHC) en trabajadoras sexuales que acuden a un Centro de Referencia de Infecciones de Transmisión Sexual (CERITSS) de la ciudad de Iquitos, Perú." *Acta Med Per* 24, no. 2: 96–100.

Bastos, Francisco I., et al. 2008. "AIDS in Latin America: Assessing the Current Status of the Epidemic and the Ongoing Response." *International Journal of Epidemiology* 37: 729–37.

Biradavolu, Monica, et al. 2009. "Can Sex Workers Regulate Police? Learning from an HIV Prevention Project in Southern India." *Social Science and Medicine* 68: 1541–47.

Bottorff, Joan L., John Oliffe, Mary T. Kelly, and Natalie Chambers. 2012. "Approaches to Examining Gender Relations in Health Research." In *Designing and Conducting Gender, Sex and Health Research,* ed. John Ollife and Lorraine Greaves, 175–88. Los Angeles: Sage.

Cabezas, Amalia L. 2009. *Economies of Desire: Sex and Tourism in Cuba and the Dominican Republic.* Philadelphia: Temple University Press.

Cáceres, Carlos, et al. 2002. *Ser Hombre en el Perú de Hoy: Una Mirada a la Salud Sexual Desde la Infidelidad, la Violencia y la Homofobia.* Lima, Peru: REDESS Jóvenes.

Cáceres, Carlos. F. and Walter Mendoza. 2009. "The National Response to the HIV/AIDS Epidemic in Peru: Accomplishments and Gaps—A Review." *Journal of Acquired Immune Deficiency Syndrome* 51: 60–66.

Campbell, Catherine A. 1995. "Male Gender Roles and Sexuality: Implications for Women's AIDS Risk and Prevention." *Social Science and Medicine* 41, no. 2: 197–210.

Casapía, Martín., Serene A. Joseph, and Theresa W. Gyorkos. 2007. "Multidisciplinary and Participatory Workshops with Stakeholders in a Community of Extreme Poverty in the Peruvian Amazon: Development of Priority Concerns and Potential Health, Nutrition and Education Interventions." *International Journal for Equity in Health* 6, no. 6: 1–8.

Chibnik, Michael. 1991. "Quasi-Ethnic Groups in Amazonia." *Ethnology* 30, no. 2: 167–82.

Connell, Raewyn W. 2002. *Gender: Short Introductions.* Cambridge, U.K.: Polity Press.

———. 2012. "Gender, Health and Theory: Conceptualizing the Issue in Local and World Perspective." *Social Science and Medicine* 74: 1675–83.

Espinosa, Cristina. 2009. "Ethnic Spirituality, Gender and Health Care in the Peruvian Amazon." *Ethnicity and Health* 14, no. 5: 423–37.

Frasca, Tim. 2005. *AIDS in Latin America.* New York: Palgrave MacMillan.

Fuller, Norma. 2001. *Masculinidades. Cambios y Permanencias: Varones de Cuzco, Iquitos y Lima.* Lima, Peru: Pontifica Universidad Católica del Peru.

———. 2004. "Contrastes regionales en las identidades de género en el Perú urbano. El caso de las mujeres de la baja Amazonía." *Anthropologica* 22: 119–36.

Galeano, Eduardo. 1973. *Open Veins of Latin America: Five Centuries of a Pillage of a Continent.* New York: Monthly Review Press.

Gerson, Judith M., and Kathy Peiss. 1985. "Boundaries, Negotiation, Consciousness: Reconceptualising Gender Relations." *Social Problems* 32, no. 4: 317–31.

Ghose, Toorjo, Dallas Swendeman, Sheba George, and Debasish Chowdhury. 2008. "Mobilizing Collective Identity to Reduce HIV Risk in Sonagachi, India: The Boundaries, Consciousness, Negotiation Framework." *Social Science and Medicine* 67, no. 2: 311–20.

Gyorkos, Theresa W., et al. 2010. "Stunting and Helminth Infection in Early Pre-School Age Children in a Resource-Poor Community in the Amazon Lowlands of Peru." *Transactions of the Royal Society of Tropical Medicine and Hygiene* 105: 204–8.

Howson, Richard. 2006. *Challenging Hegemonic Masculinity*. New York: Routledge.

Hunefeldt, Christine. 2004. *A Brief History of Peru*. New York: Checkmark Books.

Isla, Ana. 2009. "The Eco-Class-Race Struggles in the Peruvian Amazon Basin: An Eco-Feminist Perspective." *Capitalism Nature Socialism* 20, no. 3: 21–48.

Kempadoo, Kamala. 2001. "Women of Color and the Global Sex Trade: Transnational Feminism Perspectives." *Meridians* 1, no. 2: 28–51.

Kempadoo, Kamala, and Jo Doezema. 1998. *Global Sex Workers: Rights, Resistance, and Redefinition*. New York: Routledge.

Maki, Sanna, Risto Kalliola, and Kai Vourinen. 2001. "Road Construction in the Peruvian Amazon: Process, Causes and Consequences." *Environmental Conservation* 28, no. 3: 199–214.

Martínez, Andrés, Valentín Villarroel, Joaquín Seoane, and Francisco del Pozo. 2004. "A Study of a Rural Telemedicine System in the Amazon Region of Peru." *Journal of Telemedicine and Telecare* 10: 219–25.

Murray, Alison. 1998. "Debt Bondage and Trafficking: Don't Believe the Hype." In *Global Sex Workers: Rights, Resistance, and Redefinition*, ed. Kamala Kempadoo and Jo Doezema, 51–64. New York: Routledge.

Nawaz, Haq, et al. 2001. "Health Risk Behaviours and Health Perceptions in the Peruvian Amazon." *American Journal of Tropical Medicine and Hygiene* 65, no. 3: 252–56.

Nencel, Lorraine. 2001. *Ethnography and Prostitution in Peru*. London: Pluto Press.

Paris, Mark, et al. 1999. "Prevalence of Gonococcal and Chlamydial Infections in Commercial Sex Workers in a Peruvian Amazon City." *Sexually Transmitted Diseases* 26, no. 2: 103–7.

Paris, Mark, et al. 2001. "Motorcycle Taxi Drivers and Sexually Transmitted Infections in a Peruvian Amazon City." *Sexually Transmitted Diseases* 28, no. 1: 11–13.

Rao-Gupta, Geeta, and Ellen Weiss. 2009. "Gender and HIV: Reflecting Back, Moving Forward." In *HIV/AIDS: Global Frontiers in Prevention/Intervention*, ed. Cynthia Pope, Renee T. White, and Robert Malow, 61–70. New York: Routledge.

Risman, Barbara. 2004. "Gender as a Social Structure: Theory Wrestling with Activism." *Gender and Society* 8, no. 4: 429–50.

Salazar, Ximena, Clara Sandoval Figueroa, J. Maziel Giron, and Carlos F. Cáceres. 2009. "Gender, Masculinities and HIV/AIDS: Perspectives from Peru." In *Gender and HIV/AIDS: Critical Perspectives from the Developing World*, ed. Jelke Boesten and Nana K. Poku, 47–65. Surrey, U.K.: Ashgate.

Sanders, Teela. 2006. "Female Sex Workers as Health Educators with Men Who Buy Sex: Utilising Narratives of Rationalisation." *Social Science and Medicine* 62: 2434–44.

Schofield, Toni, et al. 2000. "Understanding Men's Health and Illness: A Gender Relations Approach to Policy, Research and Practice." *Journal of American College Health* 48: 247–56.

Smallman, Shawn. 2007. *The AIDS Pandemic in Latin America.* Chapel Hill: University of North Carolina Press.

United Nations Programme on HIV/AIDS (UNAIDS) and World Health Organization (WHO). *AIDS Epidemic Update 2009.* Geneva, Switzerland: UNAIDS/WHO. http://www.unaids.org/en/dataanalysis/knowyourepidemic/epidemiologypublications/2009aidsepidemicupdate/.

Wahab, Stéphanie. 2004. "Tricks of the Trade." *Qualitative Social Work* 3, no. 2: 139–60.

Zavaleta, Carol, et al. 2007. "High Prevalence of HIV and Syphilis in a Remote Native Community of the Peruvian Amazon." *American Journal of Tropical Medicine and Hygiene* 76, no. 4: 703–5.

CHAPTER 13

Sex Workers' Rights Organizations and Government Funding in Canada

Sarah Beer and Francine Tremblay

SEX WORKER–RUN ADVOCACY ORGANIZATIONS emerged in major Canadian cities throughout the late 1970s and 1980s. These small, loosely affiliated groups supported individual sex workers at a local level and promoted their rights internationally by denouncing criminalization, stigmatization, harassment, and violence directed at people who work in the sex industry (Brock 1998). The emergent movement for sex workers' rights was dramatically altered by the AIDS epidemic in the mid-1980s. Activists had to turn away from their original political goals and join public health initiatives to combat HIV/AIDS transmission, all the while disputing the image of sex workers as vectors of contagion (Beer 2010; Brock 1998; Jenness 1993).

By the late 1980s, health-based public funding became available to various advocacy groups in order to engage in direct, meaningful involvement with marginalized communities deemed at risk of HIV/AIDS. This funding was intended to encourage research collaborations and community partnerships in order to address risk factors and achieve an integrated approach to disease prevention, especially among previously unacknowledged populations such as sex workers, drug users, and gay men (Altman 1994; Rayside and Lindquist 1992). But what does it mean for marginalized political groups to accept government funding, and how does this impact the group at an organizational level?

We explore this issue by considering a case study of a long-standing and foundational sex worker organization, Stella, located in Montréal, Québec, Canada. For this, we draw on multimethod qualitative data to analyze aspects of the sex workers' rights movement to consider two key events in Stella's history. The first is the organization's pivotal role in an

Inter-neighborhood Consultative Committee on Prostitution (*Comité interquartiers sur la prostitution*), which resulted in a criminal diversion initiative suggesting a nonjudicial approach to sex work, and the second, is their role as host to the *Forum XXX: Celebrating a Decade of Action, Designing Our Future,* one of the largest international sex worker events in the last twenty years.

Our research shows that a period of dense activism caused Stella's near collapse, and reliance on government funding is partially responsible for this internal breakdown. Efforts to maintain state funding necessitated a formalized organizational structure, which in turn created internal hierarchies and divisions between paid and unpaid staff. All of this negatively impacted the already precarious positions of Stella's most marginalized members. State funding also limited Stella's capacity to contest the legal classifications of their work. We contend that all of this does not, however, depoliticize Stella, or other groups like it. In addition to promoting sex workers' rights, the services they offer are political in that they make sex workers lives safer, bring their communities together, and develop their capacity for advocacy. While there are some drawbacks to state funding, these resources have enabled Stella's longevity, positioning the organization as a key figure in the sex workers' rights movement.

The Sex Workers' Rights Movement

Before examining the impact of mainstream funding on sex workers' rights organizations in Canada, it is first important to contextualize the sex workers' rights movement. In Canada, laws regarding the exchange of commercial sexual services are located within a particular legal context. In Canada, power is shared between federal and provincial governments. Parliament creates federal legislation in matters related to the Constitution, while provincial and territorial governments are responsible for local legislation, policing, appointment of prosecutors and judges, and administration of the courts. Laws can be variously enforced, but provincial and municipal governments cannot enact legislation or bylaws that infringe on federal jurisdiction or rights enshrined in the Canadian Charter of Rights and Freedoms.

Across Canada, then, sex workers share similar grievances about the legislative structure and its impact on their work. Although the exchange of sex acts for material gain is legal (for those over the age of eighteen), provisions in the Criminal Code of Canada (1985) prohibit keeping or being found in a common bawdy house (Section 210), providing directions or transportation to a common bawdy house (Section 211), procuring or living on the avails of prostitution (Section 212), and communicating in a public place for the purpose of prostitution (Section 213). The law prohibiting public communication most directly affects street-based sex workers, who are estimated to make up 5 to 20 percent of sex industry workers, yet account for more than 90 percent of prostitution-related incidents reported by police (House of Commons 2006, 86). And although the laws apply to women and men, as well as to sex providers and customers, the women working in street-based prostitution are the most likely to be charged and imprisoned under the provisions related to adult prostitution (Duchesne 1997, 4). Street-based sex workers are also the most vulnerable to violence. In order to avoid police attention and circumvent arrest, they are displaced to remote or industrial locations, have little time to screen clients, and tend to avoid working with others (i.e., someone who could record license plates). These factors inhibit the capacity of street-based sex workers to maximize health and safety and to work with dignity. Though inhibited by these restrictions, sex worker efforts at mobilization do have a forty-year history.

Globally, the movement for sex workers' rights was initiated in the mid-1970s by protest events in Lyon, France, and the first prostitutes' rights collective, Call Off Your Old Tired Ethics (COYOTE), in San Francisco, California. This garnered international attention for the conditions faced by sex workers and launched the International Committee for Prostitutes' Rights (Jenness 1993, 42; Mathieu 2001, 54). By 1985, Amsterdam was host to the first international conference for sex workers, where attendants produced the World Charter for Prostitutes' Rights (Pheterson 1989). These events ushered in a new period of activism for sex workers, and the international movement for sex workers' rights was officially launched.[1] Canadian sex workers soon followed suit with their first national organization, Better End All Vicious Erotic Repression (chosen for its acronym: BEAVER), which emerged in Toronto, Ontario, in 1977 with the mandate "Legitimize the female sex, decriminalize prostitution" (Brock 1998, 41). Like other emergent sex workers' rights organizations, they denounced police brutality and the laws criminalizing prostitution.[2]

The onset of the HIV/AIDS epidemic in the early 1980s dramatically altered the organizational environment and focus of sex workers' rights groups in Canada. Until the late 1980s, grassroots organizing resulted in loosely affiliated sex worker collectives with small membership bases. Often these groups would disband and reemerge around specific grievances at various points in time. They supported local sex workers with information regarding laws, working conditions, human rights, and health, with a focus on political transformation. They campaigned against localized occurrences of harassment and abuse by police and resident groups, challenging the stigmatization of sex industry work in general and the criminalization of prostitution in particular (Brock 1998; Beer 2010). By the mid-1980s, public health agencies identified sex workers, alongside gay men, as probable sources of HIV transmission. As a result, newly emerging sex workers' rights groups had to mitigate their liberation goals and focus on combating the image of sex workers as vectors of disease.

AIDS, Sex Work, and a Window of Opportunity

Despite the similar impacts of federal law across Canada, Québec holds a unique place within the country due to its sociopolitical and cultural climate. The Quiet Revolution, beginning in 1960, certainly played a role in this uniqueness as the province underwent a period of dramatic social and political change. The Quiet Revolution marked the scission of church and state, the emergence of a Québécois national identity alongside a prosovereignty movement, and the beginning of the welfare state. In the early 1960s, state programs gradually replaced religious charities and a complete reorganization of health services was initiated.

In November 1979, Québec medical authorities diagnosed the first case of AIDS (Bilodeau, Lefebvre, and Allard 2002, 25). In 1982, Comité SIDA Québec (CSQ) was the first organization to address the issue, focusing on the gay population, and soon after the federal department, Health Canada, became involved on an ad hoc basis (Bilodeau, Lefebvre, and Allard 2002, 34). By 1985, medical authorities recognized that HIV transmission was not limited to the gay community. Following the recommendations of the CSQ, provincial funds were released to organize community groups deemed at risk of contracting HIV/AIDS, and between 1987 and 1992, community organizations dedicated to "high-risk" populations emerged throughout the province.

During the same period, the provincial political party, Parti Québécois, called for an examination of the province's health care and social services.

The ensuing Rochon Commission (1988) stated that health promotion was inextricably linked to social equity and justice (Bilodeau, Lefebvre, and Allard 2002, 1; Carey-Bélanger 1985, 204), highlighting the social dimension of Québec culture. Acting on the commission's recommendations, the province favored community involvement in program development and took a harm-reduction approach in an effort to reduce HIV transmission, rather than a moralized position focusing on the eradication of prostitution. From this view, sex worker empowerment was and is central to the fight against HIV/AIDS; here, sex workers are well positioned to instigate safer sex practices with clients and to offer peer education and outreach services to others working in the sex industry. Peer-based programming has been used increasingly throughout the world as a health-promotion strategy to improve knowledge of sexual health, skills for negotiating safer sex, and increased access to social supports (see, for example, Yasmin Lalani's chapter in this volume). Importantly, organizations run "by and for" sex workers reinforce the validity of sex work, which in turn increases disclosure and dialogue with health professionals.

Meanwhile, law enforcement branches of government continued to uphold a law-and-order agenda primarily focused on eradicating sex workers from city streets. It is within this contradictory governing structure—one treating sex workers as criminals and the other as empowered sexual health promoters—that government-funded sex worker organizations emerged in Canada. This has also caused an enormous amount of confusion, tension, and frustration for organization members serving sex workers with regard to their role in the community. While these issues are prevalent in sex worker organizations across the country, we focus here on how one organization in Montréal has attempted to navigate this terrain.

The Sociopolitical Climate in Montréal and Stella's Emergence

Montréal is the largest city in Québec and it is Canada's second largest metropolis. The city is reputed to be one of the safest in North America, as well as a hub for adult entertainment (Tremblay 2011). During the 1980s and early 1990s, Montréal experienced a slower rate of economic growth than other Canadian cities, and city officials responded by implementing various neighborhood revitalization programs aimed at making inner-city districts more attractive to investors. Media attention to these issues provoked public concern that Montréal's standing as a safe and family oriented city was deteriorating, and city officials adopted zero-tolerance policies based on the "broken-windows" model implemented by then mayor Rudolph Giuliani in New York City. The rationale behind the policy is that citizens do not distinguish between disorder and crime and thus neighborhoods presenting disorder and "symbols of decay," such as street prostitution, form a breeding ground for crime (Cameron 2004; Hubbard 2004; Hubbard and Sanders 2003; Ryder 2004; Sanders 2004). In an effort to make Montréal appear safer and cleaner, the eradication of street-based prostitution became a primary objective.

As law enforcement advocated a zero-tolerance stance on street-based sex work during the mid-1990s, public health and academic researchers were taking an entirely different approach. A team from the Centre d'études sur le sida (CES)[3] had been investigating HIV infection among incarcerated women in Québec (Hankins et al. 1994). The research team identified street-based sex workers as an overlooked population lacking services throughout the province and brought together community representatives to explore the feasibility of an HIV-intervention program for street-based sex workers in Montréal.

Community representatives began a series of meetings at the Public Health Unit of the Montréal General Hospital in order to explore the possibility of implementing an HIV-prevention program aimed at street-based sex workers in the central district of Montréal, Montréal-Centre (CES 1994a). Community representatives included Claire Thiboutot, a longtime activist and one of the founding members of Québec's first sex worker association, Association québécoise des travailleuses et travailleurs du sexe;[4] representatives from community-based organizations for street-involved people at risk of, or living with, HIV/AIDS, including Robert Paris of the Projet d'intervention auprès de mineu-e-s prostitué-eés (P.I.a.M.P.),[5] Thomas McKeown of the Centre d'action communautaire auprès des toxicomanes utilisateurs de seringues (CACTUS),[6] and Frances Shaver, a sex work researcher and sociology professor at Concordia University; and members of the AIDS research and action groups CES and Action sida Montréal.[7] Out of these consultative meetings, Project Stella[8] was born.

At their first meeting, organizers agreed that HIV intervention needed to address the socioeconomic environment in which sex workers operated. Risk management, often perceived as an individual issue, was reframed as a social problem. The team agreed that poor social conditions rendered already marginalized women more vulnerable to violence and health risks and, in fact, hindered their capacity to work safely (CES 1993, 4). To that end, in December 1993, after introducing Project Stella to their respective organizations, Robert Paris (P.I.a.M.P.) reported that his group was receptive as long as the project was aimed at overall health, not just HIV prevention, and included outreach services and a drop-in center. Thomas McKeown (CACTUS) wanted a project that focused not only on services but also on political action (CES 1993, 3). Professor Frances Shaver reiterated the need for a project that would address working conditions, including educating women about their rights as citizens (CES 1993, 3).

They modeled Project Stella after Maggie's, Canada's first government-funded sex worker–run education project in Toronto, and they received a $40,000 (CAD) grant over a three-year period from Health Canada to open a drop-in center and provide peer education and outreach services to street-based women and trans-identified workers in Montréal (CES 1994b, 1). Additional funding was acquired through provincial and municipal health departments and HIV/AIDS organizations, including the Ministère de la santé et des services sociaux[9], the Régie Régionale de la Santé et des Services sociaux de Montréal-Centre,[10] and the Centre Québécois de coordination sur le Sida.[11] Upon receiving operational funding, the organizers turned the leadership role over to sex workers, and on April 27, 1995, Stella opened its doors.

From the beginning, Stella set up a participatory structure where current and former sex workers would have major input at every level of the organization—as volunteers, administrators, and on the board of directors. The number of paid employees at Stella fluctuated depending on grants received for various projects. Today, in addition to contractual work, there are generally four to seven people employed in more permanent positions as director, administrators (for grant writing, evaluation reports, clerical work, etc.), and outreach workers. In 1996, of the eleven administrators, six were former or current sex workers. However, administrative tasks were overwhelming for some, and three of the six sex workers hired that year were unable to fulfill their mandate. A report produced the following year addressed this issue: "Although all levels of decision-making within *Stella* (like our Board of Directors) have been open to participants, few have taken an active role [. . .] Survival issues sex workers face on the street makes it difficult for them to participate in meetings [. . .] Those whose personal life was less turbulent [. . .] avoided *Stella* because they had no need for its front-line services" (Stella 1997, 3). Members of the board decided that rules regarding sex worker leadership needed to be relaxed until they could further develop sex worker capacity and participation (Stella 1996, 4).

Stella was originally located in a three-story building in the heart of Montréal's red-light district. The offices were on the third floor, an anarchist bookstore was on the second, and the drop-in center was at ground level. It was an ideal location for a drop-in, with a storefront window and lots of pedestrian traffic. Stella provided meals, showers and lockers, and fostered a sense of community among working women. Members framed the organization as both a public health initiative and a sex workers' rights group (Stella 1998b, 7). A few volunteers organized a "political committee" dedicated to discussing and relaying information on relevant issues (e.g., differences between legalization and decriminalization, feminist debates on prostitution and their impact on sex workers). It was an effort to build community, increase participation, heighten solidarity, and develop an understanding of the sociopolitical environment in which they were operating.

On both the national and international levels, Stella was among a number of autonomous associations of sex workers supported by HIV-prevention funding, working toward the decriminalization of prostitution-related laws. In Canada, their capacity to act politically and to push for legislative change is limited by the Income Tax Act, which prohibits registered charitable organizations from devoting more than 10 percent of their annual resources to political activities (Canada Revenue Agency 2011). In an effort to promote the health and safety of sex workers, Stella would offer peer outreach and services alongside some, albeit limited, participation in the promotion of decriminalization. Stella's team began immediately carving its place in the public sector, first municipally, with the Comité interquartiers sur la prostitution, and then at the national and international levels with the Forum XXX.

Comité interquartiers sur la prostitution
(Consultative Committee on Prostitution)

In December 1996, the City of Montréal formed the Comité interquartiers sur la prostitution. It was a nationally unique endeavor that brought together municipal officials, police officers, sex workers, researchers, and representatives from Stella and other allied community health organizations such as Séro-Zéro and CACTUS (Stella 1996, 2).[12] After three years of intense debate between city officials and community representatives the committee reached a fragile consensus on an alternative to repression. In June 1999, they published their report proposing a "Pilot Project"—a nonjudicial, or "criminal diversion," approach to sex work within one city district. The committee suggested that for an experimental twelve-month period, street-based sex workers in Hocholaga-Maisonneuve, an area already plagued with social issues such as poverty and petty crime, would not be ticketed or arrested. Instead of proceeding through the courts, lawbreakers would be diverted to social and medical programs (Stella 1998a, 5; 1998b, 7).

The committee called a public meeting to discuss the proposed Pilot Project on November 15, 1999, and three hundred people gathered, with the majority expressing their firm opposition to the proposal (Stella 2011). A nonjudiciary approach was interpreted as a "free-for-all" attitude toward prostitution in a district already struggling with various social issues; residents argued that the project would attract "prostitutes" from other regions and questioned why it had not been proposed in an upper-class neighborhood (Sansfaçon 1999, 20). As one of Stella's members described the event, "The room was divided into strict camps, with the large majority so angry with prostitutes and with *Stella* that they were resorting to boos and angry jeers. It was incredibly violent. The poor Committee on the stage was trying to keep it together, answering the questions as best they could, but seemingly trembling from anger and disappointment" (Tremblay 2011, 203). The public response was so intense that at the close of the first meeting, Stella members required police escorts in order to leave the premises. The second meeting ended with a bomb threat and city officials pulling out of the initiative.

The Pilot Project was immediately aborted, ending in what Stella members referred to as the "days of hatred" (Stella 2000a, 3). Indeed, their engagement in this process had increased Stella's visibility in the community, but in doing so, it made the organization a target for public outcry. Incidents including a brick thrown through the window, a dead bird placed at the door, and threatening messages left on the answering machine forced the organization to close for a week in order to protect the safety of its members and staff (Stella 2000b, 14). It is difficult to relay the disappointment and frustration experienced by the Stella team in the aftermath of their first collective effort to engage in policymaking processes.[13] The outcome of three years of participation in the committee left the team shaken and drained (Tremblay 2011).

The public outcry following the meeting reflected a deep intolerance toward street-based sex workers. The public meetings mobilized two residents' organizations, Corporation de développement Berri-UQAM and the Association des résidantes et résidants des Faubourgs de Montréal, that quickly and efficiently mounted a well-organized and vocal campaign against street prostitution.[14] This angry countermovement not only threatened Stella's members but also worsened the situation for other street-based sex workers. Although the community never truly welcomed street prostitution, over time they accepted it even less (Stella 2000c, 3). In response to renewed police crackdowns, which now targeted clients, street workers moved to more isolated locations in order to attract business, making their work more dangerous and Stella's outreach efforts more difficult. The consequences of engagement in the committee shattered any hope of building trust and cohesion among sex workers and police. In the end, the proposed Pilot Project instigated a powerful opposition that realigned the antiprostitution values of local residents, business owners, police, and city officials and subordinated the status of sex workers and their representatives.

Forum XXX: Celebrating a Decade of Action, Designing Our Future

In the following year, Stella went through a much-needed period of healing. At the organization's 2002 Annual General Assembly, members expressed the need to rebuild a sense of community and solidarity from within, and they contemplated potentially more fruitful collaborations with other sex workers and allies. They decided on an international conference in honor of Stella's upcoming tenth anniversary. The team successfully applied for a large grant from the federal Public Health Agency of Canada to organize an international conference on AIDS where participants would strategize on HIV prevention measures and celebrate the global fight for sex workers' rights. Preparation for the event focused a great deal of the team's energy and attention. Leading up to the conference, Stella had eighteen employees, in addition to a large number of volunteer organizers (Tremblay 2011).

In May 2005, Stella brought together 250 sex workers and activists from across Canada and around the world for Forum XXX: Celebrating a Decade of Action, Designing Our Future (Stella 2011). Over four days, sex workers and their allies took part in a series of panels, discussion groups, and workshops on three central themes: "Me and My Work," "Sex Work and Society," and "Sex Work and the Law." Forum XXX gave birth to *eXXXpressions*, a publication recalling the week's workshops and promoting sex worker pride (Stella 2006). The conference itself was deemed a huge success by attendants and put Stella on the map as an international player in the movement for sex workers' rights.

This momentum, however, was short-lived. At the close of Forum XXX, tensions within the organization began to surface. Within the following year, the director and founding member announced her resignation, some employees left, some were fired, and conflict developed among members of the board of directors. It was as if, after an intense period of activism, something had ruptured. We contend that many of these tensions were ultimately related to the impact of state funding and how it had shaped the direction of the organization and limited members' participation. After Forum XXX, money allocation became a central issue. Some members wanted more political action while others wanted more services. Moreover, reliance on state funding demanded a formal organizational structure, which was especially pronounced in the lead up to Forum XXX.

Shaping the Organization

Canadian sex worker organizations receive federal and provincial government funding to provide outreach services to the most vulnerable workers in the sex industry. In doing so, these organizations enter into a contractual relationship with the state that requires them gather data about the population they serve, produce reports justifying their raison d'être, and be assessed by a professional evaluator. It is this contractual relationship that demands a formal organizational structure, hierarchal decision making, and a clear division of labor (Kriesi 1996; McCarthy and Zald 2006; Ng 1988; Staggenborg 1988). Formalization processes involving specialized tasks with explicit job descriptions, orientation, and training procedures restrict opportunities to those who can meet these criteria (Riger 1994).

Employees were hired at Stella to perform clerical jobs, fill out grant applications, produce and distribute safe sex literature, organize events, provide outreach services, maintain the drop-in clinic, and represent the organization at public meetings, on committees, and in the media. This requires people with strong (usually bilingual) reading and writing skills who can work business hours, meet strict deadlines, speak comfortably with public figures, and risk being publically identified as a sex worker. The most "socially respectable" sex workers (such as those with formal education, who work in off-street venues, who experience fewer concerns related to health and poverty) tended to hold paid positions within the organization. For sex workers who have few choices when it comes to employment, not getting a job at a "by-and-for" sex workers organization was interpreted as betrayal, and some of the most underprivileged sex workers were left with the impression that their organization had been hijacked by the most socially respectable sex workers (Tremblay 2011). In the preparations leading up to Forum XXX, a larger operating budget allowed the team to hire more staff members who could provide the necessary expertise to carry out various tasks involved in organizing a large-scale international event. Gradually, participation at Stella came to be perceived as a privilege, and tensions between paid and unpaid members mounted. The movement of the space from a street-level drop-in center in the informal "red-light district" to a fourth-floor office building in another area of town further amplified these tensions.

Balancing Service and Politics

As members expressed divergent views as to what the organization entailed, it became evident that there was confusion over funding restrictions and how to balance service provision and political activism. They witnessed the Canadian government fund public health and harm reductions programs, such as Stella, while the legal arm of the state continued to criminalize activities surrounding prostitution. Initiatives such as the Comité interquartiers sur la prostitution had created the impression that sex workers were free to voice their opposition to the legal system, especially since criminalization undermined their capacity to provide outreach and fulfill their service provision mandate. Likewise, the ensuing Forum XXX, celebrating the sex workers' rights movement, reinforced the perception that Stella was indeed a political action group. This raises questions whether state funding, by restricting direct political action, depoliticizes social movement organizations.

Research on nonprofits from a variety of fields indicates that while resources are central to the longevity of social movement organizations (Walker and McCarthy 2010), obtaining state funding tends to initiate a process of formalization, which is often accompanied by the creation or persistence of internal hierarchies (Cress 1997; Markowitz and Tice 2002; Morgen 1990; Quinn and Andersen 1984; Reinelt 1994). Moreover, reliance on external funding can detract from broader social movement goals by forcing social movement–borne, community-based organizations with oppositional values to walk a "political tightrope" (Minkoff 2002, 33; see also Matthews 1994; Morgen 1990; Ostrander 2004; Reinelt 1994; Riger 2002). That is, in order to stabilize funding and support, community organizations must strike a sometimes fragile balance between service provision and overt political advocacy.

However, many scholars and observers of social movements contend that when they formalize their activities in service provision organizations, they are unable to strike this balance. For example, contributors to the volume *The Revolution Will Not Be Funded* (INCITE! 2007) critique what they call the "nonprofit industrial complex," arguing that state and foundation funding has depoliticized feminist social movements. The book documents a turn in the 1980s when the advancement of neoliberal policies and retraction of state protections turned many nonprofit feminist organizations into surrogates for the state. As the state relied on nonprofit organizations to provide necessary services to members of society, it actually contained social unrest resulting from inequality and a lack of social protections (see also Ng 1990). Indeed, many contributors argue that these outcomes are the result of a concerted effort by the ruling elite to ensure that broad-based movements for systemic social change are functionally impossible. Funders (state oriented or otherwise) influence political agendas and encourage organizations to adopt hierarchical businesslike practices, while the legal structure that defines nonprofit/charitable status limits, and even undermines, work for radical and systemic social change.

However, other researchers challenge the notion that external funding necessarily leads to cooptation and depoliticization of social movement organizations. In their research on nonprofits and religious congregations, Mark Chaves, Laura Stephens, and Joseph Galaskiewicz (2004) found that government funding did not suppress political activity and, in some instances, it even had a positive effect. In her research on social movements in the United States, Jennifer Jenkins (1998, 215) shows that while external funding contributed to the professionalization of some aspects of social movements, it also enabled them to protect themselves against attacks. Others have found that government funds can be more accessible than private contributions, which tend to favor noncontroversial recipients, and as such, state funding does not necessarily result in goal displacement or structural constraints but actually provides funding continuity and pre-dictability, which is necessary for organizational operations (Brown and Troutt 2004; DiMaggio 1986; Gronbjerg 1993).

State-funded groups like Stella (Montréal), Maggie's (Toronto), Stepping Stone (Halifax), and Prostitutes Empowerment Education Resource Society (PEERS; Vancouver and Victoria) are key figures in the Canadian sex workers' rights movement. Our research findings affirm the capacity of community-based organizations to serve as important spaces for margin-alized groups to develop community and advocacy capacity. With stable funding, community-based nonprofit organizations both expand the arena of social service provision and act as potential sites of civic engagement (Majic 2011; Marwell 2004; Orr 2007; Warren 2001; Wood 2002). In her analysis of nonprofit sex worker organizations in the United States, politi-cal scientist Samantha Majic identifies a process of "radical institutional-ization" whereby community organizations, "radical" in their opposition to the dominant sociomoral order, incorporate movement goals through organizational practices (Majic 2011). Similarly, we find that service-based organizations are simultaneously political because they empower sex workers and make their lives safer.

State funding has enabled sex workers and their allies to both care for and mobilize their constituency. In addition to providing direct services (i.e., distributing safe sex literature and equipment, community referrals, etc.), Stella members have supported sex workers laying charges against assailants and they regularly produce and distribute "Bad Tricks" lists, as well as material on rights, violence prevention, and tips on how to negoti-ate safer working practices (e.g., the biannual *ConStellation* magazine and the XXX Guide). These tools empower the constituency while engaging sex workers in research, discussion, and community building. Outreach workers mediate with police, local business owners, and residents, empha-sizing the social inclusion of street-level sex workers. Stella employees offer training workshops aimed at social workers, students, and health professionals to ensure services available to sex workers respond to their needs. Members who can risk public visibility maintain a media presence

asserting sex workers' rights, raising awareness of the harms of criminalization, and advocating for better working conditions. In all of this, they reinforce the idea that sex work is legitimate labor, encourage better working
conditions, promote awareness about discrimination against sex workers,
and build alliances with international networks of sex workers and other
social justice organizations.

The Implications of State Funding

There is evidence that with government funding, Stella, like many feminist
organizations, began to formalize their efforts (Matthews 1994; Morgen
1990; Ostrander 2004; Reinelt 1994; Riger 2002). However these same
grants sustained the organization during periods of growth, discontent,
and community opposition. Research indicates that resources are central
to social movement organizations sustaining themselves over the long
term, and this longevity is necessary to mobilize an autonomous voice
for disenfranchised populations in local and national politics (Walker and
McCarthy 2010). The stability and duration of the organization also lends
legitimacy to the group and positions members as key stakeholders in policymaking processes, such as the Consultative Committee on Prostitution.
Moreover, resources and formal organizational structures have facilitated
collaborations with academic researchers, like the Sex Trade Advocacy
and Research (STAR) project, and professional organizations, such as the
Canadian HIV/AIDS Legal Network, which in turn reinforce the organization's legitimacy, contribute to knowledge about the sex industry, and
develop a rights-based perspective on subjects such as HIV, feminism,
migration, trafficking, and overall working conditions.

Notably, Stella fits into a broader network of people working strategically to improve sex workers' lives. The sex workers' rights movement
in Canada is composed of closely affiliated but separate branches—
government-funded service organizations, such as Stella, and politically
focused coalitions, like the Coalition for the Rights of Sex Workers, Prostitutes of Ottawa/Gatineau Work, Educate, Resist (POWER), and Sex
Professionals of Canada (SPOC), for example. While the latter are able
to engage in direct opposition to the state, groups like these continue to
face many of the same obstacles as the activist coalitions that mobilized
before the 1980s, when state funding first became available to sex worker
organizations. That is, most continue to rely on small groups of volunteers

and their organizational stability is weakened by a lack of resources (Beer 2010). Events like the Consultative Committee on Prostitution highlight the public hostility that is regularly directed at individual sex workers and the organizations that represent them. While state funding has many limitations, a central component of sex work politics is to have sex work-ers' voices and perspectives represented in the public sphere, and this is exactly what organizations like Stella accomplish.

Conclusion

It is our contention that the services state-funded sex worker organizations provide are political, and moreover, these organizations play a central role in the sex workers' rights movement, even as they receive funding from state agencies. As social movement organizations, they set out to make the lives of sex workers better. Indeed, this has been accomplished through service provision. In addition to attending to the needs of the community by providing tools to help them work safely, use of computers, clean nee-dles, and so on, the organizations offer a home base for local sex worker movements and for connections with similar organizations across Canada and internationally. Stella was first confronted with the limitations of their political efforts on the Comité interquartiers sur la prostitution when they were informed that advocating against criminalization was overtly political, and thus restricted by their status as a charitable organization. This resulted in some members branching off to form political groups in order to move that issue forward. Without reliable funding, many of those groups have been short-lived. Nonetheless, membership is overlapping and embedded in community organizations.

It is largely out of these organizations that independent activists and political coalitions have emerged alongside empirical research studies reflective of sex worker perspectives. What were once isolated individu-als are now collectives. Importantly, sex worker organizing is complicated by the social stigma and criminality of the work involved. Government-funded organizations provide a political outlet while protecting anonym-ity and, moreover, a sense of community as opposed to isolation. Indeed, it has been through receiving and providing services that many workers have *become* politicized.

Recent police investigations into a striking number of murders and disappearances of street-based sex workers across the country have brought attention to the risks imposed by the current legal framework, yet no legislative changes have been made. In response to this inaction, in 2007, the Toronto-based Sex Professionals of Canada (SPOC) and Vancouver's Downtown Eastside Sex Workers United against Violence Society (SWUAV) brought constitutional challenges to their respective provincial courts, arguing that the laws related to adult prostitution violate the rights of sex workers guaranteed by the Canadian Charter of Rights and Freedoms. On September 28, 2010, Ontario Superior Court Justice Susan Himel decided in favor of the applicants, striking down all the impugned provisions. The federal government appealed this ruling and, at the time of writing, the case is before the Supreme Court of Canada, where a final decision will impact all Canadian provinces and territories. This initial decision, however, marks a change in the status quo and an enormous victory for the sex workers' rights movement.

The court challenges to social and political indifference to sex workers' disappearances across the country reflect the importance of sex worker organizations, as these cases rely on numerous individual testimonies provided by sex workers who are allied and/or members of these collectives. Stella, among other organizations in several provinces, has helped individuals develop in their capacity as activists, supported them through a very public litigation process, and lent a recognizable and relatively unified voice to the issues.

Small groups such as Stella need funding to function; however, to minimize the effect of formalization processes on members, particular attention must be paid to emotions and self-reflexivity. Forum XXX was a significant achievement for the organization, but it also revealed internal tensions building among the constituency, resulting in a period of unrest. Awareness of the impacts of state funding, especially with regard to formalization processes, is an important part of mitigating its effects. Over the past several years, Stella members have made a concerted effort to reconnect individuals, rebuild relationships, and develop solidarity through discussions and meetings. Through dialogue and reflexive engagement, members have slowly rebuilt cohesion and enthusiasm for the group. Stella's thirteenth anniversary party, which brought together estranged members at Cleopatra (one of the last surviving strip clubs in Montréal's historical red-light district), marks their significant efforts in this community-building work. The organization, like the movement more broadly, continues to face the challenges of increasing sex worker participation and attending to the concerns of a diverse constituency while continuing to provide essential services and support to marginalized sex workers. Though problematic, state funding has enabled these efforts, thus advancing social movement goals.

Notes

1. COYOTE members and French prostitutes recognized violence in the sex industry as a pervasive problem resulting from sex workers' criminal status and police harassment (Jenness 1993, 48–49; Mathieu 2001; Weitzer 1991, 25). Treating prostitution as a legitimate occupation was at the core of COYOTE's aims and they articulated their claims as a civil rights issue—the right of consenting adults to sell (and purchase) sexual services—and identified the taxpayer as the real victim in the regulation of prostitution (Jenness 1993).

2. Decriminalization is the preferred regulatory model among sex workers' rights advocates as it is intended to maximize sex workers' autonomy and safety. Operating without the threat of arrest reduces many of the health and safety risks currently involved in sex industry work. Decriminalization means that, rather than regulating sex workers through criminal law, they would be treated like other occupational groups—with the same rights, responsibilities, and labor protections as other workers. Decriminalization also accounts for the diversity of sex industry work by enabling sex workers to manage their workspaces in as they see fit (see Stella 2011). For an assessment and analysis of a decriminalized environment see *Taking the Crime out of Sex Work* (Abel, Fitzgerald, and Healey 2010).

3. Centre for AIDS Research.

4. Sex Worker Association of Québec.

5. Outreach Project for Minors involved in Prostitution.

6. Community Action Centre for Injection Drug Users.

7. AIDS Action Montréal.

8. The name would ultimately be changed to Stella, L'amie de Maimie (Stella, Maimie's friend), derived from the story of Maimie, an "ex-prostitute" who offered a safe haven to sex workers during the early 1900s in Montréal. In her memoirs, she spoke fondly of a sex worker named Stella, a frequent visitor to her home (Pinzer 1997). Based in this tradition, a central tenet of the Project Stella was to provide a drop-in space for women working in the sex industry to meet, develop relationships, and build a community.

9. Department of Health and Social Services.

10. Regional Board of Health and Social Services for Montréal-Centre.

11. Québec Centre on AIDS.

12. Séro-Zéro (now RÉZO) and CACTUS promote harm minimization approaches to commercial sex and illicit drug use, with specific organizational focuses on gay and bisexual men, people living with AIDS, and/or street-involved youth and trans people.

13. The sentiment is expressed in a poem, *I Remember*, by Marie-Claude Charlebois (2011): "I remember the feeling that we were about to change the world. I remember our high heels in the conference room . . . I remember other Canadian cities being envious of our project. I remember Stella's windows being smashed by bricks. I remember the dead bird placed at our door. I remember the anonymous messages left at Stella, naming us and our children . . . I remember the images of the girls all over the TV. I remember the surge in violence toward the street girls. I remember the bad date lists published the months following the withdrawal of the project . . . I remember the hypocrisy. I remember the screaming. I remember the hatred." (Translation from French to English is our own.)

14. The emergent residents' organizations were *L'Association des résidants et résidantes des faubourgs de Montréal* (The Suburban Residents Association of Montréal) and the *Corporation de développement Berri-UQÀM* (Berri-UQAM Development Guild). Together, these groups demanded stronger police presence and repression of street-based prostitution; they called for the creation of "john schools" to rehabilitate clients and took it upon themselves to publicize the license plates and photos of suspected clients. Employing the buzzword "narco-prostitute," resident groups linked street prostitution to drug consumption and organized crime and encouraged an alternate form of repression aimed at clients. In response, police launched *Operation Cyclops* the following year, an ongoing project that invites residents to submit "observation reports" to the local police station describing incidents of solicitation and noting the license plate numbers and appearances of suspected clients (Harper 2009, 5).

References

Abel, Gillian, Lisa Fitzgerald, and Catherine Healy, eds. 2010. *Taking the Crime Out of Sex Work: New Zealand Sex Workers' Fight for Decriminalisation.* Bristol, U.K.: Policy Press.

Altman, Dennis. 1994. *Power and Community: Organizational and Cultural Responses to AIDS.* London: Taylor and Francis.

Beer, Sarah. 2010. "The Sex Worker Rights Movement in Canada: Challenging the 'Prostitution Laws.'" PhD diss., University of Windsor, Ontario.

Bilodeau, Angèle, Chantal Lefebvre, and Denis Allard. 2002. *Les priorités nationales de santé publié 1997–2002: Une évaluation de l'actualisation de leurs principes directeurs.* Québec: Institut national de santé publique du Québec.

Brock, Deborah. 1998. *Making Work, Making Trouble: Prostitution as a Social Problem.* Toronto, Ontario: University of Toronto Press.

Brown, Laura, and Elizabeth Troutt. 2004. "Funding Relations between Nonprofits and Government: A Positive Example." *Nonprofit and Voluntary Sector Quarterly* 33, no. 1: 5–27.

Cameron, Sam. 2004. "Space, Risk and Opportunity: The Evolution of Paid Sex Markets." *Urban Studies* 41, no. 9: 1643–57.

Canada Revenue Agency. 2011. Policy Statement CPS-022, Political Activities: The Difference between Political Purposes and Charitable Purposes. http://www.cra-arc.gc.ca/chrts-gvng/chrts/plcy/cps/cps-022-eng.html#P107_9478.

Carey-Bélanger, Élaine. 1985. "La Commission Rochon: Enjeux pour le service social, les services sociaux et la société." *Service Social* 34, no. 2–3: 202–5.

Centre d'études sur le sida/Centre for AIDS Studies (CES). 1993. "Unité de Santé Publique, Hôpital General de Montréal." Unpublished Meeting Minutes, Montréal, September 29.

———. 1994a. "Pour une intervention en prévention du VIH/sida et autres MTS pour les femmes prostituées de Montréal-Centre Compte-rendu de la quatrième réunion des intervenants." Unpublished Meeting Minutes, PIaMP Montréal, January 27.

———. 1994b. "Pour une intervention en prévention du VIH/sida et autres MTS pour les femmes prostituées de Montréal-Centre Compte-rendu de la cinquième réunion des intervenants." Unpublished Meeting Minutes, Centre Ozanam Montréal, February 23.

Chaves, Mark, Laura Stephens, and Joseph Galaskiewicz. 2004. "Does Government Funding Suppress Nonprofits' Political Activity?" *American Sociological Review* 69, no. 2: 292–316.

Commission d'enquête sur les services de santé et les services sociaux (commission Rochon). 1988. *Rapport de la Commission d'enquête sur les services de santé et les services sociaux.* Les Publications du Québec.

Cress, Daniel. 1997. "Nonprofit Incorporation among Movements of the Poor: Pathways and Consequences for Homeless Social Movement Organizations." *Sociological Quarterly* 38, no. 2: 343–60.

Criminal Code of Canada (R.S., c. C-46). 1985. "Part VII: Disorderly Houses, Gaming and Betting." http://laws.justice.gc.ca/en/C-46.

DiMaggio, Paul. 1986. *Nonprofit Enterprise and the Arts.* New York: Oxford University Press.

Duchesne, Doreen. 1997. "Street Prostitution in Canada." *Juristat: Canadian Centre for Justice Statistics* 17, no. 2: 1–13. Ottawa, Ontario: Statistics Canada. http://www.statcan.gc.ca/pub/85-002-x/85-002-x1997002-eng.pdf.

Gronbjerg, Kirsten. 1993. *Understanding Nonprofit Funding.* San Francisco, Calif.: Jossey-Bass.

Hankins, Catherine, Sylvie Gendron, Margaret Handley, Christiane Richard, Marie Thérèse Tung, and Michael O'Shaughnessy. 1994. "HIV Infection among Women in Prison: An Assessment of Risk Factors Using a Nonnominal Methodology." *American Journal of Public Health* 84, no. 10: 1637–40.

Harper, Lina. 2009. *Montréal Mirror* 25, no. 5 (July 16–22).

House of Commons. 2006. *The Challenge of Change: A Study of Canada's Criminal Prostitution Laws: Report of the Standing Committee on Justice and Human Rights.* Report of the Standing Committee on Justice and Human Rights. Report of the Subcommittee on Solicitation Laws. http://cmte.parl.gc.ca/Content/HOC/committee/391/just/reports/rp2599932/justrp06/sslrrp06-e.pdf.

Hubbard, Phil. 2004. "Cleansing the Metropolis: Sex Work and the Politics of Zero Tolerance." *Urban Studies* 41, no. 9: 1687–702.

Hubbard, Phil, and Teela Sanders. 2003. "Making Space for Sex Work: Female Street Prostitution and the Production of Urban Space." *International Journal of Urban and Regional Research* 27, no. 1: 75–89.

INCITE! Women of Color against Violence. 2007. *The Revolution Will Not Be Funded: Beyond the Non-Profit Industrial Complex.* Cambridge, Mass.: South End Press.

Jenkins, Jennifer. 1998. "Channeling Social Protest: Foundation Patronage of Contemporary Social Movements." In *Private Action and the Public Good,* ed. Walter W. Powel and Elisabeth S. Clemens, 206–16. New Haven, Conn.: Yale University Press.

Jenness, Valerie. 1993. *Making It Work: The Prostitutes' Rights Movement in Perspective.* New York: Routledge.

Kriesi, Hanspeter. 1996. "The Organizational Structure of New Social Movements in a Political Context." In *Comparative Perspectives on Social Movements: Political Opportunities, Mobilizing Structures, and Cultural Framings,* ed. Doug McAdam, John McCarthy, and Mayer Zald, 152–84. Cambridge, U.K.: Cambridge University Press.

Majic, Samantha. 2011. "Serving Sex Workers and Promoting Democratic Engagement: Rethinking Nonprofits' Role in American Civic and Political Life." *Perspectives on Politics* 9, no. 4: 821–39.

Markowitz, Lisa, and Karen Tice. 2002. "Paradoxes of Professionalization: Parallel Dilemmas in Women's Organizations in the Americas." *Gender and Society* 16, no. 6: 941–58.

Marwell, Nicole. 2004. "Privatizing the Welfare State: Nonprofit Community-Based Organizations as Political Actors." *American Sociological Review* 69, no. 2: 265–91.

Mathieu, Lilian. 2001. *Mobilisations de prostituées.* Paris: Belin.

Matthews, Nancy. 1994. *Confronting Rape: The Feminist Anti-Rape Movement and the State.* New York: Routledge.

McCarthy, John, and Mayer Zald. 2006. "The Enduring Vitality of the Resource Mobilization Theory of Social Movements." In *Handbook of Sociological Theory*, ed. Jonathan H. Turner, 533–65. New York: Springer.

Minkoff, Debra. 2002. "Walking a Political Tightrope: Responsiveness and Internal Accountability in Social Movement Organizations." In *Exploring Organizations and Advocacy Governance and Accountability*, ed. Elizabeth J. Reid and Maria D. Montilla, 33–48. Washington, D.C.: Urban Institute Press.

Morgen, Sandra. 1990. "Contradictions in Feminist Practice: Individualism and Collectivism in a Feminist Health Centre." In "Transcendence in Society: Case Studies," supplement 1, *Comparative Social Research*: 9–59.

Ng, Roxana. 1988. *The Politics of Community Services: Immigrant Women, Class and State.* Toronto, Ontario: Garamond.

———. 1990. "State Funding to a Community Employment Center: Implications for Working with Immigrant Women." In *Community Organization and the Canadian State*, ed. Roxana Ng, Gillian Walker, and Jacob Muller, 165–83. Toronto, Ontario: Garamond.

Orr, Marion. 2007. "Community Organizing and the Changing Ecology of Civic Engagement." In *Transforming the City: Community Organizing and the Challenge of Political Change*, ed. Marion Orr, 1–27. Lawrence: University Press of Kansas.

Ostrander, Susan. 2004. "Moderating contradictions of Feminist Philanthropy: Women's Community Organizations and the Boston Women's Fund, 1995–2000." *Gender and Society* 18, no. 1: 29–46.

Pheterson, Gail. 1989. *A Vindication of the Rights of Whores.* Seattle, Wash.: Seal Press.

Pinzer, Maimie. 1997. *Letters from an Ex-Prostitute: The Maimie Papers.* New York: Feminist Press.

Quinn, Robert, and David Andersen. 1984. "Formalization as Crisis: Transition Planning for a Young Organization." In *Managing Organizational Transitions*, ed. John R. Kimberley and Robert E. Quinn, 11–28. Homewood, Ill.: Irwin.

Rayside, David, and Evert Lindquist. 1992. "Canada: Community Activism, Federalism, and the New Politics of Disease." In *AIDS in the Industrialized Democracies: Passions, Politics, and Policies*, ed. David Kirp and Ronald Bayer, 49–98. Montréal, Québec: McGill-Queen's University Press.

Reinelt, Claire. 1994. "Fostering Empowerment, Building Community: The Challenges for State-Funded Feminist Organizations." *Human Relations* 47, no. 6: 685–705.

Riger, Jo. 2002. "Organizational Dynamics and the Construction of Multiple Feminist Identities in the National Organization for Women." *Gender and Society* 16, no. 5: 710–27.

Riger, Stephanie. 1994. "Challenges of Success: Stages of Growth in Feminist Organizations." *Feminist Studies* 20, no. 2: 275–300.

Ryder, Andrew. 2004. "The Changing Nature of Adult Entertainment Districts: Between a Rock and a Hard Place or Going from Strength to Strength?" *Urban Studies* 41, no. 9: 1659–86.

Sanders, Teela. 2004. "The Risks of Street Prostitution: Punters, Police and Protesters." *Urban Studies* 41, no. 9: 1703–17.

Sansfaçon, Daniel. 1999. *Rapport du comité Montréalais sur la prostitution de rue et la prostitution juvenile*. Montréal, Québec: City Hall.

Staggenborg, Suzanne. 1988. "The Consequences of Professionalization and Formalization in the Pro-Choice Movement." *American Sociological Review* 53, no. 4: 585–605.

Stella. 1996. "La Prostitution de Rue à Montréal, L'Urgence d'une Nouvelle Approche." *Annual Report of Activities*. March 1.

———. 1997. *Rapport d'évaluation, Volet I: La participation de travailleuses and extravailleuses du sexe dans la structure de Stella et le soutien apporté à cette participation. Stella*, March 31.

———. 1998a. "Stella's Bulletin." *ConStellation* 4, no. 1: 1–8.

———. 1998b. *Volet II: La Prise en charge des travailleusses du sexe*. Minutes de L'Assemblée Générale Spéciale de Stella, L'Amie de Maimie, Stella Montréal, January 22.

———. 2000a. "États Financiers." Unpublished Meeting Minutes, Stella Montréal, March 31.

———. 2000b. "Stella, Vivre et Travailler en Sécurité et avec Dignité." Unpublished Annual Report, Stella Montréal, June 21.

———. 2000c. "Rencontre due Conseil d'Administration de Stella." *Unpublished Board* Meeting Minutes, Stella Montréal, April 20.

———. 2006. "eXXXpressions." *Forum XXX Proceedings: A Compilation of Presentations, Discussions, and Perspectives, May 18–22, 2005*. http://www.chezstella.org/docs/eXXXpressionsE.pdf.

———. 2011. "Making Space for Working Women." http://www.chezStella.org.

Tremblay, Francine. 2011. "From Prostitutes to Sex Workers: Transition and Transformation through Collective Action in a Québec Context." PhD diss., L'Université du Québec à Montréal (UQAM).

Walker, Edward, and John McCarthy. 2010. "Legitimacy, Strategy and Resources in the Survival of Community-Based Organizations." *Social Problems* 57, no. 3: 315–40.

Warren, Mark. 2001. *Dry Bones Rattling: Community Building to Revitalize American Democracy*. Princeton, N.J.: Princeton University Press.

Weitzer, Ronald. 1991. "Prostitutes' Rights in the United States: The Failure of a Movement." *Sociological Quarterly* 32, no. 1: 23–41.

Wood, Richard. 2002. *Faith in Action: Religion, Race, and Democratic Organizing in America*. Chicago: University of Chicago Press.

Contributors

CHERYL AUGER is finishing her PhD in political science at the University of Toronto. Her dissertation examines sex work policy and policy debates.

SARAH BEER received an MA in criminology and women's studies from the University of Ottawa and a PhD in sociology from the University of Windsor. She is a postdoctoral fellow at the University of Windsor and an instructor of sociology at Dawson College in Montréal, Québec.

MICHELE TRACY BERGER received a PhD in political science from the University of Michigan. She is associate professor in the Department of Women's and Gender Studies at the University of North Carolina–Chapel Hill and is the author of *Workable Sisterhood: The Political Journey of Stigmatized Women with HIV/AIDS*.

THADDEUS GREGORY BLANCHETTE has a PhD in anthropology from the Federal University of Rio de Janeiro and is a professor at the Federal University of Rio de Janeiro. He studies "gringos," prostitution, sexual tourism, and the trafficking of women in Brazil and has written on these topics for academic and popular magazines in Brazil and the United States.

RAVEN BOWEN is an MA candidate in criminology at Simon Fraser University. Her research focuses on sex work exit, reentry, and duality. She founded a number of sex worker organizations and programs in Vancouver and has many community-based publications to her credit. In 2005, members of the sex working community named a service award after her that is given annually to those who provide outstanding support to sex industry workers. She received the inaugural Naked Truth Lifetime Achievement Award in 2011.

GREGG BUCKEN-KNAPP received his PhD from George Washington University in Washington, D.C. and is associate professor in the School of Public Administration, University of Gothenburg, Sweden. His work has most recently appeared in the *Journal of European Public Policy* and *Human Rights Review*. His research for the Nordic Prostitution Policy Reform Project is funded by the Swedish Research Council.

ANA PAULA DA SILVA holds a PhD in anthropology from the Federal University of Rio de Janeiro and is a visiting professor at the Federal University of Viçosa, where she is investigating foreign men's attitudes toward Brazilian women. She also works as a consultant and has published several articles in Brazilian and American academic journals regarding prostitution, race, and the trafficking of women.

VALERIE FELDMAN is a PhD candidate in sociology at the University of California–Davis. Her research uses organizational field analysis to examine the contemporary governance of prostitution and sex trafficking in the United States.

GREGOR GALL is professor of industrial relations at the University of Bradford and a columnist for the *Morning Star*, the daily paper of the labor movement in Britain, as well a regular contributor to the *Scotsman* newspaper. He runs a subscription-based research service for unions. Among his books are *Sex Worker Union Organising: An International Study, An Agency of Their Own: Sex Worker Union Organising,* and four edited volumes on union organizing.

KATHLEEN GUIDROZ received a master of public administration degree from Louisiana State University and a PhD in sociology from George Washington University. She is an adjunct professor at Georgetown University.

ANNIE HILL completed her PhD in the Department of Rhetoric at the University of California–Berkeley. She is assistant professor in the Department of Communication Studies at the University of Minnesota, Twin Cities. She has been a visiting scholar at the Institute of Criminology at the University of Cambridge and an empirical legal studies fellow through Berkeley's Center for the Study of Law and Society.

JOHAN KARLSSON SCHAFFER received his PhD in political science from the University of Gothenburg. He is a researcher at the Norwegian Centre for Human Rights, University of Oslo. His recent publications include articles in *Review of International Studies* and *Human Rights Review*.

EDITH KINNEY received a JD from Berkeley Law and completed her PhD in jurisprudence and social policy at the University of California–Berkeley. She is a visiting assistant professor in the Social Sciences Division at Mills College in Oakland, California. Her work has appeared in the *Berkeley Journal of Gender, Law, and Justice*.

YASMIN LALANI completed her PhD at the Ontario Institute for Studies in Education at the University of Toronto. Her research examines the gender politics of HIV/AIDS curricula used by female activist-educators in the Amazon region of Peru.

PIA LEVIN received an MA in Nordic history from Åbo Akademi University, Finland, and is a doctoral candidate in the history of science and ideas at Uppsala University, Sweden. She is a research assistant for the Nordic Prostitution Policy Reform Project.

ALEXANDRA LUTNICK received an MA in sexuality studies from San Francisco State University and a PhD in social welfare at the University of California–Berkeley. She is a project director for the San Francisco–based Urban Health Program in RTI International's Behavioral Health and Criminal Justice Research Division.

SAMANTHA MAJIC received her PhD in government at Cornell University. She is assistant professor in the Department of Political Science at John Jay College/CUNY. She is the author of *Sex Work Politics: From Protest to Service Provision*. Her research on sex work, political activism, and policy has appeared in the journals *Perspectives on Politics*; *The Journal of Women, Politics and Policy*; *New Political Science*; and *Polity*.

TAMARA O'DOHERTY completed a JD from the University of British Columbia and an MA in criminology from Simon Fraser University. She is completing her PhD in criminology at Simon Fraser University and lectures on criminology at the University of the Fraser Valley in British Columbia, Canada. Her work has been used to support the legal challenge to Canada's criminal prohibitions against sex work activities, and she recently published in *Canadian Journal of Criminology and Criminal Justice* and *Violence against Women.*

JOYCE OUTSHOORN studied political science and contemporary history at the University of Amsterdam and received her doctorate from the Free University of Amsterdam. She is professor emeritus in women's studies at the Institute of Political Science, University of Leiden. She edited *The Politics of Prostitution: Women's Movements, Democratic States, and the Globalization of Sex Work* and, with Johanna Kantola, *Changing State Feminism.* She has published in many journals, including *Public Administration Review, Social Politics,* and the *European Journal of Women's Studies.*

CARISA R. SHOWDEN received her PhD in political science from the University of North Carolina at Chapel Hill. She is associate professor of political science and women's and gender studies at the University of North Carolina at Greensboro. Her first book, *Choices Women Make: Agency in Domestic Violence, Assisted Reproduction, and Sex Work,* was published by the University of Minnesota Press. Her work on third wave feminism and the relationship between feminist and queer theories has appeared in the journals *Frontiers* and *Feminist Theory.*

FRANCINE TREMBLAY received an MA in sociology from Concordia University and a PhD in sociology from Université du Québec à Montréal (UQÀM). She is part-time faculty in the Department of Sociology and Anthropology at Concordia University in Montréal.

Index

Page numbers in italics indicate photographs or other illustrations.

244; in Finland, 210–11; gender equality's role in, 172, 198–99; in New Zealand, xx–xxii, xxivn2, 102, 178, 237; in Norway, xiii, 196, 212; sex worker involvement in, xxix, 106, 115, 222. *See also* Canada, sex work policies in; criminalization of sex work; decriminalization of sex work; Finland; Great Britain, prostitution policy in; legalization of sex work; regulation of sex work; Sweden, criminalization of purchase of sexual services (CPSS); United States (U.S.); zoning of sex work

Pushor, Debbie, 59, 62

Quiet Revolution (Canada), 290

race: Brazilian migration policies, 131, 138, 139, 141n5; effects on research, 6–7, 7–8, 14–15; Netherlands' categories of sex workers, 177, 179, 183–84; sex workers' rights movement, 259, 264n39

red-light districts, 99, 173, 294, 298, 303

Red Thread (sex worker group, Netherlands), xxxii, 177, 180, 186, 189n5, 224, 226

reflexivity, 4, 18, 24–26, 40–42, 115

regulation of sex work, xxiv–xxxiv, 86, 99–100, 102–4, 112–13, 115, 116n3, 222. *See also* licensing of sex work; public policy, sex work; surveillance; zoning of sex work

rehabilitation of prostitutes: antitrafficking campaigns involving, 157–60, 162; in Great Britain, 78–79, 83, 85, 89–93, 94, 95; of sex workers, 78–79, 149; in Thailand, 149, 157–60, 159

Reid, Colleen, 59, 66, 67

repatriation of trafficked individuals, 150, 151, 153, 154, 160–62

Report of the Departmental Committee on Homosexual Offences and Prostitution (Wolfenden report, Great Britain, 1957), 80–82

rescue paradigm, in Thailand's antitrafficking campaign, 145–48, 153, 154–57, 155, 162, 163, 167n23

research studies, sex work, 3–30; assessing bias in, 40–41, 48n3, 115; boundaries in, 17, 37; feminist perspectives in, 3–5, 6–7, 19–21; field work, 8–12; funding for, 19, 25, 55, 56, 64; guidelines for, xxvii, 56–57; with hidden populations, 31–33, 39, 42, 44, 46; identity's role in, 3–4, 11, 12–18, 23, 33; male researchers' experiences, 20–21; multivocality in, 4–5, 15, 26; participatory approach to, xxi, xxvi–xxvii, 39, 115; politics-of-location approach, xxvi, xxxi–xxxii, 3–6, 10–12, 15–20, 23, 25; positionality in, 4–8, 12–18; rapport with respondents, 9, 10, 13, 15–17; reflexivity in, 4, 18, 24–26, 40–42, 115; re-presenting sex work in, 252–53; sampling methods, 8, 42, 43; sexuality in, 3–6, 8–12, 13–14, 16–18, 18–25; social value of, 68–70; stigma attached by academic community, 5–6, 9, 10, 18–23, 25, 58; subjectivity in, 16, 24, 40–41; theory building in, 4, 6, 12, 18, 22, 25, 32. *See also* knowledge production; participant-driven action research (PDAR), Vancouver example; Sex Worker Environmental Assessment Team (SWEAT), participatory research study